SLAVES TO FASHION

Slaves to Fashion

BLACK DANDYISM AND THE STYLING
OF BLACK DIASPORIC IDENTITY

MONICA L. MILLER

Duke University Press   *Durham & London*   2009

For Carl, min älskling

A body of people came down the platform, some of them Negroes. Yes, I thought, what about those of us who shoot up from the South into the busy city like wild jacks-in-the-box broken loose from our springs—so sudden that our gait comes like that of deep-sea divers suffering from the bends? What about those fellows waiting still and silent there on the platform, so still and silent they clash with the crowd in their very immobility, standing noisy in their very silence; harsh as a cry of terror in their quietness? What about those three boys, coming now along the platform, tall and slender, walking stiffly with swinging shoulders in their well-pressed, too-hot-for-summer suits, their collars high and tight about their necks, their identical hats of black cheap felt set upon the crowns of their heads with a severe formality above their conked hair? It was as though I'd never seen their like before: Walking slowly, their shoulders swaying, their legs swinging from their hips in trousers that ballooned upward from cuffs fitting snug about their ankles; their coats long and hip-tight with shoulders far too broad to be those of natural Western men. These fellows whose bodies seemed—what had one of my teachers said of me—"You're like one of these African sculptures, distorted in the interest of a design." Well, what design and whose?

RALPH ELLISON, *Invisible Man* (1952)

Contents

Acknowledgments

Dandies are, famously, men of parts; like fops, their precursors, they are "the offspring of more than one Man's labour, for certainly no less than a Dancing, and Fencing-Master, with a Taylor, Milliner, Perfumer, Peruque-Maker and a French *valet-de-chambre*" (*Love's Last Shift*, III.i). This black dandy book is no exception, and as its author I owe a debt to the many who facilitated its debut.

This book would not have been written had I not been encouraged, as a sophomore at Dartmouth College, to consider a career (now a life) as an academic. The support I received from the Mellon Minority Undergraduate Fellowship (now the Mellon-Mays Undergraduate Fellowship) in college, graduate school, and as a professor was and is absolutely essential to my personal and professional well-being. There are too many individuals involved with the program, mentors and fellows, to thank; instead, I'd like to acknowledge the program as a whole and the vision that it seeks to realize.

As a dissertation at Harvard University, this project was shepherded to completion by Henry Louis Gates Jr., Barbara Johnson, and Larry Buell, a formidable and ceaselessly encouraging triumvirate. My fellow students were my earliest and kindest critics, and the best of friends. I'd like to thank in particular Aviva Briefel, Sianne Ngai, Rebecca Walkowitz, Amanda Claybaugh, Martin Puchner, Christian Porter, Gabrielle Starr, Beth Ford, and Catherine Toal. Henry Turner also belongs in this group. The Woodrow Wilson National Fellowship Foundation and the Mellon Foundation provided fellowship support.

In more recent years, while at Barnard College, I have benefited enormously from an Andrew W. Mellon Post-Doctoral Fellowship, a year as a Fellow-in-Residence at the Schomburg Center for Research in Black Culture at the New York Public Library, and an Andrew W. Mellon Career Enhancement Fellowship. At Barnard my colleagues have been patient and endlessly supportive. I have been fortunate enough to benefit from the collective wisdom of Kim Hall, Quandra Prettyman, Margaret Vandenburg, Jim Basker, Ross Hamilton, Jennie Kassanoff, Lisa Gordis, Caryl Phillips, Lisa Tiersten, and Elizabeth Hutchinson as readers or listeners to various parts of this manuscript. I have also relied on the Barnard Center for Research on Women, directed by Janet Jakobsen, as a challenging and friendly venue in which to present this work and to discuss its implications. Barnard College internal grants have also enabled me to take a research trip to the British Library in London and to hire three detail-oriented research assistants, including Svati Miriam Lelyveld. At the Schomburg, I had the good fortune to have Colin Palmer leading the Fellows' seminar and Peter Hobbs as my research assistant. Special thanks also go to my cohort of Fellows and the dedicated folks who run the Division of Photographs and Prints.

Since living in New York, I have been involved with a number of seminars and writing and reading groups that have been inspirational, set deadlines for me, and made me a better writer, teacher, and citizen of the world. At Columbia University my colleague and friend Rachel Adams introduced me to two important groups, the New York Americanist Group and Columbia's University Seminar in American Studies. I would like to thank the University Seminars Office for its help in publication. The ideas presented here benefited from discussions in the American Studies University seminar. The Sister Scholars, especially Farah Griffin, are also due recognition for initiating a group that read, wrote, ate, and schemed in equal measure. I'd also like to thank MMUF Fellow Candice Jenkins, who read every chapter of this book, for her patience and keen editorial eye.

I also want to thank my editor at Duke University Press, Courtney Berger, for her wise counsel and for her ability to furnish me with two readers whose advice and suggestions transformed this project at a crucial point.

Special thanks also go to the artists whose work I discuss in chapter 5: Isaac Julien, Lyle Ashton Harris, Iké Udé, and Yinka Shonibare, MBE, who all generously agreed to have their captivating artwork included in this book.

Friends who have supported me over many years include Debbie Peikes, Heeten Kalan, Jenny Dahlstein, Roop Roy, Randall Quan, Subitha Subramaniam, Patricia Mengech, Rob Miotke, Russ Porter, and Pernilla Bard.

To my parents, Glenn Miller and Justine Perry Miller, I owe a debt I cannot repay. The capaciousness of this book is a result of their encouragement to dream big in all areas of my life. They have never set limits on me or my ideas and never hindered my sense of possibility. For this gift, I am eternally grateful. It is my hope that with this book, as with everything else, I can make them proud.

To my son, Langston Wennerlind, thank you for your big, beautiful smile and outrageous sense of humor. And to my husband, Carl Wennerlind, I remember that I promised to make you laugh, to make you think, and to make you happy. I hope that the completion of this book in some ways fulfills these promises. I dedicate this book to you with all of my love.

SLAVES TO FASHION

Introduction

STYLIN' OUT

I begin with two seemingly disparate images: one an eighteenth-century oil painting of an unnamed black boy dressed in a bright red jacket, gold collar, and padlock about his neck, and the other, that of the flamboyantly attired, stylistic maverick hip-hop artist Andre 3000. Can the depiction of the enslaved boy, whose life was defined by service to an eighteenth-century European gentleman, reveal anything about the magnetic appeal of this contemporary celebrity, known for his leadership of the African American Gentlemen's Movement, a recent fashion trend?[1] How has the representation of black people been transformed from images of dandified "luxury" slavery to that of self-fashioning black dandies whose likenesses are now ubiquitous on the stage and on the streets? It is this transformation in black style — from costumed object designed to trumpet the wealth, status, and power of white masters to self-styling subjects who use immaculate clothing, arch wit, and pointed gesture to announce their often controversial presence — that this book seeks to elucidate. The history of black dandyism in the Atlantic diaspora is the story of how and why black people became arbiters of style and how they use clothing and dress to define their identity in different and changing political and cultural contexts. In this cultural history, which examines moments in which black people style their way from slaves to selves in Enlightenment London to present-day Afro-cosmopolitan New York, I show the ways in which Africans dispersed across and around the Atlantic in the slave trade — once slaves to fashion — make fashion their slave.

Black people are known for "stylin' out," dressing to the nines, showing their sartorial stuff, especially when the occasion calls for it and, more tellingly, often when it does not. In contemporary culture, stylin' out takes a number of forms and happens in multiple locations, from the

1. Sir John Baptist de Medina, *James Drummond, 2nd Titular Duke of Perth,
1673–1720. Jacobite*. Scottish National Portrait Gallery.

high style seen at the famous White Parties in the Hamptons given by
the hip-hop fashion mogul Sean "Diddy" Combs, to any black church on
Easter Sunday, to the locker room after the Super Bowl championship,
when a winning player positions an oversize baseball cap forty-five degrees off-center on his head before the television camera turns to him.
In all of these situations, signals are being sent about how each dresser
sees himself and how he wants to be seen by others. For Diddy, wearing
an icy-white haute couture Valentino suit after a lifetime in track suits

and sneakers signifies his success as a businessman and his arrival on an exclusive social scene. Yet in the black entertainment industry some form of dandyism or play with costume and couture has always been de rigueur. For those attending church services, a smart three-piece suit, a hat, gloves, and maybe even a pocket square communicates self-respect, community pride, and an appreciation of the joyful solemnity of the occasion. The spiritual has always had a sartorial dimension for black people in America, as many slaves were allowed to dress in their finest clothes but once a week, on Sunday. For the football player, donning the outsized baseball hat modified out of its functionality to become a fashion accessory at once establishes individuality within a group of teammates and belonging to an urban, edgy subgroup of black athletes who, along with hip-hop and rap musicians, have been instrumental in transforming sports clothing into a billion-dollar fashion industry. In each of these cases of celebrities and ordinary people, the dandyism practiced is both personal and political, about individual image and group regard, and begs to be read from both an intraracial and interracial perspective. Stylin' out, like any performative act, needs an actor and an audience; the audience can be anything from oneself in a mirror to fellow strollers on Harlem's 125th Street to the international media. The messages sent out by the black well-dressed must be interpreted by their viewers; black dandyism takes on meaning as black style communicates moments of mobility and fixity, depending on who is looking.

Contemporary examples of black high style (particularly black urban style) are ubiquitous; but the history of black dandyism is less well known. This history begins in part with the contact between Africans and Europeans that initiated the trade in slaves. While young black boys were sometimes acquired as luxury items and used in displays of wealth far more ostentatious than that displayed in the master–servant portrait that opens this chapter, other blacks, while laboring on other shores, found themselves in a very different relationship to adornment. The travel journal of William High Grove (1732) records a scene of contact in Virginia in which clothing (or a lack thereof) communicates a great deal about status:

> The men are stowed before the foremast, the Boys between that and the main mast, the Girls next, and the grown Women behind the Missen. The Boyes and Girles [were] all stark naked; so Were the greatest part

of the Men and Women. Some had beads about their necks, arms, and Wasts, and a ragg or Piece of Leather the bigness of a fig Leafe. And I saw a Woman [who had] Come Aboard to Examine the Limbs and soundness of some she seemed to Choose. Dr. Dixon bought 8 men and 2 women and brought them on shore with us, all stark naked. But when [we had] come home [they] had Coarse Shirts and afterwards Drawers given [to] them.[2]

While the diary entry hardly seems anticipatory of any contemporary moment of black sartorial agency or stylin' out, it does, in fact, contain important elements that transform degrading aspects of this scene into a story of black dandy origins less obvious than, but similar to, that of the dandified blacks depicted in paintings of the elite. "Some had beads about their necks, arms, and Wasts, and a ragg or Piece of Leather the bigness of a fig Leafe": while not clothing proper, these pieces of jewelry and other accessories hold within them the power of memory, of a place of autonomy as the only material retention from former lives in Africa. It is small objects like these, precious or shiny bits like beads and ribbons, that slaves often collected and used to augment their standard issue "Coarse Shirts and . . . Drawers" in gestures of memory, individuality, and subversion.

The accumulation of objects of personal adornment and the nature of their display mattered to materially deprived African captives. This is as true for those who were deliberately dressed in silks and turbans, whose challenge was to inhabit the clothing in their own way, as for those who were more humbly attired, who used clothing as a process of remembrance and mode of distinction (and symbolic and sometimes actual escape from bondage) in their new environment. That the procurement of fine clothing and accessories could be important to African captives is evidenced by the need of those who absconded to have a "traveling wardrobe." In Virginia in 1769, a mulatto slave named Joe, a "genteel and active Fellow," who "has always been kept as a Gentleman's waiting Man, his Hair comb'd very nicely, [who] can write a good Hand," escaped on a fine horse with "a large bundle of Cloaths and other things with him," including, "a blue over coat and Breeches, a Lead colour'd Cloth Coat and Vest, with Metal Buttons, and Silver Lac'd Hat, several summer vests, white Shirts and Stockings, of which some are silk." Clad in such finery, Joe rode toward the shore, where, as he told some people he met on his journey, he hoped to get a ship to London and live as a free man.[3] Here, dress and fashion are practically and symbolically important to a slave's sense of individuality and liberty; captives described as "remarkably fond of dress" often style out to signal or to reach their own imperatives.[4] As the Atlantic began to connect blacks and whites in unprecedented ways, black people expressed their own sense of style in relation to that which they perceived was operating in the European societies with which they traded or in which they lived. On the backs of those on the African coast and those imported into America and England, a negotiation of identity was taking place, a visual and visible sign of how Africans cast into a diaspora would have to construct their identities literally and materially.

In this book I examine a series of transhistorical and transatlantic moments in literary and visual culture in which black male subjects can be seen understanding, manipulating, and reimagining the construction of their images through the dandy's signature method: a pointed redeployment of clothing, gesture, and wit. In choosing to concentrate on the dandyism of black men, I aim also to study the way in which the black dandy figure embodies the construction and deconstruction of masculine identity relative to negotiations of race, sexuality, and class. Because the dandy is a figure who exists in the space between masculine and feminine, homosexual and heterosexual, seeming and being, even when not specifically racialized, an investigation of the black dandy's emergence and perpetuation as a cultural sign of this indeterminacy says much about the politics and aesthetics of racialization and identity formation. I position the black dandy explicitly among other racialized performers and performers of masculinity in order to read the dandy as a complicated figure that can, at once, subvert and fulfill normative categories of identity at different times and places as a gesture of self-articulation. The negotiation of these categories has been a major task of black diasporic subject formation historically. My book narrates this process in terms of how black identity has been and continues to be stylized.

In order to illustrate the black dandy's embodiment of this intersection of identity markers, I consider the pleasures and dangers of the styling of blackness and self-fashioning as well as the performativity, irony, and politics of consumption and consumerism that define such stylization. In this book, I understand blackness as always already "performed."[5] As Harry Elam Jr. states, "The 'race question' is inherently theatrical. From the arrival of the first African slaves on American soil, the discourse in race, the definitions and meanings of blackness, have been intricately linked to issues of theater and performance. Definitions of race, like the processes of theater, fundamentally depend on the relationship between the seen and unseen, between the visibly marked and unmarked, between the 'real' and illusionary."[6] In addition to seeing blackness as a dialectic between performer and audience, I see it as a historical or even imperialist phenomenon in that black people have had to be black for white or European audiences since their designation as black or African replaced a sense of themselves as being from specific geographic regions and ethnic groups. Black and blackness are themselves signs of diaspora, of a cosmopolitanism that African subjects did not choose but from which they necessarily reimagined themselves.[7] In this book black dandyism is an interpretation and materialization of the complexity of this cosmopolitanism. I read black dandyism and the politics of its performativity as an index of the formation of this blackness—as a sign of the conceptualization of early Afro-diasporic identity, as part of a negotiation of the transition from slavery to freedom in America in the nineteenth and twentieth centuries, as an evaluation of the fact of blackness within modernism, and as an Afro-cosmopolitan critique of national identity in the late twentieth century and early twenty-first.

As a cultural history of black dandyism, this book reads dandies as knowing and telling cultural phenomena in a variety of literary, visual, and performative texts. The literary, visual, and performative "interanimate" each other here.[8] Sometimes privileging an investigation of a black dandy on stage, sometimes of one in the streets, such interanimation of dandy figures has as its goal the narration of a story about black identity that understands black style as a performance and about the performativity of blackness. This is not intended to be a complete history of black dandyism; nevertheless it is comprehensive in that it identifies and analyzes crucial moments of black stylization in the four centuries since the beginning of the slave trade. I start with the first black dandies, the luxury slaves in eighteenth-century England whose sartorial novelty and sometimes flamboyant personalities resulted in their representation in visual culture, on stage, and as literary subjects. I conclude with a group of contemporary artists whose re-vision of the history and politics of black dandyism in photography and film has the potential to redeem the use and abuse of image from which the figure has long suffered and profited. In between, in each intervening time period, I show how the dandy manifests an evolving series of debates about racial formation, class mobility, gender assignment, sexuality, and nationalism. The black dandy's deployment of sartorial style — especially the self-consciousness of his display — is of signal importance to assessing the figure's intervention in studies of identity construction. The figure's stylin' out visualizes an awareness of the way in which all identities are styled and manipulated, let out or hemmed in. Yet, since black bodies are often already "theatricalized spectacles," aware of their "third-person consciousness," the black body in the dandy's clothes, his signature use of style, displays the possibilities and impediments of this identity construction particularly for racialized subjects.[9] As he changes clothes and strikes a pose, the black dandy performs sameness and difference, safety and danger, all the while telling a story about self and society. Dandies, like the fashions that constitute them, can be transformative — I use the changing relation between the black dandy's body and the fine clothing displayed on it to tell a much larger story about African diasporic identity and the representation of blackness across time and cultures.

Black Style

The Difference that Race Makes

In an essay from 1896 entitled "Dandies and Dandies," the quintessential decadent dandy Max Beerbohm declared, "There is no reason why dandyism should be confused, as it has been by nearly all writers, with mere social life. Its contact with social life, is, indeed, but one of the accents of an art. Its influence, like the scent of a flower, is diffused unconsciously."[10] For Beerbohm, the power of dandyism lies in its status as a creative, self-defining art form that can have multiple social and political targets or themes. Though often perceived as a mere trend of fashion in late eighteenth- and nineteenth-century British culture, dandies come in different forms and are visible and visual signs of the working out of a number of societal problems or challenges. Indeed, in Western high culture, dandies are best known not only as snappy dressers, but also as beings whose self-presentation identifies them as outrageous — everything from morally bankrupt do-nothing aristocrats, aesthetes in the Byronic or Baudelairean vein, flamboyant sartorial or conversational Wildean wits, to über fey and fashionable sexual outlaws.[11] From its beginnings and certainly now, dandyism functions as a symptom of changing social, political, cultural, and economic conditions. Fastidiousness or ostentation in dress would seem to matter only to those keeping up with haute couture, but such choices are instead descriptive of radical changes in social, economic, and political hierarchies that result in new expressions of class, gender, sexual, national, and, as we will see, racial identities.

The vocabulary and grammar of dandyism say much about its function as a social semiotic important to black self-fashioning. Though often used interchangeably, the words "dandy" and "fop" came into the English language at different times and with slightly different meanings, meanings that matter in determining the significance of the figure's racialization. According to the *Oxford English Dictionary*, from the fifteenth century onward the word "fop" designated one "foolishly attentive to and vain of his appearance, dress or manners."[12] By means of affectation, fops demonstrate the derivation of their appellation in the Latin for "fool" (*fatuus*) by slavishly adopting foreign fashion (primarily that of the French) and favoring style over substance at any cost. In contrast, from at least the 1780s, "dandy" designated a "swell," one who "*studies* above everything else to dress elegantly and fashionably" (emphasis added).[13] In comparison to the definitive derivation of "fop" in "fool," the dandy's adaptability is only reinforced by its uncertain linguistic origin. Though "dandy" does not have a definite etymology according to the *Oxford English Dictionary*, it is intriguingly associated with "dandiprat," an English coin of the sixteenth century.[14] The dandy is thus one whose style is carefully considered and often, as a result, is more self-conscious and deliberate than that of a fop; this self-consciousness, one might say, mobilizes the figure's currency. Anyone can be or can be made to be a fop, but dandies must choose the vocation, must commit to a study of the fashions that define them and an examination of the trends around which they can continually redefine themselves.

Though fops and dandies are intimately related, between the fifteenth and eighteenth centuries the silliness of foppery became the potential pointedness of dandyism. This is, incidentally, the period in which European exploration of so-called new worlds turned into exploitation of those places and their people. Flooded with new images of self and other, Europeans and Africans seemingly began to pay more attention to self and societal representation, self-display, and self-fashioning. As the dandy's influence diffused from social to political life across and around the Atlantic and from white to black, dandyism becomes above all a lesson in interrogating identity (of the self, race, nation) and analyzing representation of that identity. Whether practiced on the west coast of Africa or on the streets of metropolitan Europe or America, black dandyism becomes a strategy of survival and transcendence.

Histories of European dandyism like Ellen Moers's classic *The Dandy: Brummell to Beerbohm* (1960) and James Laver's *Dandies* (1968) typically discuss the exploits of dandies as actual or fictional people as they explore the possible ideological effects of their self-conscious bodily display. Such surveys often conclude that the dandy, whether of the austere or flamboyant variety, uses his characteristic style and charisma to distinguish himself when privileges of birth, wealth, and social standing might be absent. Such cultivation and use of personal distinction serve as evidence of societal transition. As Laver puts it, "Clothes are never a frivolity. They are always an expression of the fundamental social and economic pressures of the time."[15] In these histories, the recounting of the lives of and scandals associated with such famed dandies as Beau Brummell, Count D'Orsay, Barbey D'Aurevilly, and Charles Baudelaire leads to an analysis of the kinds of social and cultural interventions their attention to a cravat, a snuffbox, and their own ennui might yield. In these histories one reads anecdotes of how the "butterfly dandyism" or femininity of a dandy such as D'Orsay, known for his hyperattention to pastel-colored clothing and "fluffy" accessories, transformed gender relations as dandies rejected increasing demands that they fill traditionally masculine roles. One discerns the ways in which a Brummellian dandy's mastery of control, his ability to tie a neckcloth perfectly, allowed him not only to dress above his supposed station, but also, by his example, to forever confuse the ability to see class through clothing. One observes how a Wildean dandy's loose bohemian dress, narcissism, and homosociality or homosexuality threatened normalizing standards of sexuality, as dandies were men who seemingly aped women while sometimes detesting them and preferring the company of men. One notices the way in which a Byronic dandy's passion for the foreign made his status as a gender, class, sex, and national traitor complete.

Even though these studies are not centered on a dandy's personal semiotic or performative power (despite the attention to biography), the dandies in them emerge as signs of a social semiotic in which they can and do signify beyond status as a "creature . . . careless of anything below the surface," or one "dedicated solely to his own perfection through a ritual of taste."[16] Whereas these histories read the varieties of dandyism as "signs of the times" or as evidence of changing trends in social hierarchies, studies of fashion, clothing, and dress see the dandy's semiotic power more as an analogue to identity construction or visible sense of self. After influential studies of fashion such as J. C. Flugel's *Psychology of Clothes* (1930), Roland Barthes's *Fashion System* (1967/83), and Alison Lurie's more popular *The Language of Clothes* (1981), among many others, cultural critics take it for granted that the combination of a self-conscious style on a performative body functions as a semiotic system of signs and referents.[17] Fashion theorists often identify the dandy's allure as emanating from the fact that the figure is both constructed and performative—a dandy is a kind of embodied, animated sign system that deconstructs given and normative categories of identity (elite, white, masculine, heterosexual, patriotic) and reperforms them in a manner more in keeping with his often avant-garde visions of society and self. Although semiotics exposes all things as signs available for interpretation and reinterpretation, considerations of dandyism transhistorically and transculturally force this interpretation to be contextual and often contingent.

As a social practice that mounts a critique against the hierarchies that order society, dandyism appears to be a phenomenon particularly suited to blacks, who experienced an attempted erasure or reordering of their identities in the slave trade. For blacks in the diaspora, the dandy's special talent—the possibility of converting absence into presence through self-display—is not only a philosophical or psychological boon, but also, initially, a practical concern. As we saw above in the case of the captives who arrived in Virginia in 1732, Africans arriving in England, America, or the West Indies had to fashion new identities and manipulate what they were given in a style all their own. Whether they were to become house slaves, field hands, or urban blacks used as domestics, apprentices, or managers, their new lives nearly always began with the issuance of new clothes. The clothing was frequently modified and augmented by the enslaved to indicate their ideas about the relationship between slavery, servitude, and subjectivity. When racialized as black, the dandy's extravagant or tastefully reserved bodily display signifies well beyond obsessive self-fashioning and play with social hierarchies. The black dandy's style is, from the beginning, always simultaneously personal, cultural, representative of "the race," and about representation even as it evaluates norms of racialization, class privileges, gender assignments, and the rules of sexuality in ways similar to that of his European dandy brothers.

Because conceptions of race are always interpolated with considerations of class, gender, sexuality, and nation, the black dandy signifies in all of these arenas at once. A racialized dandy is at once a threat to supposed natural aristocracy, he is (hyper) masculine *and* feminine, aggressively heterosexual yet not quite a real man, a vision of an upstanding citizen and an outsider broadcasting his alien status by clothing his dark body in a good suit. In that dandies of any color disrupt and destabilize conceptions of masculinity and heterosexuality, they are queer subjects who deconstruct limiting binaries in the service of transforming how one conceives of identity formation. In that the black dandy adds a deconstruction of racial and ethnic "notions" to this queerness, he might better be called "quare," or queer with a distinctly black accent. Using an African American vernacular for "queer," E. Patrick Johnson defines "quare" as "odd and slightly off kilter," a "lesbian, gay, bisexual, or transgendered person of color who loves other men or women, sexually and / or nonsexually, and appreciates black culture and community," "one who thinks and feels and acts (and sometimes 'acts up'); [who is] committed to struggle against all forms of oppression — racial, sexual, gender, class, religious, etc.," and, finally, "one for whom sexual and gender identities always already intersect with racial subjectivity."[18] For Johnson, quare is queerness with some "shade" thrown on it, a queerness that attends to the politics and performativity of identity without reifying debilitating notions of any of identity's markers. As queer or quare performative beings, black dandies are creatures of invention who continually and characteristically break down limiting identity markers and propose new, more fluid categories within which to constitute themselves.

Even though they are figures who truly challenge normalized conceptions of race, gender, sexuality, and class, black dandies are not figures who experience or perpetrate a radical or even nihilistic destabilization of identity's markers. Instead, as creatures whose quareness is performed with and on their bodies, they highlight the necessity of challenging these limiting categories and proposing new ones that are potentially progressive. For them, dressing up and acting up are similar, sometimes equivalent acts. Quare subjects' performativity necessarily holds fluid notions of race, sexuality, gender, class, and nation in concert and in tension. As queers of color, black dandies challenge what Roderick Ferguson calls "ideologies of discreteness," instead opting to "decode cultural fields not from a position outside those fields, but from within them as those fields account for the queer of color subjects' historicity."[19] The process of deconstructing identity markers from within can be read as that which "neither opts to assimilate within such a [dominant] structure nor strictly oppose it"; rather, it is what José Muñoz defines as "disidentification," or a "strategy that works on and against dominant ideology."[20] Disidentification in the dandy's hands (or closet) exposes the hybridity, syncretism, mixedness of all people, deconstructs race and blackness, sex, gender, and class into moments of productive ambivalence, agency, and capitulation.

Despite the necessity for black people to study and master methods of self-fashioning, no history of European dandyism or study of dandyism in literature has included any extensive analysis of actual or fictional black dandies and their deployment of an oppositional or interrogative black style. While literary and cultural studies of dandyism have highlighted the dandy's manipulation of the sex and gender system, these inquiries do not recognize the black dandy's challenge to racialization as well as to that system, even if they briefly mention the androgyny and biraciality of contemporary black dandies like Prince.[21] Indeed, within the field of fashion studies, black style — especially high style — and all it might reveal has received little serious attention. The scope of the few studies that investigate black style as a phenomenon with a specific history and symbolic force is often limited to contemporary times or at least to some part of the twentieth century. That is true of two museum exhibitions, *Black Style Now* at the Museum of the City of New York (2006–07) and *Black British Style* at the Victoria and Albert Museum in London (2004).[22] That both of these exhibits were wildly popular, especially with black patrons, indicates that even if cultural institutions that do not usually cater to this topic or demographic do not understand the complicated allure and symbolic presence of an exceptionally well-clad black body, many in the public, the actual performers and regular audience of these interventions into self-fashioning, most definitely do.

An exception to such oversight, with a specific reference to high style, is the anthology *Dandies: Fashion and Finesse in Art and Culture* (2001), which hopes to provide what the editor, Susan Fillin-Yeh, calls an "'outsider' paradigm of sartorial finesse detached from Western European superclass dandyism — traditional, mainstream, and gendered as male," in the hope of revealing "women's dandyism and other dandyisms" as well.[23] Employing a methodology that takes in feminist and queer theory, literary theories of deconstruction, studies in iconology and semiotics, and postcolonial studies as well as anthropological studies of status, adornment, and the body, *Dandies* includes the only essay on black dandyism in the canon of dandy histories, the art historian Richard Powell's "Sartor Africanus." Though *Dandies* acknowledges black dandyism as one such "outsider paradigm," even Powell begins his essay by wondering, why, "alongside detailed descriptions of such legendary dandies as Beau Brummell, Eugene Delacroix, and Paul Garvarni, [is] one . . . hard-pressed to find *any* references at all to black dandies?"[24] Offering a sketch of black dandyism in nineteenth-century America that includes the silent challenge that the former slave and abolitionist Frederick Douglass mounted simply by standing at a podium in a three-piece suit with all of the accessories, Powell calls for an investigation of the black dandy's ability to procure and perform "a wardrobe that speaks of modernity, freedom, oppositionality, and power."[25] My book broadens the classic volumes on dandyism and follows the lead of studies that want to uncover the power of "alternative dandyisms" and treat a dandy's race, gender, sexuality, class, and nation intersectionally. In addition, it hopes to provide a historical origin and trajectory for this investigation. In offering this analysis of black male sartorial style, I read the black dandy as a fusion and negotiation of the European dandy's more well-known social semiotics and the inherent bodily and sartorial performativity of the black diasporic cultures created by colonialism, imperialism, and the slave trade. In doing so, I explore the formation, transcendence, and ambivalence of performances of race and identity in terms of the black dandy's triumphs and travails.

Black, White, and Dandy
The Lessons of Performing Ambivalence

If, as Joseph Roach contends, "to perform . . . means to bring forth, manifest, and to transmit . . . [and] more secretly, to invent," then dandyism must be considered a major example of black performance or expressive culture, especially in the way it reveals the tenuousness of the assumed boundaries of identity and spectacularly opposes and rewrites them visually and materially.[26] Though called by many other names, black performance styles have become grouped under the general rubric of signifyin'—an intra- and intercultural aesthetic that has come to define the culture of the African diaspora. To "'signify' is to repeat, revise, reverse, or transform what has come before, continually raising the stakes in a kind of expressive poker"; signifying is thus a signature of all black expressive forms, whether music, dance, oral and written narrative, and even (especially for my purposes) dress.[27] Black dandyism is often seen as being imitative of Western dress and as a sign of one's aspiration to enter the mainstream, but when interpreted as a signifying practice, it becomes instead a dialogic process that exists in relation to white dandyism at the same time it expresses, through its own internal logic, black culture.

Black dandies may seem to mimic European dress styles in an effort to accrue the power associated with whiteness. Such repetition, however, is never a strict copy of the original style, but a black interpretation of it designed to offer the black performer a greater sense of mobility and creativity within the expressive form. If "the discourse of mimicry is constructed around an ambivalence[,] in order to be effective, mimicry must continually produce its slippage, its excess, its difference," then it is in this slippage, the space between repetition and difference, that the dandy finds and accrues power.[28] For the dandy, it is in the site of this slippage, the space between the body and its materiality, where one has "access to cultural meanings and critique."[29] For example, two men, one black and one white, dressed in the same suit and hat will almost never wear it in exactly the same way. The black body alone inside the material will alter the fabric; the interpretation continues with an added saunter, tilt of the hat, gestures in ways that make the clothing a comment on mainstream style rather than an impersonation of it. The next black man, in the same suit but with a different pocket square and a different walk, revises the pose of both of the first two men, creating two separate but intimately related conversations about image and identity. Deconstructive of the received codes of identity formation and performative of new modes of being, black dandies continually "repeat, revise, reverse, or transform what has come before," using clothing as a means to create new images and identities and revise them yet again. Each iteration of black style attempts to escape stereotypes, fixity, essentialization — signify on them — and functions as a process of identity formation grounded in irony, satire, wit, and self-consciousness.

The power and potential ideological force of the black dandy's interpretation of, rather than mere imitation of, European or white high style (his simultaneous mimicry *and* signification) should be read on a continuum between complete subversion or transcendence of that authoritative aesthetic and capitulation to it. In the absence of a proper assessment of the context in which a particular black dandy is operating, the figure's signification and expression of self can and will be seen in myriad ways. As mimicry and signification, black performativity can, like performance in general, both "conservatively re-inscribe or passionately reinvent the ideas, symbols and gestures that shape social life" even as or because it must "negotiate systems of power, cultural and social mores, values and beliefs."[30] Performing race and signifying on racialization, black performers exploit the "ambivalence" inherent in their performances, exposing race as a "device."[31] To expose race as a device and assign other signifiers of identity as devices or tools, the black dandy's method of choice is sartorial style and élan — his crafting and wielding of these weapons allow him to fashion freedom out of ambiguity. As a form of cultural resistance, black dandyism functions as a kind of fashionable "weapon of the weak," an "everyday form of resistance" (to use James Scott's terms) the enslaved and marginalized use to comment on their relationship to authority. As Scott argues, forms of resistance common to slaves — acts as simple as "footdragging, false compliance, flight, feigned ignorance, sabotage, theft, and . . . cultural resistance [such as singing, dance, dress]" — are not at all trivial; they are acts that enable everything from survival to more overt forms of protest.[32] Scott calls these acts "something of a testament to human persistence and inventiveness," even if they are not a direct confrontation with authority or oppression, rarely productive of revolution or even reform, and "typically void of any direct symbolic confrontation with authority or with elite, white norms."[33]

Because of its visual nature, its direct quotation of elite (African and European) forms, and its self-consciousness (dandies *study* "above everything else to dress elegantly and fashionably"), dandyism might productively be called not a weapon of the weak but a weapon of the stylin' because it is decidedly not an "implicit disavowal of public and symbolic goals."[34] Dandyism is, rather, a sometimes subtle, sometimes entirely obvious, but always fabulous appropriation and revision of fancy clothes that is less a "hidden transcript" with which Africans and African Americans preserve a sense of themselves, than a highly readable performative text that is subject to interpretation and translation and more often than not functions as a challenge.

Black style makes both subtle and overt challenges and capitulations to authoritative aesthetics. For Robin D. G. Kelley, the sartorial irony of African American teens stylin' out while working behind a McDonald's counter and Malcolm X's appropriation of the cool, illicit urbanity of the zoot suit serve as primary examples of this confusion, "the complicated maze of experience that renders 'ordinary' folks so extraordinarily multifaceted, diverse and complicated."[35] The complexity of the cultural expressivity and performativity of "ordinary folks" is also the subject of Shane White's and Graham White's groundbreaking history *Stylin': African American Expressive Culture from Its Beginnings to the Zoot Suit* (1998), a study that, like Kelley's work, emphasizes the absolute knowingness with which African Americans sang, danced, dressed, and strolled. In their culling of countless examples of African Americans, slave and free, dressing above their station and taking their oppositional fashion public and into the streets, White and White celebrate the way in which "black men and women developed a style that did indeed affirm their lives," even as the black body has always historically been "contested terrain."[36] This contest is not one in which black people were always victorious; as Kelley argues, "In these efforts to represent the body through dress, African Americans wielded a double-edged sword, since the styles they adopted to combat racism all too frequently reinforced, rather than challenged, bourgeois notions of respectability."[37] Black dandyism serves as both liberation and a mode of conformity.

Black dandy manipulation of sartorial style does not and cannot always lead directly to the creation of a new, wholly liberating aesthetic. As creatures of fashion who play with fashion, dandies seem to be especially adept at what Ralph Ellison might call "flipping the script" or "raising the stakes" in any representational game. Even so, like any performative act, dandyism is contingent and unstable, a liminal art, especially when that art has always had a literally material base. Precisely because the primary tools of the dandy's art—clothing and dress—are tied to consumption, the ambiguity of the dandy's political power is amplified. While examples of the dandy's political, oppositional agency abound, so too do moments of complication. For example, in the first chapter of this book, when I discuss the dandyism of Julius Soubise, an eighteenth-century black Londoner famous for cutting a figure on the social scene by completing his outfits with diamond-buckled red-heeled shoes, I also note that he often displayed his unique style in coffeehouses that were also used as slave-trading arenas at the time. While sipping his coffee, a colonial product, as he himself once was, Soubise was both a consumer and dangerously close to a commodity. When I later argue that in *The Marrow of Tradition*, Charles Chesnutt's Reconstruction-era novel, Chesnutt dresses Sandy, a former slave turned faithful old servant, in an outfit that befits his old *and* new Negro status, I also note that at the end of the novel Sandy's years of loyalty are rewarded with the inheritance of his former master's wardrobe, an act reminiscent of slavery times that repositions him firmly back into old Negro status. Thus, Sandy's efforts to redefine himself as a free man are thwarted by the persistence of the system that once defined him so differently. When I discuss the explosion of dandyism in early twentieth-century New York, I understand this outbreak of fashion with the knowledge that the department stores in Harlem, where ready-made clothing was available to the masses for the first time, often did not employ blacks, who were their best customers.[38] I measure this irony against the fact that, nevertheless, African Americans historically have spent a greater portion of their income on clothing and dress than white Americans.[39] Black dandyism has had and will always have a difficult, indeed, a tortured, relationship to consumption in that the procurement of clothing, accessories, and luxury goods that enables the performance comes literally and sometimes metaphorically at a high cost.

While it is beyond the scope of this book to examine in greater depth the tangled relationship of black dandyism to consumption and the market, in the final chapter I do attempt to understand this relationship in moments like those mentioned above and also in more contemporary times. In this chapter I discuss the performative behavior of a group of artists negotiating the increasingly globalized art market, artists who self-style as dandies and use dandyism in their work and whose style is part of their marketability and cultural cache. In contrast to some of the fictional dandies I concentrate on in other sections of the book, these artists experience a unique relationship to consumption and the market in that they are simultaneously consumers and producers, selling their particular kind of black dandyism even as they live, perform, and market it. While I speculate that dandyism's current close ties to global capitalism may signal the death of or certainly a significant change in its ideological force (Roland Barthes's axiom "Fashion killed dandyism" echoes here), nevertheless, I try to preserve a sense of what might be important about the identity and practice in this moment.

Black dandyism has always been practiced by those interested in much more than materialism and the latest style. Indeed, to borrow a formulation from another dandy theorist, Jessica Feldman, dandyism in its modern form (or within modernism) is a practice that relies on the "ability of [the dandy's] genius to see, and by seeing to create, however dimly and intuitively, at the farthest reaches of culture, and, blindly one startling step beyond."[40] For blacks, what this "beyond" looks like or could look like, when regarded as being beyond circumscribed notions of race, gender, sexuality, class, and national identity, has historically been figured by dandified appearance and been of the utmost importance in combating the injustices of the present. As such, it has functioned as a visible and visual ideal.[41] This ideal is nothing less than a truly radical kind of freedom, accessible perhaps only through a constant, playful, yet studied change of clothes.

In *Unmarked: The Politics of Performance*, Peggy Phelan issues a warning and offers hope to students and critics of the performativity that defines the black dandy's being. Throughout her analysis she warns that being visible or coming into representation does not always confer power; while many minority subjects assume that invisibility equals powerlessness, visibility can equal powerlessness, too. For Phelan, representation and visibility cannot confer identity; they can only serve as a negotiator of identity's matrices. Stating her case in linguistic terms, she avers that "the risk of visibility is then the risk of any translation. . . . The payoff of translation (and visibility) is more people will begin to speak your tongue."[42] Blacks in the diaspora have been weighing the risks and the payoffs of dandyism for centuries, in the hope of communicating the complexities of black identity as widely as possible. While Phelan understands that there is a vast space between the representation and the real, and that the visible is incapable of truly confirming the possibility of the real or a fuller sense of identity for minority subjects, she also knows that the uncertainty generated by that space can be productive, even liberating, that "doubt may be the best guarantee of real presence."[43] Therefore, even though those who perform have no guarantee that their performances do the work of imagining and therefore of creating a hoped-for ideal self, society, or world, they do so in the knowledge that their performances are nevertheless vital to the creation of new vocabularies and of an extended language with which to speak about themselves. Having these performances, one has new possibilities; without them, one recycles the same old terms.

The dandy artist Iké Udé, a subject of my last chapter, calls his performance of dandyism and use of dandyism in his work a part of his effort to image and imagine a "future perfect."[44] For Udé, a dandy's "style is not just about form and substance. It is also about the luxurious deliberation of intelligence in the face of boundaries"—deliberation that includes the past, happens in the present, and all the while looks forward, beyond.[45] That Udé describes his performative dandyism in grammatical terms, as a completed act in the future, is of signal importance to why black dandyism matters now. In the present, as black style becomes global style, the history and nature of black image making, its idioms, are increasingly important for the expression of individual and group, black, white, and other identities and desires. In a world in which the fluidity and mobility of African and African American cultural and aesthetic forms—style— constitute what can be called a major part of "black cultural traffic," one needs a facility with the language of image and identity that one can increasingly speak in and through.[46] The black dandy embodies and articulates this language, its complexities, and its futurity. The past, present, and future of this style will be our style, for many years to come.

Inside the Black Dandy's Closet

In writing the first history of black dandyism in the Atlantic diaspora, I investigate a series of crucial moments in which black sartorial style can be read as an index of changing notions of racial identity and the other identities in which race is constructed, performed, and lived—namely, gender, sexuality, class, and nation. I will look at major moments and places of transition for black people in the diaspora when they are negotiating these designations and creating new ones. England in the mid-eighteenth century is the subject of the first chapter. In this period and place the Atlantic slave trade and the rise of a culture of consumption created a vogue in dandified black servants. I locate the origins of the black dandy figure in a cosmopolitanism that was initially forced upon black slaves and servants and then capitalized on by these same figures. Through the exploits of the era's most famous black fop, Julius Soubise, and his relationship to Mungo, a well-dressed, back-talking comic slave character from Isaac Bickerstaffe's tremendously popular opera *The Padlock* (1768), I tell the story of the black dandy's origin. Soubise's extraordinary life—born a slave in the Caribbean, raised, petted, and censured by the English nobility, notorious by dint of his ironic wit, outrageous fashion, and canny exploitation of his precarious social position—is a product of the convergence of a number of historically specific factors: the spectacularization of so-called prestige slaves, black stereotypes in the theater, the relationship of gender-bending and sexuality-confusing fops and dandies to the emerging culture of consumption, and the growth of the black community in England. In a move intended to contain the confusing power of an impertinent black man in fancy dress, Soubise and Mungo became associated with each other. Instead of disarming the black fop and foppish black further, the figure of the black dandy, or "the Slavish Swell," emerges and launches a visual and verbal critique and subversion of his unusual dehumanization. By investigating the provenance and effect of associating slaves with swells, I show that black dandyism in the period is characterized by a self-consciousness about image making that requires the black subject to mobilize his spectacular outlaw nature and turn society's objectifying gaze into a social and cultural regard.

In chapter 2, I turn to the United States in the nineteenth century, where black people negotiate the transition from slavery to freedom. Here I take up the Mungo figure as he is exported to the American stage in the colonial period and joins the development of two indigenous dandyish performative traditions: carnivalesque race and class cross-dressing festivals in which black slaves and freedmen dressed as elite whites, and later, after independence, blackface minstrelsy. In the colonial period and throughout the nineteenth century, black dandyism in these indigenous festivals destabilized hierarchies of race and power, even as the emerging blackface minstrel theater developed its own black dandyism to challenge the freedom imagined and, in some cases, gained in the festivals. The chapter coins a term—the crime of fashion—to describe the racial and class cross-dressing that was, as practiced by blacks, a symbol of the self-conscious subversion of authority and, as seen in blackface, an attempted denigratory parody of free black pride and enterprise. In this period, the black dandy is thus both a victim and a perpetrator of the crime of fashion, a figure that both escapes and falls into pat definitions of blackness, masculinity, and sexuality.

That the crime of fashion and the fortunes of the black dandy figure provide a lens through which to read the relationship between image, identity, and freedom for American blacks can be gleaned from the fact that such crimes are at the center of the work of the nineteenth century's most provocative authors on the subject of race and nation—Harriet Beecher Stowe, Herman Melville, Mark Twain, and Charles Chesnutt. I focus on Chesnutt's *The Marrow of Tradition* (1901), in which the dandy figure's status as a historic, palimpsest creature is manipulated in order to portray black Americans (especially black men) and their plight outside of romantic racialist ideology and the caricatures of blackface minstrelsy. I argue that by presenting his own portraits of blacks in opposition to, but not ignorant of, minstrelsy's nearly indelible black-and-white images, Chesnutt re-dresses the efforts of Stowe, Twain, and others by imagining and imaging a meaningful change in the portrayal of African Americans as nascent "New Negroes."

Chapters 3 and 4 analyze the dandyism that emerges in the United States at the beginning of the twentieth century, when an unprecedented number of blacks make the transition from rural to urban and south to north in an effort to strive toward new images and identities personally and for the race. These two chapters concentrate on the dandyism practiced and advocated as an aesthetic ideology by two of the leading figures and proponents of black modernism in the Harlem Renaissance, W. E. B. Du Bois and James Weldon Johnson. Chapter 3 focuses on Du Bois as an unlikely, yet seminal, black dandy theorist. I argue that although Du Bois's interest in the dandy figure would seem to stem from a rejection of the blackface stereotype that mocked black efforts at education and sophistication, in fact, his conception of the Talented Tenth and other

"co-workers in the kingdom of culture" reveals his interest in rehabilitating the dandy figure in the early twentieth century as a highly educated,
refined activist for international black freedom. Although contemporary
critics have read Du Bois's essays, especially *The Souls of Black Folk* (1903),
as texts that reveal the author's "highly gendered structures of intellectual and political thought and feeling," Du Bois's concern with the connections of gender and sexuality to leadership began before the writing
of that work and continued well after it.[47] By reading essays and fiction
written before and after *The Souls of Black Folk*, I contend that in his less
well-known writing Du Bois conceived of the black male body and the
leadership style that it would seem to delimit very differently. While still
a young scholar, Du Bois began to imagine black participation in democratic institutions as a "queer" marriage between white and black cultures
or races, as he promoted an alliance between the Teutonic "Strong Man"
and his less or "differently" masculine African American counterpart.
In his novel *Dark Princess* (1928), from the Harlem Renaissance era, Du
Bois fictionalizes and internationalizes this desire, centering his novel on
a black activist-dandy whose nattily clad body signifies on, rather than
blindly accepts, masculinist tropes and the strictures of American excep-
tionalism. Du Bois's dandy leads a revolution of the Darker People of the
World and mobilizes a long-standing wish for racial leadership by what
he calls "men who were — different." These men, anxiously positioned on
the spectrums and intersections of race, gender, sexuality, and nation,
take the lead in creating a world in which people of color might claim the
ability "to love and enjoy" not as a privilege but as a right.

In chapter 4, I focus more specifically on the Harlem Renaissance and
the place of dandyism as a modernist sign and goal within black culture. I
concentrate on the dandy figure as appropriated by Harlemites to define
their own modernity away from limiting conceptions of racial and cultural
authenticity. Early twentieth-century Harlem, the New Negro Mecca, was
a place in which black people determined to remake themselves and their
images, against stereotypes and toward self-representation. As this newly
urban black community upgraded its look, black dandies exploded everywhere and became of actual and symbolic use and concern to Harlem's intelligentsia. Attempting to define blackness in a way that was representative of the New Negro and marketable to the world, principals in Harlem
wanted to take advantage of as well as police the infectious style and modern attitude displayed by fashionable Harlemites. Their efforts to do so

were necessarily fraught, as the dandies they looked to as embodiments of black modernity were themselves liminal creatures—heterogeneous and collaged, mulatto and queer—incapable of being sold uncontroversially as the New Negro or the quintessential example of Negro art.

In this chapter, I use the work of James Weldon Johnson to illustrate the challenge the dandy and his ideology of inauthenticity presented to architects of the Harlem phenomenon. Given that he was the resident historian of the Renaissance and an organizer of some of the most stylish visual protests of the National Association for the Advancement of Colored People, Johnson understood the impact of image and the necessity of capitalizing on style and visuality as evidence of a new black attitude. In fact, in his own life he had developed what his biographer called a "cosmopolite self-concept," a sense of himself unfettered by the limitations of America's racial regime, an idea that he came, in part, to express through his own self-presentation. I maintain that during the Renaissance, Johnson, like so many other artists and elites, found himself working at cross-purposes. On the one hand, he was charged (and charged himself and others) with creating and promoting Negro art that had distinct and specific "racial" qualities useful in distinguishing and promoting black humanity and cultural arrival; on the other hand, his own life and personal and artistic expression of blackness as "cosmopolite" defied easy packaging. This contrast and tension between racialized thinking and cosmopolitanism can be seen in Johnson's multifaceted literary work. While researching a history that celebrates the visual panache of black New Yorkers and writing journalism that promoted essentialist notions of racial identity and art, Johnson wrote perhaps the novel most deconstructive of essentialism (and intrigued by black looks) in the Harlem Renaissance canon, *The Autobiography of an Ex-Coloured Man* (1912 / 27). The *Ex-Coloured Man's* protagonist is not a New Negro artist who follows the race-defining dictates of the age, but a dandy who trumps the color line, signifies on it, and then queers it as he explores gender and sex categories at the same time he reimagines blackness. Finding blackness and all the other categories of identity too limiting to embody, Johnson's dandy stays true to his "cosmopolite self-concept" and passes, not for white, but against proscribed notions of race, masculinity, and sexuality. While some might label Johnson's or his dandy's inability to define or embody black modernity as a failure for the Harlem movement, I read it as a success. For when dandies pass or die in fiction of the Harlem Renaissance (I look also at Wallace

Thurman's roman à clef *Infants of the Spring* [1932]), they paradoxically preserve the multiple possibilities of and within modern black identity.

In the last chapter, which functions as an epilogue to the previous explorations of the dandy as a modernist sign, I investigate contemporary visual and filmic manifestations of the black dandy as a figure who expresses, simultaneously, cultural syncretism, racial transcendence, and late-capitalist ennui. If, in the Harlem Renaissance, the black dandy figure passed out of consideration as an expression of black modernity, then its potential as such is taken up again by a new group of black moderns in the contemporary period. Fast-forwarding from the 1940s to the early 1990s, I interrogate here the most ironic, self-conscious, and historically referential manifestations of dandyism in the late twentieth century and early twenty-first.[48] Isaac Julien's film *Looking for Langston*, which opens the chapter, brings the Harlem-era dandy back to life. A product and sign of a triply post generation—postcolonial, post–Civil Rights, post-Stonewall— *Looking for Langston* engenders a revision of the dandy figure that is historically embedded, a vision that looks back at the dandy's history while pushing forward the dandy's critique. In *Looking for Langston* and the self-portrait photography of Iké Udé, Lyle Ashton-Harris, and Yinka Shonibare, MBE, the dandy is reanimated via Frantz Fanon's pronouncement in *Black Skin, White Masks* (1967) that as a racialized subject struggling for actual and psychic freedom he "wears his blackness like a costume." I explore the efforts of these artists, a group of potentially "postblack" aesthetes, to restyle this "costume" in a way that acknowledges, confronts, and perhaps attempts to transcend its long history on the lines of color and culture. Self-styling as dandies as well as exploring the dandy figure's particular "black" history in their work, these artists, whom I dub the artists of New Dandyism, imagine the black dandy as a figure emblematic of the freedoms and limitations of contemporary Afro-cosmopolitanism. In this epilogue and, perhaps, elegy to black dandyism, I hold that these artists image a "redemptive narcissism" that at once redresses the injuries done to the black body and signifies the potential (necessary) tautology of such a gesture. Their art thus exemplifies the persistent coexistence of slaves to fashion and those who make fashion their slave.

Theorizing about black popular culture, Stuart Hall asks his readers to notice "how, within the black repertoire, *style*—which mainstream cultural critics often believe to be the mere husk, the wrapping, the sugar coating on the pill—has become *itself* the subject of what is going on . . . think of how these cultures have used the body—as if it was, and often it was, the only cultural capital we had. We have worked on ourselves as the canvases of representation."[49] By analyzing manifestations of black dandyism from Enlightenment England to the contemporary art worlds of New York and London, I hope to demonstrate that the vicissitudes of black style result less from fashion or the simple turn from one consumption-fueled trend to another than from the constant dialectic between both black and white efforts at black representation and intraracial or intrablack conversations about self and racial identity and representation. Black dandyism images survival as well as a transcendence of the overwrought debate over stereotypes versus supposedly more positive images, stylized versus self-styled images, often simultaneously. The impossibility of defining black dandyism as a wholly or completely transformative act should not lead to conceptions of its failure as a strategy of identity formation. Rather, its status as a ubiquitous, popular performance full of ambivalence should teach one about the myriad contexts in which black identity formation takes place, should visualize the limitations that black people must negotiate and recombine as part of the act of self-definition. When black people use the body as cultural capital and clothing as a necessary but unstable currency of self-worth, a dandy's style reveals the value of blackness in a global market of identity formation in which, at different times and in different places, the cost of embodying or performing blackness can be both too cheap and too dear.

1

Mungo Macaroni

THE SLAVISH SWELL

Dear heart what a terrible life I am led!
A dog has a better, that's shelter'd and fed:
Night and day 'tis de same,
My pain is dere game:
Me wish to de Lord me was dead.

Whate'er's to be done,
Poor black man must run;
Mungo here, Mungo dere,
Mungo every where;
Above and below,
Sirrah come, sirrah go;
Do so, and do so.
Oh! Oh!
Me wish to de Lord me was dead.

Sung by the slave Mungo in *The Padlock* (1768)

What was new to 18th century experience—as codes of
polite behaviours spread to broader and lower strata of society—was the frightening possibility that nothing stood
behind decorum. . . . Fashion, masquerade, theater, cross-
dressing emphasized the total disagreement between
seeming and being, the deliberately fabricated incongruity
between exterior and interior.
BARBARA MARIA STAFFORD,
*Body Criticism: Imaging the Unseen in Enlightenment
Art and Medicine*

On October 3, 1768, at the Theatre Royal, Drury Lane, a character judged "well drawn" and "almost wholly new to the stage" by the *London Critical Review* appeared on the British stage.[1] One of just five roles in *The Padlock*, a comic opera written by Isaac Bickerstaffe with a libretto by Charles Dibdin, the black servant Mungo dramatically entered London's theatrical and visual space. Clad in a tight-fitting, red-and-white-striped silk suit, Mungo strode across the stage in conversation with his master, Don Diego:

> [act I, sc. vi.] *Don Diego, Mungo with a Hamper of Provisions on his Back, which he throws down and sits upon.*
>
> *Mung.* Go get you down, you damn hamper, you carry me now. Curse my old Massa, sending me always here and dere and for one something to make me tire like a mule—curse him imperance and him damn insurance.
>
> *Dieg.* How now?
>
> *Mung.* Ah Massa, bless you heart.
>
> *Dieg.* What's that you are muttering, Sirrah?
>
> *Mung.* Noting, Massa, only me say, you very good massa.
>
> *Dieg.* What do you leave your load down there for?
>
> *Mung.* Massa, me lilly tire.
>
> *Dieg.* Take it up, rascal.
>
> *Mung.* Yes, bless your heart Massa.
>
> *Dieg.* No lay it down: now I think on't, come hither.
>
> *Mung.* What you say, Massa?
>
> *Dieg.* Can you be honest?
>
> *Mung.* Me no savee, massa, you never ax me before.
>
> *Dieg.* Can you tell the truth?
>
> *Mung.* What you give me Massa?
>
> *Dieg.* There's a pistreen for you; now tell me do you know of any ill going on in my house?
>
> *Mung.* Ah Massa, a damn deal.
>
> *Dieg.* How! That I'm a stranger to?
>
> *Mung.* No Massa, you lick me every day with your rattan; I'm sure, Massa, that mischief enough for poor Neger man.
>
> *Dieg.* So, so.

A sassy, back-talking, physically comic slave, Mungo debuted a startling voice and new look for blacks in the British theater. He spoke an identi-

Mr. Dibden in the Character of MUNGO
in the Celebrated Opera of the Padlock.

London, Printed for R. Sayer at N.º 53 Fleet Street & J. Smith at N.º 35 Cheapside.[21]

2. *Mr. Dibden in the character of Mungo.* From *Dramatic Characters, or Different Portraits of the English Stage* (London, 1770). Harvard Theatre Collection, Houghton Library.

fiable version of West Indian speech—a first for the London stage.[2] His ostentatious silk costume was even more outrageous than his confrontational, unusual accent.[3] Fabulous both for his flashy dress and extravagant speech, he was one of the first comic blackface performances on the stage of a patent theater.[4] The combination of novelties that produced this moment had an electrifying effect. In a culture that has been called "a society of the spectacle," in which "[visuality] opens up, controls, or legislates the terrain upon which a large number of concepts are articulated," Mungo and *The Padlock* became a smashing success.[5]

The Padlock was at Drury Lane only after Bickerstaffe and Dibdin (who also played Mungo) had convinced the theater manager David Garrick to take a risk. As a result, the play became "one of the most popular and lucrative works presented during [Garrick's] nine year regime."[6] Contemporary theater critics raved: "Dibdin by his music, and still more by his acting in a comic opera . . . produced that degree of sensation in the public which is called a *rage*."[7] So popular was the character of Mungo in *The Padlock* that his name quickly became representative of his type and his race; the *Oxford English Dictionary* records the usage of "mungo" generically for "Negro slave" as originating with the performance of the play.[8] By 1769 "mungo" was "a typical name for a black slave," "a Negro," as a result of the artistry of Bickerstaffe and Dibdin.

However, just a year later, in 1770, "mungo" also meant "a person of position, a 'swell.'" Soon after Mungo's initial performance, almost immediately after the appearance of the slave in a strange, glittering uniform, it had apparently become typical to think of black slaves in terms of society and fashion. How and why mungos or black slaves in England became swells—people distinguished in the eighteenth century for their unique, often flamboyant, hyper-haute dress and mischievous attitude— is the subject of this chapter. The relationship between slaves, swells, the English stage, and the British empire tells the story of the emergence of the first black dandies, captured and, later, free Africans who learned to use dress, style, gesture, and wit to redesign the roles assigned to them. These dandies illustrate and mediate the political, social, and cultural power of visuality and visibility in an age of colonialism, imperialism, revolution, and nation building.

The Padlock Open'd

Though most famous as a stage character in 1768, Mungo has origins in *The Padlock*'s source, "The Jealous Husband," a tale by Miguel Cervantes from 1613.[9] The "Advertisement" for the opera notes its provenance and indicates the nature of the changes required for the adaptation: "Some little variation has been necessary in the ground-work, in order to render it dramatic; but the characters are untouched from the inimitable pencil of the first designer."[10] Perhaps written in deference to the reputation of the source text's well-known author, this statement isn't exactly true. In fact, the variations or changes Bickerstaffe made to the Cervantes text are meaningful, especially those concerning the character on which Mungo was based. Bickerstaffe's condensation of Cervantes's morality tale turns Luis, a complacent Negro eunuch, into Mungo, a slave with an attitude.

"Render[ing] it dramatic" depended on emphasizing, exaggerating, and making spectacular the role of the slave from one text to the other. This change reflects the contemporary cultural climate in mid-eighteenth-century England and thus made theatrical and box office sense. Unsurprisingly for a morality tale, the plot of the Cervantes text turns on a consideration of rectitude in the face of temptation. Supposedly guarding the gate — affixed with a giant padlock — protecting his master's mansion and the beautiful young wife secreted inside, the slave Luis and the wife's nurse are easily bribed by a young, wealthy, handsome man plotting to gain access to the house. Eventually, the master of the house learns of the breach and of his wife's willing transgression with the interloper; a generous man, respectful of free will, he forgives everyone, blesses the younger couple, and quickly dies. Despite this turn of events, happiness eludes the new couple: the wife's guilt sends her to a convent, and the young man sails for the Indies in despair. In contrast, Luis is freed, perhaps because he had not been expected to act better — only the nurse, presumably a white, Christian woman who should know how to behave, is punished. The narrator of the story glosses the lesson offered: "All I wanted was to get to the end of the affair, a memorable example which illustrates how little one should trust in keys, revolving doors and walls when the will remains free."[11]

In his expanded role in *The Padlock*, Mungo is not at all a naïve dupe; he presents a radically new representation of black servitude. This difference is exemplified in the quantity and tenor of Mungo's speeches. As he himself announces in the song that serves as the epigraph to this chapter, he and his voice are visible and audible, "here, dere, and everywhere." Marianne Cooley, a linguist who has studied Mungo's speech, confirms that, "appearing in both acts, Mungo speaks about a quarter of the lines in the play, whereas African-American characters in other 18th-century plays usually had fewer than ten [lines]."[12] Mungo is not the first black slave to lament his abject position on stage (as some adaptations of *The Tempest*'s Caliban and the popularity of Thomas Southerne's *Oroonoko* attest), but he may be one of the first to combine the sympathy evoked by the oration of a typical noble savage with caustic hilarity. In *The Padlock*, Mungo is the source of all the comic relief. The amusement he generates is only emphasized by the incongruity of his abjection: ironic verbosity emanating from a black body in fancy dress.

Mungo obviously disappoints his duty as a faithful retainer much more than did his predecessor Luis. This disloyalty is registered verbally before it becomes action in the opera. As we can see from the banter that accompanies Mungo's initial entrance onto the stage, the relationship between Mungo and his master is figured as a contest between the master's rattan switch and the slave's surly speech. "Licked," or beaten, by the rattan, Mungo responds by playing off the other meaning of the word—he attacks with his own tongue. The slave's tendency to reposition the licks aimed at him does not always end in a verbal coup for Mungo. For a slave, or at least this one, arguably the first dramatic depiction of an insolent house Negro, the last word is difficult to secure, no matter how compelling the harangue. At best, no clear winner in this contest can be declared, despite the fact that through his own impudence Mungo demands recognition by exposing the master–slave relationship as one in which servility might not include lip service as well.

While Bickerstaffe and Dibdin did not plan to use their adaptation of Cervantes's exemplum to teach a lesson about how funny it might be to toy with the aspirations of freedom for both blacks and women, the finale of their opera nevertheless communicates just that. Both are liberated from their master's house, but neither women nor slaves gain much by the end. Though patriarchy and white male supremacy are not named explicitly as the target of their mutual revolt, an attentive, sympathetic audience understands the connection intimated between them. Indeed, when the curtain descends on the opera, Mungo does not enjoy freedom, as he did in the story, but suffers instead "bastinadoes" ("a blow or cudgell, sometimes to the feet with a stick") for his "drunkenness and infidelity."[13] His punishment, the blows to his feet, attempts to establish a distinction between his physical and linguistic or cognitive freedom. The young wife, however, suffers the opposite fate. Her newly betrothed sings the final lines of the play, adapted from "An English Pad-lock," Matthew Prior's poem of 1704 which gives the opera its name: "Be to her faults a little blind, / Be to her virtues very kind; / Let all her ways be unconfin'd, / And clap your padlock on her mind."[14] Presumably this sentiment—establishing the line between slavery and freedom as a thin one for both women and slaves—ushered in the thunderous applause accorded to this eighteenth-century rage and hit. In the end, a consider-able amount of the opera's allure included, ingeniously, the containment of subversive blacks and women in oppressive antics made palatable, even amusing. Yet, this containment is presented in such a way that it is incomplete—even though the curtain closes, Mungo was not exorcised from the public imagination. Still in his striped suit, a sensation and rage that the audience does not or cannot forget, he remains "here, dere, and everywhere."

Like any other drama that turns on characters in blackface, *The Padlock* presents a challenge to those desiring to claim the oppositional behavior of "black" characters as antislavery material or, in the case of more con-temporary performances, an ironic defense of black civil and political rights. A slave's complaint like that in *The Padlock* can seem like an abo-litionist speech or, if performed differently, an exposure of black foolish-ness. Mungo in *The Padlock* perfectly illustrates the complexity of this phenomenon as, on the one hand, his complaints are registered, yet, on the other hand, his oppositional gestures are seemingly undermined from the onset and at every turn. Indeed, depending on how you assess a seem-ingly singular element of his novelty—his costume—he might be seen to embody a critique of his own complaints. Mungo's glittering uniform can be read as either appropriate or ridiculous for a Negro slave in the eigh-teenth century, as it perhaps covers up the dehumanization and emascu-lation he already suffers as a chattel or indeed emphasizes it. The threat of this dehumanization and emasculation is clear when Mungo's master opens the opera by singing, "My doors shall be lock'd / My windows be block'd, / No male in my house, / Not so much as a mouse, / Then horns, horns, [of a cuckold], I defy you" (act I, sc. i), insisting that no man will gain entrance into his house, while also implying that no man (besides himself) already lives there. In *The Padlock*, Mungo is not a man, not a mouse, apparently not a threat to the chastity of the beautiful woman confined within. Under these circumstances, all Mungo can do is embody and display the confusion attendant to his position and identity by entering the stage scenes later cursing the burden of his blackness and servitude — on his fancily clad back.[15]

Fashioning Character, or Circum-Atlantic Suits

A reprint of *The Padlock* from 1823 boasts inclusion of "Notes, Critical and Explanatory" that advertise the play as "an amusing trifle," "favourably received," nevertheless with "nothing in the plot to distinguish [it]."[16] Fifty years after its original, sensational production, *The Padlock* became an ostensible mediocrity, a play deemed to employ the "usual stratagems."[17] Responsibility for the earlier favorable reception remains a mystery only hinted at in these "Notes": "There is some truth, and a great deal of humour, in the characters of *Mungo* and *Ursula* [the nurse]." Unlocking why there was "some truth" and a "great deal of humour" in Mungo's character is to engage, rather than dismiss, the confused genealogy of this witty and sartorially ostentatious slave.

Though the depiction of Mungo in *The Padlock* appears to simplify his character as it inaugurates the stereotype of the uppity, sassy house slave, in fact, Bickerstaffe's characterization of Mungo should be read differently. Stereotypes — true to the origin of the word in a printing process that produces a text from a *copy* of a printer's plate (not an original) — derive their force from their seemingly a priori reproducibility.[18] One recognizes stereotypical imprints the instant they are formed because of their overdetermined familiarity. More important than a stereotype's original plate is its stereotyped shadow. It is this image that gives the stereotype its currency. The date of Mungo's "birth," 1768, thirty years before the origin of the concept of stereotype, indicates that rather than considering Mungo as such, one had better think of his persona in terms of type or character. Characters and types are the literal and metaphorical elements of a stereotype's manufacture.

In the eighteenth century, character was a key element in the fashioning of identity. In *Character's Theater: Genre and Identity on the Eighteenth-Century Stage*, Lisa Freeman argues that the stage presented and explored modern identity in terms of an exploration of the "concept of character," rather than in terms of the identity formation we have come to associate with interiority.[19] In the time period, character was a much more mobile and fluid mode of subjectivity (one that may not yield a subject at all), "an experimentation with surface and depth, public and private, self and other."[20] What eighteenth-century audiences came to know about themselves and about others they learned by deploying an optic that negotiated the interaction of these surfaces and their perception. Looking at eighteenth-century theater and culture in this way allows one to see the degree to which spectacle, the accentuation and promotion of visual (and audible) surfaces, mattered in terms of defining character and identity. Recognizing self and other, sympathizing, identifying, and disidentifying with familiar and foreign images, allowed audiences to formulate their characters and those of others.

If, in a theater of character, "the only basis for assessing others consisted of multiple, contradictory and competing 'outsides,' that which can be observed, but never confidently known," then Mungo's "outsides," or his spectacular dress and speech, reveal the nature of the black and British identities being formed in the production of the play.[21] The use of dialect associated with black slaves and servants and Mungo's outrageous striped costume were the only two major features of the opera which were decidedly not part of the Cervantes story.[22] An investigation of these surfaces shows not only how the English thought about Negro character, but also, perhaps, how they imagined the presence of black people in England—the nature and extent of the mobility they would have, whether or not they could or should be marked as different, what to do about their sexuality. How Mungo was seen (and his speech is a part of his recognition and perception) reveals how he was constructed as a character and a type.

Mungo's character had very little to do with actual Negro interiority or subjectivity. Rather, it can be regarded as a particular effect of English participation in the triangular Atlantic slave trade, an element of its growing empire. This trade brought foreign people and items to England's shores and was thus one of the principal forces driving the creation of London as the center of what some have called the "world of goods."[23] In the eighteenth century, London was, according to the historian John Brewer, "the fastest-growing city in Europe . . . it stood out as the metropolis of the moment, a city of riches, conscious of its rising status and eager to clothe its naked wealth in the elegant and respectable garments of good taste."[24] Items for sale in this world included actual black people as well as representations of them, well packaged, elegantly costumed, and bought easily enough at the Drury Lane box office. It is these representations and their status as social, cultural, and economic exigencies that reveal the instability of this world and the characters and identities it produced.

Mungo in *The Padlock* serves multiple purposes in that his play is as much about British anxieties surrounding the disturbance empire brings to racial and gender hierarchies as it is about British superiority over other empires. His character, then, matters as an explanation of his enormous popularity and of what that popularity indicates about contemporary conceptions of blackness, Britishness, and their relation to each other. Although eighteenth-century theater is largely thought of in terms of social drama, with fops, rakes, and naïve socialites occupying so many drawing rooms, national identity was also at stake on the stage, as Britain expanded its empire throughout the century. Who counted as British and how the expanding category of Britons was to behave individually and with each other were salient topics for the theater. According to the theater historian Bridget Orr, the Restoration and eighteenth-century stage reflected and in some ways engendered the "on-going tensions" accompanying the development of the British empire.[25] Vision, visibility, and visuality were the impetus and mechanism through which new places and new people were presented on stage.[26] These tensions were also instantiated by the visual in that the theater was influenced by a new kind of ethnography, as the older accounts of colonial people and places were being replaced by more recent firsthand observations by those directly involved in mercantilist enterprises, especially the slave trade.[27] This update of information had the effect of changing the terms in which people were described and how they were seen.

As a play set in Spain, *The Padlock* was already part of a discussion about the inferiority of the foreign; with the addition of an actual exotic to its cast, Mungo, the play becomes about many other issues attendant to empire. By the time the opera opened, Spain and Spanish themes had been a staple on the stage for nearly a century as the British used Spain "as exemplary of the failure of an imperial state apparently blessed by many advantages but brought down by ambition and intolerance."[28] Theatricalization of this intolerance took some very specific forms. The plot of *The Padlock* was actually a common theatrical trope demonstrating Spanish incivility and enthrallment to an absolute monarch. When read as a standard Spanish play in which the despotic husband / Spanish emperor is foiled, *The Padlock* does seem to employ "the usual stratagems" as it stages a lesson about the need for moderation and civility. But when read from a domestic angle, one that considers Mungo's anomaly as part of this British group (an exotic among foreigners), the lesson learned is much less easy to discern. On the one hand, *The Padlock* dramatizes Mungo's subordination to Diego's will, the subjugation of slave to master. On the other hand, Mungo's own spectacular characterization, his saucy attitude and outrageous dress, mitigate his total domination.

In fact, it is precisely Mungo's costume and dialect that made him a spectacle that somaticized so many anxieties in this visually obsessed, imperial world. The old adage "clothes make the man" could not be more true in the case of Mungo: his costume has much to say about the patently constructed racial and gendered identities of African slaves in the early days of British imperialism. As depicted in a well-known contemporary engraving of Dibdin in the role of Mungo, the slave's costume consisted of a two-piece silk suit, pants of knee breeches and a short and collared jacket, reputedly in red or pink and white stripes. Burnt cork, white stockings, and, in another illustration from 1769, a white hat completed the costume.[29] The keeper of the costumes at Drury Lane, Garrick was famous throughout the eighteenth century as a manager who frequently mounted productions advertised as "new dress'd in the Habits of the Times."[30] Garrick's production of *The Padlock* appears in one stage history as a comedy with "New Dresses, Music, and other Decorations"; in another his costuming of Mungo appears as the principal illustration in a chapter entitled "Stage Costume and Stage Tricks."[31] Interestingly, in the latter history, *The Padlock* illustration is never directly referred to in the text, confusing its designation as an innovative costume, or an actor's "trick" used to elicit raucous laughter.

The mid-eighteenth century was a time of innovation and reform in costuming tradition. The custom of the nobility of donating their castoff clothes to the theater had ended about one hundred years earlier; since then, plays were often performed in contemporary dress, with managers relying on the public's imagination. Despite their efforts at reform, managers and dressers often produced stage costume deemed at best eclectic or at worst absurd.[32] Garrick was famous for his creativity in such situations. In fact, his costume for Mungo was part of a well-meaning but often failed effort to introduce consistency in costuming as well as historically correct costumes to the English stage. However, in the case of Mungo, Garrick's desire to avoid incongruity of dress and role seems to have failed. Mungo's glittering striped suit is altogether unfit for the likes of a slave, except, of course, if the absurdity was intended to elicit an ironic comic effect or, more intriguingly, point to more recent trends in British slaveholding.

What the manager of Drury Lane might have had in mind for Mungo bears some investigation. According to the theater critic Raymond Pentzell, Garrick was known to have chosen from the following standard conventions when dressing his characters: (1) *costume à la turque*, used in general for the exotic; (2) Spanish dress/Van Dyck, for Spaniards or villains; (3) Old English Dress, found on Shakespearean characters and other Tudors; and, (4) the "Roman shape," found on heroes, ancient and modern.[33] The character of Mungo, a black slave in a Spanish play, nominally a villain and originally an exotic, would seem to present Garrick with a challenge. Mungo's striped suit, approximately something between the Turkish and Spanish conventions, is a perfect example of how the demands of historical accuracy may have clashed with an eclecticism made necessary by the available options.

A look at the engravings of Dibdin as Mungo shows that, surprisingly, he is not dressed in a turban, caftan, baggy breeches, or cassock, clothing that traditionally signals the exotic or one from the Middle East, Near East, Africa, or the Americas. Nor is he in a strictly traditional Spanish costume, "a plumed hat with turned up brim, a ruff or broad falling collar, a short, close-fitting jacket, slashed knee-breeches, and a short cape."[34] Instead, the costume synthesizes the two, mapping the spectacular quality of the supposed oriental onto the more staid Spanish suit, producing the gaudily striped, close-fitting, two-piece ensemble. The appropriateness of this hybrid suit for Mungo—himself a cultural hybrid, an African resident in Europe—is both remarkable and accidental. Indeed, Mungo's suit is not a "new Dress" sewn just for him. In fact, the suit had a long past (and future) reflective not of cultural hybridity, but of the material limits characteristic of a dressing room in an eighteenth-century theater. As Pentzell notes, the suit can be seen in illustrations from other plays acted at Drury Lane from 1740 to 1805, including such different

Shakespearean roles as Macbeth in *Macbeth* and Viola in *As You Like It*.[35] Known as the Garrick "fancy suit," derived from Spanish dress, "distinguishable by its bright colors, tinsel striping, and usual lack of slashing," it was developed as an alternative to the Roman shape and was perhaps used in place of the Turkish costume.[36] "Its connotations impossible to pin down," Mungo's suit "supplied such needs as these": "the appearance of villainy, once Spanish suits had lost their character designation either by their increasing historic and geographical association or by their assimilation into 'Old English': the comic tenor of . . . Harlequin-esque 'villains' . . . ; the removal of characters from modern context when their historical dress was either unknown or regarded as too bizarre and unflattering; and, simply the shortest way to attract attention—by bright color and glittering stripes."[37] The costume works on Mungo precisely because it combines villainy, comedy, and spectacularity. However, it is a spectacularity that rather than removing Mungo from the modern context more firmly inserts him in it. The costume works on Mungo because of its general ability to signify a spectacle as well as its specific function as a vehicle of black spectacularity, a tradition of black dress established before the performance of *The Padlock*. The costume works on Mungo in *The Padlock* because, as many historians of black Britain note, black slaves resident in England, from the time of their first landing in the 1550s through the eighteenth century, were often used and regarded as luxury items and ornaments rather than as laborers. They were therefore dandified, dressed in hyper-haute versions of the latest fashion.[38]

Hoping to incorporate Mungo into his Spanish play more easily via costume, Garrick wittingly or unwittingly spectacularizes him, forestalling or at the very least complicating that very integration. The padlock was also an actual costuming accessory before it became a theatrical one, as padlocks adorned the necks of some slaves made to wear silver or gold collars as part of their livery. This convention obviously resonates strongly with *The Padlock*.[39] Mungo's costume attracts attention to and signifies on this phenomenon, while at the same time materializing the difficulty of incorporating exotic characters into either the theatrical or the real world.

Though the "bright color and glittering stripes" of the two-piece suit make it hard to ignore, Mungo's outrageous costume goes unremarked upon within the action of the opera. It is a costume or a trick that is not taken advantage of on the level of plot. As such, it is a silent but glaring reminder of the political and cultural context of British colonialism that surrounds the rage the play generated. Less easy to ignore is Mungo's speech, the other aspect of his singularity responsible for the British public's vision of him as "wholly new to the stage" and public life. The texts of the play make clear that he speaks an English that is definitively marked as different; after the performance of the play, the speech is heard specifically as black, as can be inferred from the *Oxford English Dictionary*'s etymology of "mungo." Significantly, Mungo's speech is not only black, but also associated with American slavery, as the character of his complaints originates in a journey made from Africa to the Americas and then to London. It is appropriate and potentially delights not because it expresses his disillusion with panache, but because it is plausible in content as well as form, part of an emerging notion of what might constitute Negro character. Again, like its innovation with costume, *The Padlock*'s novel recording of black speech styles reflects theatrically what, from the British vantage point, is reality on the world's stage.

The literary representations of Mungo's speech vary slightly, as seen in the promptbook versions of *The Padlock*.[40] Black dialect, like blackface and other performances of blackness, originates with a desire to represent aspects of blackness by actually re-presenting them, producing an impossible authenticity. In her analysis of Mungo's language in the *The Padlock*, Cooley identifies his speech as one that includes both "accurate" and "stereotypical representations" of West Indian–inflected English.[41] Cooley reads the variation present as evidence that the dialect had to be more plausible than precise—what audiences wanted was not real black speech, but something they understood as black.[42]

"Rendering [the original story] dramatic" and producing a very popular version of Negro character demanded speech and costume neither too real nor too fantastical, something recognizable but not too threatening, an "experimentation with surface and depth, public and private, self and other."[43] What might be said to be real about the fact, if not the form, of Mungo's dialect and costume is that it is undeniably born out of the British slave trade and the accompanying anxious efforts to imagine black people in Britain or as British, a constituent part of the national cast. At the time, this fiction or fantasy might be said to be part of, as Peter de Bolla argues, "an incredible pressure . . . to work out, precisely to figure a way of representing, the composure and compass of the public sphere and to conceptualize the new cultural domain in terms of visuality."[44] If so, Mungo in *The Padlock* provides an extraordinary object lesson for such a project. That a character on a London stage speaks in a recognizable and somewhat accurate rendition of West Indian or "African-American" dialect, while in a costume that simultaneously reveals his familiarity and foreignness, suggests that what is also being dramatized in this theatrical moment is the complicated prehistory of African-diasporic identity formation and representation.

If, in the eighteenth century, identity was not "an emanation of a stable interiority, but the unstable product of staged contests between interpretable surfaces," then the development of black subjectivity, as dramatized by Mungo, is a process which begins with the formation of a spectacular Negro character—performances of blackness in blackface, fancy costumes, and imitations of black speech.[45] As such, black character and identity begin as a white fantasy of black reality, which thereafter black people must confront. It is no wonder that by the time Mungo saunters on stage in 1768, he proclaims himself "lilly tire," since the journey between black character and subjectivity, exteriority and interiority, between Africa, America, and Europe, entails a *circum*-Atlantic trip. When this diasporic slave character in glittering stripes becomes associated with an actual black much more successful at taking advantage of his sumptuous visuality (he is also dressed in silks), the possibility of black dandyism—a knowingness, acknowledgment, and capitalization of the intersection of image and identity—arises.

Black Looks Onstage and Off

The black image precedes the black man in England, as the stage actually introduced black people to English audiences long before they met them in person.[46] Even a character as novel as Mungo had predecessors; certainly not the first "stage black," his character is noteworthy because unlike others he was verbal and ironic, sassy and fashionable. While Mungo may not have shared all of these character traits with his predecessors, he was part of a phenomenon they all had in common: nearly all black characters on the English stage were there because of the drama of their look and what that look implied about Britishness, blackness, gender, and sexuality. Examination of Mungo's theatrical ancestors, spectacular black slaves and servants in travel narratives, plays, masques, and pageants reveals how this black look was constructed and how black characters, fictional and actual, might fashion a look back.

Interpreted as excessive and anomalous, unorthodox and deviant, African bodies and behaviors in travel narratives provided a lens through which the English established norms of political, cultural, economic, and moral behavior in the medieval and early modern periods. Narratives such as *The Travels of Sir John Mandeville* (English translation, 1499), Leo Africanus's *Geographical History of Africa* (English translation, 1600), Richard Haklyut's *Principal Navigations* (1589, last volume translated, 1600), and Samuel Purchas's *Pilgrimage* (1626) serve as a record of what the literary scholar Kim Hall has called a "licensed voyeurism" practiced by early explorers in Africa and other non-Western places.[47] Emphasizing the excessive nature of the European response to Africa and Africans as well as its inherent basis in visuality, voyeurism connotes an interest that exceeds mere observation and reveals the role of these images in the establishment of a sense of national, ethnic, and racial identity that resulted from these narratives of exploration.[48] Perhaps because they were already rather dramatically described, the African images in the travel narratives naturally found their way to the stage. There, their potency as representations of racial, sexual, and gender difference—the contrast they provide establishing the authority of white male European normativity—was exploited. Black theatricality, in terms of physical presence, behavior, and dress, became an integral part of theater and undoubtedly influenced perceptions of blackness and Englishness onstage and off.

The characterization of the early English stage's famous Africans and Moors—Muly Hamet in George Peele's *The Battle of Alcazar* (1588–89), Aaron and Othello in Shakespeare's *Titus Andronicus* (1592) and *Othello* (1604), respectively, and Eleazar in Thomas Dekker's *Lust's Dominion* (1599)—might be said to take after one of their own, Aaron, who "puts on villainy like a costume": "Away with slavish weeds and servile thoughts! / I will be bright, and shine in pearl and gold" (II.i.18–20).[49] The separation between Aaron's character and his representation, the idea that his "villainy" functions like a costume or a mask, suggests that some playwrights understood the way in which the marginalized or oppressed can be forced to inhabit a certain position, for the sake of drama, on a theatrical or national stage. Consequently, what the "costume of blackness" came to imply proved difficult to remove from conceptions of actual black people, those for whom blackness seemingly comes *pret à porter*.[50]

Critics concerned with the "popular image of the black man in English drama," the "black presence in English literature," or "Othello's country-men" (titles of early important studies) emphasize the almost total lack of redeeming value in any of the portraits of blacks on stage: "Lust, revenge, cruelty, demonism, ugliness—these are the major qualities that compose the image of the black man as he was fashioned by the playwrights.[51] More recent studies of British theater and imperialism, such as Bridget Orr's *Empire on the British Stage: 1660–1714*, have complicated this view, arguing that critics have approached black characters in seventeenth-century drama with a too "static a view of race."[52] Felicity Nussbaum echoes this sentiment, adding that a little later in the eighteenth century proper "both an essentialist racism ('race' as a series of exclusions based on biological and behavioral traits) and the language of cultural nomi-nalism (the recognition that classifications are simply convenient labels) pertain to the period."[53] For Orr and Nussbaum, the theatricality of these black characters was of primary importance in negotiating the increas-ing "absolute difference" of black characterization and its relationship to Englishness and whiteness.[54]

At the time, race seemed to function as a costume that could be put on and taken off but never really abandoned. The idea of racial charac-teristics functioning like attire is reinforced by the fact that early stage blacks actually put on black costumes, using makeup, masks, gloves, and other fabric to mimic the blackness of skin. Blacking up through makeup began with Ben Jonson's *The Masque of Blackness* in 1605 and continued as a tradition for many centuries; the trend of using tight masks of fabric lasted until at least the late eighteenth century at masquerades. In 1768, a week after Mungo's debut in *The Padlock*, *The Gentlemen's and London's Magazine* records that a man attending a masquerade given in honor of the king of Denmark at the Haymarket appeared "in the character of an African, with a rich diamond collar round his neck; his face was so com-pletely covered with black silk, and so neatly put on (for he wore no mask during the whole night) that he could not take it off." That same night, a "Mr. Mendez" also appeared in the guise of Mungo.[55] Here blackness is an actual costume—its popularity seemingly indelible.

By the time Shakespeare was writing "there were several hundreds of

black people living in households in the aristocracy and landed gentry or
working in London taverns"; the everyday Londoner "would have had two
conflicting views of blacks, one of their savagery out of travel books and
from the stage and the other of their basic humanity as fellow citizens in
the streets."[56] Actual black people had been in England since 1555, in the
form of official delegations from Africa or serving as house and personal
servants.[57] This early acquaintance did not increase Britons' comfort with
others; they experienced a "strong sense of dissimilarity from those without."[58] This sense of "dissimilarity" seemed to prevail as English people
and playwrights integrated very little of their everyday observations of
blacks into their theatrical representations of them, with the possible exception of Shakespeare and a few others.[59] Although I will not address
exceptions to this rule in any detail, I will say that I find the two most
well-known blacks on the early modern stage, Othello and Caliban, intriguing as precursors to a figure like Mungo. Othello provides a contrast
to Mungo in terms of early models of self-fashioning as he inhabits his
Orientalist or Africanist costume in a way that provokes respect rather
than risibility, but with the same complications concerning his blackness
as a mask. Othello is also a study in the commensurability of exteriority
and interiority, as a figure who combines nobility and a desire for the
racial other, whose hotheadedness and insecurity lead him to murder.
Caliban's famous backtalk, not to mention his imputation concerning the
nature of his language acquisition—"You taught me language, and my
profit on't / Is I know how to curse. The red plague rid you / For learning
me your language!" (*The Tempest*, I.ii.365–67)—intersects with Mungo's
oppositional, complaining speech. From the stage, then, with the possible
exception of *Othello* and *The Tempest*, one learns little of the actual black
response to contact or confrontation with the white, Western world.

Dressed in turbans and wielding swords while delivering tirades, most
black characters in the theater are described as "a loud presence," who
"rant . . . and curse their way through the plays with obscene antics and
treacherous behaviour."[60] In contradistinction, silence characterizes their
counterparts in many pageants and masques. The black figures portrayed
by royal courtiers in masques, such as those in King James I's (later James IV
of Scotland) staging of Jonson's *The Masque of Blackness*, are valued more
for what they communicate visually and thus metaphorically or allegori-
cally than for what they say. According to Hall, it was well known that

King James had a "penchant for . . . exotic or unusual" spectacles in which blacks were featured as "dehumanized alien curiosities."[61] In fact, the wedding of James and Anne of Denmark in Oslo (Norway and Denmark were united at that time) had featured "four young naked Negroes" dancing in the snow, boys who died soon after from the exposure.[62] *The Masque of Blackness* that followed James's accession to the English throne served to solidify his extravagant use of the exotic in a show of personal power and national pride. Though no actual people die in *The Masque of Blackness*, the liberty taken with their representation—the masque dramatizes the "whitening" of the daughters of the River Niger, seemingly by James's own royal fiat—enables a celebration of whiteness and Englishness that undergirds the ideology of the British slave trade and imperialism.[63]

By the seventeenth century, England and English identity became increasingly defined by means of excessive responses to blackness that bear some relationship to luxury, leisure, and wealth.[64] Blackness was not a tool just of the royal, but was also exploited by the powerful merchant class in London. The economic gain to be had from the display of exotics, intimated in the court masque, is laid bare in the Lord Mayor's Pageants. Sponsored by trade guilds, the pageants commemorate the annual inauguration of the new lord mayor by yoking celebrations of civic and national pride to an early form of advertising and marketing. As many of these guilds were involved in international trade, including markets for fruit, cloth, sugar, and spices, the pageants used to great effect blacks and other exotics who hailed from those faraway places where the new luxury items originated. Consisting of a series of tableaux vivants staged atop carriages and drawn through the streets of London, the pageants found a much wider spectatorship than the masques and even the theater, including royalty, guild leaders, tradesmen, and the general public. With such a large and varied audience, the guilds were careful to control the images they offered and, as a result, left little room for ambiguity when depicting the potentially unruly inhabitants of their growing commercial empires. The pageants had perhaps the greatest opportunity to influence mass conceptions of blackness and to increase the association of blacks with spectacular performances sometimes based on the celebration of their oppression and exploitation.[65]

In contrast to the masques and the theater, the Lord Mayor's Pageants put whites in black costume and real black people, often small boys, on display with other exotic animals; together, they visually represented the power of the British merchants' reach across the world.[66] The description of an "Indian emperor" from a pageant in 1672 makes this clear: "And in the reer of the Camel, highly exalted on a silver throne and under a canopy of silver fringed, sitteth an Imperial person alone, in Royal habit; his face black, likewise his Neck and Arms . . . on his head a Crown of various coloured feathers, a rope of Pearl about his neck, Pendants in his ears, short curl'd black wool-like Hair."[67] A hybrid of Latin American and African, this king (in blackface) was surrounded by two actual black boys, described as "two Negroes, attired properly in diverse colour'd silks, with Silver or Gold Wreaths upon their Heads, as Princes of West-India."[68] According to convention, most of the white characters and those in blackface do not speak, or, if they do, they deliver monologues or sing in praise of the pageant sponsor. The actual blacks never have lines in the play. These exotic ornaments fit into a scripted scene that is both still and largely silent. Such opulent displays, then, especially those featuring blacks as part of a civic tradition, can enable a damaging deceit. The spectacle of luxurious excess, at the expense of black bodies, becomes a method of distracting a national audience away from acknowledging its oppressive tactics at home and abroad.

Later in the eighteenth century, these common ways of representing blackness in association with luxury and exploitation changed yet again before Mungo's debut in 1768. Earlier models of blacks as villains, revengeful, lustful, or silent partners of the slave trade's riches, gave way to the trope of the Noble Savage, a new model of black masculine character. A development seemingly sensitive to a deeper analysis of slavery and imperialism, the trope also responded to English culture's turn toward sentiment. Perhaps the best known of this type is Oroonoko, famous from Aphra Behn's novel of the same name (1688), whose story was first adapted for the stage by Thomas Southerne in 1695. Oroonoko was of royal birth and possessed European features both in terms of his heroic behavior and his beguiling good looks. He was "enormously attractive to eighteenth-century audiences," and the play was the "second most-produced drama in the eighteenth-century theater."[69]

As seen in engravings from the play's run throughout the century, Oroonoko cloaks his heroism and nobility in costumes that seemingly replay the associations of blackness on stage that came before: he is both in feathers and luxurious fabrics. Indeed, one might expect that Oroonoko might become less foreign and more English as the century wore on and the play's propagandistic role in the abolitionist cause grew. Instead, as Nussbaum's readings of the engravings from 1776 and 1774 reveal, Oroonoko's visual style fluctuates but remains incommensurate with his dramatic role.[70] The later image of Oroonoko and his wife, Imoinda, finds him in the latest fashion of the day, a finely embroidered three-piece suit ensemble that is finished with a ruffled shirt. Nussbaum argues that "neither [Oroonoko nor his wife, Imoinda] resembles a slave in any way, and the African origins of the couple are completely effaced."[71] The earlier portrait of the couple confuses even more. Here Oroonoko is pictured as a "dark-skinned Highlander," a "bearded, half-naked, and scowling hybrid African-Scots creature" who "wears a low-slung furry loin cloth resembling a kilt and a feather in his coon-skin cap."[72] Depicting Oroonoko as both hypernoble and unabashedly uncivilized, these prints demonstrate the seemingly fundamental division of visuality and purported character for black people.[73] What blacks look like and how they behave (even when supposedly noble) rarely correspond for those enmeshed in the slave trade. In fact, the system seems to rely on the production of this division between looks and character. Thus, Oroonoko could be savage and swell and declaim against slavery in costume associated with primitivism or, perhaps, even with luxury slavery.

The instability of the representational economy for black men symbolizes the confusion with which conceptions of race and blackness were being formed. Even so, as the century progressed, this instability comes to look more and more like a dichotomy, as black men came to be seen as "noble *and* savage, as prince *and* slave, as heroic *and* comic, as white *and* black, in blank verse *and* speaking dialect, as threatening to white women *and* forming racial alliances with them."[74] Indeed, adding a noble savage to the black male repertoire did little to change fundamentally black stage styles and their association with slavery and commerce. The creation of Mungo in the same time period as these two depictions of Oroonoko as noble and savage is surely evidence of this. All of these roles—from the masques, pageants, plays of the early modern and Enlightenment stage—and their inventive or creative costuming haunted actual black men in Britain, who were just as likely to be dressed in velvet as to be compared to "parrots, monkeys, and lapdogs."[75]

"Finest, Best Made Black Boys"

The spectacle of "Negro-boys" atop fantastical griffins in the streets of London reveals that blackness is often spectacularized in the service of establishing whiteness and European nationality as supreme, as a mode of mystifying crude economic relationships. However, this story is told not only on a public dais, but also in private homes. In costume but not wearing makeup after performances, some of these Negro boys returned to English palaces, mansions, and county seats where they lived and were treated as pets. In England, black boys and black men were sometimes luxury items, collected like any other signifier of wealth and status. Peter Fryer uses the word "vogue" to describe the period of their celebrity in British history, approximately 1650 to 1800, evidencing the fact of their status as commodities subject to the whims of fashion.[76] The first textual evidence of the black boy as pet appeared in the newspaper *Mercurius Politicus* on August 11, 1659, in an advertisement for a runaway slave: "A negro-boy, about nine years of age, in a grey searge suit, his hair cut close to his head, was lost on Tuesday last, August 9th, at night, in St. Nicholas Lane, London. If anyone can give notice of him to Mr. Thomas Barker, at the Sugar Loaf, in that Lane, they shall be well rewarded for their pains."[77]

Those privileged and wealthy enough to participate in New World exploration or the slave trade directly or indirectly—royalty, nobility, ship captains, and merchants—began the trend of keeping Africans as entertainment, curiosities, and sometimes surrogate sons. In almost all cases, these black slaves were, as James Walvin notes, "clothed in splendid and at times bizarre liveries" from the time of their earliest use in England.[78] Even Queen Elizabeth herself owned or employed a "lytle Blackamore" nattily got up in "a Gascon coate of white Taffeta, cut and lyned with tincle, striped down with gold and silver, and lined with buckram and bayes, poynted with poynts and ribands."[79] While historians of black Britain, such as Fryer, Walvin, Edward Scobie, Folarin Shyllon, and Gretchen Gerzina, have duly noted the presence of these unusual pet people in the chronicle of Britain's involvement in the slave trade and the formation of an early black British community, relatively little attention has been paid to the impact their forced foppishness has had on white perceptions and representations of black people or, more intriguingly, how such a practice affected black self-perception and representation. Revealing how black boys were packaged as prestige items also reveals the raw material they could use to reimagine themselves, reinvent their images personally and politically. As they embody emerging perceptions of blackness and masculinity as well as trends in fashion and dress, these black boys prefigure the black dandies who, in later historical moments, more self-consciously participate in their own stylization.[80]

English royalty did not originate the phenomenon of the black luxury slave—it followed a trend begun much earlier by southern European courts.[81] Britain's comparably late entry into African and New World exploration and trade prevented them from obtaining suitable subjects (or objects) earlier. Nevertheless, by the eighteenth century England was so well known for its black boys that other Europeans knew where to go when hoping to purchase "lytle Blackamores"—when "in 1769, the Tsarina of Russia wanted a 'number of the finest best made black boys, in order to be sent to Petersburgh as attendants to her royal majesty,' her agent came to London to buy them."[82] At first the playthings of royalty, black boys quickly became an affectation for the lower orders of elite society—they were, at the time, fashion forward.

The luxury black symbolizes the extreme wealth of his owner in the denial of his laboring power and potential. He is, perhaps, the perfect example of conspicuous consumption. What made these slaves conspicuous was, in large part, the irony-laden dichotomy of their status as debased beings in uniforms of sumptuous dress. Liveries played an important role in easing the transformation of black boys into objects for Englishmen, aiding in their stylization as owned. A black boy might find himself in "a blue livery suit trimmed with a narrow, closely woven braid of silk or gold, or silver thread called a galloon and lined with orange cloth, with silk-fringed sleeves and gold galloon facing; or maybe a Fustian frock with yellow Mettal Buttons, a blue livery coat lined with red, with Yellow Mettal buttons, a red Waistcoat, Breeches and Stockings, and a hat laced with Silver Orris—a kind of gold or silver lace."[83] Clad in garish but expensive outfits or in oriental apparel complete with turban and feather (as Mungo should have been), these black slaves were what Hall would call "meta-objects" whose dress primarily communicates a wealth and cosmopolitanism not necessarily their own.[84] At this time the African can be known only through his participation in an exotic display designed by the elite to feel wealthier, more powerful, and ultramodish through a process of ornamentalizing and displaying the African abject.

These images were often memorialized in the form of painting and jewelry designed to trumpet elite status, good taste, and the beauty of whiteness.[85] The portrait of Lady Mary Churchill, duchess of Montagu, from the 1720s includes just such a servant, who, in his own elegant three-piece suit, matches the sartorial refinement of his mistress. Sometimes identified as the famous eighteenth-century black writer Ignatius Sancho, who served the duchess's family in his youth, the page is dressed with a stateliness that ennobles the slightness of his office, as his only task here is to hold the duchess's yarn. Symbolically, he does much more work in that his physical disposition, the blackness of his skin, and the sumptuousness of his dress serve other purposes—he looks at the duchess, directing the viewer's gaze toward her, his skin contrasts with that of his mistress, making it appear even more white, pure, and lovely, and the almost understated sophistication of his dress indicates the truly elite, aristocratic wealth of his owners. In this domestic scene, the intimacy suggested between the lady and her servant is mitigated by the open door in which the servant stands. This portal also has actual and symbolic weight—seated and at leisure, the duchess is the only permanent part of this picture: the servant can go, seemingly at any time.[86] In art, as in life, black boys were in the background, both needed and expendable; as such, they have no look of their own.

Reinforcing the impression that the blacks in these paintings and the slaves they depict are in a kind of representational prison is the fact that they are often depicted as collared or chained. Forged in brass, copper, silver, and sometimes gold, the collars were often padlocked, reflecting actual social practice—an advertisement in the *London Advertiser* states, "Matthew Dyer, working goldsmith, at the Crown in Duck Lane, Orchard Street, Westminster, intimates to the public that he makes 'silver padlocks for Blacks or Dogs; collars & c.'"[87] Engraved with their owners' names and the family's coat of arms (if applicable) and often including a home address, the collars turn the slave chain's function into fashion in a rather astounding way. The wearing of expensive "jewelry" and clothes seemingly did little to convince the boys of the merits of prestige slavery, and they often ran away:

A black boy, an Indian [perhaps West Indian], about thirteen years old, run away from the 8th inst. from Putney, with a collar about his neck with this inscription: "The Lady of Bromfield's black, in Lincoln Inn's

3. *Lady Mary Churchill with negro page*. Attributed to Enoch Seeman. Boughton House, Audit Room. By kind permission of His Grace the Duke of Buccleuch & Queensberry, KT.

Fields." Whoever brings him to Sir Edward Bromfield's, at Putney, shall have a guinea reward.

Run away, a Tannymoor [tawny-moor?], with short bushy hair, very well shaped, in grey livery lined with yellow, about seventeen or eighteen years of age, with a silver collar about his neck with this directions: "Captain George Hasting's boy, Brigadier in the King's Horse Guards." Whoever brings him to the Sugar Loaf in the Pall Mall shall have forty shillings reward.[88]

Given that they were so overwhelmingly marked as signs of white affluence, blacks in a quest for self-representation would have to confront the growing archive of images that purportedly captured their essence. The nature of this process of black–white identity formation was perhaps understood by white observers of the prestige black boy phenomenon. Witness this letter sent to Richard Steele's and Joseph Addison's *Tatler* magazine in 1710, a letter that many feel was a satirical, ghostwritten gesture by the editors themselves:

Sir,—I am a black-moor boy, and have, by my lady's order, been christened by the chaplain. The good man has gone further with me, and told me a great deal of good news; as that I am as good as my lady herself, as I am a Christian, and many other things; but, for all this, the parrot that came over with me from our country is as much esteemed by her as I am. Besides this, the shock dog has a collar that cost almost as much as mine. I desire to know whether now I am a Christian, I am obliged to dress like a Turk and wear a turbant. I am, Sir, your most humble obediant servant, POMPEY"[89]

Whether the letter was written by Pompey or by Steele and Addison, its tone communicates a dis-ease with identity as illustrated by servitude and its uniform, a question about whether the clothing truly fits. For a black slave, the livery was a menace that could not be removed easily, especially if the outfit included the permanent accessory of a silver collar. Judging from runaway slave advertisements, slaves in livery and collars abandoned their duties, seemingly contradicting claims that the life of a prestige slave was one of relative ease. For Pompey and his ilk, the mechanisms of self-expression available to the slave are proscribed by the look of his servitude.

Since the nature and location of the labor performed by servants (in the kitchen, at the front door, in the stable) often determined what they wore, the livery communicated status both within and without the household. Employed as personal servants or valets, black boys lived in relative intimacy with their masters and mistresses. One such boy is playing a seemingly public role in a painting by Edward Matthew Ward from 1845, attending his master and mistress as they exit Lord Chesterfield's waiting room. In a bright red velvet livery trimmed with gold braid and white furs, accessorized with a matching turban with feather and red hose, this boy holds a guitar in one hand and supports his mistress with his shoulder. As in the painting of Mary Churchill with her servant, the black page in red provides not only musical entertainment, but also an aesthetic contrast to his white-clad mistress. Indeed, like their servant, the master and mistress are elegantly, if not ostentatiously, dressed—all the silks, velvets, ribbons, and laces complement and set off their white-powdered faces. While in the Churchill portrait the main compositional juxtaposition is between mistress and servant, the contrast in this painting is between the master–servant group on the right and the somber, conservatively dressed man in the brown suit seated on the left.

Titled "Dr. Johnson in the Ante Room of Lord Chesterfield, waiting for an Audience, 1748," this painting records a famous incident of misunderstanding that took place in the mid-eighteenth century. The somber man is Samuel Johnson, the compiler of the *Dictionary of the English Language*, who in 1748 came to Lord Chesterfield, a great patron of literature, to secure his subscription to the *Dictionary*. Instead of seeing Johnson, Chesterfield admitted an actor and playwright famous for his foppish comedies, Colley Cibber (likely the man on the left). Johnson wrote his great defense of letters and high art, "Letter to Chesterfield," in response to this snub. While it may seem that what is being recorded here is a contest between fashion and intellect, high and low arts, one can also read this painting in terms of what it might say about different styles of slaveholding. Though most famous for his dictionary, Johnson later became infamous for his generosity to his own black servant and personal secretary, Francis Barber. Of resolute antislavery convictions, Johnson took Barber in and later left Barber his estate when he died, including a generous yearly pension, an act unheard of in those times. Though not depicted in this painting, Barber and his sober presence are called up in the sneer

4. Ward, Edward Matthew (1816–79). *Dr. Johnson in the Ante Room of Lord Chesterfield, waiting for an Audience, 1748*. Tate Gallery, London / Art Resource, N.Y.

Johnson throws toward Cibber and his fancy family group, supported by the elegant black.[90]

Though not meant as an antislavery gesture, Johnson's sneer indicates his awareness of the true nature of this kind of clothing for the black "elite." Sumptuary laws enacted to check the magnificence of livery suggest that the servant clothing did indeed both establish and disturb social hierarchies.[91] Though masters seemingly employed livery to control their own status as well as that of their servants, their efforts at doing so were undone by the very phenomenon they sought to employ — the notoriously capricious world of fashion.

One can imagine that an amusingly dressed little black boy may have been treated like a family member, a "cherished" retainer, a plaything, a nuisance. He might have also experienced all of these roles during his lifetime, as a slave in the same family. Often slaves but sometimes servants, the liveried blacks were actually in a particularly anxious position, as English society could or would do little to accommodate them outside of the terms of their service as black servant boys. The volatility of their position can be discerned from the fate of one of their number, Sambo, servant to Elizabeth Chudleigh, the "profligate Duchess of Kingston": "She brought [him] up from the age of five or six, and . . . she was so fond [of him] that she took him, elegantly dressed, to most of the public places she frequented. He sat with her in the box at the theatre, watching the *Beggar's Opera*. Unfortunately, when he reached the age of 18 or 19 he began staying away for several days or nights at a time and associating with a set of 'whores and ruffians,' so she packed him off to the West Indies."[92] One might speculate here that the livery also functioned as a cover for the sexual threat posed by black boys as they became men. Not able to be fired like a white counterpart and having no place to go if he were let go, a maturing Sambo was sent away potentially to live a life of plantation slavery. As a solution for what to do with adolescent black boys, exile to the West Indies was not an unusual choice; those young men who were imputed to be "drunks, lechers, those who lacked a sense of responsibility, had no loyalty" were often sent back to the colonies.[93] Sambo's fate manifests the cruelty that fancy dress and a luxurious residence would seek to hide—plantation slavery in the Americas. Thus, this one life is a poignant example of the interstitial relationship between hypervisibility and invisibility, between luxury and labor, between the expression of pleasure and the policing of sexuality.

The alleged good treatment of some of these black boys further complicates their position on a figurative threshold, as some of them, including Sambo, were educated and highly cultured. When these boys were given access to education and contemporary high culture, their lives stretched the experience of slavery to include the breeding of curious creatures— black Englishmen or "darling blacks"—who lived among the elite and like the elite but ultimately without personal and collective freedom.[94] Add to this the way in which many blacks experienced slavery or servitude in Britain, isolated from each other in their masters' houses, able to meet and socialize only at their masters' whim. As Gretchen Gerzina notes, "The lives of most black people were an odd mixture of isolation and assimilation, of separation from each other and the larger society while being connected to both."[95] Thus, the threshold they stood on was not one separating the classes only (as was the case with their white coworkers), but a position of forced negotiation between an African heritage and English acculturation that resulted in the emergence of a unique worldview. A "diasporic manner of thinking," Nussbaum argues, "entails constituting oneself as located not simply on both sides of a border, but 'in-between' geographical places and available identities including a repertory of cross-racial borrowings instead of a settled hybridity."[96] Black men of some privilege, luxury slaves negotiated on and with their very bodies this "repertory of cross-racial borrowings."

Though ostensibly the most favored of their race, the liveried blacks, as we have seen, were only rarely allowed to live lives that aspired to a status beyond survival. That the English had mixed feelings about the blacks among them is obvious from the diversity of the black population resident in English-controlled territories. In the eighteenth century, of the twenty thousand blacks in London, those other than prestige slaves and servants were for the most part laboring slaves or members of the working poor who had escaped or been manumitted from slavery. They were beggars on the streets of London, stowaways from plantations in the Americas, seamen in the navy or merchant marine, musicians in military bands, laborers, craftsmen, apprentices, prostitutes, circus-type curiosities, actors, scholars, and ministers.[97] The uneasy and ironic combination of slavery and freedom, prestige and poverty, bewildered notions of the black man's place in English society. Even though the population of this diverse black community fluctuated with the demands of economics and the trends of fashion, the uncertainty about their status remained constant. England was not sure whether to welcome or bar them from their country and homes; whether to enslave, merely tolerate, educate, or befriend blacks.

In the absence of a comprehensive plan, the English seemingly accommodated all attitudes, resulting sometimes in a great deal of irony. The general indeterminacy provided opportunities for blacks to establish their own views, to add their own voices, whether in writing or gesture. For example, the black writer Ignatius Sancho spent his life after service chronicling his life of genteel poverty. Self-taught in the libraries of his masters and mistresses, Sancho enjoyed the wit and culture that provided analytical if not material solace in his quest to keep his wife and their children, known as the Sanchonettes, in food, clothing, and medicine. The letters he wrote to his fellows, men and women who occupied positions ranging from servants to literati like Laurence Sterne, exhibit a tension between the condition of black bodies (for the most part, objectified and misused in slavery and made abject in poverty) and a well-educated mind. One might read Sancho's literary record of the deterioration of his gouty body and the illnesses that befell his family as both metonymy and metaphor for the dis-ease that characterized the lives of most eighteenth-century free blacks.

The contradictory treatment of black people eventually resulted in an era of competing narratives, this time not just among British authors of black identity, but also among black Britons themselves. Indeed, rivalrous claims for black stylization and identity formation can be seen in the single figure of the man known as the Mungo Macaroni, Julius Soubise, the black companion to the duchess of Queensberry. A mid-eighteenth-century celebrity, he was a participant—rather than merely a forced patron—in the current trends of a commodity culture of visibility, luxury, and fashion that established new intersections of image and identity for the individual and groups of others.

Slave to Fashion
Julius Soubise as Mungo Macaroni

The introduction to the biography and cultural world of Catherine Hyde Douglas, known as Kitty, duchess of Queensberry, begins as follows:

> The eighteenth century appears to the eyes of the twentieth century to be more crowded than any other century with famous characters of all sorts; romantic and tragic, gallant and brutal, splendid and sordid, cultivated and barbarous. And of these the most notable have been frequently described and discussed in history and general literature. But there are others, figures more shadowy, that are seen in the background, of whom we only catch glimpses.[98]

In placing her heroine among the "shadowy," Kitty's biographer unwittingly tells the reader where to look for another "famous character," the duchess's constant companion, the black fop Julius Soubise. Known as a "mad eccentric" for her preferences in art and fashion, Kitty was not as famous as Alexander Pope and Johnson, but she and Soubise nevertheless cut a figure during their most active years on the London scene.[99] At once magnificently "romantic and tragic, gallant and brutal, splendid and sordid, cultivated and barbarous," Soubise merits the same kind of superlatives used to describe other eighteenth-century notables. Indeed, no "darling black" was "more petted, more loved, more spoilt" than he.[100] His visibility earned him the notice of the white and black elite communities and extended to the duchess of Queensberry a definite notoriety, whether she desired it or not. An elegant, extravagantly dressed and accessorized black man, Soubise was "the fop among fops."[101]

In fact, Soubise's celebrity was so great for a time that he was immortalized as *the* "Mungo Macaroni" in a caricature print from 1772.[102] Distinct from fops, members of the ruling class who were accused of being "the offspring of more than one Man's labour, for certainly no less than a Dancing, and Fencing-Master, with a Taylor, Milliner, Perfumer, Peruque-Maker and a French *valet-de-chambre*," macaronies were a group of late eighteenth-century Londoners notorious for their flamboyant appearance, performative behavior, and artificiality.[103] It is in the "Mungo Macaroni" print that the etymology of "mungo" finally makes sense, where the Mungo stage character meets its swell. Formerly a sassy but unwittingly glamorous slave, popular only after *The Padlock* had debuted the type in 1768, Mungo / "mungo" takes on a whole other dimension in association with Soubise. Bringing together the oppositional nature of impertinence with the self-conscious use of style and image, Soubise in Mungo's clothing signals the potential for a black character to constitute identity by actually and figuratively talking back, taking control of his own self-presentation and look.

A second print of 1773 takes the Soubise–*Padlock* connection even further, this time with additional implications for the history of black self-fashioning. This print, of the duchess and Soubise in a fencing contest, appears under varying titles: "The Eccentric Duchess of Queensbury fencing with her protégé the Creole Soubise (otherwise 'Mungo')" and "The Duchess of Queensberry playing at foils with her favorite Lap Dog Mungo after Expending near £10,000 to make him a—." Together, the titles reveal that the true subject of the print is the relationship between Soubise and Mungo, the play or contest being staged here between blacks,

A MUNGO MACARONI.

5. "A Mungo Macaroni by M. Darly, 1772." © Copyright the Trustees of the British Museum.

the nobility and the excessiveness ("£10,000") associated with the whole affair. Though having different titles, both prints include a tag emanating from Soubise's mouth that ventriloquizes Mungo in *The Padlock* but with an incisive difference: "Mungo here, Mungo dere, and Mungo everywhere. Above and below. Hah! Vat your gracy tink of me now?" In combat with his mistress in the print and made threatening by the complicated

The D——of ——— playing at FOILS,with her favorite Lap Dog MUNGO after Expending near 10000 to make him a——.

6. "The D_ of [erased] playing at foils with her favorite Lap Dog Mungo after Expending near £10,000 to make him a—." Courtesy of the Lewis Walpole Library, Yale University.

association with the fictional Mungo, Soubise responds here with a confrontational "Hah!" that marks a turn in the stylization of black slaves and servants. As the popularity of a real black servant and *The Padlock*'s fictional slave converge, as theatrical fantasy meets real-life theatricality, a black demand for recognition emerges. What darlings like Soubise perhaps came to know and exploit was the powerful possibility that identity, as signaled by clothing and social milieu, is at base composed of just that: signs and symbols, capable of being performed and resignified. Such an intervention takes advantage of the fact that hegemony is, as Bruce Robbins argues, "not absolute domination, but a continually fluctuating, continually renegotiated give-and-take, a dialogue that is unequal, but not quite monologue."[104] The emergence of the consciousness of such a phenomenon enables misrepresentation to betray itself.

The life of Julius Soubise, the "Black Prince" of 1770s London, carries meaning well beyond the small stage on which it was intended to be performed. Soubise outgrew his role as a prestige servant, walked out of the play that would subsume him into the self-dramatization of the white elite.[105] As a former slave, companion to a duchess, athlete and coach, entertainer, ladies' man, black fop, and quite visible member of the emerging black community, he was theatrical, spectacular, and a complication to perceptions of blackness, especially of black masculinity and sexuality. Though he himself did not leave a handwritten record of his life, he is included in the memoirs and reminiscences of some of those who knew him best.[106] Raised in an atmosphere in which "the law takes no notice of negroes," Soubise was visible in the face of official invisibility. He outstripped his origins in bondage and for a time held and returned the surveillant gaze of an increasingly visually oriented social world.[107]

Soubise arrived in England from Jamaica on April 2, 1764, at age ten, the son of a female slave in St. Kitts and a free white man. The property of a Captain Stair-Douglas of the Royal Navy, he is listed tellingly as "Othello" on the manifest of the ship that brought him to England.[108] He passed into the household of the duke and duchess of Queensberry that same year. Kitty, cousin to the captain, was so "struck with his manner and address" when she met him that she begged the captain to give her the anachronistically described "uncommonly smart and intelligent little Mungo."[109] The duchess apparently manumitted him, named him Julius Soubise (after Charles de Rohan, prince de Soubise, a courtier to Louis XV and Madame Pompadour), and treated him like an adopted son. According to the duchess's desires and in spite of the censorious opinions of others, Soubise was educated, outfitted in the latest fashions of dress, and became well versed in social convention. Some of Kitty's friends, Lady Mary Coke among them, "thought that it was all very well to give the little negro an occupation, but that fencing and riding were likely to arouse in him rather lofty expectations which might not be fulfilled."[110]

Never really a servant but not literally or properly entitled to the life of the leisure class, Soubise had to do something when he grew up, rather than merely be somebody. Despite Mary Coke's objections, he became a student of the famous Italian fencing and riding master Domenico Angelo.

Soubise was so skilled as an equestrian that Angelo hired him as one of the chief instructors at his school. His race and circumstances were no bar to his success: Angelo's son Henry notes that even though "his colour and humble birth might have made him repulsive to his high-born pupils; on the contrary, these circumstances seemed to excite a greater interest in his favour."[111] Soon popular among Kitty's friends, with his employer, and with the "young bloods" that he taught, Soubise seemingly proved himself "grateful and affectionate" for his unusually privileged upbringing.[112]

While one cannot be sure how aware Soubise was of his exceptional status or the import of such a role on his social reception, his legend does include moments of coyness on his part and that of his patrons that defy easy characterization. The dynamic between mistress and companion was difficult to determine:

> However this might be [the settling of Soubise's future at the Angelos' School], this minion, somewhat spoiled by indulgence and flattery, forgetting that he was a chance child, thrown by fortune upon the precarious bounty of strangers, began to assume unbecoming airs, and vaingloriously boasted being the son of an African prince.
>
> It was well known that the Duchess was prompt in mortifying vain assumption. "O is it so, Master Soubise?" said the Duchess, "I must lower your crest I perceive."[113]

Even so, his pretensions did not affect his popularity at home, nor did he suffer at school, as Angelo's maids found him "very attractive" and continued to call him "the young Othello."[114] The repute of his amiability and gallantry was only amplified in the larger social world when he became the talk of the town and the butt of jokes. The precariousness of his position is captured in a rather subtle, skillful joke told at a dinner given by the Angelos:

> Mr. [Thomas] Sheridan [a popular lecturer] observed to [Samuel] Foote [actor-dramatist], when dining at my father's [Carlisle House, home of the Angelos], the conversation being on the Duchess and her *protégé*, "that considering all circumstances, he was the best behaved, unassuming minion of the great, that he had ever known;" and "so modest withal," added Dr. Kennedy [a physician], who was of the party. "Yes," replied Foote; "but damme, for all his modesty, I never saw him blush."

This repartee offended the elder Sheridan, who, always pompous and ceremonious, considered his consequence assailed by any sallies of wit.[115]

The lack of clarity in Sheridan's response — does he take offense because of the excess of wit or because of incipient racism? — signals that the environment in which Soubise matured was one in which his status as an exception was provisional and dependent on capricious witticism.

For good or bad, the duchess's companion was an almost universal object of notice. Handsome and reportedly possessed of "well-formed legs and well-proportioned body," the shapely legs thought "so rare with the black sons of Africa," Soubise was sought after as an artist's model.[116] In addition, he was an accomplished musician: "He played upon the violin with considerable taste, composed several musical pieces in the Italian style, and sang them with a comic humour that would have fitted him for a *primo buffo* at the Opera-house."[117] Also known as a "favourite performer at the Vauxhall pleasure gardens, Soubise always won mighty applause and an encore for his comic opera rendering of a popular ditty called 'As now my bloom comes on apace the girls begin to tease me.'"[118] Possessed also of pretensions to a career in the theater, he studied elocution with Richard Sheridan and was known for his renditions of scenes from *Othello*. In his late teens Soubise was well in the public eye; he even managed to be promoted at the riding school to a new position at Windsor to teach the young nobility at Eton College. During this time the "attractive" Soubise was "loved by his patroness, trusted by his employer, mothered by his employer's wife, lionized by eminent actors, writers, and painters, the pet of Georgian aristocrats, . . . [and] could do no wrong." That is, until he "suddenly changed his manners and became one of the most conspicuous fops in town."[119]

Inexplicably (or not), around age nineteen, Soubise transformed himself from a black in fop's clothing to a fop who was black. Of course, the transition from one to the other was hardly smooth and somewhat impossible to complete in an age of slavery. Biographers, memoirists, and historians all note this change in his behavior, declaring it for the most part an inevitable result of "all this adulation" and of Kitty's "parenting."[120] Henry Angelo sets the scene for the fop's emergence:

> Even whilst at my father's [Domenico Angelo's], [he] had private apartments, unknown to the family, where he assumed the habits of an

extravagant man of fashion. He had a constant succession of visitors, and his rooms were supplied with roses, geraniums, and other expensive greenhouse plants, in the spring. He was equally expensive in his perfumes, so that even the frail fair would exclaim, "I scent Soubise!"

He was no less extravagant in nosegays, and never seen, at any season, without a *bouquet* of the choicest flowers in his bosom. As general a lover as Don Juan, he wrote as many sonnets as Charlotte Smith; but not in that elegant writer's mournful strain—for he was as gay as a butterfly.[121]

Apparently, a room of his own, where he could "assume habits" of his own choosing, was all that Soubise needed to fashion a social debut in his own style. His coming out also included taking boxes at the opera and membership in several fashionable clubs—the Thatched House Club in St. James's street, "a rendezvous for wits, politicians, men of fashion," the Brush Club in Long Acre, a kind of speakeasy, after-hours club, and, most important, the Macaroni Club, [which was actually just a table at Almack's Club], whose cosmopolitan, aggressively styled members he began to honor with his own dress.[122] The "gayest of the Macaronis," Soubise presented himself "dressed in powdered wig, white silk breeches, very tight coat and vest, with enormous white neck cloth, white silk stockings, diamond-buckled red-heeled shoes"—in short, just as he appears in the "Mungo Macaroni" print.[123]

When he was not touring Hyde Park in his own carriage accompanied by a white groom, he was seen riding with the duchess in her post chaise and four and dining with her (and other *chérie*) at Windsor's most expensive inns. A version of his liveried brothers but with a difference signaled by his extravagance, Soubise seemingly capitalized on his forced spectacularity. Aware of the constructedness of his position and performatively responding, he signified on his visibility and status as someone else's luxury item by meeting white excess with black luxuriance.

Soubise's tale begins and ends in boundary crossings. Initially part of a tradition that violated the sanctity of personhood through ostentatious objectification, he ends up playing the same game, but with allegedly disastrous results. Certainly his transition from slave to celebrity manifests the desire of the powerful to disarm difference; however, at the same time, as a result of the risk it entails, the same act grants to its object a measure of power. Soubise exhibited his resulting influence in both clever and regrettable ways. While his biographers treat the incident differently, they all mention that his years as London's most colorful spendthrift and foppish cad ended when Angelo finally convinced the duchess to send Soubise abroad "to mend his wild ways from the high life of the rakes."[124] According to some, the black fop actually left to hush up his rape of one of the duchess's maids.[125]

Like all young black men serving as luxury slaves or companions to the wealthy, Soubise would have had a difficult time publicly conducting any kind of romantic relationship, especially with a white woman, whether a maid or a marquess. Considered an Othello from an early age, his sexuality was as much on display as his color and foreignness. Dressed in the latest fashions as a boy while at Kitty's side, he was at once feminized and spectacularized, made into an object whose own desires could be ignored. Clad in elaborate outfits as an adult, with Kitty's purse in his hand, he was seemingly a different kind of curiosity able to act, at least sometimes, on his own will. For Soubise and all black slaves and servants, whether they labored in the fields, in country houses, or within a system of social and cultural signs, the subjugation of their race is absolutely dependent on the disciplining of their sexuality. Valued for the titillating combination of sameness and difference he added to the drawing rooms of the elite, Soubise could not express his desires in a society that continually used him to satisfy their own. Given his isolation as a black in elite society, the exercise of his sexuality could be perceived only as a threat of miscegenation. Although a product of the confused desires of the British elite and, indeed, a man whose very body and its adornment embodied that disorder, Soubise could not or would not be allowed to spread the bewilderment further. His "bloom" could not, in fact, come on apace because it had no socially acceptable place to go. Even Soubise's relationship with his aging patron Kitty was suspected of being untoward.[126]

Guilty or not of violating his patron's maid — one can imagine a number of scenarios in which Soubise's actions might have been misunderstood — he was forced into exile and sailed for Calcutta in July 1777. There, he was reportedly helped to prosperity by the duchess's friends in the colonies. He lived for twenty-one years as the master of his own fencing and riding school before he was killed at age forty-four by a fall suffered in breaking a horse for the British government in India. He is rumored to have married a woman of unknown ethnicity in India and fathered a child.[127] Kitty herself died just two days after her protégé left England, ending an era in which white and black conspired to fashion the life of a former slave like that of royalty, in the face of a culture that would demonize them both.

Soubise was perhaps self-made only after being manufactured in the service of white affluence. Just as livery can signal a servant's or slave's status simultaneously on the margin and at the center of aristocratic life, so it can function as a symbol of the servant's divided loyalties to master and self. This phenomenon finds a primary exemplar in Soubise, a free black who, though wearing fine clothes, was just a fashion trend away from being taken for a slave. Similarly, he must be remembered as a black man who sported his finery and displayed his wit and talents in the very clubs and coffeehouses where slaves were routinely put up for sale.[128] Though his look was ostensibly put together by others and then by himself to signify (and resignify) certain social absolutes, the total package — black man, clothes, performative social environment — contained a message much more complex.

Indeed, a result of taking the rakish sons of the House of Lords and other British elites as his models, Soubise's recourse to foppery and macaronic fashion — his insistent theatricality, spectacularity, performativity — was a response to cultural phenomena affecting both blacks and whites. The foppery had its origin in the theatricality and performativity of the spectacular beaux made famous by Restoration drama.[129] The fop is Restoration society's "most consummate showman," a "one-man metatheater" whose "every movement and speech brimmed with theatricality."[130] A fop on stage or in the drawing room hopelessly complicated from within the naturalness of society's organizational categories. The questioning and realignment of gender roles embodied in the fop were nurtured by increased urbanization and cosmopolitanism in England, according to the historian of masculinity Michael Kimmel.[131] Liberating women and feminizing men by means of removing them from rural environments that reinforced traditional gender roles, the city opened a window into other worlds, both domestic and foreign. The fop's effeminacy, intimated by his obsession with his own pretty person, merely confirmed the figure's supposed turn away from a number of masculine and civic norms. Fop attire and accessories — elaborately embroidered long frock coats in luxurious fabrics, long waistcoats of velvet with brocade trim, silk stockings, lace shirts, fine leather pumps, scented linen handkerchiefs, finely powdered perukes, beautiful lacquered snuffboxes — signal this man's overweening interest in self-presentation and the role that imported goods play in that distinction.[132] As an effeminate xenophile, the fop is a treasonous man on a number of levels — he is not manly enough (too busy with the self, he does not spend enough time wooing women), authoritative enough, or English enough and is thus a traitor to his class, gender, and country. Though his sexuality is not necessarily in question, the fop's failure to be a "true Englishman," a sensitive but stoic man entrusted with familial and national concerns, came to be seen as symbolic of a national crisis. Enter Soubise, imported African, "fop among fops," and point of anxiety for the white elite and for the culture at large.

That Soubise was called not only a "fop among fops," but also a "Mungo Macaroni" signifies beyond semantics. London in the 1760s knew macaronies as a group of aggressively foppish men "defined from the outset in terms of what they consumed, and particularly what they wore"; they named themselves after "returning from European tours enamoured of European style [and] set up, as a punning rejection of the robust anglophilia of roast beef, the Macaroni Club."[133] Like fops, they were ostentatious dressers and consummate consumers of foreign goods; however, macaronies intensified their engagement with the commodity culture surrounding them, fueling a midcentury debate between image and identity that was intimately related to concerns about character, especially masculine character. Whereas the presence of fops caused society a widespread but somewhat muted panic about the social roles of men, the macaronies' activities, exemplified by their exploits at Vauxhall Pleasure Gardens in London, resulted in a short-lived but profound investigation of the emerging contest between spectacularity and interiority, character and identity.

When satirists chose Soubise as "A Mungo Macaroni," the joke they intended was actually on them, since their association of an actual black fop with the macaronies served to increase the figure's oppositionality rather than disarm it. Described by some arbiters as "extravagantly outré," macaroni dress, according to the fashion historian Valerie Steele, signified on conventional Continental male dress in terms of the extremity of the cut, the rich fabrics, the distinctiveness of the accessories associated with it, and the panache with which it was worn.[134] The macaroni suit was slimmer than those of other soberly dressed men and even those of the fops, featuring "a shorter and more closely fitting waistcoat and frock coat" that, because it riffed on the long, flowing coats favored by the fops and exposed the body (coming dangerously close to showing the buttocks), was dubbed obscene.[135] Macaronies accessorized this sexy, form-fitting ensemble with "shoes with buckles and bows, light silk stockings, a variety of accessories, including a nosegay, a particular handkerchief tied into a bow, large coat buttons, a large and often tasseled cane, one or two watches . . . and sometimes a cutlass (the phallic nature of the weapon was surely intended)."[136] Of course, the crowning glory was often the macaroni's elaborate, generously proportioned powdered wig, whose grandiose appearance was augmented even more with the pun of a very small French hat placed atop it. While fops were effeminate, macaronies were seen as creatures much more ambiguous in gender and sexuality and playful—an outfit with both a cutlass and tiny French hat as accessories can be nothing but—and thus much more dangerous and desirous to civil society.[137]

Fresh from the Grand Tour, macaronies extended the fop's performative arena by taking their stylish show out of the drawing room and into the public square. Macaronies worked their fabulous outfits in gardens and parks, where they could promenade, watch others, and be watched. Vauxhall was the macaronies' haunt and the site of their intrigues, a veritable outdoor theater with daily performances by the social elite. Called by Miles Ogborn "a key site in 18th-century cultural production," Vauxhall was primarily a visual experience; its buildings and walkways presented an "array of tableaux, illusions, panoramas, phantasmagorias and automated pictures" to be navigated by the fashion-conscious.[138] Sexual frisson lurked behind every corner. Like his fashionable pals, Soubise frequented Vauxhall, even appearing there as a musician. A space populated by attractions that relied on illusion, exaggerations or diminutions of scale, and a playful banter between fantasy and reality, Vauxhall was a place where what Ogborn calls the "hungry gaze" reigned.[139] Consisting of a look employed by those eager to attain status through notice, as well as those looks designed to cut, or dismiss, someone from personal and group consideration, the "hungry gaze" was the macaronies' genius. As they added this gesture of regard to their already cultivated oppositional vestamentary look, they heightened their critique of societal reliance on the transparency and acceptability of certain social and gender norms.

The key to the macaronies' power is the return of the gaze — it is a gesture that presupposes a sense of self and is an action that performs and is a process of subjectification that incorporates, rather than denies, desire. Appetizing to look at, hungry to see and be seen, macaronies are just as much aggressive spectators as they are the "wrong sorts of spectacles" and "illegitimate narcissists."[140] Irony abounds in the imputation of such wiles to Soubise, a person who, as a former slave and a fop, was himself an object and a subject of empire.

Sensational and in vogue from about 1764 to 1774, the macaronies garnered media attention: they were seen by everyone in the pleasure gardens, in the theater, at clubs; they became the subject of society magazines like the *Macaroni Jester* that routinely inveighed against them; they were featured in a play. Already visually excessive, they were immortalized as visual objects in the later 1760s, when they "went from being something life-sized, extravagantly decked out and at court to being something small, made of paper and widely distributed" — the subjects of an extremely popular caricature print series by Matthew and Mary Darly.[141] Soubise as "Mungo Macaroni" is a Darly print. These famous prints were part of a general cultural obsession with "making persons into reading matter," with, as we've seen, discerning the surface of an individual to determine his or her character.[142] The connection between these caricatures and the then-contemporary obsession with character goes well beyond the similar etymology of the terms; eighteenth-century Britons looked to the concept of character as it was experienced textually, visually, and in the theater to make sense of a world increasingly crowded with options of who and how to be.[143] It was critical to eighteenth-century people that character be legible and that different types and characters be available for comparison — print caricature serves this comparative role as it exaggerates character, making it, putatively, easier to read.

The Darlys' print series played an extremely important role in the interpretation of mid-eighteenth-century society, its types and the relationship of character to individual and national identity. Satirical prints like the macaroni caricatures negotiated the differences between type and individual, indicating that in the period, oddness or singularity is both fascinating and troubling (especially if the anomaly depicted is race, gender, or sexuality).[144] At the time, to be an eccentric individual was to be fascinating, to be eccentric within even the outer limits of social norms was, within this small but increasingly cosmopolitan social world, to be famous.[145] To be eccentric, a former slave, and a habitué of the *ton* was to be the one and only Soubise—a man who was simultaneously a foreigner and, because of his inclusion in this series, a "real Englishman," a slave to fashion, and an early "stylist of black subjectivity."[146] As the "Mungo Macaroni" on the street and in print, Soubise "blurred the boundaries of class, gender, and nationality and acted as a cautionary tale and a secret exemplar for the rising middle classes as they debated how to become urban cosmopolites while remaining authentically British."[147]

Being the subject of a caricature was both an honor and an insult—this is certainly true of Soubise as he takes on the guise of "A Mungo Macaroni." When Darly depicted Soubise as a "Mungo Macaroni," one must assume that it was a decision made to remind the public and the ubiquitous Soubise of his lowly "Mungo-esque" origins.[148] Of course, the barb also would have been thrown at the macaronies themselves—apparently, as creatures dependent on consumption for their flare, they possess and exhibit a uniform that even Mungoes can and do emulate.[149] The spirit of farce behind the parody would definitely allow for multiple critiques. However, few would have anticipated that adding "Macaroni" to "Mungo" would actually aid, rather than hinder, acknowledgment of a Mungo's own subversive construction of black identity. Many historians of macaronies and their prints have pointed out the close connection between macaroni philosophy and another eighteenth-century social form based in part on fantasy, the masquerade. Both forms rely on self-fashioning and the fears of artificiality that such freedom generates. As an occasion in which everyone was in costume, deliberately attempting to manipulate surface and character, masquerades "celebrated so profoundly the hybrid and duplicitous nature of material appearances," that, like the macaroni prints, "dramatized the thrill and danger of self-creation."[150] Soubise himself most certainly attended masquerades in which Mungo costumes were in evidence; there must have been many occasions in which costumed Mungoes confronted this black macaroni and vice versa. At midnight, both would have removed their masks and gazed hungrily at the other's "black" face. What resulted from this confrontation was the establishment of the performativity of black identity, the fact that it can and is performed by both black and white. Soubise as "A Mungo Macaroni" is both in costume and himself—it is this possibility that disturbed and excited all participants in this society of spectacle.

"Here, dere, everywhere, above and below," blacks were initially foppish to fulfill whites' desire for recognition. However, given the opportunity, as was Soubise, blacks themselves met that desiring gaze with a
look of their own, sometimes sizing up others and their methods as they
themselves were measured. To be sure, Soubise's "hungry gaze" might
be difficult to see, as it exists between the lines as part of the will to
aggressively self-style and trope on his own visibility. Seeing and seeing
through certain structures designed to fix his identity and place in the
culture, he seemingly reached for the bigger picture, a fuller sense of
what it could mean to be a black fop or Mungo Macaroni, in contrast to
a foppish black or Mungo. Fops and macaronies understood the lesson
that foppish blacks had always known — image can and does affect identity formation in a cosmopolitan commodity culture. The fop / Macaroni
critique revealed that the emergence of new masculinities and self and
national identities were deeply implicated in imperialism and the commodity culture that it generated. These events were all too easy for the
prestige black to share and capitalize on, given that he was constituted
by them. As Mungo says in his song, "Sirrah come, sirrah go"; signifying
on foppery and the macaroni style presented one way for slavish swells in
England to dismiss those dictating their image and identity and take on
another master — themselves.

The black fop's emergence and evolution into the macaroni, a change
from being stylized to self-stylization, were not exclusive to the fashionable set. In the mid-eighteenth century, a recognizable black community with an active social and political life began to form in England. At
this time, the black population grew as loyalist refugees fled the wars in
America (especially the American Revolution, 1776–83) and legislation,
while not prohibiting slavery or the slave trade, redefined the status of
slaves on English soil (the Somerset case, 1772). The freed and enslaved
joined English-born blacks in evaluating and protesting the untenability
of their condition as both bonded and free.[151] Black protest included gestures announcing self- and group identity in the form of autobiographical narratives and other antislavery tracts like those of Sancho, Ukaw-
saw Gronniosaw (1770), Ottobah Cuguano (1787), and Olaudah Equiano
(1789). In addition, blacks organized themselves for reasons of both politics and pleasure. Francis Barber was said to hold a salon at the home
he shared with Johnson, an example of how "the houses of well-placed
Negroes often became a focal point where others met and sheltered or

simply passed their spare time."[152] Current newspapers carried notices of black social events, sometimes linked to the celebration of political victories against slavery, including a ball celebrating the Somerset decision.[153] Such events served as a notice to owners, masters, and employers and to themselves that blacks did constitute a sizable community, even though they were isolated as servants in the homes of the elite or as seamen on merchant vessels. Even exceptional individuals were now seen as part of a group newly visible not merely as spectacles but as urban denizens with an agenda. Thus representation of black individuals and of the group—long out of black control—became as important to blacks as it had been to whites.

Coda

Coming to America

The indeterminacy that surrounded the Mungo figure titillated: the slave of *The Padlock* and all that he connotes in costume and attitude fascinated the late eighteenth century. Bickerstaffe's Mungo was marketable even beyond the considerable achievement of lending his name to a new word subsequently descriptive of a whole class of black people. In 1768, Mungo achieved status as a "popular obsession"; such notoriety included his celebration in caricature—the "Mungo Macaroni" and the fencing image—the placement of his image on a "silver and blue glass tea caddy"—a photograph of which is in the Theatre Museum in London—and, for a time, a vogue of his personality as a masquerade ball costume, as garnered from contemporary press reports.[154] Mungo served not only as a disguise at entertainments, but also in print, making an appearance as the apocryphal author of a collection of essays. Called *The Padlock Open'd* (1771), the volume ironically rails against the decadence of English society and concludes with a plea to render the stage "a useful diversion" instead of a "scandal and reproach to our religion and country."[155] In addition, Mungo's signature phrases, "Me lilly tire" and "No Massa," became "part of everyday conversation"; Mungo also became a part of the official record when referenced in a joke recorded in the annals of the House of Commons.[156] Dibdin himself became obsessed as he named his first son, born in 1768, Charles Isaac Mungo.[157] Part of high, low, and popular culture, the Mungo figure became iconic. So archetypal was Mungo that even the best-known black actor of the nineteenth century, the legendary "Negro tragedian" Ira Aldridge, played him, often in performances that followed his signature role as Othello. He wore a similar striped suit.[158]

In his various incarnations, Mungo may have been omnipresent, but, as the nineteenth century dawned, the blacks he came to represent seemingly were not. Increasing legal challenges to the slave trade, which was abolished in 1807, and to slavery, ended in 1834, slowed importation and immigration; repatriation schemes to Sierra Leone and Canada depleted some of the population; intermarriage with low- and middle-class whites occurred more frequently. These developments soon resulted in the false perception that the black community in England was vanishing and, by the early nineteenth century, had disappeared.[159] While historians have assumed that black Britons descended from grace to ordinariness, from hypervisibility to invisibility, in fact, as Gerzina and others have shown, black Victorians were a small but visible part of communities as diverse as those inhabiting the Liverpool waterfront and the royal palace.[160] Blacks and especially the darlings did not lose their status as objects of scrutiny and hence the force of their collective return gaze (see especially the case of Queen Elizabeth's "adopted" daughter, Sally Bonetta Forbes)—indeed, even Mungo had a legacy. The mourners who have relegated Mungo to the vicissitudes of history have not heeded the fact that the attenuation (but not disappearance) of Mungo and his fellows from the English stage and streets did not signal the end of his journey "here, dere, and everywhere." Indeed, just months after he appeared at Drury Lane in October 1768, and despite his immediate success, he suffered the fate of some of the other errant blacks of the era: Mungo was exported to the American colonies. *The Padlock* debuted in New York City in May 1769.[161]

Born of English colonization and imperialism, Mungo quickly felt at home in America as a new stage embraced him and *The Padlock*. The play enjoyed success in America and a legacy as great or perhaps greater than that which it had experienced in England. Applause in New York earned *The Padlock* openings in nearly all of the major colonial cities. New York and Philadelphia saw forty-six productions before the turn of the century; other productions "blanketed the colonies" as Mungo carried his burden to Savannah, Charleston, Richmond, Washington (Kentucky), Baltimore, Newport, and Boston.[162] *The Padlock* was produced even when the

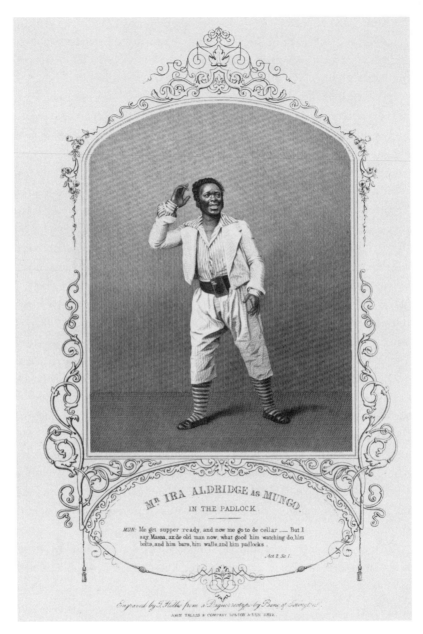

MR IRA ALDRIDGE AS MUNGO.

IN THE PADLOCK.

MUN: Me get supper ready, and now me go to de cellar ___ But I
say, Massa, ax de old man now, what good him watching do, him
bolts, and him bars, him walls, and him padlocks.

Act 2. Sc 1.

Engraved by G. Hollis from a Daguerreotype by Paine of Islington.

JOHN TALLIS & COMPANY LONDON & NEW YORK.

7. "Mr. Ira Aldridge as Mungo in *The Padlock*." Harvard Theatre
Collection, Houghton Library.

8. Mungo as black dandy appears to the far left, wielding a monocle. Detail from title page and stage directions, "The Padlock," 1823. Harvard Theatre Collection, Houghton Library.

theaters were closed during the American Revolution—soldiers at Valley Forge were said to have planned a production as a diversion "if the enemy does not retire from Philada soon."[163] It earned a rare honor for an eighteenth-century English drama when it was printed in Boston (1795) and New York (1805). In addition, one of Mungo's songs appeared in the edition of the *American Songster* published in 1788.[164] Popular before, during, and after American independence, *The Padlock* and especially its ostensible hero Mungo are credited with having a profound effect on a nascent American theater. The inaugural performance in 1769 is judged to have been "so famous and popular that it 'stands at the head of every chapter on the subject of Negro Minstrelsy in America.'"[165] Given that "Negro Minstrelsy," or the blackface tradition in America, to this day affects modes and methods of black representation and self-representation, the historical importance of the slavish swell and his American descendant, the minstrel theater's black dandy, cannot be ignored. By 1823, Mungo was being portrayed in illustrations in such a way that makes clear his provenance as a black dandy. An edition of *The Padlock* from 1823 in *Dolby's British Theatre* includes a diagram of the disposition of the main characters during the finale. Mungo is pictured at stage right in the pose of an iconic black dandy caricature—he wears a tuxedo and peers through a monocle, seemingly inspecting the crowd that has come to see him.[166]

Mungo's journey around the Atlantic—from Africa to the West Indies, where he picked up his accent, back to England, where he learned to dress and strut, and his return to America, where blackface minstrel theater was the most popular form of entertainment in the nineteenth century—testifies to the fact that the slave trade and its creation of a black diaspora have forever conditioned the way in which black people represent themselves and are portrayed by others. Negotiating, manipulating, and performing black identity, Mungos everywhere compulsively engage the aesthetics of Euro-American group and self-representation. Traveling that circum-Atlantic route with the foppish black and the black dandy under such circumstances inaugurates the seemingly never-ending contest of characterization versus self-stylization.

2

Crimes of Fashion

DRESSING THE PART FROM SLAVERY
TO FREEDOM

In order to recompense me for my trouble [the nursing of
a sick silversmith], the Captain promised me ten pounds.
. . . I thought this would be of great service to me, although
I had nearly money enough to purchase my freedom. . . . In
this expectation I laid out above eight pounds of my money
for a suit of superfine clothes to dance in at my freedom,
which I hoped was then at hand.

OLAUDAH EQUIANO, *The Interesting Narrative of the Life
of Olaudah Equiano, or Gustavus Vassa, the African* (1792)

Dere's a coat to take de eyes ob all Broadway! ah! Missy, it
am de fixins dat make de natural *born* gemman. A libery
for ever! Dere's a pair ob insuppressibles to 'stonish de
coloured population.

Zeke, a colored servant, reflecting on
his new uniform, in ANNA CORA MOWATT'S
Fashion; or Life in New York (1845)

One lady says (as I sit reading in the drawing room window
while Maum Mary puts my room to rights): "I clothe my
Negroes well. I could not bear to see them in dirt and rags;
it would be unpleasant to me." Another lady: "Yes. Well, so
do I. But not fine clothes, you know. I feel, now — it was
one of our sins as a nation, the way we indulged them in
sinful finery. We will be punished for it."

MARY CHESNUT'S *A Diary from Dixie*, March 20, 1862

Tailored for Service

Anna Cora Mowatt's antebellum play *Fashion; or Life in New York* (1845) opens with a conversation between the servants Millinette and Zeke. "A libery for ever!" wishes Zeke, the hapless black, when he sees the magnificent scarlet coat that serves as uniform for his new job. "Oh *oui*, Monsieur Zeke," concurs Millinette, the French maid; but, in an aside she admits, "I not *comprend* one word he say!"[1] The maid's comment refers to Zeke's sentiment perhaps as much as to his dialect. For her, his admiration of the gaudy livery defies explanation, as the clothes rather loudly imply servitude rather than self-satisfaction. Reactions to Zeke and his suit illustrate the differing opinions regarding the major concern of the play—the role of foreign high culture in American national identity, especially as embodied in European cultural and sartorial fashions and values. American simplicity simply will not do for the upwardly mobile in antebellum New York, be they black or white. The foreign and flashy in clothing and mannerisms are what is fashionable.

In such an atmosphere, Zeke must add a more aristocratic and dignified appellation to his livery, and so, at the insistence of his nouveau riche employers, the Tiffanys, his name is changed to Adolph. Not educated in a liberal tradition, but rather in a "libery" one, Zeke takes to subservience quite naturally. He trusts in appearances and believes that clothing and names can absolutely and uncomplicatedly transform a servant into what he calls "de natural *born* gemman."[2] Later, when Mr. Tiffany mistakenly calls him Zeke, Adolph saucily remarks, "Don't know any such nigga, Boss."[3] Duped by the coat and a new name, Zeke and his reputation, as well as the Tiffanys' fortune, falls prey to the manipulations of the confidence men Count Jolimaitre and Mr. Snobson. In the end, the Yankee Adam Trueman rescues the Tiffanys: he exercises a "Republican simplicity" that disdains the foolishness of venerating fashion, of "mak[ing] men wear the badge of servitude in a free land!"[4] This rescue is welcomed only by the ruling class as the last image of Zeke in the play finds him refusing to give evidence when the count, formerly reckoned by Zeke as "de genuine article ob a gemman," is found out.[5] The Tiffanys and Zeke both are victims of fashion, but in the end the masters are rehabilitated and only the black servant remains corrupted. Once the narrative double to the nouveau riche, Zeke ends as a confidant of the counterfeit, still firmly fascinated by and embodying fashion's follies.

As in the case of Mungo, the stage on which Zeke appeared was a space that, for the most part, worked to control the representation of blacks and others who were potentially unruly or capable of stepping out of their proscribed roles. While Zeke does not escape any of the delimiting stereotypes associated with black character at this time, the success of *Fashion* did, in fact, propel its female author to break down some barriers of her own.[6] As "the most successful play by a female American playwright in the nineteenth century," the popularity of *Fashion* transformed Mowatt's career from that of young society wife to that of a famous playwright and actress and writer on the international stage. Nevertheless, this liberation was made possible by the continued enslavement of some, especially the black servants, to the sociocultural world she mocked and escaped.[7]

Not only was the play the first hit written by a female playwright, but it also succeeded because it was "native-born" theater that dealt with the particularities of an emerging social scene and national culture.[8] Nearly all the critics, pro and con, took great pains to point this out.[9] Amazed at the dexterous use of indigenous materials, the reviews indicated that perhaps *Fashion* was "the premiere of a milestone in the development of American culture," "a complete vindication of America's claims to cultural self-sufficiency."[10] The play's popularity and sensational effect stemmed from the way in which it combined a host of novelties in American theater, especially a new relationship between author, theatrical subject and content, and audience.

The social world that *Fashion* depicts was Mowatt's native ground. Her mockery of society in *Fashion* is complicated. Depicting the transformation of a society ruled by old money to that of the nouveau riche, Mowatt both censured and took advantage of the attendant loosening up of social and moral boundaries. In *Fashion*, Mowatt accomplished something rare for an iconoclast: she brought her people along with her, earning respect for the theater in general and for women in the theater especially.[11] When the play opened in 1845, the audience, normally divided between businessmen and sporting women, was instead full of Mowatt's own set — the respectable, the fashionable, the literati.[12] Both the well established and the parvenu took Mowatt's social commentary well — her biographer records that the lawyers responded to Adam Trueman's upright attitude, while the "society belles" enjoyed the repartee between "the false count and intriguing maid, characters they recognized as part of their world."[13]

Also in this world, but not in Mowatt's expanded audience, were blacks and working-class women—the likes of Zeke and Millinette. Instead of seeing themselves reflected on stage, they provided the audience with "plenty of comedy broad enough for everyone's [else's] taste."[14] *Fashion* was a success for reasons of its supposed realism, as it was a "first attempt to view American society critically and to picture American life with some degree of naturalism," yet, for some dissenters, including Edgar Allan Poe, some of the "characters were conventional stage types."[15] Although in many respects an absolute innovation in American drama, *Fashion* was more of the same in other respects, especially in its characterization of blacks. In contrast to *The Padlock*, whose sensational success depended on the antics and attitude of a dandified black, the interest *Fashion* garnered did not rest on Zeke's behavior or costume.[16] Mungo's brashness is easy to incorporate into a reading of his potential oppositionality, which is a source of his popularity; Zeke's love of his "libery" seemingly offers no such occasion.

How a dandified black in love with his own sartorial subjugation might fit into the fashions paraded and mocked in *Fashion* says something about the naturalism effected in and by this historic American play. How and why Zeke's imbrication within racist discourse might have been a part of the play's success, why a hopelessly (rather than intriguingly) dandified black man might be part of the play's phenomenon, matters when it comes to making a true assessment of the work's historical importance. Whether or not Zeke can really be seen as having, according to one later observer, "just a touch of the trickster, not fully realized," helps one assess the complications of and for black characterization on this new national stage.[17] In America, where Africans and African Americans sometimes outnumbered the whites who owned them, where they were more often labor than luxury items, blacks would have to be depicted very differently—tricksters would seemingly have to be contained entirely. "A libery forever!" declares Zeke, more truthfully than he knows.

As in eighteenth-century Britain, depictions of dandified blacks in early nineteenth-century American theater had competition from other performative arenas—real-life personalities did intervene in this seemingly scripted fashion show. By the time of *Fashion*'s debut, black dandyism in America derived from both theatrical and actual traditions important to the formation of African American and American identity. These traditions see the dandified black, the aspirant black "gemman," very differently. Coexistent with Zeke on stage were two indigenous dandyish performative traditions that did realize the figure's potential as a trickster: the carnivalesque African American race and class cross-dressing festivals of Negro Election Day and Pinkster and the dandy character in the blackface minstrel theater. In contrast to and in conversation with Zeke's characterization in *Fashion*, both of these traditions place fancy dress and the black people wearing it at the center of a debate about Americanness and its intersection with race and class identity, styles of masculinity and sexuality.

In the colonial period and throughout the nineteenth century in America, black dandyism, as enacted at these indigenous festivals, was a practice that destabilized hierarchies of race and power even as it upheld these same strictures in the emerging blackface minstrel theater. In this chapter I take up the dandy figure as he is exported to America and experiences a number of rituals of reversal that define the figure as both liberatory and oppressive. In examining these reversals, I coin a term to describe the black dandy's antics—the crime of fashion. The crime of fashion describes the racial and class cross-dressing that was, as practiced by blacks, a symbol of a self-conscious manipulation of authority and, as seen in blackface, an attempted denigratory parody of free blacks' pride and enterprise. In this period, the black dandy is thus both a perpetrator and a victim of crimes of fashion, a figure that both escapes and falls into pat definitions of blackness, masculinity, and sexuality.

The black dandy crime of fashion is at the center of the work of the nineteenth-century's most provocative authors on the subject of race and nation—Harriet Beecher Stowe, Herman Melville, Mark Twain, and Charles Chesnutt. For these authors, placing a black dandy in the text animates his dual provenance and creates moments of instability that have the power to continually redefine blackness and masculinity, sometimes to unsettling ends. At stake in the perpetration of a crime of fashion by or on a black dandy is the status of who is or can be a "natural born gemman" as blacks transition from slaves to free people. As we saw in chapter 1, dandies can appropriate or wittily mock the status of a gentleman. As the black dandy dresses the part from slavery to freedom in nineteenth-century America, he does both, often to criminal or characteristically scandalous effect.

The King's New Clothes

An integral part of early America's performative culture, annual African American festivals like Pinkster, a holiday of Dutch origin, and Negro Election Day, an Anglo/Afro-American affair, featured class and race cross-dressing.[18] By performing who they were and who they were becoming by means of fashion and style, early African Americans redefined constricting markers of identity as they literally and symbolically changed clothes. Given the social and material conditions in which colonists lived, the high rates of illiteracy, and a dearth of written communication networks, actions often spoke louder than (written) words. If what was visible was known to be true, these festivals offered performances in which visuality and spectacle operated to both confirm and challenge social and cultural hierarchies.[19]

Pinkster and Negro Election Day featured parades and dances of slaves dressed to the nines in clothing normally reserved for their social and racial betters. Historians claim European carnivals, festivals of misrule, and commedia dell'arte as precedents for these celebrations.[20] These festivals are also related to later American expressive traditions that include the cakewalk contests that originated in the American South, Jonkonnu (John Canoe) festivals in the South and Caribbean, and festivities associated with Afro-Cuban Kings in Cuba and Kings of Congo in Brazil.[21] According to Victor Turner, rituals of reversal like those enacted at these festivals are characterized by a temporary exchange of power in which those of inferior social status "are positively enjoined to exercise ritual authority over their superiors; and they, in their turn, must accept with good will their ritual degradation."[22] For the participants, these events are a release from their respective high or low positions, at the same time they serve to increase the culture's awareness of the structural and social inequalities being mocked. A subset of these rituals includes more carnivalesque occasions when "inferiors affect the rank and style of superiors, sometimes even to the extent of arraying themselves in a hierarchy mimicking the secular hierarchy of their so-called betters."[23] Given their ubiquity in the slaveholding Americas, historians have long debated whether or not these performative race and class cross-dressing events were more than a simple example of what Frederick Douglass called "safety-valves, to carry off the rebellious spirit of enslaved humanity."[24] In many of these American festivals, however, the carnivalesque elements resonate even more deeply when one of the power-exchanging parties is of a different class *and* race as well as enslaved; thus, the mockery of power is intensified, even doubled, by the black participants in fancy dress. Indeed, recent research into the festivals has revealed that events like Pinkster and Negro Election Day offered participants a critical social outlet, opportunities for economic ventures, political organizing, and spiritual explorations.[25] The mimicry around which the festivals seemed to be organized contained other imperatives of black self-satisfaction and self-definition through the performativity of race, class, and gender. Dressing up and across class and racial boundaries, Africans and African Americans celebrated the possibilities of cultural syncretism and the power of black dandyism to visualize dignity in the face of oppression. These early black dandies perpetrated some of the first crimes of fashion in a fierce and amusing way.

Few contemporary accounts of Negro Election Day and Pinkster, regular holidays by the mid-eighteenth century, survive.[26] Historians have had to rely on diaries, memoirs, and nineteenth-century local histories and treatises on blacks in the Northeast for descriptions of the festivities. While not merely imitative, the black festivals did follow some white conventions. In colonial times, election days in the North were often festive affairs, as communities came together to canvas each other, vote, and celebrate the vicissitudes of power. As early as the 1750s, however, the election day festivities of the majority population began to include black participation, as Negro Election Day was celebrated by black slaves and free people who were, according to a nineteenth-century chronicler, "peculiarly alive to the effect of pomp and ceremony [in the white elections, and blacks] and not only made every effort to be present, but the imitative instinct stirred them to elect a governor for themselves."[27] Black election day, like the white, was accompanied by speeches before or after the voting, a parade in fancy dress or military gear commemorating the change of office, and dinner and dancing.

Originally a religious holiday associated with Pentecost or Whitsuntide, Pinkster supposedly takes its name from a Dutch corruption of the word for "Pentecost." Celebrated first in Holland, the festival traveled to America with Dutch settlers in New York and retained its religious affiliations, while expanding into more secular associations with the change of seasons and flowers that springtime brings.[28] It continued to be celebrated when New York came under British rule. Pinkster was a multicultural affair from the beginning, a holiday for masters, slaves, black and white free people, and Native Americans. However, by 1800, it was organized by blacks and included actual and symbolic bids for cultural authority as the festival featured the crowning of a black Pinkster king, a parade accompanying him to the festival grounds, and a market, carnival, and other entertainments.[29] At Pinkster, the African American participants "appropriated an alien culture and created a truly indigenous form . . . resulting in an interaction between groups involving not only power relationships, but reciprocity and competitive pursuits as well."[30]

The dress of the black participants visualized the potential parodic nature of the festivals. Had they intended a faithful, un-ironic imitation of whites, the participants would have aimed for more precision in their apparel. Instead, they are reported to have worn "uniforms—anything but uniform" and outfits in which the haphazard dominated as they "were matched with an African eye for color . . . ensembles of real style and flair."[31] A comment on African style, African American social position, and white American pomp, slave dress in the festivals indicated that the drama was one in which culture was not merely being copied, but rather negotiated on the backs of the participants. A tone of mock-seriousness pervaded, turning imitation into parody; all involved in the festivities, black and white, were satirized. African American governors and their constituents, Pinkster kings and their subjects were a little off—hilariously and strategically so.

Holding office for a full year, with limited but actual power, Negro governors ruled over an interaction in which the "release" of "society's structurally engendered 'sins'" included a mockery of the present white–black hierarchy as well as an appreciation of the American replay of African traditions of social control and self-presentation.[32] In many West African societies, satiric songs and festivals routinely took native and, later, European authority figures to task. Performances and celebrations held people publicly accountable for their actions, and they vocally and visually derided pomposity, laziness, cruelty, self-importance, and misused authority.[33] Negro Election Day and Pinkster manifest African-derived style throughout, in everything from structures of social organization to clothing practices. From its highest officials to its entertainments, the festivals in some ways preserved African traditions presumed lost in the middle passage. Indeed, the festivities, which included dances traceable to West Africa, were presided over by a governor or king who was often himself "African-born or of verifiable African lineage."[34] The duties performed by the black official—for example, settlement of disputes among blacks, mediation between masters and slaves—were similar to those discharged by the heads of more informal African governments.

And while African traditions of social organization may have met whites' needs, the election and appointment of black governors and kings was not wholly a method of social control by whites.[35] Often the slaves or servants of men important in the community—for example, Negro Governor Samuel Hunt'on in Norwich, Connecticut, was the slave of the prominent citizen and member of the Continental Congress Samuel Huntington—the Negro governors and kings "personified dignity" in that they were among the most influential, well-regarded, sage, physically strong, and cosmopolitan men in the area.[36] Governors and kings were men of achievement who were respected as community elders and represented the black community's best effort at personifying self-respect in a system of slavery designed to limit their humanity and autonomy, even in its northern domestic variety. Self-respect included feeling confident enough to be an agent of satire, a perpetrator of a crime of fashion that transformed imitation into autonomy.

The inauguration outfits of the governors and kings communicated dignity as well as the syncretic or multifaceted nature of the new African American culture being created and celebrated through the festival—all with a witty edge. Witness this account of the most famous Pinkster king, Old King Charles or Charley, an African from Angola, at Pinkster celebrations in Albany in the early 1800s:

> Never, if our memory serve us, shall we forget the mingled sensations of awe and grandeur that were impressed on our youthful minds, when first we beheld his stately form and dignified aspect, slowly moving before us and approaching the centre of the ring. His costume on this memorable occasion was graphic and unique to the greatest degree, being that worn by a British Brigadier of the olden time. Ample broadcloth scarlet coat, with wide flaps almost reaching to his heels, and gayly ornamented everywhere with broad tracings of bright golden lace; his small clothes were of yellow buckskin, fresh and new, with stockings blue and well burnished silver buckles to his well-backed shoe; when we add to these

9. "An Election Parade of a Negro Governor" by H. P. Arms. *Connecticut Magazine*, June 1899. Courtesy, American Antiquarian Society.

the tri-corned cocked hat trimmed also with lace of gold, and which so gracefully set upon his noble globular pate, we nearly complete the rude sketch of the Pinkster King.[37]

Charley's colorful, ill-fitting, spectacular uniform satisfies and plays with the multiple aesthetic expectations of the audiences he serves: African, African American, recently British, newly American. As an Angolan in pieces of British dress uniform and presiding over a black-organized, originally Dutch festival with clear African religious elements (he approaches a ring to dance some version of the ring shout, a circular dance of West African origin), Old King Charley represents the *bricoleur* style and cultural performativity of African slaves and early African Americans.[38] Obviously an amalgamation of aesthetic traditions, the black official in a riot of colors is a metaphor for the syncretism of Pinkster, the distance traveled by the multiplicity of rituals at play.

The power wielded by Africans and American-born blacks participating in these festivals originated partly in memory and a creative response to loss.[39] Africans may have arrived in America physically and metaphorically naked, a seeming tabula rasa on which European and new American fashions might be imposed, but they had likely not forgotten the customs and aesthetic practices that had governed their lives in Africa. Slave clothing, especially slave festivals that involve clothing and performativity, displays this intersection of memory and creativity. James Fenimore Cooper, the only American author to record a nearly contemporary view of Pinkster, emphasizes his sense of the festival's multiculturalism and retention of African traditions in *Satanstoe: or, the Littlepage Manuscripts, A Tale of a Colony* (1846).[40] Though written in the mid-nineteenth century, the novel is set a century earlier, during Pinkster's heyday. Cooper brings the eye of an amateur anthropologist to his account of Pinkster, called "the great Saturnalia of the blacks" in the novel:[41]

> The features that distinguish a Pinkster frolic from the usual scenes at fairs, and other merry makings, however, were of African origin. . . .
> Among other things, some were making music, by beating on skins over the ends of hollow logs, while others were dancing to it, in a manner to show that they felt infinite delight. This, in particular was said to be a usage of their African progenitors. . . .
> A party of Africans kept us for half an hour. . . . The American-born

blacks gazed at this group with intense interest also, regarding them as so many ambassadors from the land of their ancestors, to enlighten them in usages, and superstitious lore, that were more peculiarly suited to their race. The last even endeavoured to imitate the acts of the first, and, though the attempt was often ludicrous, it never failed on the score of intention and gravity. Nothing was done in the way of caricature, but much in the way of respect and affection.[42]

Accurate in its details and, for the most part, sensitive to the nature of the performance, Cooper's description merits interest for its rare glimpse at diversity within the African and African American community. Particularly intriguing is its portrayal of the African American gaze and the way in which that look matters so much to cultural identity. Trained at other Africans with "intention and gravity," "respect and admiration," this look eliminates "caricature" and lends this performance a kind of poignancy not captured in other accounts of the festival. In *Satanstoe*, blacks are seen interacting with and learning from each other, transforming themselves from Africans into blacks. What Cooper re-creates here is what Michael Gomez calls a process of cultural translation that Africans had to undergo in the Americas, a transformation of their identities from those based on ethnicity or the specifics of their African origins to race or a sense of blackness that was both imposed upon and taken on by Africans in America.[43] This process was a long, uneven, creative one, as "people of African descent were carefully selecting elements of various cultures, both African and European, issuing into combinations of creativity and innovation. . . . They borrowed what was of interest from the external society, and they improved upon previously existing commonalities of African cultures."[44]

While the description of Pinkster in *Satanstoe* does not emphasize the place of clothing these dancing blacks wore as much as the import of their bodily motions in the process of cultural translation, it was, nevertheless, the total performance—the combination of black body, movement, and costume—that communicated the acculturation taking place on the Pinkster field. The bodies were both African and African American or black; the movement was a combination of Old World and New World styles; the costumes were similarly mixed and, as garments "danced" by the body, the most obvious outward sign of the cultural fusion taking place. This Pinkster performance shows Africans and African Americans during colonial times and in the early republic "engaged in poly-cultural, rather than syncretic life-styles"; traditions of movement and dress existed side by side, sometimes blending and fusing, sometimes disappearing or superseding each other.[45] It is in the mélange of European and African (principally West African and Central West African) modes of self-fashioning that black dandyism and dandies in America developed their aesthetic. Cultural performances like Pinkster and Negro Election Day are singular elements of African and black self-fashioning, elements that produce and announce a sense of self necessarily always in translation.

While this process was an uneven one, even during the gaiety of the festivals, nevertheless, at its ground was what Gomez calls "the African antecedent."[46] As seen in their dance, African Americans like King Charley and his fellows did not "simply forget (or elect not to remember) their African background. Rather, the background played a crucial role in determining African American identity."[47] For nascent black dandies, whose dress and persons were an outward manifestation of the identity-making process, this background was both symbolic and material. Not only beliefs about which sartorial flourishes communicated authority or counted as high fashion, but also weaving, dyeing, and other knowledge useful in the production of clothes seemingly survived the Atlantic crossing intact enough to have formed the ground of black dandyism and self-fashioning.

Though early European accounts of contact with Africa often emphasize nakedness and equate the lack of clothing with barbarity, other accounts stress African excess in dress, especially among the elite.[48] John Thornton indicates that the slave coast of Africa was a place that experienced a great deal of conspicuous consumption of goods from other regions in Africa, Europe, and European-controlled areas in Asia.[49] From the point of contact, the West African elite eagerly incorporated European cloth and clothing into their wardrobes, in fact shifting their earlier interest in intra-Africa traded luxuries to those items now brought by Europeans.[50] Kings and their courts were "almost always" "outfitted in ways that marked them from ordinary people"; items of European origin quickly became part of the process of visually displaying authority and power.[51] The West African elite traded their textiles for those of the Europeans; in addition, they were given cloth and items of fancy clothing such as suit jackets, cloaks, and linen and silk shirts as gifts or in exchange for influence.[52] Most African nobility incorporated discrete items into their ensembles rather than wholly adopting European dress.[53] Foreign goods were rarely distributed to the folk, and aristocratic style and status became characterized by a combination of traditional and European dress.[54] Though elite style (flowing caftan topped with a fitted long-tail coat) may seem representative of competing values, especially as contact mutated into exploitation, the aesthetic by which the look was put together was all African.

In general, West African aesthetics allow for the "embrace of the new and unusual" and include an "ability to inventively manipulate and blend the traditional and novel"; this adaptive and creative impulse permeated all aspects of style, from the combining of actual items of African and European dress to the reworking of cloth that composed that dress.[55] Transported to the other side of the Atlantic, West Africans remembered and reinvigorated the importance that European fancy dress had had in communicating nobility, authority, respect, especially for fellow Africans, and, most important, a deeply ingrained cultural predisposition to exploring hybridity, syncretism, and displays of conspicuous consumption. Cultural exchange by means of clothing existed before the middle passage and, as we will see, continued well after it. Exchange was both cultural and material, as it was common for slaves to be bought from African traders with currency in the form of bolts of cloth.[56]

The power of clothing, cloth, and fashion found an outlet in Negro Election Day and Pinkster. While read as simple imitation by most whites, the urge of all blacks to indulge themselves in finery would have been significant in at least two systems: as possible homage to not uncomplicated African traditions of displaying status, and as a recognition and potential diffusion in parody of those who held that same status in America. Fancy European dress on a black body is less ridiculous and imitative than palimpsestic; the layers of clothing mark the complex intersections of the routes that cross the Atlantic and create the African diaspora and the identities formed therein. The use of clothing to visualize this diasporic identity or cosmopolitanism indicates that the black people involved understood intuitively that identity can be performed, that race is a fiction, and that both are culturally and historically based. Their play with clothing helped them and others to see (and accessorize) the space between seeming and being.

The anxiety produced by black dandies and dandyism in America turns precisely on the way in which a black in a seeming multifarious combination of colors, patterns, styles—or even in a well-cut, well-fitting suit—combines notions of self-respect and agency with a knowingness about the way in which visibility and consumption affect regard of the self and the group. Though officially allowed to fully express their love of the cloth on Sunday and on the occasional holiday during the year, slaves worked to signify personal and group style via clothing in smaller, quotidian ways. Slaves were given basic clothing either yearly or according to the seasons.[57] In addition, masters rewarded a small percentage of slaves, especially house slaves, with castoffs or new items of clothing.[58] Though elegant according to white standards, house slaves had less choice about what they could wear and how they could accessorize than their fellows toiling in the fields.[59] Both house and field slaves were often themselves responsible, especially during and after the Revolutionary War, when European imports slowed, and during the Civil War, for making clothes and cloth for everyone on the plantation, masters included. Even if they were not able to control the initial process in which they dressed, they could define their own style in mending, maintaining, and otherwise adding to their often meager wardrobes.[60]

In addition to flourishes achieved by bright color dyes, silver and gold buttons, and brilliant ribbons, slaves' closets were improved through shopping and shoplifting from masters. The first bit of money slaves managed to earn working on their own time was overwhelmingly spent on clothing for Sunday and other holidays.[61] Advertisements for runaway slaves record innumerable clothing thefts and identify specific slaves by their love of dress and fashion:

Parker's Weekly New-York-Gazette; or, The Weekly Post-Boy, #1008, April 29, 1762:
Five pounds reward, run away on Monday the 12th instant from me the subscriber, a Mulatto servant man named Charles. . . . He is a likely well-set Fellow, 28 or 30 years of age, and about 5 feet six inches high, and has the Smallpox. He has a Variety of Clothes, some of them very good, and effects to dress very neat and genteel, and generally wears a Wig. He took with him two or three Coats or Suits, a dark brown or Chocolate coloured Cloth coat, pretty much worn, a dun or Dove coloured cloth, or fine Frize, but little worn, and a light blue grey Summer Coat of Grogam Camblet, or some such stuff, a Straw Coloured waistcoat,

edged with Silver Cord, almost new; and several Waistcoats, Breeches, and Pair of Stockings; a blue Great Coat and a Fiddle. His behavior is excessively complaisent, obsequious, and insinuating; he speaks good English smoothly and plausibly, and generally with a cringe and a smile, he is extremely artful, and ready at inventing specious pretences to conceal villainous Actions or designs.[62]

Baltimore, Maryland, *Journal and Baltimore Advertiser*, July 13, 1781: Went away, from the subscriber . . . a well-looking Mulatto Man, named Harry, he is a slave, about 5 feet 9 or 10 inches high, not very robust made, a good house-servant and groom, and very ingenious about many things. . . . I believe he is about 33 years old, and has lived with me 22 years and some months; his wearing-apparel I cannot describe, as he got cloaths whenever he wanted them, and asked for them, he will no doubt pass for a freeman.[63]

There are so many examples of slaves who are "addicted to dress," "remarkably fond of dress," "generally dressy," "very fond of showy dress," and who "occasionally dressed gay," in eighteenth-century Maryland alone that one can surmise that clothing and appearance served as marks of true distinction for slaves in the period.[64] Slaves stole clothing not only because it was portable or their only material possession, but also because better clothing allowed them to pass more easily for freemen and to enter the market as consumers. Clothing could be sold, traded, or exchanged for other necessary items.[65] From the perspective of both masters and slaves, clothing had significance beyond functionality—at stake was nothing less than a sense of freedom, a display of the difference between purported essence, self-worth, and aspiration.

The importance of dress is also well illustrated in the fact that whites passed sumptuary laws that specifically forbade black extravagance.[66] These laws were designed to stop the performativity of identity with clothing, to arrest the exploitation of sartorial semiotics. The best-known laws were drafted in Charleston, South Carolina, in 1735 and 1740 and in New Orleans in 1786. In Charleston, the effort to prevent perceived black fashion violations was wholly ironic, for some slave masters, especially those involved in illicit relationships with their female slaves, were responsible for the distribution of finery so offensive to their fellow citizens. Additionally, male slaves were sometimes punished for their infractions by means of sartorial gender or sexual humiliation—they were made to wear female clothing or inadequate clothing. Indeed, for whites and blacks, clothing and fashion were a means by which the status of slave and master, whiteness and blackness, masculinity and femininity, Africanness and Americanness was being determined.[67] In the early American household, clothing was a weapon in the struggle for social control, individual agency, and personal integrity. As the covering of a metaphorically and actually naked black body, slave clothing represented a battle for sheer survival. Ambiguous messages and the resultant tension created not just the odd black dandy, but a social practice, black dandyism, that in colonial and antebellum America had a regular holiday devoted to it.

The abolition of slavery and an influx of European immigrants competing for jobs with free blacks and resentful of any white patronage of blacks, as well as African American efforts to restyle themselves as free and striving toward respectability all caused the performativity and visuality that characterized the festivals to play differently over time.[68] The class and racial cross-dressing came to have increased symbolic value as the status mockingly achieved in the festivals actually became theoretically, if not materially, attainable for blacks transitioning to freedom. Before this time, the festivals had not been a threat because of the relatively low numbers of slaves and free blacks compared to whites and the nature of the slave system in the northern colonies and states (domestic versus plantation slavery).[69] The end of the slave trade, and then of slavery, in all the northern states by around 1830 and, in the case of Pinkster, black public opinion played a role in the end of this phase of black sartorial contest.[70] By the early nineteenth century, Yankee Doodle's black dandy brother lost his festivals in the gap between his newly free status and the ability to express that condition.

However, the dandy's import for blacks and whites alike did not diminish with the end of the festivals. In the early American period, the crimes of fashion perpetrated by black dandies were duly punished and perpetrated again, this time on a proper stage. Coincident with the end of the festivals was the rise of America's most enduring black dandy representation, the urban, superstyled ladies' man Zip Coon, the black dandy from the blackface minstrel show. The development of blackface minstrelsy, the most popular entertainment of the nineteenth century, engendered another set of representational crimes in which fashion and folly played major roles.

"De Genteel Fine Ole Nigga"
Black Dandies in Blackface

What does a gentleman look like?[71] As Zeke inquires in *Fashion*, are all
"gemman" natural born? What visual and audible cues, accessories of
clothing, accents of language, and behavioral gestures help one decide?
That men will be scrutinized for such signs in *Uncle Tom's Cabin* is a point
that Harriet Beecher Stowe makes clear. The novel's opening scene describes two "gentlemen" bargaining over Uncle Tom, the first of whom,
"when critically examined, did not seem, strictly speaking, to come under
the species":

> He was a short, thick-set man, with coarse commonplace features, and
> that swaggering air of pretension which marks a low man who is trying
> to elbow his way upward in the world. He was much overdressed, in
> a gaudy vest of many colors, a blue neckerchief, bedropped gayly with
> yellow spots, and arranged with a flaunting tie, quite in keeping with
> the general air of the man. His hands, large and coarse, were plentifully
> bedecked with rings; and he wore a heavy watch-chain, with a bundle
> of seals of portentous size, and a great variety of colors, attached to it,—
> which, in the ardor of conversation, he was in the habit of flourishing
> and jingling with evident satisfaction. His conversation was in free and
> easy defiance of Murray's Grammar, and was garnished at convenient
> intervals with various profane expressions, which not even the desire to
> be graphic in our account shall induce us to transcribe.[72]

What the reader learns about gentlemanly status derives from the combination of the elaborate, unflattering description of the first man, the
slave trader Haley, and the almost total lack of information about his companion, Mr. Shelby. The only description given of Shelby is that he "had
the appearance of a gentleman" who lived in "easy, even opulent circumstances."[73] Shelby's relative position relies on his implicit opposition to
Haley's vulgar extravagance. Dressing above his station with too much
color and too much jewelry, comfortable in his "free and easy defiance"
of grammar and social convention, Haley falls short of the natural aristocracy of his host. Indeed, the description renders the white Haley surprisingly close to the stereotypical black aristocrat, the minstrel show's black

dandy—a resemblance not without consequence. In *Uncle Tom's Cabin*, those dandies unmitigated by sentimentalism are grotesque, while in contrast the sentimentalized are depicted as "poetical voluptuary[ies]."[74] With these portraits, Stowe establishes the visual frame through which her novel operates and the impact of that frame on conceptions of race and gender ideals.

Uncle Tom's Cabin literalizes the valuation of black people in poignant presentations of the trade in slaves. Uncle Tom's value as chattel is determined officially three times: when he is sold away from the Shelby plantation, exchanged between Haley and Augustine St. Clare, and auctioned to Simon Legree. For Shelby and Haley and to a lesser extent St. Clare, Tom's price is determined primarily by the combination of his pious character and modest appearance, which lessen the potential threat of his healthy, strong, even imposing physique. Looking at Tom and observing his behavior convince Shelby, Haley, and St. Clare that Tom is the "genuine article." Simon Legree subjects Tom to a more intense investigation, a manhandling even; before the auction, Legree "seized Tom by the jaw, and pulled open his mouth to inspect his teeth; made him strip up to the sleeve, to show his muscle; turned him around, made him jump and spring, to show his paces."[75] Such brutality is expected from a vile man like Legree. However, the other moment of Tom's assessment couldn't be less expected and, surprisingly, more appropriate.

On arrival in New Orleans at the St. Clare household, master and slaves are met at the door by the house slave Adolph, "a highly dressed young mulatto man, evidently a very *distingue* personage, attired in the ultra extreme of the mode and gracefully waving a cambric handkerchief in his hand."[76] Moments later St. Clare catches Adolph, "conspicuous in satin vest, gold guard-chain, and white pants," "negligently leaning against the banisters, examining Tom through an opera-glass, with an air that would have done credit to any dandy living." He had, moments earlier, been "bowing [to his master] with inexpressible grace and suavity."[77] Unexpected because of the comic layer it adds to these other, similar scenes of cruelty, the confrontation of Tom and Adolph, darky and dandy, resituates the frame assessing blackness and masculinity in the novel, especially since it is an image derived from a contemporaneous phenomenon that probed race, class, gender roles, and the rules of sexuality—namely, blackface minstrelsy.

In the middle of the most popular novel of the nineteenth century in America occurs an image from the era's most popular entertainment, the blackface minstrel show. The presence of the dandy and his opposite, the darky, reproduces the staging of the early minstrel show, which featured the two characters in dramas of blackness set on the plantation and in the city. Though the appearance of Adolph is claimed by some to be part of the inauguration of what would become the "stereotypical Black dandy," the presence of the Negro gentleman was in fact more likely a result of Stowe's inclusion of what was already an existing phenomenon.[78] Whether on stage or in a text or, more threateningly, on the street, the servant or slave dandy and his sartorial crimes embody the tension between image and identity produced by slavery and the hope or taste of freedom.

Even before the establishment of the minstrel show proper, white performers blacked up and dressed up in outrageous, seemingly incongruous clothing to broadcast the antics of blacks—blackface dandies were first seen individually between or after theatrical fare (like Mungo in *The Padlock*) or, alternatively, at the circus.[79] These late eighteenth- and early nineteenth-century "Negro delineators" often specialized in certain characters whose appearance and behavior were revealed in the lyrics to their signature songs. Though the outrageous popularity of Thomas Dartmouth (T. D.) Rice's comic "plantation darky" Jim Crow brought the comedic power of blackface to America's attention, dandies like Barney Burns's Long-Tail Blue and George Washington Dixon's Zip Coon were just as notorious and entertaining.[80] In fact, when the black dandy was present on stage with the quintessential darky, the minstrel show proper, as performed in a theater by a troupe supposedly sketching Negro life, was born.[81]

The popularity of the blackface dandy might be traceable to his familiarity, rather than to his novelty, at least for the first audiences in the North. Northern cities, especially New York, Boston, and Philadelphia, were home to minstrelsy's first theaters and performers, who were working- or middle-class whites.[82] In its mockery of blacks and whites alike, the early minstrel show alludes to the earlier class and race cross-dressing festivals of Negro Election Day and Pinkster. Some historians of minstrelsy wrongly blame a "general neglect of African American history" for not establishing a "definite link" between the festivals and the show.[83] But, in fact, the blackface minstrel show borrows from the festivals not only in its emphasis on the public nature of the events in which racial and class identities were fabricated and presented, but also in its echo of other features of the festivals.[84] Blackface minstrel performances often began with a parade through town that announced the arrival of the traveling show and included the presence of the interlocutor, famous for his "grandiloquent" stump speeches concerning politics, as well as burlesque skits in which white men in blackface pretended "to exhibit the refined manners of Counts, Kings, and Princes."[85] These similarities produce a genealogy figuring the blackface dandy as parody of the festival's dandyism (itself a parody). The dandy in black and blackface is a particular instantiation of "burlesque and counterburlesque," a dynamic Eric Lott finds operating generally in the show.[86] Thus, the dandy in blackface seems to take over where the black dandy left off. As soon as the festivals began to wane in the 1820s, blackface performances of dandyism were on the rise.

The end of Negro festivals in the North, in combination with the outlawing of the slave trade and the abolition of slavery, forced a reconception and reimagination of blacks in fancy dress. Once considered imitators, blacks themselves soon turned the parody associated with the festivals into appropriation, even as blackface performances worked to continually reappropriate such self-fashioning. Upon emancipation, many blacks followed Olaudah Equiano's lead and satisfied the urge to display their new status with a new set of clothes.[87] As a result, blacks in the North not only did not give up their love of finery, but, on the contrary, increased their displays of black style from once a year or every Sunday to as often as possible. Blacks' desire to express their increased fortune after the abolition of slavery in the North roughly coincided with white Americans' desire to signal further cultural distinction from Europe in the aftermath of the War of 1812.[88] Fancy clothing became implicated in both of these expressions of arrival, though to opposite effects. As we saw in Mowatt's *Fashion*, the attention blacks paid to current style became associated with the pretentiousness of whites anxious about America's short cultural ancestry. Even though blacks more regularly donned "superfine clothes" for reasons related to negotiating the specificities of *their* location in American life, when caricatured as dandies they became part of a cultural critique of perceived white decadence that becomes increasingly difficult to parse from concerns about black "striving." The dandy figure therefore unites status anxieties among whites with those among whites and blacks and later among blacks as well.

Whether on stage in the legitimate theater or frolicking through a minstrel show, the black dandy was as subject to ridicule as he was to loathing.[89] Examination of the best-known blackface dandy characters—known as Long-Tail Blue and Zip Coon from their signature songs—reveals the transformation of the figure from an ex-slave gunning for respectability to a free black intent on "broadcast[ing] 'blackness' into the public realm."[90] As one of the first blackface acts, Long-Tail Blue strutted on stage in 1827, newly free and nattily attired, potently incarnating a question that hovers over the minstrel show generally: What if?[91] What if blacks were free? And not just in the North? What if they had money, access to education, unchecked social, cultural, and economic mobility? Long-Tail Blue and Zip Coon answered these questions, simultaneously revealing and repressing whites' anxieties about race, class, gender, and sexuality. In fact, some historians claim that minstrel shows often began this investigation with skits depicting "Illustrations of the Dandyism of the Northern States," an indication that the activities of dandified black northerners was notably present for the players and audience.[92]

Freedom brought Long-Tail Blue a new attitude that he expressed with "ultramodish" clothes featuring "tightly fitting pantaloons, a lacy jabot, a silk hat, baubles dangling from his waistband, a lorgnon, which he held up with an effeminate gesture, and occasionally a walking cane." In addition, "if there was one thing he could not do without, it was a blue coat with long swishing tails," a symbol of potential animalism in both physiognomy and sexuality.[93] Blue also pursues white "galls," in particular, one already going out with Jim Crow, though, of course, the white policeman who witnesses the flirtation quickly intervenes and "splites" his long-tail blue.[94] The dandy repairs the coat and picks up where he left off—no worse for the temporary punishment, even if it is a metaphor for castration.[95] Though Long-Tail Blue approximates white gentlemanly elegance in his costume, he will not be allowed to convert appearances into realities. The blackface dandy's sartorial proximity to whiteness and wealth hardly effects his social equality.

Whereas Long-Tail Blue had been a free black perhaps overly intoxicated with liberty, the dandy's later incarnation in Zip Coon was still well dressed, even "a larned skolar," but of a much more beastly demeanor.[96] Later, in 1844, Dandy Jim from Carolina joins Blue and Zip, extending the dandy figure's portrayal of blacks as ridiculous. A narcissist intending to cut a figure at the ball and, in some versions, woo "lubly Dine" into providing him with "eight or nine / Young Dandy Jims of Caroline," Dandy Jim boasts of a sexual prowess that is definitively linked to his appearance as a "handsome nigga [who is] bound to shine."[97] Unlike that of Long-Tail Blue, Dandy Jim's lust remains within his own race and social conventions: "Lubly Dine" is a fellow black whom Jim actually marries in the song. However, despite the placement of Dandy Jim's excessive sexuality within an intraracial family structure, his quest to populate the world with as many little dandies as he can — "ebery little nig she had / Was de berry image ob de dad" — is nevertheless threatening.[98] Thus, the white fantasy of black freedom and equality that black dandies embody is not just one in which social equality leads to miscegenation, as in the case of Long-Tail Blue, but one which seems to equate miscegenation with the threat of mere black presence and visibility (Zip Coon and Dandy Jim). Long-Tail Blue, Zip Coon, and Dandy Jim menace even as they amuse, revealing the affinity between effeminacy associated with extreme attention to dress and appearance and hypermasculinity linked to a sexual rapacity that exceeds racial boundaries.

Although the early minstrel show presents the dandy in different guises, constant in its portrayal of blacks in fancy clothing is the figure's association with sexual threat and class critique. In the case of the blackface dandy, the donning of the clothing of elites translates to a desire not only for social mobility, but also for the most extreme form of integration, interracial sex. The threat of free blacks was expressed as what Lott describes famously as the "bold swagger, irrepressible desire, sheer bodily display" of the black dandy. As Lott argues, "In a real sense the minstrel man was the black penis, that organ returning in a variety of contexts, at times ludicrous, at others rather less so"; his manifestation on stage was a result of "the white man's obsession with the rampageous black penis."[99] The phallic nature of the dandy's iconography and mischief cannot be denied. What is surprising about blackface dandies is the degree to which they succeed at their plan of "insurrection and intermixture" — for example, when Long-Tail Blue's coat, a clear analog of his phallic power, is split by a watchman, it is very quickly repaired.[100] Even though Blue does not complete a conquest of any white "galls" at the end of his tale, he is still very much in the chase.

Despite the fact that blackface dandy's sexual threat is almost always

10. George Endicott.
"My Long-Tail Blue," ca. 1827.
Picture Collection, The Branch
Libraries, The New York Public
Library, Astor, Lenox and Tilden
Foundations.

11. "Zip Coon, A Favorite Comic
Song." Photographs and Prints
Division, Schomburg Center for
Research in Black Culture, The
New York Public Library, Astor,
Lenox and Tilden Foundations.

12. Barney Williams in "Dandy Jim," 1899. Picture Collection,
The Branch Libraries, The New York Public Library, Astor, Lenox and
Tilden Foundations.

figured as heterosexual, the figure has a queer, or "quare," effect because
of the way in which his racialization is so bound up in his sexuality and
vice versa. This is not to say that the blackface dandy himself is queer; to
say so would be anachronistic and limiting of the total force of his boundary crossings. Instead, the figure's excesses allow one to see from a contemporary viewpoint the way in which the minstrel show worked hard
to express blackness in terms of the other markers of identity. The black
dandy's overweening and inappropriate sexuality blackens him, just as his
blackness and fine dressing make his sexuality anomalous. Yet, even this
element of nascent queerness can and does become signified on in the

show because the "galls" being pursued here by white men in blackface are themselves white men in blackface and drag. From this perspective, the blackface dandy's antics signal the intriguing possibility and threat of both interracial and same-sex liaisons that have to be pursued through blackness. Even the defeats suffered by blackface dandies have to be analyzed in terms of how they sometimes conferred odd or "queer" victories on the whites portraying them. The blackface minstrel show was not, in any way, an arena in which the anxieties attending race, class, sex, and gender were contained. In fact, the dandy on stage, a white performer in blackface, often cross-dressing in terms of race, gender, and class, comes alive in the pursuit and performance of these anxieties, in the production of a queerness that lingers after the curtain goes down and the burnt cork is removed.

In asking What if? blackface minstrelsy also broached the question that haunted nineteenth-century Americans, a question included in an era-defining text like *Uncle Tom's Cabin*: Who can be a gentleman? The answer given by the minstrel show, in the figure of the dandy, suggested that free blacks, no matter how proper, savvy, educated, and within the law, would not be considered eligible for such a revered status. Nevertheless, the dandy's antics in the show were contrasted with the image making of northern blacks who, newly freed, began, like Equiano, to dance in new clothes at their freedom. The change in the look of the black community in urban centers like New York and Philadelphia, the result of black migration to the city as well as of some shopping or clothes swapping on arrival, did not go unnoticed. Attempts to control the perceived impertinency of these newly emboldened, newly fashionable blacks ranged from the subtle to the outrageous.[101] Excessive responses included ripping the new clothes off the backs of those blacks dressed beyond what whites could bear.[102]

The taste of independence caused blacks to examine their self-identity and image as a group—signs of social stratification present in the early black festivals gave way to a full-blown cult of respectability.[103] Elite blacks in urban centers with the oldest and best-established black populations, especially those in Philadelphia and New York, took these earlier lessons and understood that "if they and their compatriots were to have any influence in the new republic, particularly on the crucial issue of slavery, they would have to lead exemplary lives."[104] In Philadelphia, the black elite established and expanded black churches, schools, newspapers, "African" relief societies, Masonic lodges, abolition and anticolonization societies, black literary, musical, and historical societies for their own self-improvement and the uplift of the less fortunate.[105] Extremely concerned with combating stereotypes, refuting doubts about Negro intelligence, leadership ability, and industriousness, "respectable" black folk offered conservative dress as an outward sign of integrity. To that end, the elite of this emerging middle or upper-middle class dressed demurely but in fine fabrics.[106] For these Negroes, such subtle ostentation was not simply a sign of "bourgeois excess," but concerned the "display of self-made black men."[107] This new phase of black dandyism—sartorial elegance in concert with institutions designed to prove blacks' fitness for citizenship, to maintain and refine blacks' social status—emerged as an affront to elite, middle-class, working-class, and immigrant whites. All of these groups were also eager to distinguish themselves from each other and from blacks in America's so-called classless society.

Publicly less concerned with riding the thin line between assimilation and positive self- or group representation, other blacks pushed the conjunction of freedom and fashion to another level. These folks "dressed flamboyantly" as part of a "desire to present oneself as individualistically as possible, to obliterate the drudgery and submission required under slavery, or . . . the poverty and blasted ambitions of many free blacks."[108] For this demographic, the struggle for both self-dignity and collective dignity was enhanced by a flair of original self-presentation. More important than sartorial fabulousness was the communication of it—these blacks notoriously took their extravagance to the streets, strutting, sauntering, and promenading in public spaces like parks and other natural "runways" like New York's Broadway and Fifth Avenue. This "stylin' out," or rejection of decorum set by both whites and the emergent black middle-class, earned the attention of reformers in both groups, but "no amount of lecturing by black or white leaders could suppress the release that the black underclass found in wearing showy clothing to 'frolicks' and balls, in drink, and other forms of conviviality."[109] Given the precarious economic situation of most blacks, the line separating these two groups was permeable indeed; what united them was their use of clothing and dress to distinguish themselves and the majority culture's insistence on not seeing the distinctions between them at all.

This behavior, both the elegance and fabulousness, and its public nature did not go unnoticed even before the minstrel show presented it in blackface. Artists and printmakers, especially Edward Clay, famous for his "Life in Philadelphia" series (1828–30) and "Life in New York" series (late 1820s), lampooned blacks' upwardly mobile lifestyles in grotesque caricatures of supposed black society. In prints depicting blacks in elaborate costumes and bourgeois social situations the artist ridiculed again and again black pretensions, intellectual capacity, and aspirations.[110] Plate 5 from Clay's first "Life in Philadelphia" edition, "Shall I hab de honour to dance . . . ," shows a couple at a ball whose dress is aspirational, in terms of both class and, in the case of the woman, physique. When the nattily clad "Mr. Cato," dressed to the nines in a formal long-tail coat and trousers, high-collared ruffled shirt, and all the accessories, including striped hose and white gloves, asks "Miss Minta," a big-boned woman in a frilly ball gown to dance, what the viewer witnesses is a series of disconnections. Though dressed like a brigadier and ever so polite in both speech and manner, Cato's dialect belies his humble origins; though clad like a princess, Minta's portly, yet muscular physique — she is as big, if not bigger, than Cato — reveals that this leisure time contrasts with her labor. Plates 9 and 13 are similar, featuring even more ridiculously elaborate costumes that serve as visual cues to the exaggeration and abuse of social pretensions taking place here. Potent because so distorting and yet so near the reality, the broad humor of the caricatures belied the multifariousness of black life and deliberately confused the depiction of middle-class striving with other forms of self-promotion. Though blacks were practicing different forms of dandyism — sometimes firmly within social conventions, sometimes independent of respectable society's strictures — parody subsumed them into a cycle in which racism, sexism, and classism tried to keep up with the various forms black agency could take.

A black dandy strolling down the street in the early nineteenth century was an ambiguous, if not nearly unreadable sign. The importance of the gaze, or those from whose perspective black fashion and self-fashioning were being judged, was understood even by those who worked to distort black images, such as the caricaturist Clay. Although his "Life in Philadelphia" series ended in 1830, seven years later Clay issued, "Philadelphia Fashions," a final print admitting, to some degree, the power of the newly emboldened black look. Anticipating *Uncle Tom's Cabin*, this print shows an elegant black dandy couple, not grotesque like their predecessors, training their eyes directly on the viewer. The man wields an opera glass to get a better view. The woman, dressed not in an outré manner but more sophisticatedly, asks her companion, "What you look at Mr. Frederick Augustus?" Mr. Augustus, whose outfit is a tour de force of elegance, answers, peeking through his opera glass, "I look at dat white loafer wot looks at me! I guess he from New York." Highlighting the foreignness of the gaze upon him, Mr. Augustus points out here a real change in the history of black (self-) fashion. Whereas Clay's earlier Philadelphia series had been voyeuristic—one in which the viewer, presumably white, ridicules the black pretension to high society by eavesdropping on blacks' social follies and foibles—this print is confrontational. Mr. Augustus's "look" at the viewer, through a monocle, magnifies concern about the viewer's own sense of self and forces a comparison of this self with that of the nattily clad black man. Looking just at his clothes, one sees that this black man's suit is not the result of the loafing of which he accuses the white—there is the hint in Augustus's carriage, in the way his clothes conform to his body, that he earned this elegance, that it fits him properly, that he wears it as a badge of self-worth. Black dandies, especially in this example by Clay, make obvious the fact that a turf war between blacks and whites, men and women, the higher and lower classes, was taking place in the popular imagination, being worked out on the body and in the streets. The question Who can be a gentleman? is asked here—the answer is complicated at best.

As a depiction of free blacks, the dandy image encapsulated a fight for and against stereotyping. The figure embraced ambivalence and manipulated it into black style, a self-conscious process of endless resignification. Indeed, in his adaptability, the dandy figure is firmly ensconced within the flow of African American history, linking African traditions and black recognition and subversive play with white power in the colonial period to black statements of respectability and individuality in freedom. Blackface minstrelsy and other caricatures fought against this mobility even as they acknowledged the ability of the figure and its real-life counterparts to reinvent themselves. Image is counterposed against image—Dandy Jim competing against an emerging black middle class, among others—for decades until after the Civil War, and then, surprisingly, the dandy's presence in blackface as a minstrel show character began to wane.

Now in the context of a country replete with urban and rural free blacks

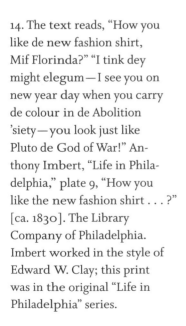

13. The text reads, "Shall I hab de honour to dance de next quadrille wid you, Misf Minta?" "Tank you, Mr. Cato,—wid much pleasure, only I'se engaged for de next set—." Edward W. Clay, "Life in Philadelphia," plate 5, "Shall I hab de honour to dance . . ." (1828). The Library Company of Philadelphia.

14. The text reads, "How you like de new fashion shirt, Mif Florinda?" "I tink dey might elegum—I see you on new year day when you carry de colour in de Abolition 'siety—you look just like Pluto de God of War!" Anthony Imbert, "Life in Philadelphia," plate 9, "How you like the new fashion shirt . . . ?" [ca. 1830]. The Library Company of Philadelphia. Imbert worked in the style of Edward W. Clay; this print was in the original "Life in Philadelphia" series.

15. The text reads, "How you like de Waltz, Mr Lorenzo?" "'Pon de honour ob a gentleman I tink it vastly indelicate — Only fit for de common people!" E. W. Clay, "Life in Philadelphia," plate 13, "How you like de Waltz, Mr. Lorenzo?" (ca. 1829). The Library Company of Philadelphia.

16. The text reads, "What you look at Mr. Frederick Augustus?" "I look at dat white loafer wot looks at me, I guess he from New York." Edward W. Clay, "Philadelphia Fashions" (1837). The Library Company of Philadelphia.

who would in some way assert their presence, the minstrel show grew nostalgic for the good old days of slavery. Deciding that the potential increase in actual dandies was a topic too alarming to consider even in a carnivalesque sense, the show phased dandies out in favor of an entertainment less focused on the conflicts that the black upwardly mobile would engender. Minstrelsy took advantage of its power as America's main source of information about Negro character; in abandoning the dandy and darky dyad for entire shows based on a desire to return to the kind of ethos expressed in Stephen Foster's "My Old Kentucky Home," the show attempted to further collapse Negro caricature and character, this time into a single category. All blacks, urban and rural, recent ex-slaves and those free for generations, would now be portrayed in a more sentimental "good ol' time" mode. Mawkishness replaced tricksterism, and what diversity the show once had was transformed into a parade of what the historian of blackface minstrelsy Robert Toll describes as "simplified caricatures that rationalized white subordination of blacks and provided the molds into which blacks were forced—on stage and off." [111]

"Now who would b'lieve clo'es could do de like o' dat?"
Black Dandy Crimes in Stowe, Melville, and Twain

No longer of much use to blackface artists in the theater, the black dandy moved from the status of theatrical and journalistic caricature to that of a character and narrative concern in some of American literature's greatest meditations on American and African American identity. In fiction, the dandy figure animates, perplexes, disrupts, even haunts the efforts of Stowe and others to depict the problematics of enmeshed race, class, gender, and sexual relations in an America making a transition from slavery to freedom. In contrast to the minstrel show and in concert with free blacks before and after freedom, authors like Stowe, Twain, and Melville preserve and extend the historical force of the figure by exploring black dandyism's power to imaginatively refashion black selves and group identities. They do this by exploring the possibility that despite the minstrel show's efforts to contain the black dandy's oppositional gaze, his nascent and inherent "queer effect" lives on. Disappearing in blackface only to resurface still dressing for success in black-and-white print, black dandies and dandyism bring with them a legacy of trickery, upsets, and expressions of dignity—all expressed through sartorial revenge.

Poised between obsolescence in the minstrel show and popularity on the page, the dandy in *Uncle Tom's Cabin* (1852) participates in the continued revolution of the figure between stereotype and self-representation, revealing the anxieties and aspirations of Americans black and white. From what scholars know about the blackface dandy's origins in a combined critique of white decadence and black fitness for inclusion in the national family, Stowe's characterization of the dandy is consistent with the blackface minstrel show. Even so, her use of this particular ready-made portrait from the conventions of minstrelsy imports a tension into the novel, insofar as the humor Adolph engenders does not at all disguise the satire directed at Augustine St. Clare and imputes a definitive queer effect to them both. Watching Adolph huffily sizing up his new counterpart Tom, St. Clare immediately registers Adolph's cattiness:

> And Adolph tossed his head, and passed his fingers through his scented hair, with a grace.
>
> "So that's it, is it?" said St. Clare, carelessly. "Well, here, I'm going to show Tom to his mistress, and then you take him to the kitchen; and mind you don't put any of your airs to him. He's worth two such puppies as you."
>
> "Master always will have his joke," said Adolph, laughing. "I'm delighted to see Master in such spirits."[112]

Adolph's saucy reply, "Master always will have his joke," reminds St. Clare that dandies will not be totally replaced by darkies, that jokes like Adolph cannot be discounted by those who have created them. A threatening and lingering presence, Adolph suggests in this moment that the black dandy figure and his function can be transformed but not forgotten or eliminated. Adolph's joke focuses attention on the dandy's survival as a slave or servant who, in freedom, promises to offer often unsolicited and always pointed social and cultural commentary. In *Uncle Tom's Cabin*, the dandy's arrogance, in combination with his sycophancy, allows for a simultaneous sneer at the modest and submissive Tom and a mockery of the ultra-gallant, übercavalier St. Clare. If, in the minstrel show, a white man in blackface conceals his critique of white decadence by means of the black mask, Stowe's rendition of the show removes the mask. The white man being referenced, parodied, he whose status as a gentleman is being questioned, is actually present. Furthermore, when one includes the dandy's full provenance, that is, his origins in African and African American race and class cross-dressing, the figure may exceed Stowe's intentions altogether—a look at Adolph in relation to dandyism in black and blackface reveals his surprising affinity to another of the book's characters who is intent on cutting a gentlemanly figure, the black radical George Harris. The unexpected relationship between Adolph and George—between the ostentatious servant-dandy and the man who, if and when he becomes free, would be the emerging middle class—mobilizes and destabilizes the caricature on which Stowe's text seems to rely.

As a black dandy valet, Adolph's stock in trade is his refined appearance, his social polish, his ability to represent his master and his household in elegance. Adolph so excels in his duties that he naturally assumes the title of gentleman, to the annoyance and silent assent of his master: "He was in the habit of adopting [St. Clare's] name and address; and the style under which he moved, among the colored circles of New Orleans, was that of Mr. St. Clare."[113] At home, he takes the gesture further, having "fallen into an absolute *meum tuum* [what's mine is yours] with regard to himself and his master, which sometimes troubled even St. Clare."[114] Clothing becomes the manifest sign of the intimacy between the two men as well as the object by which the ironic difference of Adolph's imitation of St. Clare is made obvious. On arrival at Belle Riviere, St. Clare notices that Adolph's vest looks very familiar. When he inquires as to its owner, Adolph declares that it came to him by way of a cheeky alteration: "O! Master, this vest was all stained with wine; of course, a gentleman in Master's standing never wears a vest like this. I understood I was to take it. It does for a poor nigger-fellow, like me."[115] Pleasing and troubling white gentlemen like St. Clare by means of imitation and appropriation, Adolph queries the gentlemanly status and masculine authority of men like St. Clare and himself.

Adolph's bid for equality with his master, his doubling and performance of St. Clare's identity, brings to the fore considerations of St. Clare's own fitness for the title of gentleman, a category which, in Stowe's novel, can be fulfilled only by a Christian patriarch. If one thinks of Adolph as a partial import from the blackface minstrel show, one knows that his exaggerated affectations—his love of fine clothing and irrepressible sense of entitlement to the tools or weapons of distinction, among them the monocle, cambric handkerchiefs, cologne water—derive from a simultaneous critique of white elite pretension and black self-fashioning efforts. As St. Clare's shadow, Adolph exposes his master's own dandyism and its function as a sign of their joint deviation from conventional masculinity. While Stowe's novel is traditionally read as being centered around an examination of the power of domesticity to properly order our national house, the novel is, of course, equally concerned with the exemplification of a kind of masculinity that will support such ordering. Chaos and laxity reign in the St. Clare household; the "shiftlessness" that Ophelia identifies as pervasive there owes as much to St. Clare's sensitivity as to his wife's selfishness. Even though he is described as having taken on the "rough bark of manhood" in adulthood, St. Clare still possessed at his "core" the "marked sensitiveness of character, more akin to the softness of woman than the ordinary hardness of his own sex," that had characterized him in his childhood.[116] He is, even in adulthood, a "poetical voluptuary," a term Stowe uses to describe St. Clare in his adolescence.[117] Adolph exteriorizes and exploits St. Clare's core, exposing his master as being effeminate. St. Clare's inability to be a proper patriarch ruins him financially and continues the exploitation of those in his care. But, when performed by Adolph, this effeminacy becomes even more complex.

Adolph's effeminacy makes him powerful and vulnerable at the same time; such dualism is consistent with the logic of the dandy character in the blackface minstrel show. Adolph's parody and appropriation of St. Clare remove them both from consideration as proper men or, in the case of Adolph, as an ordinary black (by virtue of his slave status, he is excluded from the category of man). Adolph's fey exposure of St. Clare's masculine weakness is not, I believe, a definitive sign of his own or his master's homosexuality; rather, it functions as a sign of the threat, both progressive and debilitating, that considering masculinity on a spectrum of possibilities brings.[118] Though perhaps not homosexual, Adolph is, like his blackface minstrel brother, the importer of a queer effect into Stowe's novel that becomes attributed to St. Clare as well. Adolph's fey attitude and doubling of St. Clare disturb the boundaries of race, class, gender, and perhaps sexuality in the novel, showing, as did the blackface dandy, the way in which a culture of slavery had to construct these categories in terms of each other.[119] In America, masters must be white and real men, upstanding Christian patriarchs; slaves must be black, or vulnerable in all ways.[120] Perhaps in spite of herself, Stowe renders this fact in Adolph's dandyism, his sartorial critique and distinction, his bid for a bit of self-mastery in a system designed to totally subjugate him. Adolph's doubling of St. Clare reveals that at least at Belle Riviere, a crime of fashion has occurred that has rent the whole system.

That this crime of fashion will only beget other violations is made clear when, after St. Clare dies, Adolph is sold to a "sprucely dressed" man at auction, after being himself subjected to an inspection by eyeglass. The eyeglass-toting man tells his friend, a young "exquisite," "Well! I was wanting a valet, and I heard that St. Clare's lot was going. I thought I'd take a look at his—."[121] In this moment, Adolph's relation to St. Clare cannot be named; the effeminate slave whose subversive sartorial and perspectival look questions the masculine potency of all within the slave system is made truly vulnerable here through sexual innuendo.[122] The trader who sells him later cautions the slave's new owner, "You'll find it'll take all you've got to keep him. He's deucedly extravagant!"[123] Requiring extreme care because of an excessiveness known to double, or "deuce," on itself, this black dandy is trapped in the performances that produced him, even as he embodies a potentially liberating difference within the very system that defines him.

Adolph's dandyism allows him to win small battles in representation, but never the war. In his exploitation of the codes of affluent behavior and dress, Adolph's parody of St. Clare hints at a critique of the system of race and class and gender but does not or cannot truly push its boundaries. Not imitating an aristocrat, as is Adolph, but passing for one, the mulatto George Harris takes the structure of dandy performance, manipulates it, and escapes with his freedom. In contrast to that of Adolph, George's race and class cross-dressing as a "Spanish gentleman" brings him very near a definite victory. George uses both of the performative traditions of nineteenth-century black dandyism, that of early African blacks in America and that of American blackface minstrels, to dandify his way out of slavery.

When George assumes the dress and character of a Spanish gentleman in order to escape captivity and join his family in Canada, he signifies on gentlemanly costume and blackface. Dressing in fine clothes and darkening his skin, he explodes the limits the text seeks to place on the relationship between racial performance and black self-fashioning. Although

George's category-defying masquerade in *Uncle Tom's Cabin* is not explicitly named as an act of dandyism, it is such, especially as it demonstrates the fugitive slave's ability to use a gentleman's clothing and attitude to derail the societal expectations of black slaves and the white men who own them.[124] In that George is captive within a system that relies on the continual performance of racial difference, his escape from slavery is a preeminently performative act, "quite literally the role of his life."[125] This role counters expectation: he does not pass for white, as his master's runaway advertisement suggests he might, he does not escape under cover of night, and, dangerously, he does not escape alone. Instead, George takes on blackness, dresses above his class, and uses a free black friend as a slave valet. These acts simultaneously reveal and conceal his natural aristocracy as an intelligent, educated, well-mannered mulatto. As a version of himself, he is as unrecognizable as he is obvious.

The disguise of the Spanish gentleman allows George to externalize a critique of the construction of his own identity and that of other American blacks. Dressing up and darkening his skin, he comments on the legacy of the slave trade and imperialism in the reference to Spain, on American racial politics—the "blackface" that gives him a racial identity that is neither black, nor white, nor mulatto—on performances of white mastery—the freeman playing a black slave, a flourish that enhances George's status as free and master of his affairs.[126] All of these acts combine into a clever manipulation of a society that simultaneously scrutinizes others, just as it refuses to really see or acknowledge them, a society in which color bears an odd relationship to invisibility.[127] In neither blackface nor whiteface, but rather a variation that trumps the color binary of racial play in America, George brilliantly passes out of slavery by means of inhabiting and superseding its mechanisms of control. The Spanish masquerade takes dandyism and blackface into a further arena, one that, if not exploding racial distinctions altogether, leads Stowe's text into a place beyond the frame of her intended portraiture of blacks as children or sentimental subjects.

In fact, George's crime of freeing himself by means of fashion aligns him with his gentlemanly king and governor ancestors, who performed an earlier version of this same act. Even so, his escape also relies on an act of blackface and thus includes some limitations as well.[128] While George escapes denigratory blackness by assuming Spanishness here, he does so in order to secure the privileges of masculinity denied to him as an enslaved mulatto. Unlike Adolph, George uses, rather than inhabits, his status as queer or out of place; throughout the novel, before his escape, he desires and works toward a masculinity much more conventional. Intent on founding or finding a place in which democracy includes racial equality, in which he would be able to be a proper patriarch, George wants nothing more than to exercise his rights as a man. His focus on being a man pits his own manhood against the relative freedom of his wife and child. George's desires uphold and align him with a patriarchal system, even as his actions — and those of his cross-dressing wife — work against the system.[129] Despite his radical deconstruction of some of slavery's necessary conventions, nothing prevents a free George Harris from taking his "patriarchal politics of ownership" into exile with him to Canada, France, and finally Liberia.[130] His performance would like to deny the volatility of blackface and other racial performances in the text but preserves it nevertheless.

To be a middle-class African American gentleman is impossible in Stowe's text and world, no matter how well one succeeds in taking on the trappings of privilege. In *Uncle Tom's Cabin*'s allegory of America, the presence of George as a self-fashioning New Negro is too volatile. For Stowe and others, there is a difference between imitating or parodying a gentleman and actually passing for one. At midcentury, on the eve of the Civil War, those blacks who pass for white or anything else will be jettisoned from the text. In contrast, those who constantly question the supremacy of the dominant race, the upper class, and masculinist gender roles, but who do so within certain limits, will not be exiled outside of the American experiment. Uncle Tom dies and George sets sail, but the black dandy Adolph remains. A short time after the final scenes of *Uncle Tom's Cabin*, the Civil War begins — soon all blacks would be free. Under these improved but still uncertain circumstances, dandyism's play with gentlemanly self-fashioning sets off in yet another direction.

What Stowe hints at in *Uncle Tom's Cabin* — that the dandy will disrupt the text and manipulate to uncertain ends the very categories constitutive of American identity — forms the ground from which Melville's *Benito Cereno* (1855) and Twain's *Pudd'nhead Wilson* (1894) explore the politics of image and identity. Though the dandyism in *Uncle Tom's Cabin* unwittingly challenges the power of racial binaries, disturbs class hierarchies and gender biases, in *Benito Cereno* and *Pudd'nhead Wilson* its deconstructive power is deliberately taken on and exploited. The gulf between image and identity, as communicated by clothing and clothing exchange between black and white, is the locus around which deception and deconstruction of racism's supposed naturalness operate in both texts. As a black body servant manipulating the stereotype of his own identity, Melville's Babo combines his fellow servant Adolph's lesson about the power of mocking white authority with the escaping slave George's method of appropriating the master's power by actually inhabiting the role. This strategy allows him to perform simultaneously submission and mastery in his orchestration and concealment of the slaves' revolt. This masquerade returns to the black dandy the power of his gaze; this usurpation is not possible without costumes.

Babo assumes and wields the body servant's intimate, potentially threatening knowledge of a gentleman's appearance and behavior. In fact, the slave's ability to tailor the expectations of Captain Delano and others is revealed as nothing less than magisterial. Boarding the mutinous ship, Delano is faced with an image whose details he does not at first suspect. Appearances are all the "undistrustful" Delano has to go on, even when later incidents rattle such "spectacles of fidelity" by means of wardrobe equally appropriate and bizarre. In Melville's own words,

> The scene [in which Babo bodily supports Don Benito, weak and re-
> covering from a fainting fit] was heightened by the contrast in dress, de-
> noting their relative positions. The Spaniard wore a loose Chili jacket of
> dark velvet; white small-clothes and stockings, with silver buckles at the
> knee and instep; a high crowned sombrero, of fine grass; a slender sword,
> silver mounted, hung from a knot in the sash—the last being an almost
> invariable adjunct, more for utility than ornament, of a South American
> gentleman's dress at this hour. Excepting when his occasional nervous
> contortions brought about disarray, there was a certain precision in his
> attire curiously at variance with the unsightly disorder around. . . .
>
> The servant wore nothing but wide trowsers, apparently from their
> coarseness and patches, made out of some old topsail. . . .
>
> . . .
>
> Still, relatively to the pale history of the voyage, and his own pale face,
> there seemed something so incongruous in the Spaniard's apparel, as al-
> most to suggest the image of an invalid courtier tottering about London
> streets in the time of the plague.[131]

Like the padlock and key Benito wears as a necklace, "significant symbols, truly," the clothing begs to be read, its fuller context discovered.[132] "Incongruous," "at variance," and "in-valid," Don Benito's attire functions as a kind of fourth wall for the performance at hand. Delano intuits and ignores the signs that identify the contrivance of the scene in front of him—he refuses to believe that the two men could possibly have a relationship other than that denoted by the hierarchy of their clothing. Unwilling to completely enter a space of discomforting suspicion, the American maintains the fiction by ignoring all the clues that would lead to the discovery of a crime of fashion. Only later, when he learns that "the dress, so precise and costly, worn by him [Don Benito] on the day whose events have been narrated, had not been willingly put on," does Delano grasp the place of style in this drama.[133] Babo's use of fine clothing renders master and slave indecipherable.

Whereas the dandy is normally dressed above his so-called station, in *Benito Cereno* Babo disguises his identity as a trickster by dressing his master in his own duplicity. Forcing Cereno to wear not only fancy clothing, but outfits too ostentatious even for the Spanish gentleman's own social position, the slave converts finery into costume, names reality as performance by means of exaggeration. His servility and excessive caretaking also allow him to wield a womanly power—he plays the servant so well that he exposes not just Delano's racism and classism, but his gender biases as well. By rights, the ship's captain—now actually the slave Babo—would wear the elegant attire of a gentleman, dress well as a sign of power. Here, Babo signifies on Delano's expectation of just such conventionality and dresses his new "slave" in a master's clothing, thereby turning the play with clothing inside out. If the narrative is, as Eric Sundquist suggests, an "entanglement in the ritual staging of authority," the ritual staged in the novel is one in which the initiate must see race and power beyond or through appearances in order to master them.[134] Those relying on minstrel stereotypes or romantic racialism to guide their reading of visual clues of identity will have the difficult task of discerning the slight difference here between power and power play.

Though Delano sees Don Benito as a "black letter text" he reads reluctantly and without confidence, the revelation of the Spaniard as the "creature of his [Babo's] own tasteful hands" reveals the servant's status as the author, subject, and deconstructor of that black text.[135] Manipulating

Delano by means of doubly signifying on costume, Babo takes the "rebellious potential within every slave," particularly dandified slaves, to a most dangerous level.[136] In linking this rebelliousness to an ingeniously self-conscious racial play, Babo's show forces white elites to experience a distance between their own images and identities. Such insistence compels black *and white* to construct new identities in this unstable, troubling, but potentially unconstrained space. But even this place has no real room for the likes of Babo; in the end, he pays for his crime with dismemberment, the separation of the dandy's head, a "hive of subtlety," from his signifying body. Restoring, in a fashion, an oppositional black gaze to class and race cross-dressing blacks, this head "fixed on a pole, in the Plaza, met, unabashed, the gaze of whites."[137]

In *Benito Cereno*, dandyism is removed from the body or abstracted; its threat is thereby only increased. The black dandy's enduring out of placeness and the relation of that queerness to cognition and interiority made him an urgent concern in later American fiction. As an allegory of the post-Reconstruction era set along the Southern antebellum frontier, Twain's *Pudd'nhead Wilson* (1894) is perhaps the most obviously dandified text of the late nineteenth century.[138] In this novel, the burlesque and counterburlesque of black dandyism are written on the body and imprinted in the mind, creating a text and describing a nation in which the definition of blackness and its possibilities become simultaneously confused and solidified.

Though named for David "Pudd'nhead" Wilson, the lawyer who eventually succeeds in identifying the dandy as black, slave, and male, the novel focuses on the black dandy character born Valet de Chambre, who eludes such classification for most of the text. The cheekily named future dandy, child of the nearly white slave Roxy, is elevated to whiteness by means of a clothing exchange contrived by his mother. Noticing his striking resemblance to Thomas à Becket Driscoll, the white child also in her care, she switches their clothing:

> "No, dolling, mammy ain't gwyne treat you [Valet de Chambre] so. De angels is gwyne to 'mire you jist as much as dey does yo' mammy . . ."
>
> By this time she had stripped off the shirt. Now she clothed the naked little creature in one of Thomas à Becket's snowy long baby gowns, with its bright blue bows and dainty flummery of ruffles. . . .
>
> She stepped over and glanced at the other infant; she flung a glance

back at her own; then, one more at the heir of the house. Now a strange
light dawned on in her eye. . . .

She began to move about like one in a dream. She undressed Thomas à
Becket, stripping him of everything, and put the tow-linen shirt on him.
She put his coral necklace on her own child's neck. Then she placed the
children side by side, and after earnest inspection she muttered—

"Now who would b'lieve clo'es could do de like o' dat?"[139]

Given the history of black dandyism, one knows that "clo'es" can create
and affect an infinite variety of subject and object positions. In this case,
Roxy's manipulation of white elite clothing both liberates her son from
slavery and makes him her own master. The irony of the gesture—she
perpetrates a crime of fashion against herself—propels the text deep into
the problematics of dandyism's combined race, class, and gender masquerade. As the new Tom Driscoll's "primal scene," this incident replays
itself again and again in the text as Tom moves between black and white,
master and slave, masculine and feminine. Though a supposed contrast
to Pudd'nhead Wilson's deterministic fingerprint technology that forms
the other half of this bizarre narrative, the dandy play or cross-dressing
initiated here cycles toward a similar, definitive, but still conflicted end.

As Tom Driscoll, Valet de Chambre unwittingly behaves just like a black
dandy or, more specifically (and importantly), as a stereotypical blackface
dandy would. A wicked, yet weak man devoted to gambling, drinking, and
general sloth, his behavior continually reveals his "true" racial identity
and sartorial masquerade.[140] As a man legally black unknowingly passing
for white, Tom can be read as a heightened example of precisely what
antebellum antiabolitionists feared and dismantlers of Reconstruction's
gains hoped to eliminate: a newly free black man who takes on and exploits the privileges of whiteness. Nevertheless, even though the locals
know him to be white, they find his demeanor excessive. When he returns from college in the East with a new wardrobe and affectations, his
friends set him straight by unknowingly mocking and exposing his "real"
identity:

He brought home with him a suit of clothes of such exquisite style and
cut and fashion—eastern fashion, city fashion—that it filled everybody
with anguish and was regarded as a particularly wanton affront. He enjoyed the feeling which he was exciting, and paraded the town serene

and happy all day; but the young fellows set a tailor to work that night, and when Tom started out on his parade the next morning, he found the old deformed bellringer straddling along in his wake tricked out in flamboyant curtain-calico exaggeration of his finery, and imitating his fancy eastern graces as well.[141]

With this—the "black" dandy being burlesqued by a dandified black—Twain simultaneously explodes and reifies notions of blackness, a category that the dandy figure in other texts works very hard to circumvent or fill with a fierce irony. By means of this particular dandy-to-dandy confrontation, one is confused by two models of identity formation—blackness is as much performed (a lesson from *Benito Cereno*) as it is inherent. Tom's status as a dandy and black is, at this point, a fact that the reader knows but that Tom does not. Thus for him, his dandyism is a habitation rather than an appropriation of an image or identity.

As if this association with curtain-calico were not clue enough to Tom's real character, it is followed by an incident in which the dandy himself "blacks up" and cross-dresses in order to commit a crime. Donning the disguise of a stooped old black woman to rob in order to pay off gambling debts, Tom shows his "color" yet again, this time by adding burnt cork to an already complicated outfit. Tom's assumption of this "disguise" exposes the black dandy's true social position as feminized, queer, and dangerous to the preservation of white power.[142] This is literalized later, when Tom's plan to rob his uncle results in the uncle's accidental murder, an act that at once liberates Tom from slavery and ultimately binds him to a legal system that simultaneously adjudicates violations of race and law. At all points in the text ambiguous, a caricature and consolidation of race and gender, Tom proves that he alone is an "extraordinary" twin of the text's original title. A self-conscious dandy only when others identify him as such, even his entrance into blackface, what could be an act of signification on his own unconventional biraciality, comes off as debilitating self-mockery. Twain's relentless use of doubling in the text prohibits a stable resignification of these identity categories; rather, dandyism in *Pudd'nhead Wilson* leads to tautology as it becomes associated not only with exteriority or clothing, but perhaps also with interiority, or character.

To have produced a farce in which race was actually meaningless, Twain would have had to make the other victim of the original crime of fashion, the white Tom or Chambers, violate or fulfill some expectations

17. "The Bell Ringer Imitated His Graces." E. W. Kemble illustration for *Pudd'nhead Wilson and Those Extraordinary Twins*. Édition de Luxe of *The Writings of Mark Twain* (1899). Special Collections, University of Virginia Library.

of mastery. Instead, as both Linda Morris and Myra Jehlen argue, "Twain shows no interest in the white baby who is raised as a slave"; "Chambers yet does not become a white man fatally misplaced among blacks, as Tom is a black man fatally misplaced among whites."[143] In the end, after Tom's guilt and racial identity are legally "verified" by means of Pudd'nhead Wilson's collection of fingerprints, both men are returned to their rightful places—Tom is sold (back) into slavery, and Chambers inherits the Driscoll estate. Whereas Tom finishes as he began, just a little the worse for wear, Chambers has been forever altered by Roxy's crime and his pass through blackness: "The real heir found himself rich and free, but in a most embarrassing situation. He could neither read nor write, and his speech was the basest dialect of the negro quarter. His gait, his attitudes, his gestures, his bearing, his laugh—all were vulgar and uncouth. His manners were the manners of a slave. Money and fine clothes could not mend these defects or cover them up, they only made them more glaring and the more pathetic."[144] Twain's relegation of both Tom and Chambers to minstrel stereotype—one of the degenerate dandy, the other of the upstart darky—indicates that while his own version of dandyism revisits the misdeeds of fashion in Stowe and Melville, it preserves none of the other texts' deconstructive bite. Indelibly associated with blackface, dandyism in Twain ridicules rather than functions as a method of critique, as its black practitioners are denied the potential of its liberating power, "money and fine clothes could not mend these defects or cover them up, they only made them more glaring and the more pathetic." Though *Pudd'nhead Wilson* begins with a clothing switch that, handled differently, would have held the promise of an extreme reconfiguration of the very building blocks of American identity (race, class, gender), its author explores and then seemingly rejects racial performance and clothing exchange as a transformative act.[145] In Twain's novel, the "we" who will be punished for these crimes of fashion are undeniably black; the victims and perpetrators of the dandy's crimes of fashion are black culturally, if not racially. They live race very differently than their white counterparts. In their attempts to rewrite the history of black images through dandyism, Melville and Twain understand that the racial play in black and white can leave a trace, a kind of smudge of burnt cork. For Melville, the residue haunts, while for Twain it must be cleaned up. *Pudd'nhead Wilson's* burlesque and counterburlesque of black and blackface dandyism in Reconstruction rewrite antebellum performances as rituals of reversal in which nothing really changes.

Charles Chesnutt Solves the Crime of Fashion

From an early age, Charles Chesnutt understood himself as someone who could and should re-dress some of these crimes of fashion. Fittingly, he expressed these thoughts in his journal on March 16, 1880, in response to the success of Albion Tourgee's *A Fool's Errand* (1879). After placing Tourgee's novel within a general trend toward northern liberal sympathy for a "colored people recently emancipated from a cruel bondage; struggling for education, for a higher moral and social life, against wealth, intelligence, and race prejudice," Chesnutt boldly declares,

> If Judge Tourgee, with his necessarily limited intercourse with colored people, and with his limited stay in the South, can write such interesting descriptions, such vivid pictures of Southern life and character as to make himself rich and famous, why not a colored man, who has lived among colored people all his life . . . why could not such a man, if he possessed the same ability, write a far better book about the South than Judge Tourgee or Mrs. Stowe has written? Answer who can! But the man is yet to make his appearance and if I can't be the man I shall be the first to rejoice at his *début* and give God speed! to his work.[146]

In promising a few lines later to write exclusively of "stale negro minstrel jokes, or worn out newspaper squibs on the 'man and brother,'" Chesnutt intuits what he is up against.[147] Entering into the discussion seemingly requires rehearsing one of the most enduring jokes concerning race and racialization: black and blackface dandyism. Perhaps the culmination of his lifelong aspiration to be an author, *The Marrow of Tradition* (1901) marks Chesnutt's most sustained effort to present Negro character while working through and beyond Negro caricature. At once staging and thwarting the association of black men with minstrel images, this text inaugurates what one might call a set of preventative measures against further crimes of fashion.

In *The Marrow of Tradition*, Chesnutt's exploration of slavery's impact on black identity formation recognizes tactics from the full spectrum of dandyism's actual and literary history. Himself a consummate trickster (as demonstrated in the conjure tales), Chesnutt manipulates the dandy figure's status as a kind of historic creature, a palimpsest, clothed as he is in many layers of apparel. The author's aim to portray black Americans, especially black men, and their plight outside of romantic racialist ideology and the caricatures of blackface minstrelsy required a thorough cleaning of the black dandy's closet.

The Marrow of Tradition follows four black men, Jerry Letlow, Sandy, Dr. Miller, and Josh Green, through a narrative roughly divided into two parts. Each man represents a different stage in the struggle for Negro progress and dresses appropriately for his particular mode of black masculinity. According to Sundquist, "Chesnutt's black characters constitute a virtual anatomy of the complicated ideology of 'progress' that surrounded the New Negro." Yet, Sundquist identifies only the roles of three men in this anatomy: "the less tractable working class [Josh Green]; the aspiring professionals of the 'talented tenth' [Miller]; and an older, more meek servant class [which he identifies primarily as Jerry]."[148] His elimination of Sandy, the dandy-servant, from this roster is strange, especially since, as he says earlier, "Sandy's place among the range of black characters that Chesnutt presents is worth more attention."[149] While Sundquist chooses to focus on the dynamic between Miller and Josh Green, the New Negro and militant, I take up his challenge to examine Sandy's place in the drama, especially his relationship to Miller, who, although a member of the talented tenth, is also a dandy.

Chesnutt further organizes his novel around the question of gentlemanly status for Negroes, using precisely the relationship between Sandy and Miller to do so. This exploration of masculine roles is also placed in an explicitly political context even within the text (in the riot). Chesnutt thus adds the question Who can be a leader? to the earlier concern of Who can be a gentleman? and what that gentleman might look like. The turn to matters of leadership demonstrates the significance of public persona in *The Marrow of Tradition* for the individual men in the text, but also for the group of Negroes comprising their community. In presenting a spectrum of male identities and a variety of leadership styles, Chesnutt dramatizes the emergence of the well-dressed black from minstrel stereotype and associates his reappropriation of the power of self-definition with what the novel's Dr. Miller would perhaps call a not "heroic" but "wise" demand for equal rights.[150] Such a move acknowledges the inherently political nature of black dandyism, a phenomenon with the power ultimately to negotiate racial play and clothing exchange into a mode of black self-definition and well-being.

Chesnutt places a rather large clue to the workings of dandyism in the text at the center of the novel, the cakewalk scene. "Figurative key to the construction of *The Marrow of Tradition*," the cakewalk appears as an event and a sign in the novel, and its presence reveals the myriad of reversals or knowing performances of race and culture that energize the text.[151] As it "fused its African roots with a satiric commentary on big house fashion," the cakewalk incorporated race and class cross-dressing into its performative properties.[152] Related to Negro Election Day and Pinkster, the cakewalk was danced by plantation blacks as entertainment for themselves (as a parody of white fancy dress balls) and their masters in the South, but by the early 1900s the dance had been through a number of other stages: it was a featured part of blackface and black blackface minstrel shows, a specialty of individual black entertainers like Bert Williams and George Walker, the focus of mixed-race and all-white dancing contests at venues like Madison Square Garden, and the subject of one of the first black Broadway hits, Will Marion Cook's and Paul Laurence Dunbar's "Clorindy: or, The Origin of the Cakewalk."[153] The combination of African and African American dance, music, and dress styles with parody as a method of recognizing and circumventing authority and authenticity made it popular with blacks and whites. Both groups saw what they wanted in the dandyism, or the dancers' imitation or appropriation of white dress and highfalutin' manners. For blacks, the performance enacted a bridge between the old and the new, slavery and freedom, while whites considered it an entertaining homage.

As a turn-of-the-century couturier interested in providing fellow blacks with fashions of their own, Chesnutt combines the patterns in the cakewalk's blackface dandyism with those practiced by other black characters. In so doing, he extends the liberating effects of the cakewalk by rehearsing dandyism's past as black and blackface, linking images of slave and free, folk and middle-class, old and New Negro.[154] This connection—possible through the genealogy of dandyism—not only allows Chesnutt to revise the "stale negro minstrelsy jokes" shared between whites or white and "black," but also allows for an exploration of issues of race, class, gender,

18. "Dancers Doing the Cakewalk." Helen Armstead-Johnson Postcards, n.d. Helen Armstead-Johnson Photograph Collections, Photographs and Prints Division, Schomburg Center for Research in Black Culture, The New York Public Library, Astor, Lenox and Tilden Foundations.

and image *within* the black community. By presenting his own portraits of blacks, outside of but not ignorant of minstrelsy's nearly indelible black and white images, Chesnutt re-dresses the efforts of Stowe, Twain, and others by imagining and imaging a "significant change" in the portrayal of African Americans. Doing so places blacks at the center of *The Marrow of Tradition*'s implied sequel, equipped with new wardrobes for a new century.

About midway through the novel, a group of northern visitors to the town of Wellington, where the novel is set, are treated to a cakewalk as evidence of the ostensible joyfulness of Negro folklife. In the cakewalk scene, fancy dress serves as both a disguise and a revelation. A black dandy gentleman enters the contest late:

> The newcomer was dressed strikingly, the conspicuous features of his attire being a long blue coat with brass buttons and a pair of plaid trousers. He was older, too, than the other participants, which made his agility the more remarkable. His partner was a new chambermaid. . . . The cake was awarded to this couple by a unanimous vote. The man presented it to his partner with a grandiloquent flourish, and returned thanks in a speech which sent the Northern visitors into spasms of delight at the quaintness of the darky dialect and the darky wit. To cap the climax, the winner danced a buck dance with a skill and agility that brought a shower of complimentary silver, which he gathered up and passed to the head waiter.[155]

Outfitted in what appears to be the blackface minstrel dandy's signature ensemble, the long-tail blue, this high-stepper is thought by most to be Sandy, Old Mr. Delamere's faithful servant. The newspaperman Ellis, also in attendance, relies on appearances as he identifies Sandy by his clothing, even though he finds the black man's behavior "strangely inconsistent with the gravity and decorum" that Sandy normally displays.[156] Initially puzzled by the man's demeanor but not by his outrageous outfit, Ellis, the novel's white liberal voice, unfortunately judges the man by his looks. Like Melville's Captain Delano, he justifies his perception by letting prejudice eliminate his doubts—the cakewalker must be Sandy, since "negroes were as yet a crude and undeveloped race," "no one could tell at what moment the thin veneer of civilization might peel off and reveal the underlying savage."[157] What readers do not know at this point and what Ellis helps them figure out later is that this savage man is in fact the town's resident rake, Tom Delamere, in blackface. Such a revelation assigns the grotesqueness of the man and performance away from Sandy, allowing one to reimagine the "negro gentleman" less connected to these images.

How Chesnutt constructs Sandy's outfit, an ensemble that works to disguise and then betray Tom, is the key to unraveling the larger effect of dandyism in the text. When the outfit first makes an appearance, as the uniform Sandy wears while serving dinner, Chesnutt writes that the blue coat "dated back to the fashion of a former gentleman," in contrast to the trousers, which were "of strikingly modern cut and pattern."[158] Later Sandy tells Ellis that the jacket was a gift from the days of slavery, forty years ago, and that he had bought the trousers recently. Incongruous in style as perhaps a result of their different eras of origin, the coat and pants seemingly pull the body wearing them in different directions, between slavery and freedom. Tom both sees and exploits the "incongruity" of what he calls Sandy's "rig." Considering that the suit "would make a great costume for a masquerade," he decides that he should use its outrageousness to ironically convince others of the outfit's consistency as Negro dress.[159] He is able to fool the northerners with it at the cakewalk only because they expect Negro entertainers like "Sandy" to combine fancy dance with funny dress. Paying more attention to the look, rather than to how it might communicate Sandy's personal style, Tom sees the clothing as only a perfectly coordinated costume, rather than an embodiment of Sandy's history and his modest ambitions.

The outfit's split personality strikingly manifests itself later after Tom uses it to camouflage his robbery and murder of Polly Ochiltree. Sandy is arrested for the crime and when questioned by his master tells a poignant tale as alibi for his getup:

> W'en I lef' home las' night after supper, my clo's wuz all put erway in de closet in my room, folded up on de she'f ter keep de moths out. Dey wuz my good clo's,—de blue coat dat you wo' ter de weddin' fo'ty years ago, an' dem dere plaid pants I gun Mistuh Cohen fo' dollars fer three years ago; an' w'en I looked in my closet dis mawnin,' suh, befo' I got ready ter sta't fer Belleview, dere wuz my clo's layin' on de flo,' all muddy an' crumple' up, des lack somebody had wo' 'em in a fight! Somebody e'se had wo' my clo's,—er e'se dere'd be'n some witchcraf,' er some sort er devilment gwine on dat I can't make out, suh, ter save my soul![160]

While the clothing exhibits the effects of an actual altercation between Tom and his plucky aunt, more important, it bears scars of a metaphorical contest between image and identity. It is with Sandy's outfit that Chesnutt stages a confrontation between very "comical" darkies (what Tom calls Sandy), "gentlem[e]n in ebony" (Old Delamere's phrase), and those others historically assaulted by minstrelsy's "mud," New Negroes with the wherewithal to outfit themselves.[161] Sandy's purchase of the trousers, along with his objection to being called a "good darky," indicates that he does not consider himself within the minstrel role, no matter how easily Tom can place him there. The outfit means something entirely different to the black who wears it and to the whites who judge the man by it. While Sandy himself may not totally escape the minstrel mask, at the cakewalk his "rig" dances without him, reproducing a separation between image — the blackface dandy's long-tail blue — and identity — the former slave's "good" pants — that already exists between the two pieces of the outfit. When the blackface body and its crime are found out, the clothing is free to be tailored for a different service. This, of course, is Chesnutt's larger aim: to restage minstrel moments like this to allow room for blacks themselves to fashion alternative public personae.

When Old Delamere discloses the mode of his grandson's wrongdoing to Major Carteret, he understates when he cries, "God alone knows how many crimes have been done in this guise!"[162] The old gentleman ostensibly speaks for Chesnutt, who, in hoping to correct these blackface violations, attends seriously to the details of the crime scene. Like Melville, he challenges the readers inside and outside of the text to reach beyond their expectations when confronted with situations that normalize black obsequiousness or ridiculousness. As a thorough investigator, Chesnutt provides background and follow-up on everyone involved, leaving clues throughout the text on how both blacks and whites might read similar moments. In his description of the ultimate fates of both Tom and Sandy, he ingeniously offers commentary on the relationship of minstrelsy and blackface dandyism to racial politics in the late nineteenth century. Though exposed as a murderer and thief by his own grandfather, who dies from the stress of the incident, Tom Delamere is not punished for his crimes. In fact, he becomes wealthy through inheritance, owing to the machinations of the white supremacist General Belmont, who destroys Old Delamere's last will granting Sandy and Dr. Miller the bulk of his estate. Banished from Wellington, Tom nevertheless gets away with murder. Sandy too is exiled in a way: Tom bequeaths Old Delamere's wardrobe, rather than his money, to Sandy, after dismissing the loyal servant from his job attending the Delamere family. As the recipient of yet another gift of his (former) master's clothing, Sandy is further relegated to the past, rewarded with items likely to perpetuate his servility. Indeed, he will certainly wear this finery at his new job as Major Carteret's butler. This new post is a complicated demotion, as Sandy exchanges work for a paternalistic "ideal gentleman" of the old South for that of a man who might be considered a scion of the new, openly racist South. Blackface performance does not pay for either the white in blackface, Tom, or for the ostensible subject of the farce, Sandy. The black, however, certainly suffers the greater consequences.

As he endeavors to put the minstrel plot of the novel to rest, Chesnutt expands his exploration of Negro character by proposing a related but supplementary narrative that explores and examines the possibilities of the dandy figure in the African American community. The link between the plots is one that the figure of the black dandy provides through its status as a menacing object for the emerging, ambitious free black community. As a caricature of free or newly freed blacks transitioning to freedom, the figure critiqued those with any pretension, serious or comical, to elite looks and manners. Himself a member of the increasingly visible but minuscule black middle-class, Chesnutt was extremely sensitive to the ironies of middle-class uplift, a phenomenon which sought to balance aid to those closer to minstrel stereotype with a resolute denial of any personal connection to such grotesquerie. The second plot of *The Marrow of Tradition* explores just this connection between the minstrel and the middle class, specifically formulating the problem in terms of the dandy's particular commentary on the contest between imposed and self-designed images of black masculine identity.

Like any dandy text, *The Marrow of Tradition* is awash in doubles—the characters and plotlines come in twos. Chesnutt's vision of the trajectory of black progress places men on either side of a divide: those who define themselves in relation to former white masters and those who are self-made. Jerry Letlow, errand boy to Major Carteret, is used by Chesnutt to explore further the difficult relationship between the old and new South. Continually bowing and scraping, gleeful at a kind word from Wellington's finest whites, Jerry understands and responds to the starkness of the racial landscape, saying, "I wush ter Gawd I wuz white!"[163] Captain McBane's effort to take Jerry as a prime example of Negro character is misguided, but his description of him is instructive: "Yes, he's one of the best of em. . . . He'll call any man 'master' for a quarter, or 'God' for half a dollar; for a dollar he'll grovel at your feet, and for a castoff coat you can buy an option on his immortal soul—if he has one!"[164] Again, Negro fashion figures as a sign of integrity. Whereas Sandy cherished but supplemented his castoff clothing, Jerry would apparently relish the possession of *any* material sign of recognition by whites. Chesnutt amplifies the hapless man's implied connection to blackface when Sandy uses black printer's ink to fill in the white spots that chemicals create on his skin. Jerry's miscalculations of racial politics eventually prove fatal: he is killed after getting swept up with the armed blacks in the riot, after futilely waving a white handkerchief, southern-belle style, in Major Carteret's direction. His feminized plea to a man he wrongly considers his friend is altogether ignored. In the aftermath of the riot, the newly outfitted Sandy takes Jerry's place in Major Carteret's employ, signaling a slight adjustment, if any, in racial relations. Not quite a dandy but having aspirations to wear elite clothing and be white exclusive of irony, Jerry mistakes the dandy figure's metaphoric use of dress in relationship to white power for an unreflective imitativeness or metonymy.

Chesnutt proposes self-respect or, more specifically, a self-regard that understands and manipulates sartorial looks, cutting glances, and oppositional views as a tonic to blackface exploitation. Displays of self-respect earn the blacks in the novel explicit designation as New Negroes, a group whose even subtle bids to change the social and political structure constitute a grievous affront to whites. The white supremacists form their plan against the Negroes in their midst as part of a multipronged effort to issue a warning to the city's blacks, who are finally coming into their own. By deposing elected Negro officials and running the professional class out of town, the "Big Three"—Major Carteret, General Belmont, Captain McBane—would once again be able to control the black population's efforts to regard themselves differently. Chesnutt signals the novel's shift from examining the Negro past to the New Negro's future by stating that only a temporary lull followed the resolution of the "Ochiltree affair," or Tom's blackface murder: soon citizens were refocused on their "obscure jealousy of the negro's progress, an obscure fear of the very equality so contemptuously denied."[165]

Representing this transition from blackface to New Negro is Dr. William Miller, a man "raised to be a gentleman in the town where [his] ancestors had once been slaves," the man McBane identifies as the "colored doctor" with the "hospital, and the diamond ring, and the carriage, and the other fallals [finery, frippery, or showy adornment]."[166] Having an education and accomplishments that even the Big Three acknowledge benefit Wellington, Dr. Miller nevertheless produces a crisis for them. Within the white group, Miller is viewed paradoxically as a "very good sort of a negro, [one who] doesn't meddle with politics, nor tread on any one else's toes" and also a "bad example," as precisely "that sort of nigger" that makes it "all the harder to keep the rest of 'em down."[167] The newness of his status as an accomplished free Negro, especially in the South, makes Miller a man whom the white supremacists deign to retain only as long as he remains "mighty quiet" and a "smart nigger without a constituency."[168] But, as we have seen before, the mere appearance of a free Negro is an inherently political statement. "That sort of nigger," a man given to frippery and uplift, will be hard-pressed to remain inconspicuous.

As exemplified in the character of Miller, Chesnutt's rehabilitation of the dandy involves not only a clothing change (the abandonment of the long-tail blue), but also an adjustment in the attitude that accompanies the change. In the novel, devilish and parodic performance is replaced by what appears to be a more conventional effort to communicate group and self-respectability. In some ways, Chesnutt's dandy attempts to convert racial and sartorial play with elite clothing into a greater sense of entitlement to that garb. Entitlement means an end to a sense of self as performative and clothing as a sign or element of that performativity; instead, Chesnutt seems to be arguing for much more transparency in the relation between seeing and being. Chesnutt's formulation of the New Negro as the new dandy contains an irony—his desire to expand the roles black men could occupy operates on the limitation of what a sign (clothing) can signify. Additionally, Chesnutt's hope for a world in which gentlemen who look and act like gentlemen are taken for nothing else, regardless of their color, includes obvious class biases. Yet, Chesnutt does acknowledge the inadequacies of the New Negro figure he employs, even as he uses the respectable dandy to comment on the artificiality of racial and social markers. The contrast Chesnutt draws between Miller's immaculate self-presentation and his feelings of profound incongruity signals the author's understanding of the continued difficulty or impossibility for the black dandy to break out of an ironic structure, to be naturalized or considered anything but anomalous, queer, even to himself. Seeing himself as "a sort of social misfit, an odd quantity, educated out of his own class, with no possible entrance to that above it," Miller updates Sandy's transitional outfit to the degree that he becomes avant-garde.[169]

Educated in Europe and in the North, Miller is first described as "looking so well—and so prosperous," a state attributed to the fact that he "inherited both health and prosperity," a certainly unusual circumstance for a black man in the 1890s.[170] Sitting with Dr. Burns on the train, he forms one half of a duo who "seemed from their faces and their manners to be men of culture and accustomed to the society of cultured people."[171] Indeed, the only discernible difference between the two doctors, both intelligent, well dressed, and accomplished, is race: Burns is white and Miller mulatto. A member of the second postslavery generation, Miller had benefited from the hard work and ambition of his ancestors; such quick progress after emancipation meant that, according to his own estimation, he had grown "above it [the color line]."[172] Though sometimes incredibly savvy about racial politics, Miller also exhibits the tragic but common naïveté of a New Negro when he thinks, "Race antagonism . . . [was] bound to disappear in time, and . . . when a colored man should demonstrate to the community in which he lived that he possessed character and power, that community would find a way to enlist his services for the public good."[173] Whereas in other dandy texts, authors like Melville and Twain dared readers to question the relationship between seeing and believing, *The Marrow of Tradition* has Miller searching for a public that would take his appearance at face value. Yet Chesnutt includes a number of elements in the text, including Miller's status as a mulatto and Sandy's debacle, to indicate that such straight readings of black people will not be possible in the post-Reconstruction era.

The mulatto-ness of the first black dandies and dandyism in America—exemplified by Africans or early African Americans manifesting their cultural identities through a mix of African and American, black and white fashion—literally gets beneath America's skin in Chesnutt's novel. In proposing a mixed-race man in a good suit as a natural outgrowth of Afri-

cans in "mixed-race" outfits, Chesnutt updates the look of black dandyism while acknowledging that the miscegenation threat surrounding the
figure had actually materialized. As a dandified mulatto, Miller is unsurprisingly concerned with his public persona, his standing in the black and
white communities. Despite the dandy's and mulatto's special affinity for
understanding and manipulating distinctions of race and class, Miller,
as a man who wants to be judged and judge others at face value, feels
less qualified and obligated to do so. This belief is tested by a situation
in which a straightforward reading of appearances proves impossible, in
which Miller must take advantage (and suffer the consequences) of his
sometime ability to bridge categories of race and class.

It is during the riot, started by the Big Three, that Chesnutt analyzes
the convictions of his New Negro while simultaneously providing commentary on the action by means of Miller's unintended but serendipitous
racial and sartorial masquerade. Even though Chesnutt was perhaps not
aware of the early relationship between black dandyism and black community leadership, his redesign of the dandy also inserts the figure back
into leadership debates during the riot. Driving into Wellington from an
appointment in the country on the day of the riot, Miller approaches a
group of obviously distressed black men and women who run at the sight
of his carriage. Confused, the doctor stops and waits for the hidden blacks
to emerge and confirm what "his slumbering race consciousness which
years of culture had not obliterated, that there was some race trouble on
foot."[174] In this scene, Chesnutt begins his correction of Miller's earlier
placement of himself above the color line, forces the dandy to acknowledge and act on his status on the color line, which intersects with the lines
of gender and class. Miller's "slumbering race consciousness" is awakened
in a counterintuitive way—he begins thinking about his own relationship
to race or blackness when the terrified folk run away from him, ostensibly
acting on the "presumption that a well-dressed man with a good horse
and buggy was white."[175] This irony engenders a number of others, all
related to the way in which the doctor's public persona, inextricable from
the combination of his dress and his skin, intersects with considerations
of himself as a good New Negro. At stake in the riot is whether or not
Miller's "years of culture" will benefit anyone but himself, whether or
how dandyism's insurgency can translate to New Negro uplift.

Taken for white and powerful, Miller has many options in this violent episode. Told by his friend, the minister Mr. Watson, that "if you put the hood of your buggy down, and sit well back in the shadow, you may be able to reach home without interruption," Miller can pass perhaps unharmed through the city if his clothing but not his face is visible (he is slightly too dark to pass for white).[176] Minutes later, he is entreated by the would-be folk hero and militant Josh Green to lead the black community against the armed and inflamed whites. Miller is honored but also surprised that his fellow blacks would choose him as a leader; this is the first time, apart from the racist Big Three, that others, especially blacks, have taken Miller's obvious self-mastery as evidence of his potential as a leader. Agonizingly contemplating a turn from exemplarity to authority, in true dandy style Miller chooses the middle way, telling Josh and the others, "I should like to lead you; I should like to arm every colored man in this town . . . but if I attempted it . . . my life would pay the forfeit. Alive, I may be of some use to you, and you are welcome to my life in that way, — I am giving it freely. Dead, I should be a lump of carrion."[177] Adept at an aggression more subtle and complex, dandies, especially the New Negro variety, tend to avoid direct confrontations, preferring to dismantle the system from within. An attempt to negotiate his way out of a situation in which he might be called a "coward, morally or physically," Miller's choice to follow a "wise" but "not heroic" path does not actually save him or his would-be constituency from actual or psychic harm.

Relying on his appearance as the key to his safety, Miller begins his journey home to find his family. As the riot worsens, and civil and human rights are thoroughly abandoned, Miller's disguise as a white gentleman in his buggy begins to fail. Reaching home only to find that his wife and son earlier had gone to visit friends, the Butlers, he is stopped three times on his way, told to dismount since "a nigger must obey" no matter what he is wearing.[178] Accompaniment by a man actually white, not just one dressed in elite clothing, is required for Miller to traverse Wellington. Even so, "white" turns out to be a term undergoing active definition in the violent fray. After his last altercation with a Jewish merchant who "had so far forgotten twenty centuries of history as to join in the persecution of another race!," Miller meets Ellis, who volunteers to escort him.[179] Finding that his family is not at the Butler's after all, Miller abandons his buggy, which he realizes "had been a hindrance, rather than a help," and starts out on foot, still hoping that "his own skin color, slight in the daytime, would not attract attention and that by dodging in the shadows he might avoid those who might wish to intercept him."[180] Finally arriving home again, he learns that his son has been killed. Janet, Miller's very light-skinned wife, had been wrong to take the chance of crossing the city with their son.

With a wardrobe that protects and then fails him, material possessions like the buggy that hinder him, and, finally, a racial identity or skin color that does not spare him or his family, Miller suffers as the pressure of the riot unmistakably separates race from class in the end. Slipping in and out of class and racial identities and thus states of masculine power throughout the melee, the doctor becomes a victim (through his son) in spite of and perhaps because of his changeability. Though the minstrel dandy had been put to rest, allowing the New Negro to claim and retool the figure's powers for his own, Chesnutt indicates that the racial and political climate is not yet ready for such a transition. Just as Miller and his wife are granted the recognition they had craved—Miller as an upstanding citizen and accomplished surgeon, Janet her birthright as Olivia Carteret's half-sister—when Olivia begs them to help her ailing child—they sustain the loss of what the New Negro, especially the New Negro leader, wants most: heirs, embodiments of progress.

Dressing his dandies in outfits that range from the incongruous to the ambitious, Chesnutt uses them in *The Marrow of Tradition* to examine not only the effect of the minstrel past on black representation and identity, but also the challenge New Negroes face in working through such stereotypes as part of their program of uplift. Given the dandy's location between black and white, upper class and lower class, masculine and feminine, it is not surprising that, in the end, Chesnutt ties issues of race and class to considerations of black masculinity. When Miller is asked by Josh Green to lead the Negro resistance, "every manly instinct urged him to go forward and take up the cause of these leaderless people, and, if need be, to defend their lives with his own—but to what end?"[181] At stake in the novel as a whole is the black man's ability to transcend debilitating stereotypes and forge new roles for himself. To do so would be to exercise one's masculinity, to do so insurgently would be to obey one's "manly instincts." Significantly, Chesnutt does not allow Miller to lead the rebellion. In holding him back, he leaves readers to decide whether accomplished blacks are more effective in their roles as model citizens and black-white facilitators, whether Miller's personal loss can or should be considered a payback for his cowardice. What is manly and who decides are not clear in *The Marrow of Tradition*.

Having worked through the crime of fashion, Chesnutt creates Miller in order to address questions of group leadership, inquiring "to what end?" do New Negro dandies style themselves? Is a black man's immaculateness only selfish? or potentially beneficial to others? Is it possible for New Negro dandies to combine these instincts? In addition, Chesnutt begs a question essential to dandyism itself: can the black dandy's performativity or queerness ever really be arrested? As the major tension at the end of the novel, and perhaps at the end of the century for the black community, the figurative potency of the new dandy figure—once African, then blackface, now newly Negro—remains dormant, uncertain.

Where Charles Chesnutt left off narrating black dandyism's challenge to African American self- and group fashioning, W. E. B. Du Bois begins with reverence for a man Du Bois eulogizes in 1933 as a "genial American gentleman and dean of literature in this land"—Charles Chesnutt.[182] Just as Chesnutt re-dressed the dandy figure he had inherited from Stowe and others, Du Bois similarly modernizes the figure for use in the Harlem Renaissance and beyond. As told in essays on masculinity and cultural nationalism that culminate in 1928 in the novel *Dark Princess*, Du Bois's New Negro story begins in a striking echo of Chesnutt's novel: the first page introduces the reader to a mulatto medical student fleeing a racist America for Europe, a man beginning a life as a cosmopolitan activist-dandy involved in a revolution of black people worldwide. Intensely focused on this figure's ability to be a different kind of man, as well as a different kind of leader, *Dark Princess* propels the black dandy figure back into Europe and Africa in order to continue redefining notions of race, class, gender, and sexuality. From these places, the black dandy takes on an additional task: figuring African identity in the diaspora, celebrating a potential reconnection of Africans and African Americans by means of and perhaps in fancy dress.

3

W. E. B. Du Bois's "Different" Diasporic Race Man

The Negro has always been interested rather in expression than action; interested in life itself than in its reconstruction or reformation. The Negro is, by natural disposition, neither an intellectual nor an idealist, like the Jew; nor a brooding introspective, like the East Indian; nor a pioneer and frontiersman, like the Anglo-Saxon. He is primarily an artist, loving life for its own sake. His *métier* is expression rather than action. He is, so to speak, the lady among the races.

ROBERT E. PARK, *Race and Culture*

Masculinity is not a given, but always a form of interrogation.

HOMI K. BHABHA, "Are You a Mouse or a Man?"

The Lady Among the Races?

Stopping at a cafe in Berlin, Matthew Towns sports a "cane and gloves" and "wears a new suit," smartly accessorized with a "dark crimson tie" that "burned with the red in his smooth brown face."[1] Confident in the knowledge that "he would be treated as he was dressed," he is "served, politely and without question."[2] A melancholic brooder, self-diagnosed as "a mass of quivering nerves and all too delicate sensibility," Matthew seemingly takes up vocations as he does moods—a former medical student, in the course of his career he becomes a radical, a Pullman porter, a convict, a politician, and a museum-going ditch digger.[3] In sensibility, Matthew strikes others as "curiously weak and sensitive in places where he should not have been"; he is "all sympathy, all yielding, all softness," prone to patronize art galleries when he should be at work.[4] Who is this

differently masculine, dandified man? He is the revolutionary hero of
W. E. B. Du Bois's "favorite" of his books, his own contribution to the
Harlem Renaissance, the novel *Dark Princess* (1928).[5]

Du Bois's dandy, who looks much like his author did in the early twentieth century, provokes as many questions as he was designed to answer.[6]
Created during a "time of [artistic] crisis," which, according to Arnold
Rampersad in *The Art and Imagination of W. E. B. Du Bois*, often necessi-
tated a turn to fiction for Du Bois, this Harlem Renaissance–era figure extraordinarily embodies long-standing Du Boisian preoccupations, not the
least of which was a concern with the interstitial relationship between
race, gender, nation, and art or, more specifically, black masculinity and
cultural nationalism.[7] In *Race Men* (1998), Hazel Carby cites this relationship as the true subtext of *The Souls of Black Folk* (1903), Du Bois's earlier
explication of his anxiety about the future of the race. Carby reads in that
book Du Bois's rhetorical "emasculation" of Booker T. Washington and his
metaphorical exclusion of women as potential race leaders as examples
of what can be called an anxious masculinism that *The Souls of Black Folk*
at once stages and perpetuates.[8] As he rhetorically eliminates "Booker T.
Washington and Others" from consideration as leaders, Du Bois establishes a legacy of leadership based on a decidedly masculinist potency of
intellect that, as Carby goes on to argue, is still present today. In a search
for black leadership that can explain "how it feels to be a problem" and
also find a way to "attain self-conscious manhood, to merge his double
self into a truer and better self"—to quote Du Bois's famous elaboration
of double-consciousness—Du Bois finds no one other than himself sufficiently representative, or racial and masculine, to do the job.[9]

Carby illustrates her point about the longevity of the masculinism of
The Souls of Black Folk with a startlingly apt portrait of Du Bois's disciple
Cornel West's embodiment of black intellectual style as an explicitly male
one. Her reading of Du Bois's sartorial dandyism as having a direct influence on that of West focuses on masculine style as a medium that determines the Du Bois genealogy of black intellectuals. Comparing iconic
photos of Du Bois and West wearing three-piece suits, Carby takes issue
with West's statement that "the Victorian three piece suit—with a clock
and chain worn in the vest—. . . dignified his [Du Bois's] sense of intellectual vocation, a sense of rendering service by means of a critical intelligence and moral action."[10] Carby claims that statements like this reflect

a larger feeling that the black male body, when finely clothed and well educated, comes "to secure these qualities [the critical intelligence and moral action] as irrevocably and conservatively masculine."[11] Therefore, the Race Man's uniform, as designed by Du Bois, is a well-fitting three-piece suit, symbolic of normative masculinity and authority itself. Carby warns that those who would require alterations to this costume should apply elsewhere, as those who do not fit this masculinist mold will be excluded from the intellectual family of black leadership.

Race Men focuses exclusively on *The Souls of Black Folk*, which is, as Carby argues, the text that most effectively "creat[ed] and imagin[ed] a black community in the early 20th-century," specifically "through a complex evocation of race, nation, and masculinity."[12] In an issue of *Public Culture* celebrating the one-hundred-year anniversary of the publication of *The Souls of Black Folk*, Henry Louis Gates Jr. echoes Carby, stating, "No other text, save possibly the King James Bible, has had such a fundamental impact on the shaping of the African American literary tradition."[13] Given the prominence of *The Souls of Black Folk* in African American literary and political culture, indeed, the culture of American modernism more broadly, it is, as Carby argues, a "necessary critical task" to examine the work's "highly gendered structures of intellectual and political thought and feeling," in order to assess the impact of its legacy.[14] The place of *The Souls of Black Folk* as a foundational text in the study of black culture and literature cannot be disputed; neither can Carby's reading of Du Bois's overall focus on exploring and establishing masculine power and privilege in the text. However, as Vilashini Coopan argues, also in *Public Culture*, Du Bois's long career presents one not with teleological thinking on gender, race, and nation, but with an "ongoing contention, collusion, and coexistence" of seemingly diverging ideas on these topics so central to his lifework. For Coopan, reading Du Bois's work is the "intellectual equivalent of living with double consciousness: sustaining two opposed allegiances, choosing neither, thinking through both."[15] In the spirit of Du Bois's own logic of working in and through contradiction and spurred on by the careful attention Carby pays to the central concern of the intersection of gender and race in *The Souls of Black Folk*, I turn to other parts of Du Bois's oeuvre from before and after that crucial text and to another version of the book's gender politics to argue for additional forms of "anxious masculinism" that might be present in Du Bois's work. In Du Bois's less well known writing and in the most literary chapter of *The Souls of Black Folk* ("Of the Coming of John") Du Bois conceived very differently of the black male body and the leadership style it would seem to delimit. Later, with Matthew Towns in *Dark Princess*—a kind of activist-dandy, whose nattily clad body signifies on rather than blindly accepts masculinist tropes, Du Bois most fully explores his long-standing wish for racial leadership by what he calls "men who were — different."[16]

The conception of Du Bois's "dandy" and the ideals for which he stands can be marked as early as Du Bois's senior year at Harvard College, in 1890. While at Harvard, Du Bois was in the midst of what Kim Townsend calls the making of "the masculine ideal of America," a time when Cambridge housed a group of men who were influential in the creation or questioning of "a patriotic American manhood" useful as "an opportunity and a responsibility to foster and spread what they thought of as civilized life."[17] Du Bois describes himself during this time as "in Harvard, but not of it."[18] He struggled with his professors, some of whom were Social Darwinists, to find an idea of manhood that would acknowledge the equality of Negroes and grant humanity to those previously worth just "three-fifths" of a man. As the idea of masculinity and manhood was being formed at the time, Du Bois used his ironic place at the center and on the periphery of this larger discussion (at the center in the way in which this discussion took place in order to exclude black men from the category of man and peripheral in that he was physically present but intellectually absent from the debate) to propose a sense of masculinity that could serve as a progressive ideal for his people and for all people.[19] Du Bois's program for fostering an inclusive Americanness debuted in his Harvard commencement speech in 1890. A critique entitled "Jefferson Davis as a Representative of Civilization," the speech sought to define a sense of American culture in which all races could participate. Of particular significance is Du Bois's conception of how this could materialize — in strikingly gendered and even oddly or "queerly" sexualized language, he proposes a marriage between an "imperious" Teutonic civilization, and a "submissive" Negro civilization as a way to achieve American democracy.[20]

In the "Jefferson Davis" speech, the oddness of Du Bois's democratic ideas begins with an attempt to turn a perennial contest between what he labels Teutonic "Strong Man" (exemplified by Davis) and Negro "Sub-

19. The young
W. E. B. Du Bois
in a plaid suit,
ca. 1890. Depart-
ment of Special
Collections
and University
Archives, W. E. B.
Du Bois Library,
University of
Massachusetts,
Amherst.

missive Man" into a cooperative relationship resulting in a viable and productive American culture. The Teutonic Strong Man brings to this relationship as his raw material stereotypically masculine traits: the mentality of a soldier and lover, a personality at once "fiery and impetuous," "cool and ambitious," brave and generous—traits which, in excess, have the potential to be a dangerous example of "individualism coupled with the rule of might."[21] Du Bois then offers to this figure the Negro as the "check and complement of the Teutonic Strong Man."[22] The Negro gift to civilization, then, is something opposite or at least complementary to the conventional masculinism of his Teutonic counterpart. While Du Bois explains that, "through the glamour of history, the rise of a nation has ever been typified by the Strong Man crushing out an effete civilization," he proposes that instead of destroying the "effete," as is his wont, the reformed Strong Man now has the opportunity to recognize the utility of the patience and forbearance brought by the Negro. "This Ethiopia of the out-stretched Arm, who has made her beauty, patience and grandeur, law," when combined with the Teutonic, constitutes a transformative imperative toward a decidedly less or "differently masculinist" world.[23] In Du Bois's speech, Strong marries Submissive, Might and Meek conjoin, white and black cooperate in a union in which it seems clear that the Negro is here the lady among the races.

Even within the address, Du Bois recognizes the strangeness of championing the Submissive Man; indeed, he adds, as a caveat to all who would question the salutary qualities of compliance, that the Negro personifies an idea of submission "*apart* from cowardice, laziness or stupidity, such as the world never saw before" (italics added).[24] This kind of vulnerability seems difficult to conceptualize, as it is a call for the "submission of the strength of the Strong to the advance of all," and a belief that "civilization cannot afford to lose the contribution of the very least of nations for its full development: that not only the assertion of the I, but also the submission to the Thou is the highest Individualism."[25] In this essay, the Negro Submissive Man is heroic by means of his acquiescence to the American project. Indeed, democracy itself is a product of the deference of both men to an idea larger than themselves and the interests or histories they might represent. Intriguing and enigmatic in Du Bois's formulation are the implications of the language that he uses to describe the ideal democratic state. In "Jefferson Davis," he assigns gender to and then sexualizes the work of racial cooperation through the rhetoric of marriage (the I and the Thou). In the speech, oddly or queerly enough, Teutonic and Submissive Men join in a civil union. This merging of men—one Strong and the other, still a man but more like a lady—enables a revision of the anxious masculinism in Du Bois's later writings. For Du Bois, taking the lady's part and taking it *as a man* becomes an important way for him to express patriarchal, but still intriguingly "differently masculine," political and cultural goals for America.[26]

In the "Jefferson Davis" essay, Du Bois imagines the nation as "a collaboration among men" or, more specifically, what Charles Nero identifies as "a patriarchal union of black and white men," in which "biracial, homosocial desire" can be expressed.[27] In the 1890s, as he is launching himself into the world from the Harvard platform, Du Bois is so idealistic about the potential for cooperation among black and white men that he manipulates his rhetoric into an unwittingly queer place to make this bond possible. A decade later, in *The Souls of Black Folk*, Du Bois finds himself less sanguine about the alliance but still desirous of the match. In a reading of the penultimate chapter of *The Souls of Black Folk*, the short story "Of the Coming of John," Nero sees the disappointed denouement of Du Bois's earlier hope, the lack of fruition of the "pregnant" partnership between Strong and Submissive or "the round and full development" of American democracy resulting from the union of black and white men.

"Of the Coming of John" details the prejudice faced by an ambitious, well-educated black man named John, who, after being put out of one too many segregated spaces in the North, returns home to Georgia, reluctantly resolved to a circumscribed world and a life of quiet toil for the work of uplift. He comes to grief when he confronts a white man from his hometown also named John, whose life Du Bois details as a double and contrast to that of black John: they both go North to attend college, attend the same opera in New York, return home at the same time. Black John kills his other while saving his sister from a rape attempt by white John; his "revenge" realized with white John's death, at the end of the story, black John himself awaits death (the arrival of a lynch mob is implied) while singing verses of Richard Wagner's *Lohengrin*, "The Song of the Bride." While Wagner or even *Lohengrin* might not be an odd choice for Du Bois, given his familiarity with and complicated veneration of German culture, his specific citation of "The Song of the Bride" (more familiar as "Here Comes the Bride") seemingly begs exploration.[28] Nero argues that in light of Du Bois's careful attention to black John's desire to have the opportunities and mobility of white John and perhaps his unexpressed desire for white John himself, one cannot help but conclude that black John is the bride here, "coming" to meet his partner in death. For Nero, the violent denouement of the potential of their relationship — together they might have rebuilt the southern town they call home, together they might have provided a model for racial cooperation that must be constitutive of true freedom in America — demonstrates Du Bois's understanding that his earlier plan for the union of black and white men would not be realized.

What seemed possible in 1890 is impossible in 1903; the Negro Submissive Man will not have a productive marriage with the Teutonic Strong Man. In "Of the Coming of John," black John is doubly queered by Du Bois, resulting in the death or attenuation of the Submissive Man's odd potential of years earlier. On the one hand, as Du Bois chronicles John's experience with discrimination, he demonstrates that a well-educated, well-traveled black man will be forever out of place, queer even if he is heterosexual.[29] This out of placeness results from continually dashed hopes of establishing at least homosocial bonds with white men in order to do the work of social justice. On the other hand, a well-educated, well-traveled black man whose desire for communion beyond the homosocial will also be read as queer in the more conventional, that is, sexual, sense.[30] While most critics attribute John's murderous impulse to a desire to save his sister, Nero reads it instead as a desire to shore up his manhood, after realizing this double queerness and violently acting out against it.[31] The Johns die in a moment of panic at the possibility of "gender inversion," because of the unrealized meeting of masculine and feminine, masculine and "differently masculine." They die because of the necessity and impossibility of black John taking the lady's part.[32]

Just as Du Bois was at the scene of the making of American manhood, he also appears to have been at the scene of the construction of contemporary notions of sexuality—these scenes obviously overlap and are mutually constitutive.[33] A man both of his time and often ahead of it, Du Bois entertained millennial theories of race, gender, and sexuality that were simultaneously conventional and progressive. While intervening in debates about Social Darwinist conceptions of racial hierarchies and arguing for more modern conceptions of race as historically and culturally contingent, Du Bois found himself also contending with new ideas about the social construction of gender and sexuality. Though "Jefferson Davis" and "Of the Coming of John" can be read as the proposal and subsequent "death of queer desire," that if successful would have ameliorated America's racial divisions, it is not at all the end of Du Bois's exploration of "differently masculine" leadership styles.[34] Despite or perhaps because of the way in which the figure deconstructs and reifies masculinity, Du Bois would never "entirely abandon this seemingly feminine man."[35] Striving for personal and cultural recognition, for status as a "co-worker in the kingdom of culture," the "feminine man" continues to probe his manhood in *Dark Princess*. In 1928, Du Bois brings the lady of the races back as the activist-dandy Matthew Towns. In *Dark Princess*, Du Bois's dandy finds himself at another productive but complicated intersection. In this text, the indigenous black dandy tradition, a negotiation of hypermasculine and effeminate black male stereotypes and self-fashioning, meets a more European dandy tradition, an exploration of the revolutionary potential of art and the aesthetic. The result is the production of an anxious masculinism readable both sartorially and rhetorically, an intriguing queerness of body and affect.

Dark Designs for Revolutionary Change

In *Dark Princess*, Du Bois transforms the "feminine man" into a dandy in an effort to exemplify a theory of art potentially productive of a cultural nationalism essential to the expression of democracy and freedom. In the novel, the sensitive and soft Matthew learns and promulgates an aesthetic theory expressed in two of Du Bois's most well-known essays, "The Negro in Literature and Art" (1913) and "The Criteria of Negro Art" (1926). In these essays and the later novel, optimism once again supersedes pessimism in terms of Du Bois's hope for radical cultural change. This optimism is embodied in Du Bois's dandy, an odd or queer Race Man with revolutionary ideas about race, gender, sex, and nation.

"The Negro in Literature and Art" announces a crisis for African American artists—economic hardship and racial prejudice have barred the production of Negro art, preventing Negroes from exemplifying their humanity. The essay surveys Negro literary achievement and finds that even though "in America the literary expression of Negroes has had a regular development," by 1913 the "great development" had yet to come. Declaring that artistic production is both the vehicle and index of racial progress, Du Bois argues for an explicit link between art, beauty, and political recognition and power. According to Du Bois, Negroes should make best use of the so-called negative racial qualities and insist on the positivity and necessity of those traits thought to be unique to Negroes: innate artistic ability, a "sensuous nature," "a slight compensation of a sense of beauty, particularly for sound and color"—a description that echoes the Submissive Man's contributions to American culture and also Du Bois's description of Matthew that opens this chapter.[36] The beautiful object(s), literature, and other pieces of art produced with this racial raw material would epitomize their creator and earn him or her and Negroes as a group recognition as artists and Americans. Such an accomplishment would signal the acquisition of a cultural and political environment for which Du Bois longs: the time when the "economic stress" and "racial persecution" of blacks will have been relieved, and the time when "leisure" and "poise" would be the privilege of all and not the luxury of the few.[37]

A little more than a decade later, Du Bois's "The Criteria of Negro Art" indicates that the predicament of the previous decade had become urgent. The urgency was not, however, due to a paucity of Negro artistic achievement, but to a perceived emptiness in the cultural authority given to the black artist, newly fashionable in elite artistic circles. With the Harlem or New Negro Renaissance in full swing around him, Du Bois realized that the "great development" of arts and letters he spoke of earlier was possibly nigh; he judged that it was up to him and other intellectuals to guide it to fruition. Du Bois challenges himself in the beginning of "The Criteria of Negro Art" to formulate an aesthetic theory that takes advantage of his earlier argument and combats the perceived mutual exclusivity of the realms of politics and culture. Hoping to articulate a way for a "group of radicals" to move beyond mere appreciation of art to a perception of its potential for embodying and wielding cultural and political power, he promotes art and beauty as constituent parts of the arsenal needed for the "pushing onward" or the continuation of the struggle for African American civil rights.[38] To this end, he brings art and politics together in the most memorable statement from the essays: "All Art is propaganda and ever must be, despite the wailing of the purists. I stand in utter shamelessness and say that whatever art I have for writing has been used always for propaganda for gaining the right of black folk to love and enjoy. I do not care a damn for any art that is not used for propaganda. But I do care when propaganda is confined to one side while the other is stripped and silent."[39] Du Bois objects here to offensive white-positive propaganda (with its implicit black negative) that denies "a similar right of propaganda to those who believe black blood human, lovable and inspired with new ideals for the world."[40] In 1926, Du Bois understands black art as propaganda insofar as it is produced in a highly contested political and social climate that works against its creation and originality. Hardly outside the purview of former slaves, not a distraction from political concerns, the aesthetic matters to black folk not as an escapist dream, but as a weapon.[41]

Indeed, Du Bois's statement, "But I do care when propaganda is confined to one side while the other is stripped and silent," provides a context for investigating the relationship between politics and art by intimating a connection between propaganda and a seemingly unimportant, sometimes aesthetic object—clothing. In his formulation, centuries of racist propaganda have naturalized black depravity, creating conditions in which African Americans have been naked or without propagandistic cover of their own. "The Negro in Literature and Art" and "The Criteria of Negro Art," in concert with *Dark Princess*, aim to remedy the situation by producing an example of theory and praxis—a promotion of the power of the aesthetic by a race man deeply implicated in the aesthetic—that combines art and politics on a narrative, metatextual level. In *Dark Princess*, Matthew Towns as a dandy embodies the Negro artist and symbolizes the power (and problematics) of recognizing art's potential in the fight for racial justice. With an activist-dandy as race man, Du Bois looks to revise nearly all the categories that describe modern identity: race, class, gender, sexuality, and nation.

In the novel, Matthew functions to elucidate a logic of dandyism that reveals Du Bois's thinking as revolutionary, but also historically contingent. In his hands, the figure of the black dandy is both retrospective and prescient, provincial and cosmopolitan, in short, oxymoronic. These qualities, as we'll see, seem absolutely essential to Du Bois's goal of opening up aesthetic experience broadly defined to African Americans and to defining these experiences as ways to imagine and experience life beyond the limitations of the color line. Within the text, these ambitions are linked precisely to one of the dandy's traditional concerns, the use of beauty as a primary mode of self-definition. In Du Bois's work, the dandy becomes a race man when he converts veneration for the beautiful thing to a philosophical realization of a universal right to access (and even luxuriate in) the beautiful as a category. An important political moment is inherent in this transformation: Du Bois is careful to champion the dandy as a new kind of race man only when he modifies an ideology of self-culture to promote art not for art's sake, but for the sake of all.

Du Bois's characterization of Matthew relies on the cut of his figure, his vulnerable masculinity, and the challenge it presents to his position and potential in society. Matthew's lifelong goal, at least at first, is to "compel recognition!," be noticed for the way in which his ensemble and differently masculinist character signal his difference from conventional ideas about black masculine political agency or the lack thereof.[42] Although Du Bois repeatedly remarks on Matthew's attractiveness, noting his "well-fitting uniform" when he is a Pullman porter and touting the beauty of the "tall and impressive" young man when dressed in a "gray suit [that] lay smooth above the muscles and long bones of his close-knit body," he dresses Matthew not only out of vanity, but mostly to imply the intricate relationship between clothing, gender, race, and class.[43] It is this complicated connection between seeming and being that the black dandy historically confronts, as necessary to the process of self-articulation.

Before his self-exile in Europe, Matthew appears in *Dark Princess* as a kind of unwitting spectacle, a man whose appearance and demeanor do nothing to ameliorate his treatment. When Matthew flees racist America "in a cold white fury," his presence aboard a transatlantic ship creates a crisis, rather than a compulsion, of recognition: "He glimpsed faces at times, intelligent, masterful. They had brains; if they knew him they would choose him as companion, friend; but they did not know him. They did not want to know him. They glanced at him momentarily and then looked away. They were afraid to be noticed noticing him."[44] Du Bois's depiction of the problematics of being looked at and being seen, here centered on the figure of a black man in a good suit, seems to complicate notions of dandyism that often rely on an extremity of self-culture and self-as-spectacle. On board the ship, reversing the transatlantic journey in which Africans lost, at least temporarily, their ability to self-fashion, Matthew had hoped also to reverse this process and be recognized as intelligent and masterful and not be merely seen as anomalous in this bourgeois scene. However, because of his race and social location, his dandyism is read not as evidence of his middle-class status and education, but perhaps as a pretension too odd to process.

Once in Europe, seated in the German cafe, Matthew appears to be a gentleman by virtue of style. Here, his ability to pay for his purchase matters more than his skin color; he understands this as readable from his clothing. Although he appears to be nothing other than a symbol of pretension to ease, or one who cultivates the self in a conscious critique of the vulgarity of others, he is still a figure enmeshed in a negotiation of

20. W. E. B. Du Bois in top hat, Paris Exposition, 1900. Department of Special Collections and University Archives, W. E. B. Du Bois Library, University of Massachusetts, Amherst.

racial, cultural, and class-based signifiers of identity. A dandy, but atypically so, Matthew achieves comfort in his costume, even though he relies on it as a kind of armor, an exterior manifestation of his hard-won self-regard. These foreign and domestic views of Matthew suggest that Du Bois uses him and his dandyism primarily as a way to discuss the styles of black masculinity extant and possible at home and abroad. At once invisible and hypervisible, a spectacle and socially and politically inconsequential, Matthew personifies the estrangement or the queerness of the "intelligent and masterful" black man in transatlantic modernism. He is out of place in America and in Europe, not able to actualize his desires or ambitions in either locale.

The emphasis on Matthew's exterior and the crisis of recognition it bespeaks is just the beginning of Du Bois's use of dandyism in *Dark Princess*. Matthew's treatment of Sara Andrews, his wife during the time he is a politician in Chicago, even further elucidates the complicated logic of dandyism and its relation to the race man's anxious masculinism at work in the text. With Sara, Du Bois begins an investigation and redefinition of the dandy's expected milieu, usually taken to be far removed from the political. Occurring in the vagaries of a narrative that is itself stylistically indulgent, this redefinition appears as an effort to define the work of an activist-dandy, the seemingly oxymoronic figure who would fulfill Du Bois's goal, stated in *Dark Princess* as "do[ing] something tangible, accompanied and illumined and made holy by the vision of eternal beauty."[45]

The realization of this "something tangible" in *Dark Princess* entails both transatlantic crossings and a passage from character to character. In Berlin, Matthew had joined the Council of the Darker People of the World, a group plotting a worldwide revolution of people of color, headed by the South Asian Indian Princess Kautilya (the Dark Princess of the title). Whereas in Du Bois's earlier work, social and political change would come to America through a marriage of Teutonic and Submissive, here revolution will happen as a result of cooperation among black or dark peoples. Previously a homosocial bond had been the key to realization of political goals. Here, it is a union between Matthew, a "differently masculine" man who exteriorizes his difference through his soft character and sharp dressing, and two masculine women — representing two widely divergent political possibilities — who potentially can enable black people freely "to love and enjoy." Although Matthew is involved in heterosexual relationships in Europe (one of which is interracial), he still plays the lady's part—the liaisons turn on "gender inversion" and are still queer. African America will arrive on the world stage after Du Bois's dandy takes action, "accompanied and illumined and made holy by the vision of eternal beauty," promoting an atypically masculine but still weirdly patriarchal mode of leadership.

Du Bois begins his exploration of the power of aesthetic beauty with a negative example. In Berlin, Matthew is deputized to investigate the readiness of African American participation in the revolution and subsequently returns to America; when the revolution stalls, he turns to machine politics in Illinois. As Matthew makes a difficult transition from exiled revolutionary to local and state politician, he meets Sara, his impeccably dressed, Pygmalion-esque future wife. Du Bois showers Sara with so much vivid, intricate description that one might wonder if he himself harbored fantasies of styling haute couture. A "thin, small, well-tailored" woman, Sara is frequently attired in the likes of a "black-crepe dress, with crisp white organdie collar and cuffs, chiffon hose" or "a new midnight-blue tailor-made frock with close-fitting felt hat to match, gay-cuffed black kid gloves, gun-metal stockings, and smart black patent leather pumps."[46] Throughout the novel, Du Bois's attention to outward appearances proves a kind of narrative of its own, as it continually indexes other twice-told tales concerning the tension between Negro interiority (or suspected lack thereof) and darker-hued exteriority, especially when fine in clothes or sensibility.

Clearly interested in the relationship between character and clothing, activism and *accoutrement*, Du Bois creates in Sara a female dandy in looks and attitude, one who sets the fashion with her personal and social grooming. So "capable and immaculate," her "exclusive receptions for the smarter set were the most notable in Colored Chicago."[47] Both the well meaning and the corrupt are attracted to her, as the disjunction between her objectionable actions and beautiful appearance allures and confuses. Sara's qualifications as a dandy extend beyond her attention to surfaces and her ability to disguise politics as a game in which she always gains the advantage. Indeed, her remarkable facility for dissemblance enables her to collect a husband as an object, albeit one with an unforeseen penchant for the beautiful all his own. Intrigued by Matthew because of his intelligence, his usefulness to the political machine, and his "very good" looks — although she says he requires "a good barber and a better tailor" — she trades on his admiration of her own intelligence, work ethic, and ability to "look . . . simple, clean, and capable."[48] Contracted by Sara in the spirit of what she describes to Matthew as "enlightened self-interest" rather than love, the marriage between them disappoints: "But behind Sara's calm, cold hardness, he [Matthew] found nothing to evoke. She did not repress passion — she had no passion to repress. She disliked being 'mauled' and disarranged, and she did not want any one to be 'mushy' about her. Her private life was entirely in public; her clothes, her limbs, her hair, her complexion, her well-appointed home, her handsome, well-tailored husband and his career; her reputation for wealth."[49] Sara is utterly disinterested in the comforts and complications of an interior, whether habitable or psychological. Surely a dandy insofar as her "private life was entirely in public," she nevertheless fails to fulfill the political program of making beauty "tangible" and relevant to the struggle. Sara has little interest in art and politics as anything other than self-propaganda. Sara-as-dandy is not a fictive personification of the kind of critical cultural program for which Du Bois calls in "The Criteria of Negro Art." But, before letting go of Sara, Du Bois explains the nature and importance of her failure to be the Submissive Man's complement.

Du Bois calls attention to the provenance of his dandy as he chronicles her inability to be exemplary. Confident and self-reliant, Sara is a self-made woman who rises from a childhood in poverty to eventual success as a stenographer earning a "fabulous" salary. Her move "Up from Anonymity," coupled with her choice not to pass (though she could have done so easily), finds her very near another Du Boisian ideal, the "Talented Tenth." "Leaders of thought and missionaries of culture among their people," the Tenth are charged with being "a saving remnant [that] continually strives and persists, continually aspires, continually shows itself in thrift and ability and character," as examples and servants to the larger black mass.[50] Essentially a member of the growing but small black middle class, Sara is a great disappointment to Du Bois because she is part of the Tenth who fail to make a transition from self to service. In that she "craved wealth and position . . . got pleasure in having people look with envious eyes upon what she had and did," and that she was "always unconsciously showing off, and her nerves quivered if what she did was not noticed," Du Bois indicates that Sara is one who puts more stock in envy than admiration.[51] She fails to meet the standards of the Tenth because she desires a kind of recognition that disallows any potential for exemplarity. Although she takes pleasure in regarding herself as object rather than subject, Du Bois does not. Du Bois opposes her to Matthew in terms of sensibility—this opposition, as it turns out, can be seen in their differing conceptions of beauty and the beautiful. Unwilling to turn her attention from beauty as thing (self as object, actual objects and surfaces) to beauty as philosophy or the aesthetic (which Matthew eventually advocates), Sara is unable to abstract dandyism to its potential political ends. An inability to do so makes beauty unavailable for use in a larger African American struggle for social, political, and cultural equality. Sara is unwilling to submit to a higher, more beautiful purpose than the fulfillment of her own selfish desires; Du Bois charges her husband, more at ease with his vulnerability and more focused on what the work of beauty can do, with that task.

As Du Bois makes clear in his essays, attention to beauty and art as well as artistic production can and should be part of Negro emancipatory efforts. Sara's engagement with politics and art, action and beauty, produces little that can aid Matthew in the production of propagandistic cover. Matthew's European experience has given him what America denies Sara: access to the aesthetic that bears a direct relation to politics and even revolutionary change. In fact, in Europe, he follows his creator's footsteps, finding there the potential "of looking at the world as a man and not simply from a narrow racial and provincial outlook."[52] This new perspective allows Matthew the psychological space he needs to be inspired politically by aesthetic experiences, to focus his energy on fighting for the right of black (and darker) people to "love and enjoy," as Du Bois puts it in "The Criteria of Negro Art." In the following conversation in a cafe Princess Kautilya explains the origin of her interest in Matthew as a representative of African America and the African diaspora:

> "We represent—indeed I may say frankly, we are—a part of a great committee of the darker peoples; of those who suffer under the arrogance and tyranny of the white world."
>
> Matthew leaned forward with an eager thrill. "And you have plans? Some vast emancipation of the world?"
>
> She did not answer directly, but continued: "We have among us spokesmen of nearly all these groups— of them or for them—except American Negroes. Some of us think these former slaves unready for coöperation,

but I just returned from Moscow last week. At our last dinner I was telling of a report I read there from America that astounded me and gave
me great pleasure—for I almost insisted that your group was worthy of
coöperation. In Russia, I heard something, and it happened so curiously
that—that I should meet you today.

I had gone up to the Palace to see the exhibition of new paintings—you
have not seen it? You must. All the time I was thinking absently of Black
America, and one picture there intensified and stirred my thoughts—a
weird massing of black shepherds and a star. I dropped into the Vik-
toria, almost unconsciously, because the tea there is good and the muf-
fins quite unequaled. I know that I should not go there unaccompanied,
even in the day; white women may, but brown women seem strangely
attractive to white men, especially Americans; and this is the open season for them.

Twice before I have had to put Americans in their place. I went quite
unconsciously and noted nothing in particular until that impossible
young man sat down at my table. I did not know he had followed me
out. Then you knocked him into the gutter quite beautifully. It had never
happened before that a stranger of my own color should offer me protection in Europe. I had a curious sense of some great inner meaning to
your act—some world movement. It seemed almost that the powers of
Heaven had bent to give me the knowledge which I was groping for; and
so I invited you [to have tea] so that I might hear and know more."

She rose, insisted on paying the bill herself.[53]

Matthew's presence in Berlin seems providential to Kautilya not only because she had recently been debating American Negro readiness for the
revolution, but also because of the epiphanic moment in the Palace of
Art, followed by Matthew's beautiful, gallant act. Gazing at the "weird
massing of black shepherds and a star" produces in the princess not only
an affective response to the art, but also an intellectual and tangible one.
She is overwhelmed by thoughts that seem to confirm and inspire her
revolutionary project and her search for another dark messiah charged
with stewardship of Africa and the diaspora. Her explanation in this scene
reveals that she not only desires diversity within the movement, black or
African participation, but that she will also value what Matthew would
bring to that movement—as a messiah here, surely he comes bearing
a gift. Du Bois's inclusion of art in this discussion seems, at first, to be

unnecessary—the chance meeting between Matthew and Kautilya is all that is required by the plot. However seemingly extraneous, the scene establishes a phenomenon on which the aesthetic philosophy of the text turns: engagement with actual pieces of art, coupled with a sense of the potential liberating and focusing force of affect inspired by the aesthetic, serves rather than hinders the revolutionary cause. For Kautilya and the Council of the Darker Peoples of the World, only those of a refined nature who appreciate the interrelation between the aesthetic and the political can partake of their revolutionary work.

Later, at a council dinner designed to introduce and integrate Matthew into the group, Kautilya and the other council members attempt to teach Matthew the mechanism of this relationship between art and political action. However, they fail to anticipate the historical and cultural circumstances that might trouble his execution of it. At the dinner, Matthew reveals his difficulty with the philosophy and triumphantly refashions it, molding the council's theory and praxis into a more inclusive place. At the table, Matthew is impressive in a "dinner jacket of the year before last"; though "not new . . . it fitted his form perfectly, and his was a form worth fitting."[54] Amazed at the culture and refinement around him and entirely captivated by Kautilya, Matthew listens intently as Kautilya explains his presence:

> "Our point is that Pan-Africa belongs logically with Pan-Asia; and for that reason Mr. Towns is welcomed tonight by you, I am sure and by me especially. He did me a service as I was returning from the New Palace."
>
> They all looked interested, but the Egyptian broke out:
>
> "Ah, Your Highness the New Palace, and what is the fad today? What has followed expressionism, cubism, futurism, vorticism? I confess myself at sea. [Pablo] Picasso alarms me. [Henri] Matisse sets me aflame. But I do not understand them. I prefer the classics."
>
> "The Congo," said the Princess, "is flooding the Acropolis. There is a beautiful Kandinsky on exhibition and some lovely and startling things by some newcomers."
>
> . . .
>
> Here again, Matthew was puzzled. These persons eagerly penetrated worlds where he was a stranger. Frankly, but for the context he would not have known whether Picasso was a man, a city, or a vegetable. He

had never heard of Matisse. Lightly, almost carelessly, his companions leapt to unknown subjects. Yet they knew. They knew art, books, and literature, politics of all nations and not newspaper politics merely, but inner currents and whisperings, unpublished facts.[55]

Interaction with this group seems in some way contingent on an ability to speak a cosmopolitan language of art, politics, and other "fads," be they of governance or fashion. Given their mission, the cartel ironically cultivates a familiarity with avant-garde Western art, represented by modernists like Picasso and Matisse, and they also remain keenly aware of the non-Western inspiration (some might say origin) behind the current trends. Clever and urbane, some on the council deem cultural production and cultural literacy proof of the attainment of what might be called a level of civilization recognizable to Western or Western-educated eyes. They are worried about the fitness of their new African-diaspora delegate, who, as we have seen, at first has a few reservations about his competency. Not a sophisticate in their way, Matthew nevertheless desperately wants "just to do his part, any part!" despite feeling "his lack of culture audible."[56]

Long-standing cultural achievement gains respect in this group; the council members have come to believe that millenniums of history have produced a "natural aristocracy" of darker people who carry their nobility in their blood.[57] With the princess as ally, Matthew spends the dinner party trying to battle this debilitating new "color line within the color line" that would exclude Africans and African Americans from this group. Finally insulted one too many times, Matthew silences the table by singing a Negro spiritual, "Go Down Moses," in defense of African American civilization, thereby literally by giving voice to his culture. Initially dumbfounding the audience, the song becomes convincing only as it receives an exegesis: concluding his performance, Matthew adds, "America is teaching the world one thing and only one thing of real value, and that is, that ability and capacity for culture is not the hereditary monopoly of the few, but the widespread possibility for the majority of mankind if they only have a decent chance in life."[58] The subsequent enthusiastic approval of this slave song, forged out of African and American experiences—Matthew's "racial gift"—gains him access into "the kingdom of culture" as defined by these potentates of taste. The acceptance of his talent elevates Matthew's heretofore provincial people to the world's stage. He and the diaspora triumph not in a flashy display of polyglot proficiency, but in the exhibition of homegrown beauty and a reminder of its polyvalent historical and ideological force.

Matthew's experiences with the council signal not only his engagement and revision of an aesthetic ennui associated with a European dandy tradition and modernist aesthetics more specifically, but also a potential revision of the most popular form of dandyism in America, the blackface minstrel tradition. The late nineteenth century had seen the European dandy figure mutate from, as Sima Godfrey puts it, a "mindless model of vanity to the model of the repressed dreamer and intellectual rebel," as a result of asking questions concerning the relationship between the aesthetic and intellectual and existential freedom.[59] Such an emendation emphasized philosophical principles and convictions around the liberatory force of beauty in an increasingly mechanistic, bourgeois society; the veneration of beauty was thus changed from an activity of leisure into a defiance, in the hands of the likes of Oscar Wilde, Charles Baudelaire, and, later, Albert Camus. All of these dandy models expressed new ideas about self and society in terms of play with gender roles and the rules of sexuality.[60] The council has absorbed some of this teaching, and it attempts to incorporate Matthew and the African diaspora into its purview. But, it is this relationship between the political potential of the abstraction of beauty and the real need for black civil rights, including an ability to self-represent in the face of racist stereotype, that fuels, in part, Du Bois's progressive conception of the nature of art as embodied in his dandy as race man. Taught to be a dandy in the council's way, to find in art a beauty that liberates the soul from bourgeois life, Matthew also finds himself implicated in, referencing, and revising another dandy tradition to which he is unwittingly linked—blackface minstrelsy. To be a race man of the diaspora, to exemplify Du Bois's interest in reforming gender roles and his advocacy of the aesthetic as political practice, Matthew will have to reconcile his dual provenance as a black dandy.

As the moment when dandy-as-rebel meets and revises dandy-as-caricature, the wonder of Matthew's Sorrow Song performance is not to be understated. Odd, like the interjection of the prophetic painting in the earlier episode, the intrusion of this artifact into a board meeting resolves some issues for Matthew's adversaries while provoking others for the reader. Even Matthew himself wonders, "How had he come to express the astonishing philosophy which had leapt unpremeditated from his lips?"[61]

A look at Du Bois's best-known treatment of the Sorrow Songs, his chapter in *The Souls of Black Folk*, in concert with the council's art lesson, reveals the strategy behind the presence of the song and its emanation from Matthew's mouth. "The most beautiful expression of human experience born this side of the seas," the Sorrow Songs are for Du Bois "weird old songs" that spoke the souls of black folk, former slaves, to men.[62] Many scholars advocate the absolute centrality of Du Bois's disquisition on the Sorrow Songs in *The Souls of Black Folk* to the author's goal of expressing black humanity through black cultural achievement. In addition, Du Bois had planned for the songs to be an aid in strengthening links between the heterogeneous black community, as he imagined the songs as a wholly sincere connection to the best artistic effort of the folk, a rallying point of sorts.[63] In "The Sorrow Songs" Du Bois not only celebrates the remarkable African American triumph over adversity that the songs record but frequently refers to challenges the songs themselves faced in the American cultural marketplace. He singles out especially blackface minstrelsy's burnt-cork imitation of black life. Indeed, in "Du Bois and the Minstrels," Scott Herring reads "The Sorrow Songs" as "Du Bois's project of retaking Black American music" from "minstrelsy's variegated appropriation and distortion of black culture."[64]

Du Bois's fashioning of Matthew's performance at the council dinner, then, might be seen as a similar reclamation, a response to corrupting effects of blackface minstrelsy on music and man. At the dinner, representing the interests of the African diaspora in an international revolution, asserting cultural longevity and confidence with a song, Du Bois's dandy is doubly updated. As he separates and recovers the spiritual from its more familiar blackface form, the "coon song," Du Bois also recovers the black dandy as striving Negro from its blackface critique in the character Zip Coon. As we saw in chapter 2, the minstrel show's blackface dandy was used to riff on northern blacks who were thought to be overstepping the bounds of their newly won or imminent freedom.[65] Onstage originally as the suave, urbane, sexually cunning comic figure playing opposite his plantation parody cousin, the dandy in the guise of Long-Tail Blue quickly degenerated into the grotesque, lascivious Zip Coon, a figure illustrative of all that white men feared about actual or potential black freedom and mobility. Often onstage delivering mock speeches about "ebucation," dressed ostentatiously in plaid tuxedos, accessorized with top hats, gloves, and canes, effeminate in both senses of the word (hypersexual and womanly, illustrated by their attention to appearance), these dandies were designed to ridicule the small but seemingly dangerous black middle class, a group that often combined respectable looks with political activism for abolition and, later, the maintenance of civil rights. In modifying this provincial figure with a cosmopolitan imperative to make black culture audible, the dandy in *Dark Princess* forces the reader to see the black performative body differently.

Aware of, but not limited by blackface stereotype, this black dandy fully participates in a modernist moment in which the performance removes the blackface taint from the art and the ridicule from the upwardly mobile, politically astute person. Matthew's defiant performance not only enables the artistic efforts of the plantation to join those in the Palace of Art, but also emphasizes the importance and necessity of self-fashioning and self-re/presentation in the African diaspora's response to slavery and oppression. It is this meeting between the European dandy and the black dandy that Du Bois wants to use as part of a truth-telling propagandistic politics. Here, the feminine man asserts himself, his culture, his cause, but without "imperiousness"; he dignifies his sense of self and purpose with a simple song.

Du Bois's conception of the dandy uses and specifically reforms arguments about art for art's sake by emphasizing the relationship between art and the establishment and legitimacy of black cultural nationalism, while at the same time insisting on the humanity of black folks rather than on their blackness, as in "The Criteria for Negro Art." He understands that black dandyism as embodied by Matthew must claim a dual heritage in order to modify the limitations of its American manifestation with a liberatory difference. To do so means affirming the place of beauty and the beautiful in the service of black equality, while at the same time redefining and broadening traditional notions of the beautiful and art beyond the bounds of race. Therefore, instead of simply removing the burnt cork from the dandy figure associated with minstrelsy or inserting Matthew and African America into a European aesthetic philosophy with no real provisions for race, Du Bois creates a dandy who, in this moment, racializes his aesthetics with significance for the uses of art on both sides of the Atlantic.

Always didactic, Du Bois must put Matthew through other trials in order to illustrate how his dandyism might work as a critique. Despite his triumph in the board meeting, on his return from Europe, this revised dandy has a difficult time transforming banter about modern art into concern about the aesthetic and politics. While in Europe and immediately afterward, the princess and her fellows represent to Matthew a sexy combination of refinement and revolution, inspiring him to declare that "his sudden love for a woman [Kautilya] far above his station was more than romance—it was a longing for action, breadth, helpfulness, great constructive deeds."[66] Unfortunately, this frisson of aesthetics and politics does not last.

Jailed and exiled from the group as a result of a botched political action, Matthew deserts international revolution, "[gave] up all thought of a career, of leadership, of greatly or essentially changing this world," in favor of organizing votes for the Chicago political machine.[67] One might expect this change would also be the end of the dandy who had hoped to find a place for beauty in the "pushing onward." In fact, art still has a place in Matthew's life, but one that has little political thrust. Though he has been introduced to the connection between artifacts and revolutionary action in Europe, Matthew's sense of the function of art and beauty appears not to have progressed beyond that of escape from struggle rather than engagement with it. In Chicago, he is inspired only to beautify his "bare, cold, and dirty rooms" by placing a rug that "burned him with its brilliance" over a newly built parquet floor.[68] Though the rug reminds him of one he saw in Berlin, he quickly "shook the memory away with a toss of his head."[69] Over the course of months, Matthew's materialism increases at the same pace as his political game playing. Later, in a fit of frustration, "half-consciously trying to counteract the ugliness of the congressional campaign" in which he is a candidate, Matthew runs downtown to buy another rug and a copy of a Picasso, a "wild, unintelligible, intriguing thing of grey and yellow and black," which he adds to "the flame of a genuine Matisse" already hanging in the bachelor pad he still maintains.[70] The activist may be gone, but the dandy seems to live on.

However, a closer look at Matthew's work as a politician does reveal his concern with aesthetics and the appreciation of beauty as a philosophy rather than as a mode of personal style. Throughout the second half of *Dark Princess*, Du Bois redeems his dandy by having him establish a relationship between political progress, freedom of the soul, and the value of contemplating the beautiful. This is accomplished by the visitation of a curious dis-ease, an "esthetic disquiet" upon Matthew. Although he takes up politics in the knowledge that it is corrupt, he nevertheless feels a discomfort with his political work:

> It was no moral revolt. It was esthetic disquiet. No, the revolt slowly gathering in Matthew's soul against the political game was not moral: it was not that he discerned anything practical for him in uplift or reform, or felt any new revulsion against political methods in themselves as long as power was power, and facts, facts. His revolt was against things unsuitable, ill adjusted, and in bad taste; the illogical lack of fundamental harmony; the unnecessary dirt and waste—the ugliness of it all—that revolted him.
>
> He saw no adequate end or aim. Money had been his object, but money as security for quiet, for protection from hurt and insult, for opening the gates of Beauty. Now money that did none of these was dear, absurdly dear, overpriced.[71]

Du Bois insists on a distinction between the moral and esthetic here; it appears as if the problem is the process, rather than the goal—Beauty. Although probably an eccentric remnant of his rather Victorian education, Du Bois's capitalization of "Beauty" might indicate consideration of it not merely as the pleasing, but, as Matthew defines it, as the broadly comforting, "security for quiet," "protection from hurt and insult." Matthew's conception of the beautiful is not just that which enriches him personally or adds to his knowledge of art history, but is instead something that would, perhaps, if able to free him from "hurt and insult," transcend the bounds of race. This place would contrast greatly with the world Matthew knows, as it would not be "unsuitable, ill adjusted, and in bad taste," full of an "illogical lack of fundamental harmony." In this scenario, Beauty looks like a privileged place to which Matthew thought he could buy access; what he does not yet understand is that if he seeks it another way, outside of the politics and money of the machine, he can claim it as a right and not a privilege.

As a Chicago politician, Matthew tries not to be sold while he himself is "buying and selling" influence; nevertheless, he determines that "he was paying a price for power and money. . . . He had sold his soul to the Devil. . . . He had sold it for beauty; for ideal beauty, fitness and curve and line."[72] This relationship between beauty and the marketplace reveals that the "esthetic disquiet" cannot be solved materially, with objects connotative of actual wealth. Submission of the soul does not bring "ideal beauty, fitness and curve and line"; rather, it brings what Matthew himself anticipated, a kind of slavery he describes as the sale of "bodies, souls, and thoughts for luxury and beauty and the joy of life."[73] Selling one's humanity as well as that of others precludes the attainment of the "joy of life" for all. Disquiet turns to bliss only with the replacement of one kind of political work with another—the abandonment of the political machine for a return to the revolution of Darker People. The difference between the aesthetic logic of the machine and that of the council is made clear on Kautilya's eleventh-hour arrival in Chicago, just as Matthew is about to compromise himself irrevocably in order to gain the statehouse. Bursting into a campaign party, Kautilya reunites with Matthew, the revolution is reinspired, and Sara and her influence are thrown over:

> And he cried, "Kautilya, darling!"
> And she said, "Matthew, my Man!"
> "Your body is Beauty, and Beauty your Soul, and Soul and Body spell Freedom to my tortured groping life! . . ."
> "The cause that was dead is alive again; the love that I lost is found!"

As he walks out the door, abandoning his life as a politician and husband, Matthew as dandy is all principle, his soon-to-be former wife all clothes:

> He [Sammy, a member of the Chicago political scene] found her [Sara] standing stark alone, a pitiful tragic figure amid the empty glitter of her triumph, with her flesh-colored chiffon and her jewels, her smooth stocking and silver slippers. She had stripped the beads from her throat, and they were dripping through her clenched fingers. She had half torn the lace from her breast, and she stood there flushed, trembling, furious with anger. . . .
> And suddenly Sara crumpled to the floor, crushing and tearing her silks and scattering her jewels.[74]

Matthew's reunion with Kautilya signals the hoped-for beginning of a new world order, the revolutionary possibility of change inspired by the interracial, multicultural, gender-inverted meeting of a headstrong, powerful, politically radical princess and a gallant, beautiful, artistically subversive, "differently masculine" man: a different relationship for different times.

After the reunion, art and aesthetic experience reenter the life of Du Bois's dandy as part of a program to restore lost souls. This program includes and insists upon some time-honored dandy activities: Matthew and Kautilya indulge themselves in sensual lovemaking and leisurely activities of the cultured life such as visits to museums and art galleries, dining on fine wines and food, listening to classical music. Kautilya explains that "gentle culture and the beauty and courtesies of life — they are the real end of all living."[75] The hyperbolic language used to animate the relationship between Matthew and Kautilya (seen in the reunion, "Soul and Body spell Freedom," etc.) may obscure the fact that the text's depiction of the good life means much more than a potential fictional exposé of Du Bois's alleged sybaritic inclinations.[76] Instead, what is being depicted is not merely the praxis of an aesthetic theory in which access to the pleasures of leisure signals freedom to those denied it, but the fictional attainment of the state Du Bois hoped for in "The Negro in Literature and Art" — a way of life without the color line.[77]

"Messenger and Messiah to all the Darker Worlds!"

In his discussion of the centrality of the aesthetic in Du Bois's early political thought, Ross Posnock identifies a strain of Du Bois's politics as emanating from a belief in "the aesthetic as the condition of human freedom."[78] Focusing on Du Bois's elitism, or "distinction," Posnock similarly finds that the aesthetic in Du Bois's writing functions critically in a number of ways: aesthetic production invites its creators into the "kingdom of culture" (as we have seen already in "The Negro in Literature and Art" and "The Criteria of Negro Art"), and aesthetic contemplation reveals previously repressed souls to themselves. Indeed, while working as a manual laborer, Matthew wakes one day feeling drawn toward a museum rather than toward his job: "There was a new exhibit of borrowed paintings from all ends of the world. After mud and filth and grayness, my soul was starving for color and curve and form. [As a result of seeing the exhibit] I . . . bathed myself in a new world of beauty . . . I was a more complete man — a unit of real democracy."[79] Du Bois's assertion here is that aesthetic experience, to quote Matthew, "adds width to [one's] world."[80] This opening up of the quotidian or parochial enables democratic thought that stands on a foundation of respect for the humanity of all. As the path to a higher collectivity, aesthetic experience redeems the "human condition under capitalism," and "renews democratic possibility," as it is the path to a higher, anticapitalist individualism.[81] Hence, Du Bois's creation and promotion of what Posnock identifies as "the political aesthete," a figure that uses beauty to liberate and empower efforts for justice. In the spirit of a semantics that adds rather than obscures meaning, I propose "dandy" over "political aesthete" as a designation for this figure; it recognizes Du Bois's long-term wrangling with the ever-entwined issues of race and gender as well as the negotiation of high and low art required by the figure. Du Bois's dandy—embodying and troping on the effeminate man, descendent of Long-Tail Blue, Zip Coon, and continental aesthetic philosophy—engenders a concern with aesthetics, politics, and masculinity.

Posnock's attention to the centrality of Europe—its aesthetic philosophers and a tradition in which experiences of beauty reaffirm humanity—in the formation Du Bois's "political aesthete" or dandy is essential to understanding why insistence on the aesthetic matters to those whose bodies and even imaginations have been unduly surveilled. However, as we have seen, Du Bois's reference to the aesthetic explicitly emphasizes the provinciality of American race relations as its nemesis. Throughout his writings on beauty, as in "The Criteria of Negro Art," Du Bois rarely finds it in America or in American things apart from the Sorrow Songs.[82] To be sure, Posnock identifies the racial color line as Du Bois's target, but he fails to mention another uniquely American tradition that played a leading role in defining that line: blackface minstrelsy. American traditions figure in Posnock's work mostly in the form of Du Bois's use of William James's pragmatic philosophy to energize the aesthetic, thereby turning art into that which produces "a productive skepticism toward the fixity of essence and identity."[83] In Posnock's work, pragmatic political thinking in the realm of the aesthetic leads more often to the transcendence of the color line than to confrontation with it. However, American popular philosophy, especially the discourse of race, gender, and sexuality embodied in the tradition of blackface minstrelsy, matters at least as much to Posnock's "political aesthete." For this reason, he is better called a dandy, which realizes the fullness of Du Bois's act of troping on the figure. Free of the color line, the aesthete turns the appreciation of the artifacts of a European high art or avant-garde tradition into a political act that references, but does not confront, popular culture representations of that same aesthete as dandy in America. The aesthete as a type for those racially or culturally Negro in America may be new, but the black dandy has a long history by the time Du Bois idealizes him in *Dark Princess*. Favoring dandy over aesthete also renews attention to Du Bois's hope, as expressed in *Dark Princess*, for what the dandy himself calls "men who were — different."[84]

That it is the dandy rather than the aesthete who is the object of Du Bois's revision becomes clear when one sorts out the extremely curious ending of the dandy's book, *Dark Princess*. The "esthetic disquiet" calmed, a dizzying array of other issues rise to the surface, issues that confuse the level of irony at which the figure and its author should be taken. A "high ideal of manhood" and an incarnation of the world's potential — according to Kautilya, Matthew "signif[ies] and typif[ies] . . . this world, and all the burning worlds beyond, the souls of all the living and the dead and them that are to be" — Matthew suffers the fate of many a man before his time: he is woefully misunderstood.[85] Though finally realizing the necessary place of the aesthetic in his reformist efforts, he gains few followers as he loses his job for taking a week off to visit the museums and even temporarily loses Kautilya, who feels that the couple's use of the beautiful too nearly approximates the decadent. Writing to his lover after she leaves, Matthew outlines a program of work ("hilariously" for six hours a day) and play (warm baths, clean sheets, Tschaikowsky [sic], films, plays, novels) designed to redress his own mistakes as well as the lack of beauty in the lives of ordinary folk.[86] Knowing that such a plan "would call for a kind of man different from [spendthrift profiteers or loafing workers]," with "a different set of values," "a new dream of living," "men who were — different," he tries nevertheless to effect the plan in a seemingly intractable world.[87] Exemplification of this idea of the new man had clearly been the task of Du Bois's dandy; his difference challenges not only a humanity-sapping economic system, but also, implicitly, an idea of manhood exclusive of vulnerability, seen here as a kind of feminine sensibility. In so doing, this new man, this black dandy — by taking his place in a project that in humanizing blackness creates a situation in which black people and their culture are "lovable and inspired with new ideals for the world" — fulfills the objectives of "The Criteria of Negro Art."[88] Poised to offer an alternative to a perhaps hopelessly compromised system of black (male) representation, the heroic feminine man in *Dark Princess* ultimately does falter—and tellingly. His failure exposes the complex workings of the signifying systems in which he is imbricated.

Despite the programmatic effort to stave off the reality of negative ideals of blackness and masculinity, Du Bois's dandy and the Council of Darker People never manage to bring off their revolution, at least within the bounds of the text. What Du Bois does accomplish is a confusing commentary on the progressive potential of reconfigured notions of blackness, masculinity, and cosmopolitanism. The final scene, in which Matthew is reunited with Kautilya and presented with his newborn son Mahdu, does justice to the novel's subtitle, *A Romance*. The couple is married in the presence of an international contingent and, as a family, inaugurated into a new world by a lavish pageant:

> Then the ancient woman [Matthew's mother, a former slave] stiffened, closed her eyes and chanted to her God:
>
> "Jesus, take dis child [Mahdu]. Make him a man! Make him a man, Lord Jesus—a leader of his people and a lover of his God!" . . .
>
> . . . A score of men clothed in white with shining swords walked slowly forward a space, and from their midst came three old men: one black, shaven and magnificent in raiment; one yellow and turbaned, with a white beard that swept his burning flesh; and the last naked save for a scarf about his loins. They carried dishes of rice and sweetmeats, and they chanted as they came.
>
> . . .
>
> They gave rice to Matthew and Kautilya, and sweetmeats and blessed them as they knelt. . . . Then the Brahmin took the baby from his grandmother. . . . Swaying the babe up and down, east and west, he placed it gently upon Kautilya's outstretched arms. . . . She raised her son towards heaven. . . .
>
> Then from the forest, with faint and silver applause of trumpets:
>
> "King of the Snows of Gaurisankar!"
>
> "Protector of Ganga the Holy!"
>
> "Incarnate Son of the Buddha!"
>
> "Grand Mughal of Utter India!"
>
> "Messenger and Messiah to all the Darker Worlds!"[89]

As the novel flips from idealist exercise to a kind of allegory, chaos of meaning is produced in the effort. The marriage and its heir are, if nothing else, queer. A male child, Little Madhu inherits Kautilya's kingdoms, which had been in protectorate. Kautilya explains to Matthew, "For had it been a girl child, I must have left both babe and you. Bwodpur needs not a princess, but a king."[90] As a biracial, bicultural hereditary king, an African American leader in the prophetic tradition *and* Buddha "incarnate," Madhu at once affirms and destabilizes notions of racial and gender essentialism. African American and South Asian Indian, Madhu defies racial categories—he embodies a deconstruction of racial barriers as well as solidarity among darker races. Participant and benefactor in perhaps the oldest system of male privilege, royalty, father and son inherit the mantle of masculinity as Madhu is crowned king. Certainly, Madhu's sex, not gender, enables his ascendancy, but his maleness gives him access to patriarchal power, which, as a system, empowers a range of masculine gender identities. Thus, the dandy's son both affirms and corrects his father's effeminacy. The "new man," in all his vulnerability, is a patriarch, but only because in his relationship with Kautilya, Matthew takes the lady's part. Because her son Madhu is a boy, Kautilya chooses to marry his father, exercising a privilege normally reserved for men. Matthew's only power here comes through assent, to not assert the I but submit to the Thou.

The figure of the black dandy, his vulnerability as the feminine man, his advocacy of the place of beauty in black cultural and political life, his plea for revisions of provincial notions of blackness and masculinity emerge as commentary not only on the way in which categories of race and gender attempt to fix essence and control access, but also as evidence of the extreme difficulty of effecting revolution when working within a dialectical regime. Even though the figure's dandyism, in Du Bois's hands, leads to a realm beyond race, it also always references its own origins in a field in which representation—blackness, whiteness, masculinity, femininity, queerness, normativity—is always actively being defined. As both critic and product of a system which seeks to limit identity, the black dandy both creates and embodies the kind of vagueness and difficulty left at the end of even a fictional struggle, like that in *Dark Princess*. With reference to *The Souls of Black Folk* and other works, Posnock identifies the ambivalence at the end of these texts written by black intellectuals as instantiating a "new authenticity" of vulnerability that can be read as a "political strategy of denaturalization in a society where racist stereotypes reigned serenely as nature."[91] Certainly this "illegibility" can be read as "potent possibility in Jim Crow's identitarian regime"; this is especially so if, as I argue, one looks to Jim Crow's show, blackface minstrelsy, as partial source of that empowering instability.[92] Attendance at that performance, and its constant replay in a world in which identity is both constructed and political, mightily tempers the joy one brings to a notion of Du Bois and others as "prophets of post-ethnicity," as they are called by Posnock.[93]

In his book *Color and Culture: Black Writers and the Making of the Modern Intellectual*, Posnock refines his notion of the "political aesthete" and "prophet of post-ethnicity" by inventing a more capacious and deliberately oxymoronic figure to describe blacks' intellectual response to racism and the burdens of representation—the "anti-race race man." The mission of this figure is described as follows: "To escape the pressure to conform to the familiar and recognizable, to stereotypes, is to be free to delete the first word or to accent the second in the phrase black intellectual or to vary one's inflections at will or as circumstance dictates. To impart something of this liability and this ambition is to interrogate the very category of race."[94]

The designation of "anti-race race man" contains in its inherent contrariness a gesture toward emancipating race men from the burden of working within restrictive dialectics, especially those of race. *Color and Culture* targets the "ideology of authenticity" that haunts black intellectuals, who are frequently perceived as being detached from the black community (the site of racial authenticity) and therefore insufficiently responsible to the race. Black intellectuals like Du Bois exemplify for Posnock a long-standing tradition of race men whose work against racial essentialism not only deconstructs stereotypes designed to validate negative or false images of black people, but also takes that work to the next level. Outside of the binary of positive versus negative images, these race men inveigh against race as a category of inquiry altogether; instead they call for a world of "cosmopolitan universalism" (a code word for the substitution of "culture" for "race") to replace the world of the color line. For example, Posnock cites strains of Du Bois's work, such as moments of freedom "above the Veil" in *The Souls of Black Folk*, as those in which Du Bois is himself theorizing as a "prophet of post-ethnicity." Additionally, he identifies *Dark Princess* and Matthew as examples of Du Bois's willingness to go beyond "the props of essentialism."[95] However, as I have demonstrated with *Dark Princess*, Du Bois does not do so without seriously *engaging* a variety of so-called props, working in and through a history of strictures of race or stereotypes in the hopes of truly disarming them. The vehemence of the liberatory force of phrases used to describe such intellectuals and their milieu—"anti-race race men" and "prophets of post-ethnicity" who espouse a "cosmopolitan universalism"—ultimately prohibits a sustained engagement with the complexity of the burdens faced by the philosophy and lived experiences of Du Bois and others. Witness Du Bois's admittedly tumultuous, but long and dedicated service to the NAACP, in which a wish for black souls to be "above the Veil" never superseded an understanding of their existence within and behind it.[96] In Posnock's argument, the practice of "cosmopolitan universalism" accesses a philosophy of culture that supersedes race, therefore ushering African American culture and its race leaders away from prejudices demanded by the particular and toward a communitarian universal. Given the denigrating rhetoric surrounding race, of course Du Bois and others worked against biological determination of group affiliation and toward a group consciousness based on common social and political experiences, or culture. However, Du Bois did so while holding an idea of culture that continually strives toward the goal of attaining cultural equality, or status as part of a universal, in tension with the particular historical circumstances that add their own demands to what constitutes that universal. He is an *antiracist* (vs. anti-race) Race Man.

Postlude to the Future
Race / Men in the Twenty-First Century

In his groundbreaking study of the crosscurrents of the black diaspora, *The Black Atlantic*, Paul Gilroy reads the "extravagance" of the conclusion of *Dark Princess* as "a beginning rather than an ending" of considerations of black Atlantic politics and cultural theory.[97] Though fictionalized in 1928, Du Bois's pan-Africanism and concern with the black diaspora dates to much earlier than the publication of *Dark Princess*. Du Bois's time as a student in Europe, the origin of his dandyism and accompanying aesthetic philosophy, also enabled him to discern the transnational nature of the color line and its role in European imperialism. In fact, Brent Hayes Edwards begins his exploration of black transnational culture *The Practice of Diaspora* with the observation that Du Bois's most famous phrase, "The problem of the twentieth century is the problem of the color line," predates its publication in *The Souls of Black Folk* and was actually uttered not in reference to African America, but in an international context, in a speech at a Pan-African Conference in London in 1900.[98] In the sentence before this most prescient statement, Du Bois describes this meeting in terms very familiar to readers of *Dark Princess* when he says, "In the metropolis of the world, in this closing year of the nineteenth century there has been assembled a congress of men and women of African blood, to deliberate solemnly upon the present situation and outlook of the darker races of mankind."[99] Placed in its original context, Du Bois's signature phrase, one sees, was not only not about America solely, but it was not even first uttered in America. For Du Bois, Europe and the pan-African plans made and realized there were part of millennial planning—new ideas for a new century.

In his biography of Du Bois, David Levering Lewis records Du Bois's recollections of his time in Europe, recorded in his notebooks and his *Autobiography*, in order to describe the "epiphany of liberation" Du Bois felt away from American soil.[100] The joy was palpable even in anticipation, as can be seen in the gleeful, celebratory purchase of a delectable (Du Bois's word), extremely expensive shirt in a New York shop immediately after being awarded a fellowship to study in Europe.[101] This change of clothes presaged an adjustment in character as well. The way in which he describes his European experiences implicitly contains a comparison to much less refined, vulgar conditions in America. Du Bois explains:

> Europe modified profoundly my outlook on life and my thought and feeling toward it . . . something of the possible beauty and elegance of life permeated my soul; I gained respect for manners. I had been before, above all, in a hurry. I wanted a world, hard, smooth and swift, and had no time for rounded corners and ornament, for unhurried thought and slow contemplation. Now at times I sat still. I came to know Beethoven's symphony and Wagner's *Ring*. I looked long at the colors of Rembrandt and Titian. I saw in arch and stone and steeple the history and striving of men and also their taste and expression. Form, color and words took new combinations and meaning. . . .

. . . I felt myself standing, not against the world, but simply against American narrowness and color prejudice, with the greater, finer world at my back.[102]

In his *Autobiography* and in *Dusk of Dawn*, Du Bois credits the Europe of the 1890s with teaching him not only to open his soul to elegance and his mind to the realization of the interconnected nature of international economic and cultural politics: "In this social setting, I began to see the race problem in America, the problem of peoples of Africa and Asia and the political development of Europe as one."[103] Thus Europe functions once again as a stop on a triangulated route between Africa and the Americas. This time, however, the journey produces a sense of unification that challenges American and European racism, rather than a feeling of irrevocable separation between Africa and America.

The contemporaneous origin of Du Bois's dandyism and his antiimperialist, diasporic thinking figure prominently as an inspiration for *The Black Atlantic* as a whole. At the outset, Gilroy declares that an "outernational, transcultural reconceptualisation" of black Atlantic culture must include assessments of the transatlantic movement, past and present, of black people and their cultures. Du Bois and his traveling are singled out specifically as essential to charting the cross-national and intercultural influences, personal and cultural hybridity, such travel records and produces. This "outernational, transcultural reconceptualisation" of black culture or modernity itself "will require comprehension of such difficult and complex questions as W. E. B. Du Bois's childhood interest in Bismarck, his investment in modeling his dress and moustache on that of Kaiser Wilhelm II, his likely thoughts while sitting in Heinrich von Treitschke's seminars, and the use his tragic heroes make of European culture."[104] A confusion of heroic, masculinity, nation building, and selfpresentation—in the single figure of Du Bois—greets those desirous of taking the black Atlantic seriously. Though he does not call Matthew Towns a dandy, Gilroy nevertheless claims that Du Bois's dandyism figures prominently in the conundrum that the black Atlantic presents to conceptions of modernity and the place of black people within it. As Du Bois's own dandyism demands attention, the fictional, revolutionary rendering of it in a text like *Dark Princess* similarly begs consideration. The black dandy—as race man—confronts modernity's challenge to acknowledge the multiplicity of forces that construct a personal, cultural, and national identity, in this case blackness, masculinity, and Americanness or nationality.

Gilroy takes very seriously Du Bois's larger gestures toward a fictional realization of interethnic and transnational alliance among "darker people" in his dandy novel, despite his gentle mockery of the smaller manifestations of cross-cultural sympathy contained therein.[105] For Gilroy, the importance of the final moments of *Dark Princess* rests not only on its production of a remarkable moment of "hybridity and inter-mixture" in the wedding pageant, but particularly in the production of another kind—the birth of a multiracial, multicultural, pan-African, and pan-Asian leader of the Darker People's revolution. Indeed, the ending of *Dark Princess* brings its dandy to a reckoning point by, contrary to dandy tradition, producing an heir. For Gilroy, Little Mahdu is a "startling portrait of procreation—cultural formation and transformation" that does not offer a "cultural fusion" plagued by "betrayal, loss, corruption or dilution."[106] An elegant declaration of *Dark Princess*'s denial of the one-drop rule and its consequences, Gilroy's praise of the novel's vision implies that Du Bois has successfully and subtly negotiated modernity's contradictions. Himself an aberration of prevailing American racial codes, the dandy's son does not signal "a fusion of two purified essences but [is] rather a meeting of two heterogeneous multiplicities that in yielding themselves up to each other create something durable and entirely appropriate to troubled anti-colonial times."[107] Though Du Bois's text presents a dandy whose legacy enables leadership out of racial binaries and nationalist exceptionalisms—traits exemplary of a diasporic race man in the Gilroy vein—it does not forgo compromise in all arenas. The dandy heir seemingly loosens many of the restrictions placed on men who work in the service of the race. Nevertheless, as a race man and potentate, Matthew and Mahdu reserve certain masculine privileges for himself.

Gilroy's celebratory analysis of *Dark Princess* allows for a consideration of dandy and son as figures exemplary of new formulations of race, nation, and the expressions of masculinity. Yet, Du Bois's fictional realization of the potential fruits of modernism dissolves some boundaries while preserving others. What seems to inhibit even one of the most radically deconstructive texts of the Harlem Renaissance—one that realizes even the great opportunity of including concerns about the diaspora—is, once again, the troubled relationship between race, masculinity, sexuality, and nationalism. African America's union with India masculinizes the feminine man as he takes on hereditary aristocratic status; however, as it is an alliance between a "feminized race" and an "oriental" one in the early twentieth century, one might find the resulting hybrid culture still challenged in so-called potency despite its vehement antiessentialism.[108] Depending on point of view, this amalgamated culture either revises the gender rhetoric of nationalist projects, or—because it is perceived as (doubly) weak and impotent—perpetuates the crisis. Indeed, as a product of two races, both of which might be considered effete, a hybrid like Mahdu bears the hopes as well as the burdens of his genealogy.

To be fair, *Dark Princess* ends precisely at the moment in which its feminine protagonist, the model for a new kind of man, produces an heir whose relationship to gender and nationalism remains uncertain and ambivalent. Like his father, the son as future race man exemplifies that doubleness can enable the liberation of signifying on race and masculinity as well as occasionally contradict the fulfillment of double aims. This might seem too fine a lens through which to regard the ending of Du Bois's novel; however, such scrutiny seems absolutely necessary if *Dark Princess* is to occupy the place of importance in the black diaspora that *The Souls of Black Folk* occupies for African America. Ironically, examination of the gender / nationalism nexus, as exemplified in Du Bois's work, is called for in Gilroy's text, even if he himself does not specifically attend to it. He writes presciently of Du Bois's formations of African American culture in the feminine, noting that "the ambiguities that spring up around his presentation of racial culture, kinship, nationality, and community in gendered form are a big problem lying dormant in the critical writing about his work."[109]

The search for and fashioning of these differently masculine Du Bois heir(s) and the inheritance such figures offer the world preoccupy Gilroy's analysis of *Dark Princess*, Carby's investigation of race men through the gender politics of *The Souls of Black Folk*, and Posnock's attempted reevaluation of Du Bois as an "anti-race race man." Despite other shortcomings, Posnock does not altogether miss the dandy's power. As a result he praises the resulting Du Boisian formulation of the dandy as employing "multiple strategies of denaturalization."[110] He names these strategies and their ultimate effect for Du Bois and his fictional hero:

The "Talented Tenth," the cult of distinction, aesthetic education, the flaunting of mulatto status, the ritual of choice to dramatize race as chosen rather than a biological given, and the construction of representation as troping rather than transparency—all work to turn race leadership from the eliciting of conformity and loyalty to the provocation to think and debate. And to experience the beauty in everyday life. The capacity for aesthetic experience insinuates new possibilities beyond the utilitarian routine of enforced labor and habit and the debasement of the rule of thinking by stereotype.[111]

Posnock rightly describes Du Bois's dandyism as a combination of personal cultivation, service to the race, and philosophical intervention concerning African Americans and aesthetics. Yet, despite his recognition of this, he fails to take full advantage of his deft analysis by literally footnoting and not taking seriously Du Bois's equal and forced investment in the complex history of the black dandy and the black modern. Of course, the history of black modernity tells a story of stereotype and self-representation of individuals and groups, "the construction of representation as troping rather than transparency," well before the time of James and other philosophers who, according to Posnock, are the predecessors to Du Bois's thought. When investigated from the perspective of black modernity, the black intellectual or race man as black dandy becomes a point of inquiry—past, present, and future—for addressing the representational structures, received and self-defined, that constitute blackness: the tension between race, gender, sexuality, and nationalism; the perceived split between aesthetics and politics; and the place of high and low art in the formation of cultural nationalism and a strategic sense of community in diaspora.

One learns from Du Bois's imbrication in the long history of dandyism and black modernity the limitations of analyzing a culture in diaspora from too narrow a critical geography. Both *Color and Culture* and *Race Men* look back only to early twentieth-century intellectuals and race men in order to trace a line of descent to the contemporary, a time in which the variegated black community has often been perceived to be in crisis at home and abroad, a time in which this crisis appears as a lack of black masculine integrity and black leadership savvy. Whereas Carby would reject black dandyism as a version or symptom of black masculinism, Posnock locates within the dandy's modern milieu a set of phenomena useful in totally liberating him from the race man's burdens. Each critic would like to use black dandyism and Du Bois's performance of it to put issues of black masculinity, racial responsibility, the status of Negro art, the place of black bodies, and the nature of the ambitions of the African diaspora to rest. However, Du Bois's uneven but optimistic exploration of such issues remains, as Gilroy argues, a challenge to all interested in reconceptualizing modernity and the place of blackness and maleness within it. As constituted in the black Atlantic, black modernity and perhaps modernity in general cannot be better investigated than by probing the figure of the black dandy—especially as one must consider the black cultural nation in an increasingly cosmopolitan context in which race and the history of its use and abuse matter. In utilizing a dandy figure, Du Bois looks back or looks black to the earliest moments of anxiety about black presence and mobility in global economic and political networks. While he may have been unaware of the full spectrum of that of which he reminds readers, he nevertheless hands down a set of parameters, terms, and categories through which to imagine and greet present-day representations of race "men who are—different." Figuring out how and why these men matter as heirs to Du Bois's dandy, at once the world's potential, a "perfect unit of democracy," and queer, will go a long way toward staving off the perennial crisis of black masculine leadership without restoring manhood to its uninterrogated rights.

4

"Passing Fancies"

DANDYISM, HARLEM MODERNISM, AND
THE POLITICS OF VISUALITY

As she lighted the fire under the coffee-pot, she looked at him
hard. Why don't you write about us? she demanded.

Us?

Yes, Negroes.

Why, we're not very different from any one else except in
colour. I don't see any difference.

I suppose we aren't, Mary spoke thoughtfully. And yet figures
stand out.

Figures?

Conversation between Mary and Byron,
CARL VAN VECHTEN'S *Nigger Heaven* (1926)

Modern Articulations

In his first disquisition on African American modernism, *Modernism
and the Harlem Renaissance* (1987), Houston Baker sets out to save black
America's first modernist movement, the Harlem Renaissance, from
consideration as a failure. He identifies Afro-American modernism as
a movement separate from modernism, a stance he later revises. For
Baker, in 1989, modernism is associated with the following successful
"objects or processes": the "collaged allusiveness of T. S. Eliot's *The Waste*

Land and [James] Joyce's *Ulysses*, the cubist reveries of Picasso, the imagism of [Ezra] Pound, the subversive politics of the surrealists."[1] Because modernism is so much the product of a "bourgeois, characteristically twentieth-century, white Western mentality," it is a record of the breakdown of the cultural confidence in "an assumed supremacy of boorishly racist, indisputably sexist, and unbelievably wealthy Anglo-Saxon males," rather than a "threat" to "the towers of civilization."[2] Modernism is not only elitist and inviolable but, as such, irrelevant to the cultural condition of those like African Americans for whom there is not the luxury or "need to pose, in ironical Auden-esque ways, questions such as 'Are we happy? Are we content? Are we free?'"[3] In *Modernism and the Harlem Renaissance*, Baker insists that in order to recognize the way in which the artists and intellectuals of the Harlem Renaissance may have succeeded in "defining themselves in 'modern' terms," one must "listen" for the modern in the Harlem Renaissance, the emergence and critical use of "*modern Afro-American sound*, as a function of a *specifically* Afro-American discursive practice" (the former his italics, the latter added).[4] For Baker, the sound of Afro-American modernism emerges as black artists learn the "mastery of form" and "the deformation of mastery," the former beginning with black-authored confrontations with the representational strategies of blackface minstrelsy, the latter with a turn to indigenous art forms, particularly the blues, as a basis for an authentic black modern identity.

In a more recent discourse on modernism, *Turning South Again: Re-Thinking Modernism / Re-Reading Booker T.* (2001), Baker changes his mind about that which would be the "marker" of black modernism and, as a result, the very definition of modernism itself. He will no longer listen for a separate black modernism or that which sounds or seems authentically or "*specifically*" black, but will look for modernism in examples of "the achievement of a life-enhancing and empowering public sphere mobility and economic mobility of the black majority."[5] This change in his definition of modernism, from the sociocultural to the more political, and the change in his methodology in seeking it, from listening to looking, bring him, surprisingly, to the figure of the black dandy. In particular, he illustrates the failure of his previous conception of black modernism in the dandyism and performativity of Booker T. Washington. Baker reads Washington's dandyism—his performativity and ambivalence—as dangerous and even treacherous to a black modern project.[6] For him, dandyism can be this and nothing else because Washington "performs" in his white father's "weeds," "the black dandy (kid-gloved ghost of the 'educated black man' in the white imaginary) . . . all dressed up without any fully modern, urban place to go."[7] Baker calls this Washington's "mulatto modernism," "a bourgeois, middle-class individualism, vestimentary and hygienic impeccability, oratorical and double-conscious race pride and protonationalism."[8] According to Baker, such dandyism obviates modernist possibilities for the black majority as well as any productive connection between modernism in black and white.

Though Baker would dismiss the black dandy and his mulatto nature as an example of the failure of African America to reach the modern, I will argue that looking to other manifestations of black dandies and dandyism, especially as they espouse a "cosmopolite self-concept" (a term associated with James Weldon Johnson, the historian of Harlem), discloses a certain black modern identity and potential for mobility while grappling with an "acknowledgement of radical uncertainty" in a newly established urban locale—Harlem, the "Negro capital of the world."[9] A few years after Washington's death, Harlemites began practicing a different, more subversive dandyism that helps one revise the perception of both black or mulatto modernism and modernism generally as exclusive phenomena. A concentration on the dandy's cosmopolitanism establishes the black dandy as a figure with both European and African and American origins, a figure who expresses with his performative body and dress the fact that modern identity, in both black and white, is necessarily syncretic, or mulatto, but in a liberating rather than constraining way. The way in which Baker and I read that dandy and his mulatto nature in the early twentieth century matters much to our respective analyses of his effectiveness as a modernist sign. For Baker, dandyism is betrayal and mulatto modernism is insufficient in the sense that it has no group objective. For me, the dandyism that erupted in early twentieth-century Harlem is not a group performance of whiteness or a staging for the benefit of the individual only, but a visible sign of the modern black imaginary, a kind of "freedom dream."[10] This other dandy's syncretic nature enables the figure to display a knowingness about representation; this knowingness makes the look of black modernism much more complicated than an explanation of white imitation suggests.

In fact, one can look to the modernist dandy's intersection with gender to uncover something about modernism's and the dandy's intersection with race. In *Gender on the Divide: The Dandy in Modernist Literature*, Jessica Feldman does delimit, for a moment, the dandy's multiplicity as she elaborates on the figure as a sign for modernism, particularly in relation to performances of gender.[11] Feldman's insights on the dandy as a figure that reveals the cultural transition that modernism embodies adds an important footnote to Andreas Huyssen's famous observation that modernism has woman or the feminized as its "Other."[12] The dandy is, for Feldman, primarily a figure that could embody the displacement of binaries that this otherness implies: "He is the figure who practices, and even impersonates, the fascinating acts of self-creation and presentation. He is the figure of paradox created by many societies in order to express whatever it is that the culture feels it must, but cannot, synthesize. This dandy is neither spirit nor flesh, nature nor artifice, ethical nor aesthetic, active nor passive, male nor female. He is the figure who casts into doubt, even while he underscores, the very binary oppositions by which his culture lives."[13] If the dandy's attention to style and cultivation of artificiality of the self is traditionally labeled a feminine trait in a patriarchal world, then the figure's status as an analogue to women and the feminine rather than an opposite, breaks down the gender divide, presenting a liberating challenge to patriarchy for women and men. Dandy style in the modernist period highlights the presence of a cultural condition in which the binaries that unnecessarily limit identity can be and are being challenged. Modernism is a state in which "a true change of style implies the ability of [the dandy's] genius to see, and by seeing to create, however dimly and intuitively, at the farthest reaches of culture, and, blindly one startling step beyond."[14] Beyond male and female, beyond black and white, beyond success or failure?

If woman is modernism's other, and the dandy modernism's subversive sign of a mediation between identity's potential binaries, then can one not see blackness and the black dandy as modernism's other "Other"? If the "radical uncertainty" of the times is now associated with "the fear of the masses . . . always also a fear of woman, a fear of nature out of control, a fear of the unconscious, of sexuality, of the loss of identity and stable ego boundaries in the mass,"[15] then can one not look to the black dandy figure to simultaneously mitigate and exaggerate this fear through an absolutely dogged sense of self-invention? As a creature of the streets, the paradigmatic actual and philosophical flaneur, the dandy in black and white can help one look at the mass, the crowd, not as a space of fear, but as a revelation, an experimental space, a place to challenge conventions of identity—can help one to look, as Feldman suggests, "one startling step beyond." Therefore, dandyism matters not just to those keeping up with haute couture; instead, fastidiousness or ostentation in dress, arch social and personal style, biting wit and gesture describe radical changes in social life, new expressions of class, gender, sexual, and racial identities, for black and white, especially in the period called modernist. It is this style of critique, the astute cultural observation that it requires, in addition to its textual or literary quality, that defines the dandy's fitness as a discursive sign for black and white modernisms and as an articulation of the relationship between these modernisms. This is especially so if one remembers that, according to Baudelaire, the dandy "cherche ce quelque chose qu'ons nous permettra d'appeler la modernité" [seeks that indefinable something we may be allowed to call modernity].[16]

Because the provenance and escapades of black dandies in early twentieth-century histories and fiction about Harlem both permit and disturb the fit between European and African American modernism, the black dandies I find there will allow me to argue for a certain presence of a black modern consciousness. The suitability and dissonance of the black dandy figure as a modernist or black modernist marker—ironically through his antiessentialist, often queer, or "quare," character—produces a productive struggle between the movements rather than a separation between them or the denial of the very existence of Harlem's modernist moment. Such a tension identifies black modernism, with the black dandy as its sign, as that which challenges the conventional wisdom about modernism's success and the subsequent failure of the Harlem Renaissance, just as it enables their mutual redefinition. The mixed origins of the movement and its dandy inextricably connect African American modernism and modernism. By concentrating on the dandy figure as appropriated and articulated by African Americans who sought to define their own modernity, I aim to demonstrate the importance of the black dandy's failure to embody authenticity of race and culture (and the relationship of race and culture to conceptions of gender and sexuality) and thus create fixity of these ideas. Although deeply regrettable and troublesome to the architects of the Harlem Renaissance as well as to more contemporary critics, this failure to espouse or promulgate a blackness that could be packaged as "the" or "a" New Negro aesthetic is precisely that which identifies the movement as a success.[17]

The Black Dandy as New Negro

Though not at all new to Americans as a figure of racial, cultural, and social conflict and negotiation, the black dandy—a widely resonant symbol of the history of the black community's negotiation of aesthetics and politics—was nevertheless taken on and embodied by Harlemites eager to exhibit a new self- and cultural regard in the early twentieth century. As Henry Louis Gates Jr. has aptly demonstrated, Negroes are called or call themselves new at what might be considered moments of crisis or times of strange, interesting, and often arresting opportunity. Used to describe an African recently arrived in eighteenth-century England, a newly emancipated slave in the 1870s, or, variably, a political radical or poet in the Harlem of the 1920s, the term "New Negro" carries with it an "eighteenth-century vision of utopia with a nineteenth-century idea of progress to form a black end-of-the-century dream of an unbroken, unhabituated, neological self."[18] As an appellation originating in a "will to power," the phrase "New Negro" "dare[s]to recreate a race by renaming it," invests rhetoric with the hope of reality.[19] With former plantation denizens and social conservatives filling out the ranks of the supposedly deferent old Negroes at the beginning of the twentieth century, the latest new Negroes were their seeming opposites: confident, optimistic, newly sophisticated, demanding equal rights, and determined to remake themselves and their images. A critical mass of these "neological people" being resident in an urban area for the first time, African Americans seized the potential to refashion themselves as a group. Newly visible to the world and to each other, African Americans discovered their own class, ethnic, and gender diversity, began both to show off themselves and to convert their visibility into social and cultural regard.

A mecca for early twentieth-century blacks, Harlem was a place that Johnson described in his history of Harlem, *Black Manhattan* (1930), as the locus of a new style of blackness, a place capable of "strik[ing] the uninformed observer as a phenomenon, a miracle straight out of the skies."[20] In *Black Manhattan*, Johnson insists on communicating and assessing the impact of this "miracle" and its relation to a modern identity for blacks, when, for example, he opens his discourse on Harlem culture as follows:

> If you ride northward the length of Manhattan Island, going through Central Park and coming out on Seventh Avenue or Lenox Avenue at One Hundred and Tenth Street, you cannot escape being struck by the sudden change in the character of the people you see. In the middle and lower parts of the city you have, perhaps, noted Negro faces here and there; but when you emerge from the Park, you see them everywhere, and as you go up either of these two great arteries leading out from the city to the north, you see more and more Negroes, walking in the streets, looking from the windows, trading in the shops, eating in the restaurants, going in and coming out of the theatres, until, nearing One Hundred and Thirty-Fifth Street, ninety percent of the people you see, including the traffic officers, are Negroes. And it is not until you cross the Harlem River that the population whitens again, which it does as suddenly as it began to darken at One Hundred and Tenth Street. You have been having an outside glimpse of Harlem, the Negro metropolis.[21]

This remarkable portrait of African Americans and other members of the black diaspora "everywhere" in Harlem streets, shops, and restaurants emerged primarily as a result of the Great Migration and an advantageous real estate market in Harlem that opened up modern apartments to blacks for the first time.[22] However, the phenomenon that began in the procurement of better places to live was not limited for long to the practicalities of shelter. As soon as groups of blacks moved into the neighborhood, churches, fraternal organizations, social welfare associations, and political organizations followed, as did the institutions for which Harlem became most famous (or infamous)—speakeasies, nightclubs, and theaters. Although most blacks in New York lived above 110th Street, their cultural influence spread all over the city, beckoning whites uptown to experience the origin of the musicals and Negro-themed comedies and dramas also playing in midtown and venues in Greenwich Village. The large Negro presence in New York (in terms of numbers) coupled with the increased prominence of black culture made Harlem and the African Americans there emblems and purveyors of a particularly American urban identity.

21. *Armistice Day*, Lenox Avenue and West 134th Street, Harlem, 1919. Photographs and Prints Division, Schomburg Center for Research in Black Culture, The New York Public Library, Astor, Lenox and Tilden Foundations.

It was not just sheer numbers of people and finely constructed apartments situated on grand avenues that brought the Harlem Renaissance and its dandies into being; it was the diversity of the people there and their collective outlook that was the crucial factor—regardless of whether they came from Alabama, Georgia, Florida, the Village, 52nd and 8th, the West Indies, or even Africa, what this group had in common was attitude. For all, no matter what geographic or ethnic background, class or educational level, sexual preference or proclivity, Harlem was a new opportunity. While certainly not all Harlemites lived in fancy brownstones (and the brownstones that were once fancy did not always stay that way), nevertheless, the people understood that they had a chance to revise their self-image and their image in other people's eyes, in both small and significant ways. A people subjected regularly to horrific racial violence, whose civil rights had been questioned and denied for most of their history in America, whose culture and character had been ridiculed and demeaned in blackface in print and on stage, African Americans had, until the migration, toiled for rights and against stereotypes for years, but not in the numbers or the diversity of strategies Harlem made available.

Indeed, display and demonstration of the new Negro attitude, made possible by the people and potential that Harlemites saw around them, are characteristic not only of the Harlem Renaissance, but also of the place of dandies and dandyism, or group and self-fashioning, within it. Three public exhibitions or parades of black cultural self-assurance offer evidence of the power and variety of visual display in the era — the Silent Protest Parade of 1917, the march celebrating the return of the heroic 369th Infantry Regiment from France at the end of the First World War in 1919, and the Hamilton Lodge drag ball, one of Harlem's most famous and well-attended annual events in the 1920s and 1930s. These three mass events — signatures of an emerging Harlem style — demonstrated to Harlem, New York, and the world that this new Negro metropolis was indeed a particular and peculiar place to seek modern blackness. Harlem was a place, according to Johnson, that was "more than a community; it is a large scale laboratory experiment in the race problem," in which the outcome of the experiment could not be or would not be controlled easily.[23]

Organized by Johnson with the help of his colleague W. E. B. Du Bois, the Silent Protest Parade, designed to be a show of black resilience and integrity after a series of race riots, took place in July 1917. Given that Johnson was field-secretary for the NAACP and responsible for information gathering and marketing of the organization, presumably he wanted the parade to make a strong political or antiracist statement. That Johnson would stage "the first massive Negro protest in American history" with what would be an era-defining style might seem incidental, but is, rather, a result of his understanding of the necessity of style as a bid for power for African Americans.[24] Featuring thousands of African Americans marching down Fifth Avenue, the parade proceeded in absolute silence, the protestors holding placards and flyers decrying the brutality and complacency they would normally have vociferously denounced. The men were dressed somberly in black, women and children in white, providing a

22. Silent protest parade on Fifth Avenue, New York City, July 28, 1917. Photographs and Prints Division, Schomburg Center for Research in Black Culture, The New York Public Library, Astor, Lenox and Tilden Foundations.

visual complement to the black and white text of the placards in their hands, two of which asked, "Mother, Do Lynchers Go To Heaven?" and "Mr. President, Why Not Make *America* Safe for Democracy?"[25] "Something like organized and conspicuous theater" and "an advertise[ment of] their precarious psychological location between justified rage and creative restraint," the silent spectacle was invigorated by the pointed visual synergy of people and text.[26] A visual precursor to Claude McKay's combination of rage and restraint in his militant sonnet "If We Must Die" (1919), the Silent Protest Parade highlighted the visual presence and defiant attitude of deliberately clad black bodies. If "in the dawning age of the mass media and an all-out consumer society, culture was itself a palpably important form of politics," then Harlem's newly visible black population, "barred from the most meaningful direct political activity," created and occupied their own stage by infusing it with looks not easily forgotten.[27]

23. Lieut. "Jimmy" Europe and His Famous Band (369th Regiment). General
Research and Reference Division, Schomburg Center for Research in Black Culture,
The New York Public Library, Astor, Lenox and Tilden Foundations.

A little less than two years later, in February of 1919, another parade of
stylish African Americans traversed Manhattan, once again joining culture and politics in an exuberant theatrical display. Though it too could be
interpreted as a balance of "rage and creative restraint," this parade mo-
bilized the tension between those impulses into a new expression of African American consciousness that the earlier Silent Protest Parade had so
quietly and forcefully predicted. This demonstration could not have been
more different from the earlier one—this time the mood was serious
but festive, the marchers dignified but not unduly solemn. Proceeding
up Fifth Avenue toward Harlem, the victorious and highly distinguished
369th Infantry Regiment, known as the Harlem Hellfighters, headed
majestically north in celebration and recognition of its heroic service in
the trenches of the First World War. In a "tight formation," resplendent
in battered uniforms that gained elegance in their disrepair, they passed
and were saluted by the governor of New York and other dignitaries at

60th Street. Seventy blocks later, at 130th Street and Lenox Avenue, the regimental band, led by the famous trumpeter Lt. James Reese Europe, abandoned its military march for the jazzy "Here Comes My Daddy," and the ranks broke into dancing, singing, and laughter.[28] This display of pride mixed with joy would become a signature—for Harlemites, the era after the war promised to be one in which protest and flamboyance would co-exist. Less than sixty years out of slavery, Negroes were proving that even public revelry was not inconsequential—"juking" in the street sent an exuberant message of cultural and racial self-confidence.

While not as overtly political as either of the previous events, another parade in Harlem was just as important in describing Harlem style and its relation to conceptions of black modernity—the famous parade of "fairies" at the annual Hamilton Lodge Ball. Staged every spring since 1869, by the early 1920s the Hamilton Lodge Ball had institutionalized a new, urban, and modern street-based display of black extravagance. According to the historian of gay New York George Chauncey, in the early twentieth century "drag queens appeared regularly in Harlem's streets and clubs," and outside of the restaurants, clubs, and cafes on Seventh Avenue gay men were to be seen "cavorting with wild and Wilde abandon."[29] As it celebrated the visual display of Harlem's most controversial new Negroes, the Hamilton Lodge Ball was perhaps Harlem's most notorious event during the years in which its modernism was in the making. Gaining in popularity steadily from the early 1920s, when its status as the preeminent drag ball in New York and the nation was emerging, the affair drew as many as eight thousand participants and observers in the mid-1930s. A drag ball in which female impersonators, black and white, competed for prizes based on fabulousness of costume and comportment, the Hamilton Lodge festivities demonstrated, annually, the fact that at times Harlem "was wide open" to those interested in gender performance and sexual experimentation and that this experimentation was often marked by a combination of fancy dress and saucy attitude.[30] Stylish display was de rigueur, as the ball was attended by a decidedly "mixed crowd," full of "ofays in drag and dress . . . Harlem's dressed and undressed," male and female straights and "inverts" crossing the lines of race, gender, sex, and class.[31] High society folks, actors, entertainers, local and national celebrities dressed to the nines joined the queens at the Rockland Palace (and once in Madison Square Garden). The "ladies" were clad in the likes of "a low-cut gown with a silver fox fur yoke," and other "original creations," such as "a white gown with pleat ruff of the same material—and backless my deah."[32]

The main event, a grand march or display of what black newspapers called "pansies on parade," proceeded with "much laughter, hip-slapping and head-tossing," past official and nonofficial judges eager to appreciate the "gorgeous thrilling spectacle—a veritable glimpse of fairyland. Whoops!"[33] While at best signaling an ironic playful tone in the reportage of a contemporary observer, the "whoops" intimates the slippage going on here as Harlem, the black mecca, became a gay metropolis or experimental site for redefining those categories by which we constitute identity. In early twentieth-century Harlem, an explosion of organza and a finely tuned attention to the politics of dress indicated a change in conceptions of blackness and the relation of race to sex, gender, and class. While the "creative restraint" of the Silent Protest Parade and the self-celebratory stroll of the 369th Infantry shifted earlier American scrutiny and surveillance of blacks into a curious attention, the Hamilton Lodge Ball "queered" that attention as thousands of "spectators took delight in watching the transgression of racial boundaries that seemed to accompany the transgression of gender and sexual boundaries."[34] In the Silent Protest Parade, men and women used gender-specific style to address racial violence; in the Harlem Hellfighters' juke, black men inserted a culturally specific pleasure into their definition of heroism; in the balls, the immense popularity of an interracial event featuring cross-dressing "inverts" demonstrated that Harlem had indeed become a queer place at least "one startling step beyond" black and white, masculine and feminine, modern and avant-garde. "Whoops!"

"Striking the uninformed observer as a phenomenon, a miracle straight out of the skies," Harlem and its spectacles were signals of a mass realization of the potential of a newly visible people negotiating and redefining the formation of modern identities. While the Harlem Renaissance was certainly distinguished by the new audibility of African American culture in the form of jazz and the blues—well illustrated by the triumphant strains of "Here Comes My Daddy"—its look and the exaggeration or embodiment of that category-exploding look in the drag balls played at least as crucial a role in establishing the movement as that which once again would define African Americans as new. As the black community studied, adjusted, upgraded, and queered this look in 1920s Harlem, New Negro dandies erupted everywhere. They could be seen in groups and as individuals, as protest marchers and those parading joy, in the guise of well-dressed doctors and lawyers inhabiting brownstones on Striver's Row, as flamboyantly dressed street peddlers of women and "hooch," beautifully clad cross-dressing dancers, musicians, and patrons at speakeasies, and artists ensconced in salons. Of course, the majority of Harlem's residents were not aware of themselves as dandies, but many could be seen that way because of the new experimental ethos they communicated through their style.

Given their ubiquity, dandies now confidently sauntering down the streets of Harlem soon became of actual and symbolic concern to Harlem's intelligentsia and the world. Then and now, reading the dandy's self-fashioning impulse as an exemplification of modernity requires an analysis of the figure's long-standing play with race, class, gender, sexuality, and dress. However, even though Harlem's look emerges in much the same way as Baker's modern sound—in a negotiation of earlier stereotypes and a visitation of indigenous forms—it reveals anything but a championing of modern black culture as a return to the authentic. In fact, when these modern Harlemites throw off the minstrel mask, they find their authenticity in multiplicity, not imitation, in indigenous traditions of race, class, and gender performance characteristic of African American expressive culture from the days of slavery. The Harlem dandy's look is a sign that blackness has been and always will be syncretic, necessarily collaged and intersected by literal and symbolic or metaphorical manifestations of gender, sexuality, and class. It is a modern identity constructed by those who, once forced to fashion lives in the diaspora, now hoped to capitalize on the potential of this complicated and creative task.

"Cosmopolite Self-Concepts"

As an architect of the Harlem Renaissance, James Weldon Johnson worked hard to transform Harlem's unprecedented African American presence and the consequent explosion of urbane sophistication into cultural regard and eventual social and political power. As a composer and musician, politician, editor, poet, novelist, and historian, he himself

24. Photograph of Harlem Easter Sunday, 1938–39. Copyright © Morgan and Marvin Smith, Photographs and Prints Division, Schomburg Center for Research in Black Culture, The New York Public Library, Astor, Lenox and Tilden Foundations.

seemingly experimented with the many ways in which black New Yorkers could harness this unique cultural and historical moment. In one of his last guises as black Manhattan's cultural historian, Johnson looks back at recent Harlem history and, as we've seen, deliberately highlights the striking visual impact of black New Yorkers as part of his attention to documenting the origin, growth, and later explosion of black style exhibited by the masses in the Negro metropolis.[35] In uncovering the origins of this "miracle straight out of the sky" and the spread of black cultural influence, especially via theater, music, and literature, all over the city, Johnson explicitly hoped to provide a record of black survival and cultural achievement that countered prevailing stereotypes. That African American identity and the public face of African American culture are formed in the tension between stereotypes and self-representation is clear to Johnson—his best known works, *Black Manhattan*, *Along This Way* (1931), and especially his novel, *The Autobiography of an Ex-Coloured Man* (1912 / 27), all explore this tension in terms of the importance of image making. Dandies and dandyism, as a sign of interest in self- and cultural (re)presentation, thus figure prominently in Johnson's work and later as a general concern for his fellow Renaissance architects attempting to turn Harlem's critical mass into an artistic movement demonstrative of black cultural arrival. Hoping to reform themselves into modern people or cosmopolites not actually or psychically subject to the provincial narrowness of the color line, these new Negroes tapped into a long tradition of African American use of style as subversive in their focus on externalizing and performing modernity.

Given his biography, that Johnson would choose to narrate the New Negro's progress as a chronicle of increasing visibility or arrival on the world's stage is not surprising; but what makes this choice fascinating is the way in which it unites Harlem cultural phenomena with a style of self-definition in Johnson's own life. *Black Manhattan* is Johnson's love letter to the city and to Harlem specifically, the only place, perhaps, where Johnson felt he and others could fully exercise what his biographer Eugene Levy calls his "cosmopolite self-concept." What cosmopolitanism meant to Johnson, how it was or could be manifested, and what its acquisition and performance could mean for the black community more generally are, in fact, signal concerns in Johnson's autobiography, *Along This Way* and the overall theme of *Black Manhattan*'s cultural history. From an early age, Johnson had been enthralled by the city and its potential as a magical space. His parents, of Haitian / French, Bahamian nationality and ethnicity, had met in the city before moving to the segregated southern town of Jacksonville, Florida, and they "talked about the city much in the manner that exiles or emigrants talked about the homeland."[36] His memory of his first visit without his parents in 1884, when he was nearly thirteen, centers on the conviction that he had come home and that "being a New York means being born, no matter where, with a love for cosmopolitanism; and one either is or is not [a cosmopolite]."[37] At the time, Johnson associated cosmopolitanism with definitively urban phenomena, less known to blacks elsewhere: an unprecedented amount of actual, psychic, and symbolic mobility. In New York, he is thrilled to travel the boroughs and bridges by boat, stagecoach, horse, and car, and, as he travels, he remarks on the manifestation of this freedom in finery as he accompanies his Brooklyn-based step-uncle, a tailor of secret society regalia, on his shopping trips to Lord and Taylor.[38] What New York cosmopolitanism meant was the absence of a sense of restriction and the stylish celebration of dignity, self-respect, and consciousness of community. Johnson's early experiences in New York left him "with a taste for cosmopolitanism, which he sought to develop, consciously and unconsciously, in his adult years."[39]

Throughout *Along This Way*, Johnson figures his growth and increasing worldliness in relationship to his exposure to, acquisition of, and analysis of cosmopolitan style. As the son of Caribbean colonial subjects, Johnson had a Victorian upbringing in which the manifestation of respectability and refinement was paramount; Johnson was, in some ways, trained to be attentive to those who cut a figure and what that visual sign could mean. He notes that he was highly impressed with his step-grandfather, John Barton, a Bahamian, who was "dapper; I might say elegant. He was a grand sight, I thought, in his long-tailed, black broadcloth coat on Sundays."[40] The year after his return from his trip to New York in 1884, perhaps inspired by his great uncle's assemblage of the "gorgeous paraphernalia" of the Masons, their "bright-colored silks," "gold and silver braid and fringe and tassels and . . . various emblems and insignia," Johnson himself wanted to procure a more sophisticated everyday uniform—a pair of black broadcloth, "spring-bottom" trousers, to him "the acme of elegance."[41] Although his family later declared nearly unanimously that he "looked funny" in his new trousers, Johnson worked his first job in a brickyard to pay for the fourteen-dollar "fancy" pants.[42] These were Johnson's first long pants and therefore, in the tradition of his forefathers, a self-authored announcement of his maturity and hoped-for sophistication.

Though Johnson thought he had reached the height of elegance with his

25. James Weldon Johnson. Yale Collection of American Literature, Beinecke Rare Book and Manuscript Library. Photograph of James Weldon Johnson by permission of Dr. Sondra Kathyrn Wilson, Executor for the Estate of Grace and James Weldon Johnson.

new trousers, he was surpassed by a young boy named Ricardo Rodriguez who came to live with his family in Jacksonville. A Cuban and the son of a business associate of Johnson's father, Rodriguez increased James's burgeoning worldliness by his presence in the Johnson household. He taught James to speak Spanish fluently; in addition, his family sent "packages of Cuban sweets and preserves, and fresh supplies of fine linen handkerchiefs, hand-made shirts, initialed underwear, French neckties, French lisle socks, high-heeled Cuban shoes" to their scholar.[43] Commenting on the richness of his friend's sartorial splendor, Johnson laments, "Rosamund [Johnson's brother, the famous composer] and I had always thought of ourselves as well-dressed boys—our mother spent a good part of her salary on clothes for us—but such finery, as this, *for a boy*, we had not even imagined" (italics added).[44] Therefore, as he mastered another spoken language, he also further honed his understanding of another semiotic system, the language of clothing, image, visibility. As Johnson remarks here, in recalling Rodriguez's trousseau-like trunk, such attention to image was unusual for a boy. Johnson used these languages for the rest of his life, as both taught him valuable lessons about being black in America and allowed him to teach America a lesson about the way regard is racialized and gendered, as well.

As defined by Levy and illustrated by Johnson's recollections of his childhood, Johnson's cosmopolite self-concept was, on an elementary level, a kind of psychological shield, an attitude and set of skills Johnson was encouraged to use to protect and preserve and exercise his humanity as he grew up in the segregated South. It allowed him to see beyond the strictures of race and to intimate that beyond those strictures were also different conceptions of nationality, class, and masculinity. While instilled in him by his proud parents, his cosmopolite self-concept was really tested and solidified only when Johnson met Rodriguez, a boy raised outside of Jim Crow expectations. As a Cuban, Rodriguez was certainly not of an environment free from racial or color prejudice, but he was free at least from its American manifestation. His utterance of a different language can, perhaps, be read as a sign of that difference. When he taught Johnson Spanish, Rodriguez gave his friend a key to another world, a world that had as just one of its signs "fine linen handkerchiefs, hand-made shirts, initialed underwear, French neckties, French lisle socks, high-heeled Cuban shoes." On a literal level, Spanish fluency allowed Johnson a measure of freedom—when speaking Spanish, he passed or was taken for a foreigner, a fact that helped him avoid segregated railway cars and hotels.[45] Johnson's fluency in a foreign language simultaneously exposed and allowed him to bypass the turgidity, arbitrariness, and cruelty of America's racial system and color line, the full experience of which his larger cosmopolite self-concept and its psychosocial sign, dandyism, was designed to avoid.

The fashion sense reinforced in Johnson another valuable lesson—the importance and power of externalizing a positive self-regard, despite of or in defiance of predominant stereotypes. For Johnson, looking good, cutting a figure, compelling recognition signified a desire to see the self and be seen outside of a limiting lens that relegated him and other African Americans to fixed roles. His cosmopolite self-concept defied those strictures and expanded his potential artistic, social, cultural, and political prospects. An internal attitude that could be manifested externally, at least in Johnson's account, cosmopolitanism was not only a bid for equality, but also an assertion of it. Later, when Johnson himself left Florida to go to New York to participate in the birth of black vaudeville in the early 1900s, his description of the black bohemia he found anticipates his later pronouncement about the force of black visibility and mutual recognition in the city: "The sight offered at these hotels, of crowds of well-dressed colored men and women lounging and chatting in the parlors, loitering over their coffee and cigarettes while they talked or listened to music, was unprecedented. The sight had an immediate effect on me and my brother; we decided to give up our lodgings . . . , and move to the Marshall. We took the large backroom on the second floor, put in a piano, and started to work. This move had consequences we did not dream of."[46] Among the many results was the brothers' extremely successful career as composers; along with their partner, Bob Cole, the Johnsons "were the musical Moses to lead the coon song into the Promised Land," the means by which "coon song lyrics became noticeably more genteel."[47] Johnson once again marked his success, his conquest of limitation, by means of dress — "contemporary photographs show him as an impeccably dressed young man with a Van Dyke beard."[48]

Johnson's life story is in some ways a chronicle of his assumption and deployment of a cosmopolitanism that characterized the Harlem Renaissance. His narrative of the life of the city, *Black Manhattan*, records this achievement for the race at large. What Johnson felt himself trying to do, first in the 1900s and then more self-consciously in the 1920s and 1930s, was to rectify a situation in which the black on the street, on stage, and in print was seen only as what he himself identified as "impulsive, irrational, passionate, savage, reluctantly wearing a thin coat of culture."[49] What he hoped to do and to later chronicle for posterity was the exchange of that thin coat for, perhaps, the "gorgeous paraphernalia" of a society of Negroes no longer "secret" but "in vogue." Johnson's narrative in *Black Manhattan* is a story of black presence and visibility, the artistic potential of that presence as it organizes first in midtown and then in Harlem, and the consequent self-stylization that was the hope and character of the Harlem Renaissance era. While endeavoring to tell a story of increasing freedom for African Americans in and via the arts, Johnson details a time in which African Americans "moved on up" geographically and culturally—all through creative, strategic self-fashioning.

If the cultivation and promotion of a cosmopolite self-concept was the hallmark of Johnson's development as an artist, intellectual, and politician, and if he sought to replace the perception that a "thin coat of culture" left African Americans isolated from a broader American cultural regard, then the attention he paid to the nature of the figure cut by African Americans in the Negro metropolis seems not only apt, but necessary. In *Black Manhattan*, Johnson trains his eye on almost all the places evidencing the presence and potential of his fellow cosmopolites, alternating scenes of the streets with those of the theaters and music halls. His gaze across New York history intensifies as he nears Harlem in the early twentieth century. As a cultural history, *Black Manhattan* is a curious book: though starting out as a rather straightforward history of African Americans in New York, in its later chapters it increasingly focuses on black self-representation, especially in the arts, as it arrives at the formation of Harlem, "the Mecca for the sight-seer, the pleasure-seeker, the curious, the adventurous, the enterprising, the ambitious, and the talented of the Negro world."[50] According to Johnson, by the time the black population in New York had migrated from Wall Street to San Juan Hill and was pushing ever upward, Negro numbers and talent were sufficient enough to create an early black bohemia whose artistic effort on the theatrical stage supplied an alternative to degrading representations of African Americans. As he well knew, the debilitating stereotypes of blackface theater had hardly been limited to the stage; in his account, this early black bohemia acted as a transitional stage, literally and figuratively, between blackface-derived images so pervasive onstage and off and those more self-determined. Therefore, the figure that African Americans cut was one that delicately balanced cultural baggage with cultural arrival, dandies in blackface with black cosmopolites.

Fascination with Harlem and African America's new look, the cultivation of a cosmopolite self-concept as part of that new look, a concern with self- and cultural regard as expressed in cosmopolite signs—these are all the hallmarks of black New York in the 1920s. As Johnson begins to tell the story of the Renaissance proper, he is quick to acknowledge and revel in its reputation as "exotic, colorful, and sensuous; a place of laughing, singing, and dancing, a place where life wakes up at night," a place in which citizens express and experience a gaiety that is "peculiarly characteristic of Harlem."[51] Again, the visual, sensual, and affective are constituent parts of this new experience: "A visit to Harlem at night—the principal streets never deserted, gay crowds skipping from one place of amusement to another, lines of taxicabs and limousines standing under the sparkling lights of the night-clubs, the subway kiosks swallowing and disgorging crowds all night long—gives the impression that Harlem never sleeps and that the inhabitants thereof jazz through existence."[52] Johnson's description of Harlem as a place of "jazz" recognizes not only the prevailing musical mood, but also the dynamism of the culture found there. Harlem is a place in which the newly urban Negro population riff off of each other and mainstream culture in the creation of a new visual and artistic culture. While Johnson admits that most in Harlem struggle "to make ends meet," that many "ordinary hardworking people" may have not seen the interior of a nightclub, nevertheless, "the people who live here are a pleasure-loving people," and, as we'll see, entirely aware of the visual and cultural cues around them.[53] Central to this story of visuality and aesthetics during the Renaissance are the ways in which the ordinary folk express this pleasure, ways that once again call attention to how Harlem looks and how African Americans want to be seen. What is important about Harlem is not just that, for the first time, African American actors "felt free to do on the stage whatever they were able to do," to express love and respect for self and others, but that Harlem was itself a theatrical, spectacular place, one in which black people manifested self-regard, explored and redefined the relationship of race, gender, and sex through their elegant, sophisticated, and playfully fine self-presentation.[54] Johnson characterizes Harlem, "miracle straight out of the sky," as a place in which black self-expression had a license to perform on its biggest stage yet: on the street, on stage, and in print. Bringing these expressive genres together in the fight against stereotype would, he hoped, prove that Negroes were "creators, as well as creatures."[55]

If, as Ann Douglas asserts, "to be black in modern America was a command to strategize, and . . . [early twentieth-century] New York was the place to do it," then Johnson's tactics for himself and African America focused on dandy-like skills: a cosmopolite self-concept, jazz sensibility toward art and life, attempt to balance stereotype and self-representation, become and promote creative, "pleasure-seeking" creatures.[56] Attuned to the subversive potential of manipulating visual and material signs, Johnson, in his chronicle of the growth of the Negro metropolis, institutions, and artists, dramatizes their potential in a particularly optimistic (perhaps misleading?) way. Pleasures abound in *Black Manhattan*, pleasures specifically associated with the acquisition and display of self- and community identity and spirit. Johnson says that as early as 1919, Negroes everywhere, especially in Harlem, "felt strange stirrings of aspiration and shed that lethargy born of hopelessness," and in Harlem, they "had begun to dream of greater and greater things."[57] This dream was externalized as style; two of the three favorite pastimes of Harlemites, strolling and parading, surely have the same effect as the other, churchgoing, which Johnson describes as "an arena for the exercise of one's capabilities and powers, a world in which one may achieve self-realization and preferment."[58] "Not simply going out for a walk" but "more like an adventure," strolling combines fancy dress and public announcement of arrival:

> One puts on one's best clothes and fares forth to pass the time pleasantly with the friends and acquaintances and, most important of all, the strangers he is sure of meeting. One saunters along, he hails this one, exchanges a word or two with that one, stops for a short chat with the other one. He comes up to a laughing, chattering group, in which he may have only one friend or acquaintance, but that gives him the privilege of joining in. He does join in and takes part in the joking, the small talk and gossip, and makes new acquaintances. He passes on and arrives in front of one of the theatres, studies the bill for a while, undecided about going in. He finally moves on a few steps farther and joins another group and is introduced to two or three pretty girls who have just come to Harlem, perhaps only for a visit; and finds a reason to be glad that he postponed going into the theatre. The hours of a summer evening run by rapidly.[59]

Part of a long history of African American expression in the streets, the stroll was a cultural practice born out of exigency that was as much an emblem of African American claims to urban space as a celebration of the creativity and freedom seen and exercised there. According to the cultural historians Shane White and Graham White, the stroll and the parade had origins in the early African American festivals and flourished in the nineteenth century when many poverty-stricken free blacks were forced to spend their leisure time in the street—it was the way in which they transformed this necessity into an advantage.[60] As threatening as comic to white onlookers, well-dressed blacks sauntering down shared city streets in their Sunday best or Saturday night special represented an actual and symbolic contest for territory. The nature of the world which they inhabited and wanted to claim was visible on their bodies: their clothes were variably actual haute couture, a knockoff of high fashion, or, most often, a combination of pieces exemplary of white fashion and a more African-based sense of bright color and varied pattern. As in the Silent Protest Parade, the Harlem Hellfighters march, and the nightly or annual presence of drag queens on Harlem's avenues, the parade operated on a similar phenomenon as African Americans deliberately marched all over town in militia uniforms, formal dress, simple suits, ball gowns, or any combination of these, "not only emphasizing differences in the way they looked and moved, but also insisting that they had a right to the streets and that milestones in their collective past were a part of the city's history."[61] What were competitive, defiant performances of freedom, dignity, self-worth, and cultural syncretism in the nineteenth century became more of an intragroup celebration of the use of style and clothing as expressive of individual and group identity during the early twentieth. As blacks moved north in increasing numbers and established their own neighborhoods and thoroughfares, a trip down "African Broadway" in Harlem dressed to the nines in fancy or "fixy" clothes asserted not only the collective black ownership of a piece of Manhattan, but also the cultural potentiality associated with that claim of space and the intrablack looks and looking taking place there.

That "what was valued highly on the Stroll [in general, but here with specific reference to Seventh Avenue in Chicago] was not only the stylish ways young black men about town presented their bodies, but also their verbal agility and quickness of wit," hints at the relationship between actual and cultural visibility that Johnson and others hoped to take advantage of during the Harlem Renaissance.[62] This relationship is one that Johnson intimates in the structure and content of *Black Manhattan*. As mentioned previously, what begins as a history of Africans and African Americans in New York and continues as an exploration of representation in the arts (especially music and theater) ends with the discovery of "the most outstanding phase of the development of the Negro in the United States during the past decade [the 1920s] . . . the recent literary and artistic emergence of the individual creative artist."[63] The emergence of the literary artist strikes Johnson as the signal that by the 1920s in Harlem, African Americans had become cosmopolites, rather than merely imagining themselves as such. As they manifested this status in their strolls and parades in black Manhattan, mass cultural displays for each other, they claimed geographic territory that could become a space of personal and group creativity and exhibition—a kind of studio—for them. Johnson recognizes this when he ends *Black Manhattan* with the pronouncement that "Harlem is still in the process of making. It is still new and mixed; so mixed that one may get many different views—which is all right so long as one view is not taken to be the whole picture."[64] The business of this laboratory or studio would be the communication of black America's new "mixed" attitude about itself via the arts; especially important in this revision of African Americans and their culture would be fiction writing, which Johnson describes as the artistic arena that has seen the most progress during the 1920s.

A move born of optimism, Johnson's turn to art and culture, perhaps at this time "the only horse willing to run under their [African Americans'] colors," was a bet that "artistic and literary achievement could do more for the black cause at this particular historical moment than any economic or political gains they might achieve."[65] If in the African American tradition black dandies continually rewrite the story of their own actual and representational subjugation by reanimating the tools of their oppression, tailoring their supposed uniforms for other tasks, then they seemed perfect as authors, subjects, and symbols for the New Negro literary renaissance. After all, the figure's sartorial, attitudinal, and verbal wit had been historically both mark and process of black signification on tests of cultural literacy and sophistication. While at once acknowledging that Harlem was "still in the process of making" and that "it is still new and mixed," Renaissance architects nevertheless pressed for the production of art that would communicate and demonstrate a *particular* black aesthetic, one that was ultimately too focused on illustrating authentic or marketable blackness. In fact, Johnson concentrates on this necessity very early in his Harlem literary career: in January 1915, in a column in the *New York Age* establishing a "Poetry Corner," Johnson states that, "We have often heard the prophecy that we as a race are to furnish the great American poets, musicians, and artists of the future. There is every reason for this prophecy to come true; we are more richly endowed for such work than the white race. We have more heart, more soul; we are more responsive to emotional vibrations; we have a larger share of the gifts of laughter, music and song; in a word, we are less material and we are, by nature, more artistic than white people."[66] While Johnson's own sartorial and representational concerns may contradict his claim about African American materiality, his play with essentialist notions of racial identity—the "natural" "gift" of laughter, the excessive emotivity—seemingly complicates his own sense of himself and other Harlem Renaissance types as cosmopolites, people operating outside of imposed boundaries. Though here dictating those "essentially" Negro qualities authors should be employing in their fiction, Johnson had himself, just three years earlier, written a novel in which he not only does not follow, but very much argues against, such limited, racialized thinking. In fact, in *The Autobiography of an Ex-Coloured Man*, a novel ostensibly about racial passing, Johnson's dandy protagonist trumps the color line, signifies on it, and queers it as he explores gender and sex categories at the same time that he reimagines blackness in the novel. In *The Autobiography of an Ex-Coloured Man*, he reaches for a wider world, a place of unassailable black dignity, impregnable self-respect, and freedom from the limitations of caste, color, and normative notions of masculinity and sexuality.

Inspired by the opportunity to fashion black modern identity but pressured to translate artistically a presumed blackness that everyone could recognize, New Negro artists were challenged to fulfill the confused directives of the age. Their use of the dandy as a means of expressing black cultural arrival or the New Negro aesthetic illustrates the potential and difficulty of such a task. Initially, Renaissance architects seemingly hoped that expressing a cosmopolite self-concept via the black dandy would define black modern identity away from stereotypes. Having transcended the limitations of blackface, the figure would then be capable of exemplifying the striving that was initially mocked by caricature: desire for education, social mobility, a cosmopolitanism not prohibited by the color line. However, in spite of the apparent auspiciousness of black Manhattan as a cultural laboratory for literary experimentation and the amazing fit of the dandy figure as a sign of cultural aspirations, artists in Harlem were not able to use the era's most self- and image-conscious figure to the specifications of Renaissance leaders. What they did not realize, perhaps, was that the effort to modify the dandy for modernity would also, in some way, uncover the dandy in black, an earlier version of black self-fashioning that would be difficult to channel into a definitive, marketable statement on blackness or serve as an untroubling sign of the emergence of modern black voices. This dandy in black brought along with him a destabilization of other categories of identity; he was essentially nothing but mixed, a product of interracial relations, a sliding point on the spectrum of gender and sexuality, a class aspirant and pretender.

As the dandy expressed cosmopolite desires or the possibility of a life lived beyond boundaries, the figure, its queerness, prevented the Harlem Renaissance from defining blackness in a way that satisfied either its prohibitive architects or future critics. Therefore, despite the seeming happy relation between Harlem and its dandies, these figures so prominent and playful throughout the 1920s proved to be fancies that would have to pass, literally and figuratively, out of the era and, for a time, out of black consciousness, especially when treated in fiction dealing with the demands a cultural renaissance makes on new or modern people.

Passing Fancies and the Pressures of Authenticity

Harlem in the 1920s was a world in which, Johnson and others believed, "it is no exaggeration to say that one colored American poet or dramatist or novelist of the first magnitude; that is, one that would command the attention and recognition of the world, would do more to batter down prejudice against the race than ten colored millionaires."[67] Harlem's literati struggled to produce the literature regarded by Johnson and others as proof of racial and cultural sophistication. For New Negro authors, a successful deployment of dandyism required a work of art or character to effect a delicate balance between a vehement antiracism (in the combat of stereotypes) and a cultural nationalism or authenticity based on the Negro's supposedly inherent racial gifts. If handled well, this display would somehow elevate the art and its people from the particular into the realm of the universal, prove that African America was or is civilized. Though not successful in this task, the dandy in the Harlem Renaissance—a figure who opposes rather than unites signs of cosmopolitanism and authenticity—nevertheless failed in an instructive way. Johnson's choice to fight stereotypes primarily by "copyright," as David Levering Lewis describes the New Negro tactic in *When Harlem Was in Vogue*, and with the dandy as a modernist sign led to the reissue in 1927 of his novel of 1912 *The Autobiography of an Ex-Coloured Man* at the height of the Renaissance's literary production. One of a group of novels self-consciously dealing with the problem of "making a poet black and bidding him to sing," *The Autobiography of an Ex-Coloured Man* defies Johnson's own proscriptions for the Renaissance as it dramatizes the difficulty that New Negro dandies would have embodying and translating supposed racial instincts into culture-confirming, race-marketing art. When also cast as a decadent in Wallace Thurman's *Infants of the Spring* (1932), the figure of the black dandy seems to capture not the proscriptive demands of the age, but rather its spirit and modernity—the way in which race, gender, sex, and class are intermixed in conceptions and presentations of blackness.

As the fictional record of a life lived on the lines of color and class, *The Autobiography of an Ex-Coloured Man* uses the historical tension between dandyism and passing to deconstruct racial stereotypes and the idea of identity categories altogether, challenging the Renaissance's call for authentically black texts (or authenticity at all). Though marketed and critically received as a book about racial passing, critical consensus about the novel now recognizes that the book passes for or over many of the other categories in which it is implicated. Even the novel's genre, never mind its subject, was initially uncertain; when *The Autobiography of an Ex-Coloured Man* was first published anonymously in 1912, it was assumed to be an actual, rather than fictional, account of racial passing. As Johnson's unnamed, dandified protagonist negotiates black and white worlds, the destabilization of his racial authenticity upends the rigidity of categories of gender and sexuality as well. Traversing and defying truth claims from its inception, the novel uses the dandyism of its protagonist to illustrate the mobility associated with his character—throughout the text, just as the Ex-Coloured Man is about to enter into stability in terms of an aspect of his identity, his dandyism, in the form of narcissism, dilettantism, class aspiration, and gender/sex performance, prevents him from normatively occupying the category. Mulatto or mixed in nearly all ways, the

Ex-Coloured Man comes to embody an extreme form of Harlem's modernism, but one necessary to the task of revisioning the race.

The dynamism between dandyism and the deconstruction of race is well illustrated in a scene at the beginning of the novel. The Ex-Coloured Man begins his story by recounting his early childhood in Georgia. Living in a small house with his black mother, surrounded by a kind of Edenic garden, the young man recalls a regular visitor, "a tall man with a small, dark moustache." An early observer of what one might call cosmopolitan signs, the boy's singular memory of this man, his white father, is that he was well accessorized, so much so that the Ex-Coloured Man found his "admiration was equally divided between [his father's great gold] watch and the [gold] chain and the [shiny] shoes."[68] When the young boy and his mother are about to be exiled north, his father bids him a heartfelt goodbye and gives him a token of their relation, a ten-dollar gold piece into which he has laboriously drilled a hole so that the boy can wear it around his neck with a string.[69] An attempt by the Ex-Coloured Man's father to bestow on his son a token of whiteness, this gesture also creates a link between father and son that undoes the supposed purity of the gesture and highlights its dandyism. Though "dandy," as noted earlier, does not, according to the *Oxford English Dictionary* (OED), have a definite origin, possible derivations include its status as a cognate of "dandiprat," a "small coin, worth three half-pence, current in England in the 16th-century." The dictionary disclaims the connection with the coin, stating that the possibility has been "guessed, but without any apparent ground"; yet the applicability of this dandy origin to the Ex-Coloured Man's self-definition is striking.[70] That the white father chooses a coin to embody his paternity or the passage of whiteness to his mulatto son is the sign of the confusion of the gesture; this bestowal will miscarry because the coin is currency, therefore expendable or transferable, and at the same time as worthless as the charm on a necklace.

Inextricable from the gesture's racial gift is its attempted gendering; when the father gives the coin to the son, he wants to pass on not only whiteness, but also an unassailable form of masculinity, heteronormativity, or mastery (master-status) as well. A transfer between men, but with a woman of color as witness ("my mother stood behind his chair wiping tears from her eyes"), this aspect of the gift fails as well, as the masculine and heteronormative emblem is rent, contains a problematic hole.

Not a sign of mastery but of penetrability, the coin worn as a necklace attaches vulnerability to the Ex-Coloured Man's body, a vulnerability he never overcomes. Recalling that he had often "wish[ed] that some other way had been found of attaching it to me besides putting a hole through it," the Ex-Coloured Man disdains the coin's false promise of genealogy, wealth, whiteness, and masculine privilege; nevertheless, he remains attached to it, declaring that he had "worn that gold piece around [his] neck the greater part of [his] life."[71] His dissatisfaction with the gift implies that the privileges of race and gender cannot accrue or endure, unlike the coin's very materiality, or its dandy connection. For this young man, blackness, racial authenticity, or authenticity in general will prove as illusive; what the boy inherits here is not what the coin might be worth, but what it fails to signify.

In a study of passing that is essential to understanding the importance of dandyism in *The Autobiography of an Ex-Coloured Man*, Samira Kawash redefines passing from black to white not as an act that "obscures a true black identity," but as an action that questions the basis of "true identities" outright. She writes that "passing insists on the fallacy of identity as a *content* of social, psychological, national, or cultural attributes, whether bestowed by nature or produced by society; it forces us to pay attention to the *form* of difference itself. In the case of the United States, difference is named and produced on the 'color line.'"[72] In her reading of passing narratives, Kawash finds that the story is not simply the exchange of one racial designation for another, but the erasure of race as a reliable category of identity. What passing teaches its participants and observers is the possibility that a disjunction between form and content, exteriority and interiority, signifies beyond assessing the veracity of "what you see is what you get." Passing denies the possibility of identity being authentic, as it forgoes rigid definitions of blackness and whiteness for an exposure and exploration of the mechanism of racial difference, the color line. In the case of the Ex-Coloured Man, the coin exchange from father to son does not benefit the boy because the coin's symbolic value as whiteness has no real function in this passing text; it cannot embody or even symbolize the content of identity. The coin is important not for its relationship to identity's interior factors, but for the externalities to which it points, the form of difference, the social, cultural, political, and legal fact of the color line. Wearing a sign of the conflation of the dandy and the color line around his neck, the Ex-Coloured Man spends his childhood and then his adult life trying on racial identities like costumes, exposing race as performative and the color line as oxymoronically capricious and definitive.

A "perfect little aristocrat," possessed of "that pride which well-dressed boys generally have," the Ex-Coloured Man becomes more self-consciously a dandy than white or black as a young man.[73] As we've seen, his first experience with whiteness disappoints; blackness comes to him in a much different but no more permanent or uncomplicated way. Identifying himself as a good student, fun-loving, and sly, he passes his early childhood without incident until an unforgettable day near the end of his second school term. One day, the school principal inexplicably asks all of the white children to rise in class. The Ex-Coloured Man "rose with the others," and innocently creates a scene: "The teacher looked at me, and calling my name, said, 'You sit down for the present and rise with the others.' I did not quite understand her, and questioned, 'Ma'm?' She repeated, with a softer tone in her voice, 'You sit down now, and rise with the others.' I sat down dazed. I saw and heard nothing. When the others were asked to rise, I did not know it."[74] According to Barbara Johnson, racial difference resides in the simple textual repetition of the command "to rise with the others"; in commanding that he rise twice the teacher unwittingly asks the Ex-Coloured Man to perform both blackness and whiteness, even if he will not be counted in both categories.[75] It is at this moment that the Ex-Coloured Man is taught a second lesson about racial authenticity: he learns both of his blackness and of its arbitrariness. Destined always to be placed with the other "others," the Ex-Coloured Man will have his identity constituted not in an "authenticity" that passing denies, but in continual displacement of the would-be signs of racial and cultural identity. In fact, he does not hear or acknowledge the teacher's second call that he rise again; "I did not know it" he claims, unable or unwilling to see himself as other in the way that authority demands.

Not aware of this displacement (although, as a concept, it is the dandy's lesson), the boy rushes home to study his otherness in the mirror. What he sees is his beauty, its feminine nature, not his race: "I noticed the ivory whiteness of my skin, the beauty of my mouth, the size and liquid darkness of my eyes, and how the long, black lashes that fringed and shaded them produced an effect that was strangely fascinating even to me. I noticed the softness and glossiness of my dark hair that fell in waves over my temples, making my forehead appear whiter than it really was.

How long I stood there gazing at my image I do not know."[76] Not blackness, but a narcissism that respects no racial boundaries emerges in this self-admiring gaze. In the "liquid darkness of his eyes," the distinction between self and other, black and white, masculine and feminine cannot be fathomed and disappears.[77] Race and gender cannot be located in something as changeable or unreadable as one's image, but is found instead in that which should be more illusory but seems more permanent: the discretion of outside observers, or, in this context, the comments of the boy's classmates, who always knew or suspected he was "coloured," who understand him as other. Seeing himself as at least doubly other and, according to his mother and his own inspection, "not a nigger," the Ex-Coloured Man is given cause never to name himself as black, white, or anything else.[78] His reticence translates the problem of his identity out of the rigid categories of black and male, into another, more performative arena: into, say, dandy.

Even though the Ex-Coloured Man intuits the fact that blackness and perhaps masculinity are fictions, he spends much of his life trying to find a satisfactory way to embody an acceptable form of both categories. As a schoolboy, he does research into black masculine identity, reading *Uncle Tom's Cabin* and Frederick Douglass and Alexander Dumas; as a result, he begins to take pride in his colored status, wishing to be "a great man, *a great coloured man*, to reflect credit on the race" (italics added).[79] As the Ex-Coloured Man studies blackness and masculinity in order to access them, he admits the vexed, ironic nature of the gesture—as a mulatto narcissist, overwhelmed by the beauty of his own image, he is always already outside of authentic or essential expressions of these categories. Yet, as one might expect from a man unable to align himself truly with a group, a man who is also a young dandy, he is quick to add aspirations of being noticed and becoming famous to his desire to be an exemplary black man. The boy's combined search for a racial self and social regard is later recognized as the mere fantasy of one who "dwelt in a world of imagination of dreams and air castles—the kind of atmosphere that sometimes nourishes a genius, more often men unfitted for the practical struggles of life."[80] Genius maybe, dandy definitely, the young boy grows up to explore his identity and that of his people, by continually traveling and mapping out a terrain of sameness and difference in which he is always slightly out of place, odd, queer.

The Ex-Coloured Man "is never *in* a place as he is, to turn a phrase, passing through"—his geographical moves parallel his identity process.[81] Each new place to which he travels also introduces him to another segment of the black community and another standard to which he might and does not conform, from southern gentility in Florida, to northern bohemianism in New York, to European cosmopolitanism in Paris. Accordingly, he assumes different racial, gender, and even sexual identities in each new location, as his racial inauthenticity leads to gender trouble and then, "whoops!"—his sexuality comes into question as well. Arguing that the novel passes as a heterosexual narrative in addition to the many other categories of genre and identity that it engages, Siobhan Somerville argues that if the novel rests definitively anywhere, it does so in its queerness. Noticing not only the confusion around the Ex-Coloured Man's race and gender, but the way in which the confusion intersects with his "perverse" desires, Somerville points out the dandy's same-sex "attachments" (to Red-Head and Shiny) from an early age.[82] These attachments find their fullest expression when the Ex-Coloured Man travels to Paris with his white patron, a connoisseur of music who admires the Ex-Coloured Man's virtuosity, to whom "he [the Ex-Coloured Man] looked upon as . . . all a man could wish to be."[83]

Abroad, he enjoys an existence that brings leisure, art, the good life, and a wardrobe that seemingly outfits him with equality—"The next day [after arriving in Paris] we spent several hours in the shops and at the tailor's. . . . He [his benefactor] bought me the same kind of clothes which he himself wore, and that was the best; and he treated me in every way as he dressed me, as an equal, not as a servant."[84] During the journey, the Ex-Coloured Man and his patron share passionate exchanges, both musical and verbal, hinting at a connection between them that not only goes beyond the sartorial, but which the sartorial perhaps is designed to reveal. Reminiscent of his relationship with his father and the true inheritance he gains in the coin exchange, the Ex-Coloured Man's relationship with "his millionaire" similarly reveals a confusion about mastery. Their relationship fluctuates between that of intimates, operating on a kind of mutual respect, to that of father and son, master and slave, or, perhaps, even master and slave mistress. A companion in cafes by day, the entertainment by means of his piano playing in the evening, and a "drug" in the wee hours of the night when the patron demands a private concert, the Ex-Coloured Man occupies all of the roles that were implicit in his dandy "primal scene" with his father. He is at once in a proposed place of equality as recipient of the patron's generosity, a bastard in terms of his inherent inequality, subject as he is to the wealthy man's whims, and the weeping woman, his mother, complicatedly abused as a lover.

The Ex-Coloured Man is extricated from this situation by two events, each of which diminishes the multiplicity inherent in his odd or queer relationship: first, he discovers his true vocation as a translator between musical genres: assuming a black identity, he will now focus only on transforming ragtime rhythms into classical idioms; and, second, after he returns to America to do this work, the millionaire commits suicide. The combination of these two occurrences causes the Ex-Coloured Man to revise his conception of himself, his profound mixedness. After this interlude the Ex-Coloured Man's queerness seemingly disappears, as does his versatility as a musician. As Somerville argues, this queer interlude becomes almost "unspeakable" for the Ex-Coloured Man, as he has a diffi-cult time articulating its impact on him.[85] When remembering the patron later, he says that he prefers to be silent about this profoundly influen-tial man rather than detail his "affection for him," which was "so strong," and his "recollections of him," which were "so distinct."[86] What he does articulate is the aspect of his dandyism that is speakable: the fact that his sojourn in Europe had, if nothing else, heightened what one might call an aspect of his cosmopolite self-concept, "because through my experience with my millionaire a certain amount of comfort and luxury had become a necessity to me whenever it was available."[87]

Deciding to return to his people, in the United States, he does not so much assume a position or stance of racial authenticity as much as he does the role of a translator or bridge between the races. But even his comfort in this liminal position — which is so beneficial to him in terms of his music because by the end of a trip he takes to the South he had found a "mine of material" and was in a "frame of mind . . . which amounts to inspiration" — cannot be maintained in America's stark racial landscape.[88] The lynching he witnesses on the very last part of his journey forces the Ex-Coloured Man to concede the false safety of those on the line of color in a country in which color is determined not by choice or appearance, but by the law.[89] Plagued by the shame that he belongs to a people who "could be dealt so with," he decides to pass again, this time into indeter-minacy; he will neither "disclaim the black race nor claim the white race," and "let the world take [him] for what it will."[90] To pass, unnoticed, may seem like the opposite of the dandy's often flamboyant visual critique of societal restrictions, but in fact it is the ultimate dandy act, the feared end of increased black mobility and self-consciousness concerning race, gender, and sexuality as performance. Dressed and educated well above his supposed station, he is easily taken for being white and heterosexual. This final transformation finds him at the heart of whiteness itself. Full only of racial and sexual panic (he fears that his white fiancée will think of him as an ape if his racial identity is revealed) and an unsettled desire for difference (the "strange longing for my mother's people"), this place turns out to be full of continued conflict and hardly a neat resolution to the demands of race and culture in a world bisected by the color line.[91] Indeed, despite the white, heteronormative position he occupies at the end of the novel, the Ex-Coloured Man wonders if there is still not "an indefinable something which marked a difference" in his identity.[92] This is a stark echo of the very definition of the relation of a dandy's art to modernity, according to Baudelaire.

Neither black nor white, yet dandy, the Ex-Coloured Man finds stereotypes but not authenticity at the end of his journey. In theory, race may be just that, an idea, a matter of performance, but racism, of which the formation and promulgation of stereotypes is a part, has real effects. As a figure who exists in a "certain relation" not only to whiteness but to "niggers," (the children's rhyme "Nigger, nigger, never die" echoes throughout the text), the black dandy assumes that race is a fiction and, when confronted with the lines of color, rummages in his closet, as does the Ex-Coloured Man, for a defiant, destabilizing look. While the Ex-Coloured Man's dressing the part from black to white, feminine to masculine, straight to queer exposes the futility of searches for authentic identities, it does in turn suggest that what authenticity there is adheres in changeability, adaptability, role play, masks. As this figure flaunts the color line, its relation to the spectrums of gender and sexuality, he both exposes and conceals what it might mean to embody cultural arrival and social regard. A dandy and passing, the figure doubly affirms the impossibility of personifying race by remaining altogether enigmatic, cannily ahead of the trends.

If the Ex-Coloured Man's experience on the lines of color and class can be read as a life lived within a "cosmopolite self-concept," then Johnson's novel affords access to the anxieties and contradictions unvoiced in his history and literary essays promulgating an aesthetic program for the Harlem Renaissance. For Johnson, it seems, the irony of the New Negro artistic position—the fact that just as African Americans reached their height of sophistication, a height that should free them from living narrowly or racially, they are called upon to produce a racial art that would prove their status as worthy of universal regard—proves too much. Not only does Johnson's dandified character resists such identity politics, but so did his creator—one must remember that the novel was published anonymously in 1912 and brought out under Johnson's name only in 1927. Urged into reprint by Carl Van Vechten, himself certainly a dandy and Harlem's most famous honorary Negro, *The Autobiography of an Ex-Coloured Man* was reissued only when, according to Arna Bontemps, the reading public "had . . . become ready for it."[93] Also ironic and instructive, then, is the fact that what the reading public had become ready for was not a text that communicated a kind of racial essence thought to evidence African American humanity and civilization, but rather a text that describes blackness or race in general as entirely resistant to quantification and expression. If Johnson's book can be read as a theory of race that thwarted what the architects of the Renaissance, including himself, advocated to replace African America's "thin coat of culture," then one can read later novels featuring dandy figures in Harlem's vogue as texts that show Johnson's antiessentialist, queer theory in practice.

Negroes Not Standardized

By the 1930s, despite the popularity of the Renaissance's most outrageous cosmopolite sign and manifestation of modernist style, the Hamilton Lodge Ball, the literary dandy was in trouble—so much so that by 1932, Wallace Thurman puts him out of his misery in an unmistakably ironic roman á clef entitled *Infants of the Spring.* Niggerati Manor, Thurman's fictional portrait of a rooming house that reportedly harbored some of the period's leading artists, closes its doors as the proprietor decides that her experiment in supporting Negro art has failed. Tired of late rent payments or none at all from her boarders, all-night parties, and especially the predominance of an air of decadence versus racial progress, she will convert the manor from a "culture maker" into a "money maker," that is, a dormitory for working girls.[94] The transformation of this "miscegenated bawdy house" ends the salon sometimes attended by thinly disguised versions of Alain Locke, Zora Neale Hurston, Langston Hughes, Claude McKay, and Thurman himself.[95] Having no safe haven and no local address, this decidedly bohemian branch of the movement seems destined to wane. Raymond, (the Thurman character), a novelist and nominal leader of the artists' group, is spending his last night in the house when he receives a late night phone call concerning another former resident. The group's inspiration, the poet and painter Paul Arbian, a devotee of the dandies Oscar Wilde, Andreas Huysman, and Baudelaire, has committed suicide. On the way to claim his friend's body, Raymond wonders, "Had Paul the debonair, Paul the poseur, Paul the irresponsible romanticist, finally faced reality and seen himself and the world as they actually were? Or was this merely another act, the final stanza in his drama of beautiful gestures?"[96] Whether a performance or a "beautiful gesture," the dandy's suicide figures as the end of an era, the end of the Harlem literary renaissance.

A "most charming parasite" "with more talent" than the rest of them, Paul is a self-declared genius modeled on the poet Bruce Nugent (who, incidentally, lived until 1987).[97] A painter of impressionistic erotic portraits and weaver of avant-garde sensual tales, he has talent but scoffs at satisfying the demands of others, never mind the competing aesthetic demands of the age. Something of a dilettante, wont to "employ every other conceivable means to make himself stand out from the mob," Paul defies all social conventions, even those of the rather liberal artist group to which he belongs.[98] He is highly unconventional even as a dandy, effecting a "habit not to wear a necktie because he knew his neck was too well modeled to be hidden from public gaze," and "no sox either, nor underwear, and those few clothes he did deign to affect were musty and disheveled."[99] At a salon set up by Dr. Parkes (Alain Locke) in order to convince the group that the "future of the race" rests on their efforts, Paul is the first to refuse the burden the times would place on them to elevate artistically the Negro to full citizenship. To ensure success, Parkes insists that the program include a visitation of the artists' "racial roots, and [a] cultivation [of] a healthy paganism based on African traditions."[100] Facetiously asking if his "German, English and Indian" forefathers also would be included in the ancestral heritage he would bring to his work, Paul then declares that he "ain't got no African spirit" and spends the rest of the meeting listening amusedly as the group fights over the possibility of establishing any concert in their efforts, regardless of whether or not they are based around African tradition.[101]

Paul's unwillingness to sacrifice individual expression to a fantasy of group liberation may strike Renaissance architects as rebellious and counterproductive, but it is consistent with this poet and painter's general policy of indeterminacy. Exclusivity in artistic medium, aesthetic style, celebration of ancestry, and even the gender of his sexual partners bores him. A man who "wooed the unusual, cultivated artificiality, defied all conventions of dress and conduct," he is a spirit, who like his dandy patron saints, will not be limited in any way.[102] An odd or queer New Negro with an aesthetic sense, racial ideology, and sexual practice out of sync with the proprieties of a program of uplift, Paul is on the margins of the map of Renaissance progress, even as he remains a symbolic center for the other artists. Against Dr. Parkes, Paul insists on a definition of modernity that will take advantage of the fact that, as Raymond later declares, "Negroes are the only people in America not standardized."[103]

Paul's passing from life to death arises from his refusal to tow the lines of color and culture, sex and gender. His suicide, of course, becomes a metaphor of the self-implosion of the Harlem Renaissance, the implied failure of its practitioners to balance individuality and group identity, authenticity and multiplicity in their articulation of a modern African American aesthetic. "Debonair," "poseur," unique in fashion and manner, Paul shares the implied antiessentialist stance of the Ex-Coloured Man and demonstrates their affiliation by means of his articulation of the ambiguity of the Ex-Coloured Man's race, gender, and sexuality. Despite its seeming appropriateness for the age, his bohemian life and attitude garner mixed reviews; according to some, Paul's genius has not yet blossomed and "someday he will surprise us all," while others feel that "he had never recovered from the shock of realizing that no matter how bizarre a personality he may develop, he will still be a Negro."[104] Misconstruing his unconventional aesthetic for a frustrated wish to be white, his friend Stephen fails to see that Paul's "bizarre personality" and image as a "most unusual Negro" are instead manifestations of a desire to escape the demand that he personify a certain kind of blackness. Though not a stellar example of a New Negro artist or even a "good Negro" at all, this dandy is truly avant-garde, ahead of the game in his refusal to be a New Negro whose cosmopolitanism must be constituted within oxymoronic limits.

These limits are such an anathema to Paul that, instead of towing the line, he decides instead to cross the line—this time not the lines demarcating black and white, heterosexual and homosexual (which he already defies), but the line between life and death. Indeed, "queers must die" in Harlem Renaissance literature, according to Michael Cobb, in punishment for being those "who wander away from the symbolic and physical Harlem organizing the artistic and emotional lifeworld of the [New Negro] novel."[105] In his reading of the Renaissance's "Impolite Queers," the era's most elegant death, the fantastic suicide of Thurman's Paul, serves as retribution for Paul's inability to "employ a more coherent and clean version of New Negro literary expression."[106] Consequently, Paul pays for the fact that he and others were too "satisfied to woo decadence . . . rather than mingle with the respectable elements of their own race," as an editorial about Niggerati Manor quoted in *Infants of the Spring* claims.[107] Paul's failure to come clean and be respectable in terms of Renaissance aesthetics derives from his penchant for what Cobb calls his literal and symbolic wanderings away from Harlem and its artistic demands.

While Cobb concentrates mostly on Paul's vocal wanderings or his impoliteness, Paul's physical mobility and status as a critic of nearly all kinds of fixity turn him into a flaneur, an analytical stroller through modern New York's physical and ideological space. Unlike many of the other characters in the novel, Paul is extraordinarily mobile, resident in the Village and flitting in and out of Niggerati Manor, while the others seem much more confined within its walls. In his mobility, he resembles Johnson's dandy, the Ex-Coloured Man, who similarly wandered north and then south, east to Europe, and back again, only to settle into indeterminacy, to "let the world take him for what it would." Like the Ex-Coloured Man, Paul gets around; but unlike that of the Ex-Coloured Man, the mobility of Paul's sexuality is not implicit, but explicit. His physical mobility serves as a metaphor for the undetermined path of both his artistic and sexual desires; this is illustrated by his provocative narration of a dream of a sexual encounter that he says begins with the feeling that he "had been walking miles, it seemed . . . somehow or other I didn't want to come home either," and ends in intimacy with a white figure of indeterminate gender.[108] In this dream and elsewhere, Paul will not be confined by heteronormativity or by a facile notion of race loyalty and artistic decorum. His dreams also include travel plans that index the trajectory of his desires and artistic proclivities: in his notebook, he reproduces letters he has sent to the decadent Italian author Gabriele d'Annunzio and the Shah of Persia (then exiled in Paris), in which he declares himself "an artist. A genius. A citizen of the world," who is prevented from joining either of them only by a "financial difficulty" that could certainly be alleviated by their generosity.[109] As a citizen of the world, Paul has visions of a life beyond Harlem and its demands of respectability, beyond black and white, beyond straight and gay. He is an embodiment of modernity, a man with "the ability . . . to see, and by seeing to create, however dimly and intuitively, at the farthest reaches of culture, and, blindly one startling step beyond."[110]

Whereas Harlem architects like Du Bois, Johnson, and others would want to limit the parameters in which New Negro artists work, they cannot, in the end, contain this new or alternative vision of modern blackness. The dandy's multivalent mobility is perilous to New Negro artistic ideology. Even though it seems as if Thurman and others kill the queer or dandy figures in their novels in order to illustrate the potentially grave results of stifling artistic inclinations that wander away from the official program, the dandies in these texts do get the final word. Riding the train downtown to Paul's apartment in the Village, Raymond imagines that his friend's death would be, like his life, a "fascinating spectacle"; as a result, his thoughts are focused not on the reason behind the dandy's "beautiful gesture," but on the manner of its execution. On arrival, Ray discovers that Paul had indeed died in rare form. The mise-en-scène for his final act had been elaborately contrived: the poet and painter had "donned a crimson mandarin robe, wrapped his head in a batik scarf of his own design, hung a group of his spirit portraits on the dingy calcimined wall [of the bathroom], and carpeted the floor with sheets of paper detached from the notebook in which he had been writing his novel."[111] Only a single miscalculation marred the scene, heightening, rather than spoiling, the pathos of the event—while drawing a bath, Paul had slit his wrists and bled to death, causing the tub to overflow, consequently soaking and erasing his novel. It had become totally illegible except for the first page. Indicating the title, "Wu Sing: The Geisha Man," and a dedication to Paul's patron saints Huysmans and Wilde, the page also retains an illustration of a single skyscraper with an eroding base, seemingly spotlit from behind. "At first glance it could be ascertained that the skyscraper would soon crumble and fall, leaving the dominating white lights in full possession of the sky"; but, however much it seemingly foreshadows destruction, the page is perhaps significant more for its mere survival than for its illustra-tion.[112] Once belonging to a nearly complete novel, it is, after all, now the first page of a blank book. The dandy's narrative will seemingly continue, though its author dies.

Although Paul "passes on," he leaves behind both his "ruined" book and a wanderlust common to avant-garde "citizens of the world." Even before his death, Paul affects the more staid Raymond and contrasts with the artistic ambition of the other dandies.[113] Rambling around in Cen-tral Park, avoiding the trip uptown to Harlem, Raymond decides that "he wanted to do something memorable in literature, something that could stay afloat on the contemporary sea of weighted ballast, something which could transcend and survive the transitional age in which he was living," yet he is unsure if he has the talent.[114] As Cobb proclaims, "If one queerly wanders in and out of Harlem, then the solid artistic frame of Harlem begins to disappear."[115] For these dandy queers, mobility engenders ques-tions about the possibility of surviving the transition between old, New, and even newer Negro aesthetics with one's convictions and desires in-tact. Although it may seem as though the dandy is sacrificed in Harlem to maintain a kind of provinciality and rigidity about its artistic project, instead, the dandy's disappearance should be read not as sacrificial but as potentially salutary. After all, it is the combination of his contrariness and mobility that really defines the dandy's dangerousness and makes possible his return from elsewhere.

At the end of *Infants of the Spring*, the future potential and legacy of Paul's dandyish philosophy of black modern identity seems, at best, at risk. Even so, one might more productively read this death and the pass-ing of other dandy insurgents during the era as "not really murders but metaphors."[116] Though Paul's life and death are perhaps meant to dem-onstrate the "toxicity of a queerly-inflected conception of race and art," one actually has both toxicity and a more hopeful organicism at the end of *Infants of the Spring*.[117] In her study called "Harlem's Queer Dandy," Elisa Glick points out that the nature of the dedication Thurman affixes to Paul's novel challenges a reading of the ending of *Infants of the Spring* as one in which the dandy becomes a martyr. She argues that the book's dedication, especially its final lines, shows that "Thurman himself under-cuts a tragic reading of the queer aesthete" by ending his book and begin-ning Paul's legacy with the following:

To
Huysmans' Des Esseintes and Oscar Wilde's Oscar Wilde
Ecstatic Spirits with whom I Cohabit
And whose golden spores of decadent pollen
I shall broadcast and fertilize.
It is written.[118]

Though dead in body, the dandy will live on, as he remains both an artist and an author of unfinished projects: "golden spores of decadent pollen" are released in this moment, and "these spores will take root in the new dialectical consciousness engendered by the culture of modernity."[119] These spores will be nurtured and blossom elsewhere, travel, necessarily, across time and genre. For though Paul dies here and the content of his story is erased, one might consider the afterlife of the actual story upon which much of Paul's ideology is based: Richard Bruce Nugent's short story "Smoke, Lilies and Jade" (1926), the first literary piece in the African American tradition with openly queer content. It is this story that forms the set piece of the subject of my next chapter, Isaac Julien's *Looking for Langston*. It is Julien's visual styling of "Langston's" search for the deferred dream of Nugent's "Beauty" that brings the black dandy back.[120]

While the dandy in Thurman's book makes a claim for Harlem's modernist aesthetics as that which should not or cannot be standardized, this lesson is one that applies to modernism in general. The dandies in these books perform a black modernism that places modernism in conversation with the Harlem Renaissance while at the same time proposing a black modernist discursive practice that finds its specificity in heterogeneity, not authenticity or imitation. What the black dandy reveals — the productive necessity of play and indeterminacy — forces one to see modernism as modernisms, and modernisms in *and as* both black and white, mulatto. The figure's redefinition of blackness and modernism does not allow for either concept to be entirely recognizable — for to present blackness as something discernible would be to play too close to the lines of stereotype, to present modernism as that which is the concern of those on "High," as audible as a distinctive sound or as a derivative look would limit its power as a tool of group and self-fashioning. Instead, when looking through the lens of the black dandy in the modernist period, what one sees are performances of modernity in, to borrow a description of an earlier mode of black performance, Negro Election Day, "uniforms—anything but uniform." Harlem's black dandies communicate a sense of self and culture, in black and white, that is experimental out of fear, necessity, strategy, and joy. When one searches for signs of modernist arrival and participation, what emerges is a sense of what modernism means for blackness and what blackness means for modernism: a notion that modern identity is—if at all definitive—essentially mixed. As such, the black dandy affirms the importance of the mix to the cultural survival and evolution of all, while arguing for a conception of blackness and modernity as perceptible processes—across the lines of gender, sexuality, and class—rather than voices or looks one has heard and seen before.

5

"You Look Beautiful Like That"

BLACK DANDYISM AND VISUAL HISTORIES
OF BLACK COSMOPOLITANISM

I ask you to note how, within the black repertoire, *style*—which
mainstream cultural critics often believe to be the mere husk,
the wrapping, the sugar coating on the pill—has become *itself* the
subject of what is going on . . . think of how these cultures have
used the body—as if it was, and often it was, the only cultural
capital we had. We have worked on ourselves as the canvases of
representation.

    STUART HALL, "What Is the 'Black' in Black Popular Culture?"

The dandy is far more than a stylish person with a unique approach
to his ciphered vocabulary of wardrobe choice. A dandy's clothes
are a reflection of his individual disposition in sharp relief to the
clothed masses of designer-clad armies. Within a dandiacal context, the use of clothes goes beyond the traditional class / designer
status symbol. A dandy's insignia of sartorial eloquence is a distinct art which eludes critical taxonomy. . . . In the end, a dandy's
style is not just about form and substance. It is also about the luxurious deliberation of intelligence in the face of boundaries.

    IKÉ UDÉ, "Post-Colonial Flaneur"

The aesthete does not have to be reactionary. My reclamation of
aesthetics has more in common with the strategies of a trickster
who is utterly impossible to place because he is a fun-lover who is
at home with confusion, but politically astute. Beauty is political
when it is appropriated by the "other," of course. The trickster is
unknowable because he is always in disguise.

    YINKA SHONIBARE, "Global Tendencies: Globalism
    and the Large-Scale Exhibition"

Are we post-black? When we think about blackness and its relationship to literary and visual culture in the early twenty-first century, have we, perhaps inevitably, come to post-blackness? If so, how do we read post-blackness? What does it look like? All of this depends, of course, on how the terms are defined. In 2001, Thelma Golden, the head curator of the Studio Museum in Harlem, coined the phrase "post-black" to describe the work of a group of young, emerging black artists whose works she had assembled for an exhibition titled "Freestyle." Originating in conversations with the artist Glenn Ligon as a kind of shorthand for "a discourse that could fill volumes," "post-black" began, at first, as a description of "artists who were adamant about not being labeled as 'black' artists, though their work was steeped, in fact deeply interested, in redefining complex notions of blackness."[1] Since the average age of the artists in the show was about thirty, they had come up in a world that had weathered "the vital political activism of the 1960s, the focused, often essentialist, Black Arts Movement of the 1970s, the theory-driven multiculturalism of the 1980s, and the late globalist expansion of the 1990s."[2] Golden's implicit question to the art world at the beginning of a new millennium—What next?—generated a group of unbelievably intriguing and diverse answers, perhaps not quantifiable or able to be labeled by anything other than the provocative term "post-black." For Golden, a post-black aesthetic, like its creators, "embrace[s] dichotomies of high and low, inside and outside, tradition and innovation, with great ease and facility"; it is, unsurprisingly, a freestyle.[3] Yet, as hinted above, this style is purposeful in that it "speaks to an individual freedom that is the result of this transitional moment in the quest to define ongoing changes in the evolution of African American art and ultimately to ongoing redefinitions of blackness in contemporary culture."[4] "Post-black," then, is a term that allows contemporary artists and cultural critics to potentially delimit blackness from both a subjective and objective perspective.

In her introduction to the exhibition, Golden calls attention to the way in which black dandyism could be a part of this discussion when she unwittingly invokes the language of fashion in the exhibition's title. While for her "freestyle" is primarily a musical metaphor applied to fine art, the concept also invokes style as a mode of self-presentation as well—*freestyle*. As part of a group often forced to use the self as a canvas for representation, as Stuart Hall mentions above, dandies have historically experimented with style as an articulation of freedom and self-possession. When Golden said of the "Freestyle" exhibition that "post-black was the new black," her parody of the old-fashion maxim begs the question of what kind of relationship a free style can or should have to notions of black self-presentation, within and without the black art world. Can black dandies, in their aggressive critique of the categories that constitute identity, fill in some of the chapters of this post-black "discourse that could fill volumes"? Here I want to discuss how dandies and their representation in contemporary art embody the debates around black identity in the late twentieth century and early twenty-first and the way in which they experiment with their bodies and the history of black fashion and self-fashioning.

Throughout this book, I have attempted to read the black dandy and dandyism as strategic, as part of a negotiation of oppressive ideologies and degrading images of blackness. I have described black dandyism as part of a process of imagining and imaging the black body and conceptions of blackness as, to borrow a phrase from chapter 4, "one startling step beyond" the limitations of contemporary practices. In eighteenth-century England, this "beyond" allowed so-called prestige slaves to turn their forced foppery into a self-spectacularization that complicated their commodification and role as "objects in the midst of other objects."[5] In the transition from slavery to freedom in nineteenth-century America, forms of dandyism enabled Africans and African Americans to imagine themselves as new people by confronting essentializing blackface parodies of black progress with memories of the syncretic nature of African style. Black dandyism in the early twentieth century emerged as a sign that these new people now considered themselves modern, cosmopolitan, urban, part of a debate on how to reform, worldwide, conceptions of blackness and of black people in the diaspora. Here, dandyism functioned as a kind of eye on a world beyond the color line, a world in which the limitations imposed by race, gender, sexuality, economics, or the demands of an artistic movement were, for moments, not impermeable. In all of these instances, black dandyism functions as a kind of visible sign of the modern black imaginary, a kind of "freedom dream."[6] This dream is dreamt with knowledge of its limitations, but it is dreamt nevertheless, to imagine and then find ways to go beyond.

A mode of self-creation, a type of cultural capital, a way to express the potential political nature of black beauty—as the epigraphs to this chapter indicate, this is a story of black dandyism in the late twentieth century and early twenty-first. I say "a story" rather than "the story" because, after the explosion of black style on the streets and in the imaginations of the residents of Harlem and of the artists of the Harlem Renaissance, the concept of black dandyism itself experienced a significant change—another type of explosion. Its supposed death in the literary culture of the Renaissance era would not be nearly the end of the dandy's story—the dream would take a slightly different, even more visible or visual form. While the circumstances that led to the cultural renaissance in Harlem—the mass influx of black people versed in the use of style—prompted black writers to use the dandy figure as an expression of black modernity, many other blacks of that time took the practice of dandyism, the strategic mobilization of style and appearance, into other arenas also invested in redefining blackness. In the early twentieth century, it was principally within the gay and lesbian community and the entertainment industry that black dandyism flourished; later, the art world too became an arena in which dandyism presented a challenge to notions of blackness from within and without the heterogeneous black community. Over the course of the century, the rise and then predominance of mass consumer culture and the politics of consumption have, at every turn, complicated dandyism's critical acumen. One wonders if, in the early twenty-first century, we might be both post-dandy and post-black.

Post-black and Pre-black

"What ever happens to a dream deferred? / What ever happens to a dream deferred / The life that was hidden / That you felt was forbidden / We're seeking the truth, because we want to know you": these lines from Blackberri's "Blues for Langston" are the refrain of the soundtrack of Isaac Julien's film from 1989 *Looking for Langston.* An emendation to Langston Hughes's classic poem "Montage of a Dream Deferred," these lyrics accompany scenes of handsome, elegantly dressed black gay men dancing in an underground club, making love in a sparsely furnished bedroom, confronting their desires in a field of poppies and calla lilies. The "we" of the song seems to direct its inquiry at these men and, consequently, at their appearance; "the life that was hidden" is lived both subversively and, sometimes, in fancy dress. While it is now a commonplace to say that the Harlem Renaissance was "surely as gay as it was black, not that it was exclusively one of these," in 1989, when *Looking for Langston* was first screened, such a statement created much controversy within the African American community and the African diaspora.[7] Even though the sound-track intones that "we're seeking the truth, because we want to know you," the truth sought is specific not to the nature of Hughes's sexuality, but to the history and legacy of a queer presence in African American and African diaspora culture and to the way in which that presence modifies past and present conceptions of black identity. Even if the gayness of the Harlem cultural world had long been an open secret, Julien's decision to tell the secret in the form of a truly gorgeous black and white medita-tion on Harlem culture, equal parts documentary and historically based fantasy of the politics of self-fashioning, caused a great uproar. Provoca-tive to the film's detractors and champions alike was its alleged outing of Hughes, who had been declared to be asexual by his biographers and, perhaps more controversially, its absolute insistence on portraying the beauty of the black body, both clothed and naked. That Julien decided to portray this presence with a pronounced attention to black male looks in terms of both fashion and the gaze indicates that the dandy certainly did not die as a purveyor of modern ideas about blackness in the Harlem era. Rather, as Julien recovers this presence and legacy, *Looking for Langston* allows one to connect this meditation on race, sexuality, and the politics of art with the more recent debates on post-blackness. Do the post-black aesthetic and its potential problematics originate in the Harlem Renais-sance? Is post-black the new New Negro?

If the literature of the Harlem Renaissance dramatized the death of the dandy, then art house cinema and its subsequent reverberations in the art world of the 1980s re-create both the dandy's funeral and his res-urrection. Fittingly, the dandy's return begins, in fact, where he left off and remarkably combines mourning for the figure's lost potential in the Harlem Renaissance with a present-day reunion of the African diaspora. Extending an "invitation to see oneself in a dream of the Harlem Renais-sance," *Looking for Langston* strategically locates that reverie not exclu-sively in the home of its eponymous lost object, Langston Hughes—that is, in Harlem Renaissance–era New York—but also in what its director calls the "mid-Atlantic."[8] The film is conceived and directed by Julien, a black British filmmaker, and combining African American cultural history with narration and voiceover in British English. Past meets present, and black Britain reaches out to African America as the film "looks" for Langston from a black, gay, diasporic perspective in the speakeasies of 1920s Harlem, in the words of Bruce Nugent, James Baldwin, and Essex Hemphill, in the artwork of James Van Der Zee and Robert Mapplethorpe. In *Looking for Langston*, black dandies come to life on the screen as commentary on the connection between these past and present black gay and diasporic identities and the challenge they present to contemporary notions of blackness and masculinity. This connection is signaled by the film's first sequence, which seamlessly joins together archival film footage of a train arriving at (or leaving) 125th Street station, a constructed vignette of a group of highly stylized mourners gathered over the casket of "Langston," and a scene of a romantically lit, smoky, seemingly underground club full of slow-dancing gay male couples. All of these men are exquisitely groomed and in tuxedos, arrested in mid-dance. When the jazzy refrain of "Blues for Langston" sounds out, the men start dancing, as if on cue—Harlem's dandies are thus reanimated, reembodied.

The Langston figure and the mourners are associated with the dandies in the club by means of the camera movement, the black-and-white film stock, and, most important, their elegant costumes. Perhaps signaling his desire to fashion a history of the diaspora and to do so partly by means of dress, Julien styles this opening sequence not only as both historical and contemporary, but also as diasporic in that he himself portrays the mourned Langston lying in the casket. This telescoping of past and present and its association with dandyism then and now unites aesthetic issues of the Harlem Renaissance era with contemporary concerns about a black artist's negotiation of his or her sexual, racial, gender, and national identities. The film locates and fantasizes about the possibilities of a transatlantic modernity and a new definition of blackness and masculinity for the black community and its artists through its striking mise-en-scène and its styling of the black male body. Rather than a gratuitous over-aestheticization of the era and its personalities, the stylization of the film is an integral part of a reformative effort. The malleability of the black male images is part of the film's overall quest to reinsert imaginatively black gay bodies into the Renaissance, to assert their influence and presence and those of less "masculinist" men in the artistic life of the black diaspora. In fact, their malleability signifies in both the past and the present; they are necessarily supple as figures teased out of a fantasy, a reconstructed past, as much as they are present-day alternatives to "a hardened convention of [black male] representation."⁹ Throughout the film, these seemingly sophisticated men, embodiments of what Manthia Diawara calls "plastic beauty," confront both the power and the failure of their own ability to embody some of these debates.¹⁰

In revisioning the Harlem Renaissance from his late twentieth-century vantage point in the diaspora, Julien works under the sign of Langston Hughes, but not at all under the image of the avuncular older poet shown in the film. Instead, he takes his inspiration from Hughes's words, and not just his poetry. Hughes's poem collage "Montage of a Dream Deferred" is an obvious influence in the film, as a sense of deferral, longing, and disappointment dominates each vignette within it. Indeed, longing or deferral is also communicated by means of montage; as José Esteban Muñoz argues via a fittingly fashionable metaphor, Julien's film weaves together "fabrics that are not traditionally found within the tapestry of montage cinema: materials that include poems, experimental fiction, still photographs, vintage newsreels, and blues songs."¹¹ Less obvious an influence but as important is Julien's debt to Hughes's defiant essay "The Negro Artist and the Racial Mountain" (1926). Written in response to an essay by the conservative George Schuyler entitled "The Negro Art Hokum" (1926, originally published in *The Nation*), which rails against the proscriptiveness and Victorian nature of the aesthetic aspirations of Alain Locke and Du Bois, "The Negro Artist and the Racial Mountain" changed the course of the Harlem Renaissance. Speaking for "the younger negro artists," Hughes publicly announces in the last paragraph of the essay a generational split in aesthetic ideology and calls for freedom from self-consciousness at last: "We younger negro artists who create now intend to express our individual dark-skinned selves without fear or shame. If white people are pleased we are glad. If they are not, it doesn't matter. *We know we are beautiful.* And ugly too. The tom-tom cries and the tom-tom laughs. If coloured people are pleased we are glad. If they are not, their displeasure doesn't matter either. We build our temples for tomorrow, strong as we know how, and we stand on top of the mountain, free within ourselves" (italics added).[12] Positioning himself, like Hughes in 1926, as a critical young gun, Julien adopts and transforms into images Hughes's desire for artistic expression "without fear or shame" and heedless of the consequences.

In interviews, Julien indicates that with *Looking for Langston* he had aspirations of impacting the "black literary academy": "There were debates I wanted to be a part of, discourses that had yet to be written. . . . The heterosexism of black studies and the homophobia of the black nationalist framework of looking at black texts limited the whole debate."[13] Telling Paul Gilroy in 1993 that he hoped to use this last paragraph of Hughes's essay in the film but was prevented from doing so by Hughes's estate, Julian prompts one to see the film in light of Hughes's words as it dares to visualize what is unable to be said, even within the film itself—"We know we are beautiful . . . we stand on top of the mountain, free within ourselves." Believing that "the image could provide a much more powerful intervention than the written text,"[14] Julien fantasizes about the Harlem Renaissance and the queer subjectivities that populated it, bringing Langston back to life more as a Nugent-inspired bohemian than as the sweetly charming black cultural icon with which readers have become comfortable. Julien's decision to rehabilitate black literary culture visually allows him to represent this defiant voice and its call for an unashamed, fearless artistic expression by means of and as a queer, black beauty. Much more concerned with staging a vision of the milieu in which these Harlemites lived and created their work than with outing Hughes, Julien "'looks back' and finds a history of black art, a history of representations of blackness and a history of black homosexuality . . . and 'talks back' these histories by collating them"—collating them in the collaged structure of the film that centers itself on dandified images of blackness.[15]

Blackness *is* beautiful in *Looking for Langston*.[16] In fact, if one is to see Julien's contribution to the potential of post-black art, one might start by recognizing that in *Looking for Langston* he uses a cue from Hughes himself to revise the homophobia and sexism of the black arts movement that initially coined the "beautiful" phrase. If the slogan "black is beautiful" "cleared the ground for the cultural recognition of a positive self-image . . . at the expense of black women, gays, and lesbians," then, as it is animated by Julien in *Looking for Langston*, it becomes a statement on a new sense of empowerment and history making for black and gay nearly three decades later.[17] Not simply the result of portraying "positive images" of black gay life, the beauty in this film and its embodiment in the well dressed and the naked matter much more. Both pleasurable and confrontational, simultaneously subversive and potentially deadly, beauty seduces in *Looking for Langston*, in terms of form and content. Julien's stylish, sophisticated mise-en-scène and his use and revision of Nugent's story "Smoke, Lilies and Jade" associate beauty with a desire to defy filmic, narrative, aesthetic, and nationalistic expectations. Indeed, Nugent's provocative story centers around a young, queer Harlemite's pursuit of a man named Beauty. *Looking for Langston* thus becomes not only a queer film about queer history, but also a dandyish film about the dandy as symbol of modern black aesthetics. In exploring the work as a film about dandyism, one should not forget that *Looking for Langston* begins with an extremely elegant funeral and ends with an image of a black Narcissus, and in between is a melancholic search for beauty / Beauty.

"We know we are beautiful" — the film's visual style is as much a part of its meaning as its subject and action. As Kobena Mercer says of Julien's work in general, "Pleasure is at the heart of the work, beauty a quality of critique."[18] A meditation rather than a documentary, *Looking for Langston* metafilmically performs its subject and the phrase that seems to have inspired its look. The look of the film and the looks between men are the film's narrative elements as much as the voiceover that explicitly juxtaposes what one might call pre- and post-black attitudes to racial definition. In fact, Stuart Hall's British voice in the film quotes the black nationalist Amiri Baraka as understanding Harlem as "vicious modernism," a combination of opportunity and peril, and then asks if, given this sentiment, Baraka "could understand the beauty of people with freakish ways?" Julien's visual styling of the film asks one to ruminate on one's own identification and disidentification with this "freakish" beauty. Though opening with a scene of mourning, the film is a memorial for the gay luminaries of the Renaissance (Hughes, Thurman, Cullen, Nugent, etc.), their descendants (Baldwin), and the sufferers of the AIDS pandemic, but it is also a "hyperbolic expression of a stereotypically faggy sense of style" that some critics have found both enervating and liberating.[19] bell hooks writes, "There is so much beauty and elegance in the film that it has the quality of both spectacle and masquerade, all of which can obscure the ways this beauty has tragic dimensions, elements of longing and loss, that lead to depression and despair."[20] Though hooks fears that Julien risks a too-close association between desire and death, spectacle and masquerade, I argue that when read through the lens of dandyism Julien's effort to visualize a queer aesthetic of blackness is visionary, a vital precursor to an aesthetic of post-blackness, the "re-defining of complex notions of blackness." Important in communicating the plasticity and viability of this beauty and its life-affirming potential are costume and a discourse of dressing and undressing that pervades the film.[21]

Choosing first to portray the "freakish" beauty of Harlem's gay underground in the tuxedo, perhaps the most recognizable and accepted uniform of masculine respectability, Julien begins the recovery of what Diawara calls the "Absent Ones" conventionally, it seems, with the replacement or masking of transgression with propriety.[22] However, the look in *Looking for Langston* cannot be so easily read, especially if one thinks of the bodies within these sexy suits as being queer and dandy, bodies who have a history of infiltrating, mocking, and establishing new conventions, primarily through the exploitation of a look. Though it seems as if Julien begins the film with a discourse on positive male images, he endeavors to go well beyond that subject, as he not only queers the Renaissance visually, but does so at the level of wardrobe. When trying to read this aspect of the formal beauty of *Looking for Langston*, one should remember, as Diawara notes, that Locke argues in *The New Negro* that the true novelty of the Harlem Renaissance "has been their [blacks'] achievement in bringing the artistic advance of the Negro sharply into stepping alignment with contemporary artistic thought, mood, and style. They are thoroughly modern, some of them ultra-modern, and Negro thoughts now wear the uniform of the age."[23] In Julien's film, the uniform of the age(s) is the tuxedo; when worn by the gay men representing, in part, Harlem's early twentieth-century queer artistic underground, the tuxedo becomes an ultramodern uniform designed to disturb rather than neatly align conventional "Negro thoughts" about art and identity.

I say the tuxedo represents the queer artistic underground "in part" because, as historians of gay New York and the Harlem Renaissance have shown, Harlem's gay culture was not most visible in the speakeasies in which gay couples are presented in this film. Rather, gay Harlem was more famously on display at the drag balls, like the Hamilton Lodge Ball discussed in chapter 4, at which men appeared in sequined dresses, not

26. Isaac Julien and Sunil Gupta. *Looking for Langston Series (No. 8) Portrait No. 2 with Flowers*, 1989. © Isaac Julien and Sunil Gupta.

suits. In *Gay New York* George Chauncey indicates that working-class Harlem generally tolerated gay men, especially drag queens in clubs and speakeasies, as female impersonators, other entertainers, and hostesses, and even, for the most part, on the street as ordinary citizens.[24] Respectable Harlem could not tolerate openly homosexual people, even if they were "cultured folk," as Julien makes clear with his focus on Hughes and his assumed social circle. Regardless of their look and the social circle to which their dress might relegate them, openly gay Harlemites were denounced publicly by journalists and ministers, Adam Clayton Powell among them. They were more quietly dismissed by the respectable classes—the middle-class, professionals, and the intelligentsia—even though this group often knew the open secret of many of its members and of the gay social and artistic networks they formed. "There was a difference between the public styles of middle-class and working-class gay men," according to Chauncey; although the "serene elegance and pomp" of the film might suggest otherwise, this is a difference Julien uses here to aesthetic rather than classist effect.[25] In order to visualize the depth of Harlem's closet and to recover a theory of beauty there, Julien searches way inside of it, past the sequins to the suits. The tuxedo's role in the film is the clue to its potentially democratic purpose as "ultra-modern uniform" and unexpected symbol of a more inclusive aesthetic theory that uses formal beauty to queer purpose.

Important to this reading is the fact that tuxedos, and even black tailcoats with white tie, are never worn at funerals; rather, they are more often the uniform of celebrations, of stepping out. Black tailcoat and white tie had been de rigueur for gentlemen as formal wear for centuries, but the short, black dinner jacket is a modern invention. According to legend, the tuxedo originates as an elite garment whose provenance is transatlantic (like *Looking for Langston*): inspired by a short dinner jacket first worn by the Prince of Wales in 1886, the tuxedo was named after the home city of the American socialite who brought it back to America and popularized it for the fashionistas of New York—Tuxedo Park, New York.[26] Blacks had been in formal dress as servants and entertainers for hundreds of years before the tuxedo's appearance, as countless paintings, prints, and illustrations of blackface and black minstrel music can attest. Despite the black tailcoat's place in communicating this social and racial hierarchy, the tuxedo and formal dress in general can be, by virtue of their very uniformity, more egalitarian garments. When tuxedoed, the poor can pass for rich, men for women; class, gender, and perceived racial hierarchies can be disguised, confused, unintentionally or deliberately transgressed. Therefore, the seeming exclusivity that the uniform represents can be infiltrated. In *Looking for Langston*, this is precisely what happens: the tuxedo that enables passing and disguise is here also a mark of belonging, a mode of connection — to get into this club, one must wear the ultramodern uniform. Doing so allows and even demands that one appropriate and transform its power.

In the film, the tuxedo as uniform of convention is challenged by the same-sex desiring bodies who wear and manipulate it. Worn exclusively by gay men and a pair of lesbians (two tuxedoed women appear in a joyful dance scene at the end), the uniform is queered and performed; as the story of the film progresses, it is used, abandoned, and taken up again, though slightly differently, by these same figures. Since *Looking for Langston* is not a true documentary but a meditative fantasy, one can see what one critic calls its "1920s costume" as not merely historical but symbolic, an analog for desire.[27] When worn by these men as the dress code of their club, it manifests a desire to belong — not to mainstream society but to this particular club. As David Deitcher argues, the lily worn by the Langston figure in his lapel "signals more than a funerary context," referring instead to "Oscar Wilde's favorite floral accessory," to "Smoke, Lilies and Jade," the title of Nugent's queer story, and to Jack Smith's film "Flaming Creatures" (1962), one of the first underground films of "perverse" pleasures.[28] As such, the suit and its accessory literally materialize the community Julien seeks. When abandoned, as in the vignette in the "field of dreams," its lack communicates a further desire, as Hughes states in "The Negro Artist," to be "free within ourselves." When critics reflect on the beautiful look of the film, they cite both the fancy clothing and the nakedness of the elegant male cast; Julien does not privilege one over another. Both can be, simultaneously and alternatively, the ultramodern uniform.[29] In *Looking for Langston*, the beautiful is both dressed and undressed, dandy and naked. Thus, the aesthetics valued here are not only those associated with the respectable, queer, or those stripped of masks and spectacle, but all three; this multiplicity opens up space for a radical revision of black aesthetics.

In *Sex and Suits*, the fashion historian Anne Hollander argues that the enduring popularity of the male suit is due to the fact that "among all the more showily revealing varieties of current male dress, it has kept the ability to make [that] nude suggestion."[30] For her, "the naked male body, coherent and articulated, must still be the ghostly visual image and the underlying formal suggestion made by any ordinary male Western costume."[31] What Hollander claims for all suits is certainly the case for the tuxedo here. As we've seen in the case of the blackface minstrel dandy, the "nude suggestion" motivated the excitement and fear of black men in fancy dress, as their clothing was associated with transgression and sexual power in songs like "Long-Tail Blue." In *Looking for Langston*, Julien uses the "nude suggestion" slightly differently, presenting it in a way that allows the black gay men in the film and the film viewer to luxuriate in it, celebrating the aesthetic freedom it might symbolize. Just as one must look carefully at the tuxedo in the film and ruminate over its several meanings, the nude, naked, or (un)dressed bears the same scrutiny.[32] Crucial to reading the "nude suggestion" in this film is reading its impetus—nearly all of the undressed scenes in the film function as a dream within the film's already dreamy atmosphere and arise from other moments in which pointed, desirous, and sometimes cutting looks are exchanged. The most consequential of these scenes, which eventuates in a meeting of the tuxedoed and naked, occurs near the beginning of the film when the pivotal moment of "Smoke, Lilies and Jade" is dramatized and Beauty is discovered.

The scene shows Alex, the Langston figure, sitting at the club bar, smoking and drinking champagne. He looks out into the crowd and locks eyes with a man seated at a table with his white lover. Alex's interest in the man is noticed and dismissed by the white lover; unable to pursue their momentary connection, Alex and the man turn away from each other. Alex remains at the bar and watches another man be similarly chastised by the white lover (with the bat of an eye heavy with mascara) for looking at his date. Alex continues to look at the interracial couple and sips a glass of champagne while the camera rests directly on his face. The scene cuts to a long pan over a naked male body lying face down on a bed, while the white man and his lover, standing behind the bed, undress. Next, Alex, in his tuxedo, with a lily in his lapel, is walking through a field, past small pools of water reflecting the sunlight, determinedly following a path delimited by flags. Eventually he stops in front of the sculpted, naked body of a light-skinned black man (in Nugent's story, he is Latino) also standing in the field; he smiles and finds his smile returned. The narration of an excerpt from "Smoke, Lilies and Jade" begins:

> He was in a field . . . a field of blue smoke and black poppies and red calla lilies . . . he was searching . . . on his hands and knees . . . searching . . . among black poppies and red calla lilies . . . he was searching . . . pushed aside poppy stems . . . and saw two strong white legs . . . dancer's legs . . . the contours pleased him . . . his eyes wandered . . . on past the muscular hocks to the firm white thighs . . . rounded buttocks . . . then the lithe narrow waist . . . strong torso and broad deep chest . . . the brown eyes looking at him . . . his hair curly and black and all tousled . . . it was Beauty . . . and Beauty smiled and looked at him and smiled . . . said I'll wait. . . . And Alex became confused and continued his search . . . on his hands and knees . . . pushing aside poppy stems and lily stems . . . black poppies . . . and . . . lilies . . . red lilies . . .

As these last lines are being said, Alex turns away from Beauty, retraces his steps past the flags and the pools of water. The scene cuts back to the bedroom; this time Alex and Beauty are naked, in the bed together. Alex is smoking, Beauty sleeping, and the narration continues:

> And he awoke. . . . Beauty was smiling in his sleep . . . half his face stained flush color by the sun . . . the other half in shadow . . . his eyelashes casting cobweby blue shadows on his cheek . . . his lips were so beautiful . . . I would kiss your lips . . . he *would* like to kiss Beauty's lips . . . he flushed warm with shame . . . or was it shame . . . his pulse was hammering . . . from wrist to fingertips . . . Beauty's lips touched his . . . his temples throbbed . . . Beauty's breath came short now . . . softly staccato . . . Beauty's lips pressed cool . . . cool and hard . . . how much pressure does it take to awaken one . . . he could feel his breath on his nostrils and lips . . . Beauty's breath pushed hard against his teeth . . . he trembled . . . he could feel Beauty's body close against his . . . hot . . . tense . . . and soft . . . soft . . .

The scene shifts back to the club, where the slow dancers are now kissing, embracing, and dancing drunkenly. Alex remains at the bar talking and drinking.

A discourse about clothing maps on to a discourse about aesthetics

27. Isaac Julien and Sunil Gupta. *Looking for Langston Series (No. 5) Masquerade No. 4*, 1989. © Isaac Julien and Sunil Gupta.

throughout the film and especially here, as the exchange of looks in the club prompts a reverie in which Alex and Beauty, tuxedo and nude, confront one another. The dreamy nature of the film and Beauty's name encourage the viewer to read Beauty's interaction with Alex as allegorical. Thus, this confrontation is not one between the characters Alex and Beauty only, but also that between hard and "soft . . . soft" black male images, Langston and his deferred dream, and the Harlem Renaissance aesthetics and its ultramodern other. If, during the Harlem era, dandies in texts had attempted to promote New Negro expression free of the demands of respectability, in *Looking for Langston* Julien achieves this expression by using the figure to imagine and image the possibility of a definition of blackness and masculinity outside of this positive-negative, respectability debate. Like Hughes, Julien labels this possibility beautiful; following Nugent, he personifies it as Beauty. When the two meet in the field, after Alex's search, the dandy confronts not his traditional other, that is, racist, homophobic, misogynist stereotypes designed to vilify the image of the black, but a new other—a naked, desirable self-other, a manifestation of an ultramodern conception of black identity that cultivates black beauty not as a reaction, but for its own sake. This dream is a vision of blackness constituted outside of binaries. In presenting the dandy as both a response to stereotypes and in a potential union with a new, naked vision of the possibilities for black identity and aesthetics, *Looking for Langston* resurrects and actually re-presents the power of the dandy figure to image black identity "one startling step beyond" New Negro convention—outside of a discourse of fear and shame. This meeting is not, as hooks argues, the mere vision of a "counter-aesthetic,"[33] but the discovery of an alternative or future aesthetic that values beauty for beauty's sake, art for art's sake, all the while being attentive to the historical, racial, and sexual politics that inform the radicality of such a claim. Functioning as an example of "masculinity unmasked," these "vulnerable, soft, even passive" black male bodies provocatively take up the question Fanon poses (but never answers) in *Black Skin, White Masks*— "What does a black man want?"[34] As it stages a confrontation between these differently masculine men, *Looking for Langston* recognizes and encourages self-fashioning as a redemptive practice across time and space, transtemporally and transatlantically.

At the moment this possibility is presented, it is ostensibly delayed when Beauty says, "I'll wait." Even though Alex and Beauty reappear in the bedroom, this time together, the ending of the scene is haunted by the unanswered question, "How much pressure does it take to awaken one?" While many critics read this line primarily as a rejection or denial of sexual desire (hooks argues that "the seeker must confront a desire that has no end, that leads him to situations where he is acknowledged and abandoned, yet he must continue to search"), Julien's staging of the entire sequence in which it appears encourages a broader reading.[35] The "one" here can be both Alex and Beauty; if Alex, then the line refers to Langston's difficulty in fulfilling his desires; if Beauty, the line references the difficulty of realizing the new aesthetic vision this meeting offers. Looking at Langston and Beauty, the dandy and his "nude suggestion" together, desiring one another, one can see that Julien is not "imagina-tively constructing an aesthetic universe where beauty merges with death and decay,"[36] but imagining an aesthetic universe in which an earlier, exclusionary version of "black is beautiful" has been appropriated and re-presented. Julien might be seen here, in Deitcher's words, as a "roman-tic and visionary who uses film to imagine the way that things can be," rather than only a purveyor of "what happens in a racist and homopho-bic world."[37] In *Looking for Langston*, one sees blackness and masculinity being defined in a truly revolutionary manner, inclusively and not in terms of opposition (whether between black and white, straight and gay, male and female)—hence one arrives at a moment of post-blackness that is still grounded in, but not limited by, history—beautiful *and* still black. This possibility is, admittedly, arrested in *Looking for Langston*, but it is not dead or murdered, as in some of the Harlem-era texts that inspired it. That it is seen and stilled, visualized and arrested, matters because, as such, like the dancing dandies at the beginning of the film, it can be reanimated in the future.

A pervasive sense of longing for this unrealized future does envelop the film, nevertheless. Julien associates such longing with arrest and still-ness, as both dandies and nudes find themselves in limbo and in mo-tion, forestalled and animated as ideas. As it moves from club to field and back to club, the film becomes an elaborate tableau vivant in which past, present, and future conceptions of black identity and consciousness are seen. Just as Hughes's "The Negro Artist and the Racial Mountain" and Nugent's "Smoke, Lilies and Jade" inspired Julien to see the aesthetics of the Harlem Renaissance differently, the actual still images in this motion picture, the photographs Julien imports into the film, perform a similar talismanic function. When Julien stages Alex's search for Beauty in the poppy field as a metatextual moment of looking in the film, he places photographic portraits of the "Absent Ones"—represented by Hughes, Nugent, and Baldwin—alongside those of striving early-century Harlem-ites by James Van Der Zee and those of black men by Robert Mapple-thorpe in order to teach the viewer how to read them.[38] One searches with Alex, here, one looks and remembers with Julien—one must regard these images, consider them. That one notices the ways in which both sets of portraits have the ability to bring back the dead is the ultimate goal of their presence in *Looking for Langston*. The nature of the photograph as

28. Isaac Julien and Sunil Gupta. *Looking for Langston Series, (No. 17) The Last Angel of History*, 1989. © Isaac Julien and Sunil Gupta.

a memorial and motivation allows it to anchor dreams and, as Julien adds his own still images to these, extends the archive of images that arrest one's attention.

Early twentieth-century Harlem is remembered primarily through its visual representation. The nature of that representation, its status as a particular site of memorial for this period, is the result of the meeting of two historical phenomena important to the development of Harlem's mystique: the history of photography and the Great Migration. The history of photography, especially the moment of its birth and the technical innovations that made it a major twentieth-century art form, correspond to pivotal moments in the history of African American representation. The daguerreotype process was introduced in the United States in 1839, the same year as some of the first performances of what came to be known as blackface minstrelsy. By 1840, black photographers began fashioning images of the black community, providing an immediate visual counter-

narrative to derogatory images of blackface. The irony of the closeness of
the birth of photography and blackface is not lost on Robin Kelley, who
notes that from the early nineteenth century "the same technology responsible for the circulation of minstrel caricature . . . was used to create
counter-images of African American life—images of dignity, pride, success and beauty."[39]

Thereafter, in the later part of the nineteenth century, "photographers
played an integral role in how blacks visualized themselves. Photographs
provided accessible imagery for virtually all levels of the community . . .
the photographer could also project how the client wanted to remember
the event [or him or herself]," or, as hooks puts it, "Images could be critically considered, subjects positioned according to individual desire."[40] At
the beginning of the twentieth century, coinciding with the Great Migration and the eventual rise of Harlem and other New Negro centers,
photography in general and African American photographers in particular flourished. Since "photography did not discriminate and its low cost
made the portrait available to many" and because a change in printing
technology made it possible to print photographs in newspapers and
magazines more easily, black-authored images proliferated—Harlemites
and others all over the United States could now see ordinary folk eager
to capture their big city lives as well as the black intellectual and artistic community hard at the work of uplift. When one thinks of Harlem,
one thinks of images of the ordinary and famous by Van Der Zee, Carl
Van Vechten, Morgan and Marvin Smith, and countless others—through
these images "we connect ourselves to a recuperative, redemptive memory that enables us to construct racial identities, images of ourselves that
transcend the limits of the colonizing [or objectifying] eye."[41]

Julien's debt to Van Der Zee and his stylization of early twentieth-
century black life is obvious from the first frame of *Looking for Langston*,
featuring the elegant mourners over the coffin of Julien as Langston. A
signature of a Van Der Zee portrait is the stunning elegance of its sitters—his portraits always present Harlem's strivers looking their absolute
best, in fashionable clothing and dignified carriage, posing in one of his
Victorian sets or in their exquisitely designed homes. According to the
photography historian Deborah Willis, Van Der Zee was an extremely di-
rectorial photographer. Although primarily a commercial photographer,
he was always interested in artistic effect. Van Der Zee often styled his

sitters and subjects, portraying them as "heroic and self-aware," in environments that communicated "partially real pride and partially carefully
constructed artifice."[42] The art of Van Der Zee and other African American photographers was often commemorative of life and death, as the
assemblage of portraits in Van Der Zee's *Harlem Book of the Dead* (1978),
featuring beautiful black-and-white images from the 1930s and 1940s of
funeral homes, the dead in their coffins, mourners contemplating their
lost loved ones, reveals. This life–death nexus is communicated in two
main ways: through the presentation of the mourners and through Van
Der Zee's artistic choices about the disposition of the living and the dead.
If Julien's technique sounds like this description of Van Der Zee's, the
homage continues when Julien portrays the dead. Van Der Zee's funerary
portraits often utilized Julien's favorite photographic technique: montage. Mourners in a Van Der Zee print are often accompanied by super-
imposed images of their "absent ones," or the dead themselves are presented both in the coffin and, in another part of the picture, alive — what
is remembered in these photographs is not the afterlife but an image of an
idealized present in which the dead accompany the living, long after they
are physically gone. In these pictures, the photographer makes manifest
the belief that the "spirit lives after the body is broken."[43] Julien imports
both the form and content of these photos into *Looking for Langston*, emphasizing the sense of the film as being much more than merely a funeral;
it is a meditation on life, death, pride, and artifice.

While Van Der Zee's photographs lend a decidedly numinous air to the
film, Mapplethorpe's black male nude images from *The Black Book* tell
a different, but related, story. Released in 1986, a time when the AIDS
crisis was at its bleakest and most devastating, Mapplethorpe's images
courted controversy immediately. Given that they were taken by a white
gay male artist and featured black men, some of whom were gay porn
stars, many wondered if they were images that celebrated or further objectified the black male body, whether viewers could look at them and
enjoy the "perfectly chiseled black male bodies" without what Hemphill
calls "guilt or capture" in the poem that accompanies their display in the
film.[44] When Julien projects these photos onto screens and has the white
male character caress them as he walks by each one, he encourages viewers to see them from an objective and subjective position, to interrogate
the politics of the way they look at images of self and other. They are to

experience a dangerous, ambivalent pleasure when looking at them. This ambivalence, though different from that experienced in the Van Der Zee photographs, also brings the images alive, makes them meaningful not as captured images of black male beauty, but as contemplations.[45] For Muñoz, Van Der Zee's photos help the queer spectator visualize a past and thus enable an "imaginary coherence that makes the visualization of a present and future possible"; when "redeployed by cultural producers like Julien [Mapplethorpe's portraits] become meditative texts that decipher the workings of mourning in our culture."[46] Again, there is more than despair and mourning here, for in his use of these photographs Julien transforms the arrest or sense of melancholia in the film, what is normally a "pathology or self-absorbed mood that inhibits activism . . . [into] a mechanism that helps us (re)construct identity and take our dead to the various battles we must wage in their names."[47] As such, these pictures become weapons; Julien is "re-using the archive," as he says, "but in a slightly more transgressive way."[48]

Julien's use of these photographs helps one to see the scenes of arrest in *Looking for Langston* and indeed the tableaux vivants of the entire film as inquiries rather than dead ends. Given that the film offers an ultramodern aesthetic vision in the form of confrontations between the elegant (dandy characters, Van Der Zee photos) and nude (Beauty, Mapplethorpe photos), the image that haunts the ending of the film is an interesting combination of these—that of a highly stylized black Narcissus. In the film's last sequence, which juxtaposes shots of the tuxedoed men dancing blissfully inside of the club with those of skinheads trying to break into the club from the outside, a fleeting image appears—Beauty as Narcissus, lying down, his cheek pressed to a mirrorlike surface that is surrounded by flowers, drawn to, captivated, and arrested by his own likeness. Though not an actual photograph like those of Van Der Zee and Mapplethorpe that inform the mise en scène, this image is presented in snapshot form and, as such, can be read as part of this photographic legacy or the last piece of a powerful triptych. In *Looking for Langston*, Julien forces one to look differently at history, at the lives of gay people in the black diaspora, at the black body, black masculinity, and black aesthetics—this different optic is both suggested and presented in three highly stylized images of the tuxedoed Langstons, Beauty, and, finally, Narcissus. Julien's goal in the film of rehabilitating "freakish beauty" is accomplished by affirming the pathological, both in terms of melancholy and, with this final image, narcissism. The Narcissus image suggests the importance of looking at and for lost black histories, across time and geographical space, and of the necessity of self-regard for both the individual and the group (the image being regarded here is not that of Langston, but of Beauty). When one sees oneself and one's history through this lens, melancholy can become "identity-affirming," narcissism "redemptive," self-regard absolutely necessary though admittedly dangerous.[49] Julien avers that the risk is worth taking, in the hope of creating and imaging an aesthetic ideology that does not stop at re-dress but strives for that "one startling step beyond."

Julien set out to make a film that is a meditation on Hughes and becomes a statement on Beauty, but perhaps he did not think he was making a film that would also be a singular intervention in the history of black aesthetics, the dandy being the embodiment of that intervention. Dandyism, narcissism, and self-regard have always been negatively associated; in *Looking for Langston* Julien uses the dandy not to champion vanity as such, but to present visually a "stylized presentation of the act of looking" that potentially has liberating power.[50] Black dandyism has long been a mode of discerning and analyzing black aesthetics, a way of measuring how black people as individuals and as a group are seen and how they see themselves; here, Julien uses the dandy to recover a history that revises black cultural and literary history and shows its visionary nature. The importance of black self-presentation to this project can be seen not only in Julien's use of clothing, dress, and self-regard as central points of his film, but also in the film's decidedly dandyish legacy. Julien presents the Narcissus image and the idea of redemptive narcissism as a provocation at the end of his film. This gauntlet was taken up almost immediately by a group of contemporary photographers from the black diaspora, artists who self-style as dandies and explore dandyism in their work as their primary mode of challenging and reenvisioning black aesthetics and black consciousness. When asked about his plans immediately after *Looking for Langston*, Julien replied poignantly, "I am only beginning to deal with questions of the black family."[51] In the work of Lyle Ashton Harris, Iké Udé, and Yinka Shonibare, MBE, the visualizing of the black dandy as redemptive narcissist becomes a cosmopolitan, family affair.[52]

"Look! A Dandy!"

Describing the nature of the "operation" he performs on late twentieth-and early twenty-first century aesthetics, the artist Yinka Shonibare asserted, "To reclaim aesthetics for the left (as opposed to its traditional home on the right), I will begin with some surgical work. In the mid-80s, my generation of artists encountered the discourse around deconstruction, postmodernism, post-structuralism, and postcolonial theory."[53] In fact, Shonibare is the latest of a group of artists whom I call artists of New Dandyism, practitioners who self-style as dandies or take dandyism as a topic in their work. While as a group both fey and fabulous, they are bound together by the fact that their artistic training included an encounter with literary theory and cultural criticism that had a certain vogue in the late 1980s and 1990s. These theories constitute Shonibare's surgical instruments. In fact, I see this group's vision of dandyism, its potential and the limitations of its critique, as coming out of an encounter with some of postcolonial theory's seminal texts, especially Fanon's exploration of the visuality of blackness in *Black Skin, White Masks*. A clue to the importance of Fanon to Julien in particular, for example, is the fact that his most recent feature-length film is a bio-pic of Fanon (1995); as he works on "the black family," Julien's oeuvre in part links "two salient conjunctures within black modernity: the Harlem Renaissance and the African struggle for liberation."[54] When these new dandy artists follow in Julien's footsteps, they too bring together an attention to the way in which the vision of a fuller definition of blackness through the dandy figure requires an acknowledgment of a queer black presence and also an attention to the politics of the gaze.

Even though Julien and his coproducer, Mark Nash, say, in reference to their Fanon film, that their method could be called "doing theory on film," what I want to argue is not that these artists similarly exemplify Fanon, but rather how they use Fanon and others to create in their photography and sculpture a black diasporic aesthetic that uses the dandy and dandyism to communicate their vision of contemporary black identity. For these artists, Fanon's text represents a first step toward redemptive narcissism, a strategy of black visualization designed to be not merely what Fanon critics like Homi Bhabha would call "a look from the place of the Other," but even a dandyish look "one startling step beyond" that vision of otherness. The dandyish images these artists present are not merely a vision of the empire looking back, but a vision looking *through* a shared history of black representation toward an image of black cosmopolitanism that is simultaneously rooted and detached, celebratory and censorious.

In an essay from 1989 entitled "New Ethnicities," the dean of black British cultural studies, Stuart Hall, famously declared "the 'end of innocence,' or the end of the innocent notion of the essential black subject."[55] While one may now accept Hall's elaboration of this turn in his work as a "recognition of the extraordinary diversity of subjective positions, social experiences and cultural identities which compose the category of 'black'; that is, the recognition that 'black' is essentially a politically and culturally *constructed* category," I would like to point out that Hall and other cultural critics arrive at this point partly through a reading of Fanon, particularly a rereading of Fanon's *Black Skin, White Masks*.[56] What these rereadings posit is that Fanon uses a rhetoric that references a critical analysis of the look in *Black Skin, White Masks* as he explores the objectification of blacks imposed by colonial power and highlights the visual nature of this objectification. It is the politics of this look and the potential subversiveness of the act of looking back that these artists work to visualize or manifest via dandyism in their work. Though Fanon might seem an unlikely progenitor of a kind of vogue in the critical return of the black dandy and dandyism, especially the figure's coy use of masquerade and spectacle, his concentration on the look in *Black Skin, White Masks* does, nevertheless, call for a deep exploration of the artifice of blackness, an artifice in which and with which these artists cloak their queer, subversive bodies. As they interrogate stereotypes of blackness and masculinity through a Fanonian lens, these dandies, like Julien, image a redemptive blackness that might be beyond the stereotypes—it is precisely their practice of dandyism and redemptive narcissism that allows them to experiment with "the extraordinary diversity of subjective positions" that characterizes a black diasporic consciousness.

Hall has said that what has intrigued artists and filmmakers about Fanon's text is that in its "persistent instabilities," *Black Skin, White Masks* is a kind of "*open text*, and hence a text that we are obliged to go on working *on*, working *with*."[57] These artists and critics, for the most part second-generation postcolonials who read Fanon with new eyes, learn from and resignify Fanon's discussion of "the fact of Blackness" by working on Fanon's description of the way in which he and others wear their blackness like a costume. Indeed, for Fanon the process of colonial objectification of blackness has the effect of metaphorically turning him into a servant of the colonizer's desires—leaves him and other colonials cloaked in a discursive uniform of stereotypes, wearing "willy-nilly . . . the livery that the white man has sewn for him."[58] Few options are open to him in the small space between this black skin and its discursive uniform of stereotypes. Indeed, Fanon laments, "All this whiteness that burns me . . . I sit down at the fire and I become aware of my uniform. I had not seen it. It is indeed ugly. I stop there, for who can tell me what beauty is?"[59] This process of being "fixed" by the "glances of the other" and by the stereotypical uniforms that these glances impose is famously communicated in the pivotal scene of *Black Skin, White Masks*, in which the colonial subject realizes the small distinction between his skin and the black uniform he is made to wear. Walking down a street in France, a recent émigré, Fanon hears

> "Look, a Negro!" It was an external stimulus that flicked over me as I passed by. I made a tight smile.
> "Look, a Negro!" It was true. It amused me.
> "Look, a Negro!" The circle was drawing a bit tighter. I made no secret of my amusement.
> "Mama, see the Negro! I'm frightened!" Frightened! Frightened! Now they were beginning to be afraid of me. I made up my mind to laugh myself to tears, but laughter had become impossible.[60]

Unable to escape his hypervisibility, Fanon is completely prevented from forming a self-identity or putting together his own look, as it were. In his experience, the colonial situation does not have room for black self-consciousness or black self-fashioning. Clad in this uniform that paradoxically makes him invisible as a political subject and hypervisible as a servant of white power, Fanon makes the only decision he can: he will remain "forever in combat with his own image."[61] It is in this combat, staged in the space between skin and uniform, that the artists of New Dandyism see a possibility for intervention.

While Fanon himself is not able to find a way to negotiate this "epidermalization" or, indeed, "costuming" of identity, the artists of New

Dandyism, with some help from Bhabha and Hall, do. Their readings of Fanon actually engage what they see as an unrealized "emancipatory wish" within the text by re-presenting the narcissism that Fanon finds at the heart of the colonial project. Whereas Fanon figures colonial authority as turning on a limiting, self-constituting "dual narcissism"[62] that promotes the fiction that black and white racialization are separate processes (that racialization indelibly separates black and white identities from each other), he encourages these postcolonial artists to propose a different kind of narcissism or self-regard in response when he says, "I grasp my narcissism with both hands and I turn my back on the degradation of those who would make a man a mere mechanism."[63] The potential for this redemptive black narcissism, a look from the place somewhere between the self and the other, arises from a reading of *Black Skin, White Masks* that insists that within the text Fanon achieves something far greater than the most profound and poetic account of colonialist identity politics. Indeed, what the text teaches in its examination of how fear of the Negro is an indelible part of the Western imaginary is a "deeper reflection of their [master and slave] interpositions, as well as the hope of a difficult, even dangerous freedom."[64] Therefore, despite Fanon's insistence that colonial authority is unassailable, that the black man's livery will be a permanent uniform, rereadings of *Black Skin, White Masks* propose that Fanon's rhetoric betrays him and that he does, actually, hint at an ambivalence in colonial power that unwittingly acknowledges a potential mode of refashioning the self.[65] It is in reading between the lines of Fanon's text that the dandy—a figure who traditionally works between the skin and its costume—returns, anxious to refashion new black diasporic identities, eager to alter stereotype's "ugly" livery and escape this "dual narcissism" for a narcissism more compensatory. In fact, *Black Skin, White Masks* ends in a plea for a continued inquiry into identity's matrices as Fanon implores, "O my body, make of me always a man who questions!"[66] The origins of this desire are located in a preceding statement, "The real leap consists in introducing invention into existence."[67] It is this "invention" that opens up a space between skin and uniform, transforming the body from a cliché into an interrogation.

While Fanon himself does not take up this possibility, he nevertheless prepares the way for these artists to take this liberatory "leap." He announces the potential conversion of what was once the overwhelming

yet limiting excessiveness of his visual impact to a different kind of extravagance—a constant reformative refashioning of himself, which he expresses by saying, "In the world in which I travel, I am endlessly creating
myself."[68] When the artists of New Dandyism figure the black body as this
space for transformation, a "'canvas,' light-sensitive 'frame,' 'screen,'" as
Hall has claimed, they begin what Hall and the artists themselves call the
"production of a new 'black narcissus.'"[69] These artists very consciously
enter into Fanon's images and fantasies and propose new ways of seeing postcolonial identity and black cosmopolitanism. For these artists,
dandyism and cosmopolitanism seemingly have a natural affinity; when
they style themselves as dandies or invoke the dandy in their work, they
gesture toward a knowledge that the dandy, especially the black dandy,
is born out of an originary moment of imperialism and globalization and
that his identification and signification across the boundaries of race,
class, and culture are seemingly as intrinsic to the figure as his subversive
style. They image this cosmopolitan identification, what Bruce Robbins
would call a "reality of (re)attachment, multiple attachment, or attachment at a distance," not only by means of dandyism, but through a dandyism that reimagines the black diasporic family and, as Shonibare hopes,
reclaims aesthetics for use by black people for the expression of their
multiple communities and complex selves.[70] This combination of desires
finds expression in Harris's work, especially his mid-1990s series of prints
depicting his real and imagined black family. As a kind of caption to his
work, Lyle Ashton Harris has said, "I have been very influenced by the
writings of Frantz Fanon, particularly his book *Black Skin, White Masks*
. . . his fierce decolonization of interior spaces provides an elasticity, a
return to the self as a site of interrogation."[71] For Harris, interrogation
of the self inevitably means interrogation of ancestors, the family, alternative selves—his self-portraiture is a familial, diasporic enterprise that
depends on dress, drag, props—on dandyism.

Future Perfect

The term "redemptive narcissism" was coined by Harris. In fact, in the
same interview in which he speaks of the way Fanon influences him, he
defines "redemptive narcissism," saying that "self-love is a form of resis-

tance to the tyranny of mediocrity. I see the mirror not only as a site of trauma and death—Narcissus falling in to drown—but as a space for rigorous meditation, cleansing and recuperation."[72] That the mirror is important to Harris and other dandy artists as a space of contemplation rather than a mere display for vanity is clear from the fact that all of the artists discussed here are photographers (two have a background in painting) whose primary medium is the self-portrait. In their work, they image a history of black representational practices by means of portrait series that add up to a gallery of collective selves. These selves are images of past, present, and future identities, in dialogue with their own, specific autobiographies as African American, American African, Afro-British, and, increasingly, as they resist these labels, Afro-cosmopolitan. As a series, the portraits form a kind of biography of the race, of the kinds of selves that are born out of forced and voluntary global migration; the kinds of selves that are potentially within and constitutive of all people. For all of these artists, the self that is the switch or the prism with which one accesses and views this transhistorical and diasporic study of the black family and aesthetics is the dandy, who, as resurrected by Julien and performed by Harris, Udé, and Shonibare, both is and images a "space for rigorous meditation, cleansing and recuperation" of black identity. Their use of the dandy—a figure whose history crosses the borders of nations and violates the rules of social, cultural, and sartorial fashion while performing a masquerade of race, gender, and sexuality—allows one to see the figure as constitutive of the possibilities (and perhaps the limits) of diasporic identities. This post-Fanonian project utilizes Fanon's own work on the visual impact of the black body against the homophobia and sexism not only of "family-oriented" black nationalist movements that make claims for unity and black beauty, but also of *Black Skin, White Masks*.[73]

As Harris insists in conversation with his brother, the artist Thomas Allen Harris, who is one of his collaborators and, like his brother, gay, African Americans have traditionally used autobiography as a primary means of self- and group expression: "Historically, the black literary tradition of autobiography as self-creation and self-fashioning had been a necessary and radical act."[74] The black diaspora's first literary expression, the slave narrative, is at once a personal history and a record of a racial and class condition; as such, for the global black community, self- and group expression are intimately tied as authors and artists negotiate the necessity and burden of representing the race. For Harris this burden has been more of an inspiration than an encumbrance, as he and his brother as well as their collaborators aim in their work to "engage autobiography as a liberating strategy."[75] When Harris styles and shoots self-portraits, he enters a long aesthetic tradition that has both literary and visual precursors. The narrative impulse in autobiography and portraiture is seemingly an attempt at a resolutely modernist act, the presentation of the "ruins" and "fragments" of modern identity within an aesthetic frame, in the hope of ordering it, making it symbolically whole. For Harris, the wholeness depends on what he describes as an "awareness of beauty as a subversive strategy, as an instrument of seduction, a way of drawing people into a space where you can begin a dialogue and exchange."[76] Harris's oeuvre creates this space as a hall of mirrors, replete with images of himself / himselves.

The art historian James Smalls has said that the "act of self-portraiture has become particularly meaningful to the African American artist" precisely because it is a "viable means of psychic negotiation, adjustment and intervention" in these fragments and the images others have constructed with them.[77] Negotiation and intervention in the realm of the visual began as soon as blacks had the means to counter extant stereotypes of themselves. Early African American art, photography mainly, is powered by a documentary impulse both to record everyday black life as seen from the perspective of the people who lived it and to fashion a self in as ideal a manner as possible. As Smalls argues in Fanonian terms, "It is the condition of the black subject to be splintered into multiple fragments of identity, to be identified from without, that becomes the basis for the formation and deformation of identity in the act of portraiture"; "in this situation, the African American self-portraitist is obliged to overcome objectification as well as subjectification in the process of self-imaging."[78] While Smalls reads self-portraits that visualize this fragmentation as sometimes dangerous instances of an obsessive self-objectification, he reads those that subvert this process as redemptive, displaying a knowingness about the process of subjectivity, of imaging conceptions of blackness and individuality that are complementary rather than oppositional, necessarily fragmented rather than tragically so. For him, Harris's practice, its "persistent emphasis on masquerade and disguise . . . expands the notion of self-portraiture by considering the entire body in gestures of self-conscious enactments before the camera, theatricality, and artificiality in the (de)construction of identity."[79] While Harris's combination of dress, gesture, and performativity has not been labeled dandyism, his campy practice works to juxtapose uniforms imposed on him—stereotypes of blackness, queerness, masculinity, Americanness—and those he more readily chooses. His portraits thus enact a dandyism that, like that in *Looking for Langston*, argues for a black beauty and self-regard that are inclusive, affirmative, subversive, and sustaining.

If Julien's work is both literary and filmic, so too is Harris's: he describes the preparation for his shoots as "very intense, very charged . . . a lot of pre-production, setting up what was basically a movie set."[80] In these large-format self-portraits, Harris literally and figuratively stages a reunion between members of his personal and cultural family. The filmic narrative that results from this practice also similarly revives the dead, "giving life back to the black male body," figuring it as a challenge to normative conceptions of blackness, masculinity, heterosexuality.[81] Of primary importance in this resuscitation is a sense of history: when Harris mounted the exhibit that would launch his career, "The Good Life" (1994), at the Jack Tilton Gallery in New York, the main wall of the exhibit was framed by what would become two of his signature self-portraits. The first features Harris as a beautifully made-up Toussaint L'Ouverture, dressed in a dark, double-breasted military jacket with golden epaulets and buttons, finished with white cravat and plumed hat, seated on a golden throne, looking defiantly into the camera. In the second, Harris and Iké Udé, a Nigerian-born artist based in New York, are pictured side by side in a portrait entitled "Sisterhood," which features the two men dressed in velvet and silk—Udé in a black three-button jacket and red vest and Harris in green jacket and red paisley cravat—and elaborately made-up.[82] Udé's left arm is resting on Harris's shoulders, while Harris's right arm cinches Udé at the waist. They sit on the same golden throne of the first portrait. The backdrop of the two portraits is a velvet cloth striped in red, black, and green, the colors of Marcus Garvey's black nationalist Universal Negro Improvement Association (UNIA) flag. Between these portraits hung pictures of Harris's family, taken from the rich archive assembled by his grandfather, a prolific amateur photographer. As it intervenes and expands debates about family, diasporic and cosmopolitan identity, masculinity, sexuality, beauty of the black body, the span of

29. *Toussaint L'Ouverture*, 1994. 24 x 20 inches. Dye diffusion transfer print (Polaroid). Courtesy of the artist and CRG Gallery, New York.

30. *Sisterhood* [Lyle Ashton Harris in collaboration with Iké Udé], 1994.
24 x 20 inches. Dye diffusion transfer print (Polaroid). Courtesy of the
artists and CRG Gallery, New York.

this wall not only communicates Harris's aesthetic philosophy, but also beautifully presents the dandy and dandyism as confrontational yet playful negotiators of blackness transhistorically and multiculturally.

Before "The Good Life," Harris had been engaged in a series of black-and-white portraits featuring himself and his collaborators in various states of dress and undress, blackface and whiteface; as the photographic medium and content suggest, these portraits artfully critique racialization, gender construction, heteronormativity. In "Construct #10," Harris styles himself as a perverse, saucy ballerina, hand on hip, clad in nothing except a disheveled dark wig and too-short leotard and tutu disguising and exposing his muscled body and manhood; in "Construct # 11," Harris poses in a door frame with his back to the camera and wearing a blond wig, naked except for a piece of tulle stretched across his buttocks and tied at the side, exaggerating his hips in midswish. In another portrait he is a whitefaced black man frowning like an unhappy clown, bowler hat and white-gloved "jazz hands" framing his face, an Al Jolson in reverse. In these images, Harris plays the hysterical queen, one who sashays and pirouettes between masculinity and femininity, denying the viewer easy access to either; alternatively, he is the sad sack child of American race relations, seeking his mammy in a circuslike atmosphere in which the media play a prominent role. These images and those in "The Good Life" come out of a personal and professional desire to experiment that has a long history. In conversation with his brother Thomas, Harris reveals that as children, every weekend after church they went home and turned their hallway into a runway, dressed in their mother's "fabulous early-1970s pant-suits and African garb," fought with their imaginary boyfriends, and performed blackness, gender, and sexuality under the watchful eye of a cousin who, Harris says, "was the first to really mirror and affirm my awkward sensitivity, my pleasure in narcissism, and my outlandish, naïve queerness."[83] "Seminal experiences of play and performance," these weekend drags find their most mature expression in "The Good Life," which, in twenty-by-twenty-four-inch Polaroids that burst into color, interrogate the many ways to constitute family out of the multifarious fragments and histories comprised by in modern black identity, the lives and experiences of the "colored."

"The Good Life" and an important series within the exhibit, "Brotherhood, Crossroads, etc.," began more specifically when Lyle Harris invited his brother to collaborate on what he calls a meditation on the famous portrait of the founder of the Black Panthers, Huey Newton. Styled by Eldridge Cleaver, the portrait features Newton seated in a high-backed rattan throne, a gun in his left hand, an African spear on the right, defiant in the Panthers' signature uniform of black leather jacket and beret.[84] Harris's response to this image and to that crafted by him and his brother take Newton's revolutionary politics into new territory, most obviously by means of pose and props.[85] "Toussaint L'Ouverture," "Sisterhood," and "Brotherhood . . ." echo Newton's physical disposition here, but with a decided, equally confrontational difference. In "Toussaint," Harris finds an image of the earlier revolutionary in himself and vice versa as he takes on the identity of the leader of the Americas' most successful slave rebellion, the first black head of a democratic Haiti. Harris's Toussaint is both regal and lovely, all the more powerful, perhaps, for the bold iconoclasm of his dress and lipstick. Harris-as-Toussaint-as-dandy asks the viewer to see so much differently: at once, one is prompted to rethink the masculinist revolutionary politics associated with Newton and the Panthers, to consider Harris's multiple connections to the trajectory of Haitian history (from revolutionary state to a particular victim of the AIDS crisis), and to think of Harris himself as revolutionary, as claiming Toussaint for queer black culture. In this self-portrait / portrait of Toussaint, a sense of self, nationalism, and citizenship is questioned and redefined, opened up by the stylization of the image's foreground (Harris in revolutionary drag) and background (this drag framed by the golden throne, in front of the red, black, and green flag).

If one thinks about this image as a kind of stage set, the mise-en-scène within the portrait and the placement of the portrait on the wall of the gallery are as important as the actor and action within it. At the time of its original display, the Toussaint image was flanked by "Sisterhood"; both images were on a wall also painted red, black, and green. Just as the nationalist backdrop is designed by Harris to "challenge a construction of African nationalism that positions queers and feminists outside of the black family," it can reconstitute family as well, as seen in "Sisterhood." Here, as the two dandified men embrace, Harris stares absolutely blank-faced into the camera, while Udé looks slightly to the right. Fossilized, absolutely still, one African American, the other an American African, the dandies of the diaspora reunite in this portrait. Udé, a self-proclaimed "artist, aesthete, and writer," is Harris's sister here. The two are family because they seemingly share a secret knowledge about the potentially subversive and affirmative effects of self-regard. In this double portrait, Udé and Harris add new images to the black diasporic family album, take Toussaint on the other side of the wall as inspiration when they revolutionize family and identity politics. As they look out from in front of the black nationalist flag, they stare through and beyond the frame that would limit any of their affiliations, especially to each other. Here, sartorial and aesthetic style signals intimacy between the men and connects them to Toussaint and all of the Harris family members pictured in between.

As teenagers, the Harris brothers moved their childhood experimentations with masculinity, blackness, and sexuality to Tanzania while their mother was working there. Here they became comfortable publicly expressing the male intimacy displayed in "Sisterhood," a comfort that was ruptured when they returned to the United States. In Tanzania, they were able to walk down the street holding hands, enjoying each other's company and companionship.[86] While Thomas Harris does not want to "mythologize a purity, or indulge in nostalgia around our version of the mythic utopia of Africa," when Lyle Harris references this intimacy in "The Good Life" it is displayed in a diasporic context through portraits like "Sisterhood" and becomes visible as a concept when placed in contraposition to the portrait of Toussaint. On its own, "Sisterhood" speaks volumes about the affirmative, familial, associative potential of diaspora and narcissism as Harris brings a sensibility nurtured in East Africa into this portrait with the West African Udé. They style their discovery of each other in New York in terms of the black dandy. What Udé and Harris stage in this photograph is the history of black stylization through the dandy figure and their place in it as African and African American artists choosing to, as Fanon says, "endlessly create themselves." In their double portrait, one sees the ways in which redemptive narcissism can constitute kinship — they are sisters in terms of race as well as in their play with sexuality and gender, siblings united in attempts to revisualize black representation in a fashion-conscious, transatlantic world. When doubled again, on display with "Toussaint," the portrait gains yet another sister and places this larger sisterhood within a revolutionary history — as such, a dandy's narcissism counterintuitively creates family and transforms identities born out of the desolation of the slave trade and imperialism into alternative images of an affirmative black cosmopolitanism.

At work on this wall and in the series of portraits that use the red, black, and green flag as background is a sense of historicity—of a transtemporal sense of mourning and affirmation.[87] When Harris poses as Toussaint, as sister to Udé, as "Saint" Michael Stewart (a young black artist mistakenly gunned down by New York City police), or with his brother in "Brotherhood, Crossroads, etc.," while not himself portraying the dandy, as a photographer he uses the dandy's theatrical talents to visually narrate both a personal and cultural identity. His masquerade restores a lost lineage and expresses future aspirations. Whether embodying the dandy or styling images from the dandy's family album, he engages in a project that, like *Looking for Langston*, uses the dandy figure to mourn lost connections (Toussaint), to assess and critique current notions of masculinity, blackness, heteronormativity and the value of art (Michael Stewart, Brotherhood). Part of this process includes also a look forward that is based on affirmation; this is best expressed in "Sisterhood." Borrowing a phrase from Udé, Harris calls these images "future-perfect" because they feature "mourning as a perverse celebration of life. And time . . ." as they "speak to the need for an immediate political, aesthetic, and psychic intervention . . . a new framework in which to refashion the body and mind."[88] While Harris speaks to the futurity of these images, the perfection of them might come from a consideration of their affirmative quality. As more than one critic of "The Good Life" has pointed out, what is so especially provocative about Harris's aesthetic is not that it fulfills what was, at the time, a "party line" of interrogating identity, but that what emerges from Harris's self-portraits and constructed family album is a sense of acceptance and solidarity, one for the others.[89] This is, surely, narcissism with a difference—the difference blackness can make for dandyism and vice versa.

Deliberate Intelligences

"Stylist of subjectivities," Iké Udé artistically subscribes to the ameliorative concept of redemptive narcissism, but in addition, as we'll see, he lives it.[90] A signature piece, the mock movie poster "The Regarded Self," features two images of Udé. In one he is in a dark men's suit and in the other he wears an antique white Japanese kimono in a way that is reminiscent of Joan Crawford at leisure in the 1940s. In both images, Udé's hair resembles a jaunty black beret. The Udé in the white outfit faces right and peers into a compact, gazing introspectively at his perfectly painted face; the Udé in the suit, positioned directly behind the first subject, seemingly looks over his shoulder into the same compact, hand raised, about to adjust his hair.[91] They both wear ascots. In the essay that inspired this piece, also titled "The Regarded Self," Udé explains that, in the main, he deploys narcissism as a strategy to negotiate stereotypes of masculinity and sexuality while interrogating the relationship between public and private selves. For him, "the self can be devoured by public scrutiny, it can be saved by private self-objectification."[92] Self-love is a need for Udé, even though he knows that in popular parlance it can be perceived very differently. In the essay, he contemplates this discrepancy, defiantly naming narcissism not only as healthy, but even heroic. Once again, the key to understanding this is the self's disposition to the mirror:

> Is this [the vilification and necessity of narcissism] a case of Caliban and the mirror? Perhaps it may be that for most people locating themselves in that "Mirror of my familiar" issues painful feelings of insecurity, pathology, ambivalence as if it were a direct reminder of a grotesque existence. Thus established, narcissism in and out occupies a performative space in the narcissistic psyche. So it is worth bearing in mind that this psychic space is not a vain space, but rather a chi-oma or God's-beauty-in-me space. A sort of sublime awareness of the self inhabited by the self and nourished with appropriate fastidiousness.
>
> The mirror for the redeemed narcissist is not a mere site at which he can perform such base functions as decoration or adornment. Rather the mirror serves as a location that allows "The Regarded Self" a sacred and intense solitude by which he can negotiate and renegotiate his superior self at all cost. Hence, the "narcissist" is always a hero in essence, exactly because he typifies the opposite of a daring appearance. . . . The best hunt or bargain for love is not outside but within and around the self. The mirror is only one side of the coin.[93]

A well-considered self-regard takes on a spiritual function; here, Udé's explanation of the power of self-love recalls the pivotal scene in *Looking for Langston* in which self-love is valued for its own sake even as it becomes and includes love of the other. Again, self-scrutiny is unapologetically affirmative and not reactive. This "appropriate fastidiousness" never considers the self as an object of scorn.

31. Iké Udé, "The Regarded Self" from *Celluloid Frames* (1995).
Courtesy of the artist.

The key elements producing this worldview are also those that define Udé's aesthetic practice: the history of Western and black dandyism; the Nigerian/Igbo concepts of chi-oma, which Udé describes above as a sense of immanence in the self; *adanma*, an Igbo masquerade in which men "perform" femininity in a "glamourized, idealized, parodied, and controlled" manner; and the world of global fashion and media.[94] In fact, while the double image of Udé in "The Regarded Self" film poster tells this story visually, the credits for the film poster wittily reiterate his artistic debts, indicating that the film's star is "Iké Udé and Mua" (moi); that the screenplay is based on Iké Udé's essay "The Regarded Self"; that the production design is by "adamma" (adanma) and the choreography by "chi-oma." Udé's self-regard is not narcissism for narcissism's sake; instead, self-scrutiny and self-love are courageous, daring, defiant, necessary in a world in which most media images are overwhelmingly not self-generated, in which the mass market and mass media make self-fashioning seem both compulsory and impossible. Though a committed proponent of self-regard, Udé claims convincingly that "my use of myself is more a mode of performance than sheer narcissism or vanity. In my work, the self is far more subordinate. The self becomes a transformative vehicle, a mask with which to enact, parody, satirize, and check varying stereotypes, icons, heroes, and such."[95] However, even as he takes his aesthetic ideology and practice to its limit—living his life as a dandy, dressing as a dandy, performing multiple traditions of masquerade in his art and life, setting, regaling, and critiquing the material and symbolic fashions that make dandyism possible—he pushes the dandy's art to a dangerous, titillating edge. After all, this play with self and society, fashion and freedom can come off as cute and coy. Ultimately, as he states, "The mirror is only one side of the coin."

Of all the dandy artists cited here as examples of post-black artistic practice and as examples of the visualization of Afro-cosmopolitanism, Udé distinguishes himself by living life as an unmitigated aesthete.[96] Describing his plans for the day in an essay titled "Magnificent Futility," he muses, saying, "Today, on the side of my picture window, a brilliant sky floats perfectly. The clouds have given way to a dazzling sunshine and everywhere a riot of vivacious colors: flowering plants, thrum of fabrics, cruising cars and clothes abound irresistibly. I'm gamely infected. Before I take my stroll, however, I shall bathe, prepare my face, hair, nails and spruce myself up."[97] Although also an artist and writer, he seemingly lives these roles from within his dandyism. One can see the centrality of dandyism in his life in one of his early pieces, "Uses of Evidence" (1996–97), an installation that was added to the permanent collection of the Guggenheim Museum in New York after it appeared in the museum's groundbreaking exhibit of 1996 "In/Sight: African Photographers, 1940 to the present." In this piece, Udé created a self-contained room within the exhibit that featured stereotypical or familiar images of Africa and Africans on the outside, among them pictures of lions, gorillas, everyday people, and warriors in the style of the *National Geographic*. Viewable through small windows into the space were images of Udé's Africa, including candid and formal portraits of his family, scenes of vibrant cities peopled with modern African people of various ethnicities, portraits of famous Nigerians like the poet Christopher Okigbo, the painter and fashion designer Afi Ekong, a scene from a match at the Lagos polo club, and a black-and-white self-portrait of Udé himself. Standing in the middle of a cobblestone street, resplendent in a formal, dark, three-piece suit, flamboyant white shirt, and cravat, Udé wears a monocle, a highly appropriate accessory for an exhibition titled "In/Sight." In this piece, Udé presents his dandy persona as the central piece of evidence, the lens through which he will read the images assembled around him and, especially, the perspective from which he will confront those primitivizing and exoticist images present on the outside of the structure. Though Udé disclaims the label of queer to describe his life and work as an aesthete, critics nevertheless describe his practice as "a restaging or queering of the African in the Western Imaginary," and, I would add, via his practice as dandy, vice versa, a queering of the West in an African Imaginary.[98] The self-portrait as dandy in "Uses of Evidence" offers insight into Udé's conception of his Africanness and Americanness (the portrait seems to have been shot in a Western, metropolitan area) as well as into his practice as an artist—both are simultaneously real and dependent on artifice. "There is no true accountable self," he says. "The self is a bargain of sorts. Like the adanma masquerade, my work addresses itself to uses such as propaganda, ambivalence, vanity, denial, glamour; all the contradictions of our society—the mere artificial constructs of our everyday consumerist culture in which anything can be bought and everything is for sale."[99]

In contrast to Harris, who was at the time also bringing his personal

32. Iké Udé, "Self-Portrait" from *Uses of Evidence* (1996). Courtesy of the artist.

and cultural history to bear on his art practice in "The Good Life," Udé never dresses as a discernible other in his work—he is always himself, the dandy, even when modeling as the cover girl for his parodies of *Glamour*, *Time*, and *Condé Nast Traveler* or playing aspects of himself in his fantasy film posters. In his work, Udé takes on roles, "tends to quote formal . . . and some subcultural archetypes" which he approximates by dress and describes as everything "ranging from the gentleman, the dandy, the aesthete, the CEO to the yuppie, the hip-hopper, the athlete, the derelict, the bohemian, the chanteuse, the club kid," rather than other specific identities.[100] While Harris refashions a family with his dandy masquerade, Udé operates from within that family, aiming his wit at fashioning an American African dandy's "discrepant cosmopolitan" world.[101] In describing his relationship to dandyism, Udé explains that despite his choice to live as a "writer, artist, and aesthete," he feels that "consciously or not, there is always a critical difference between the artist and the work of art, between a dandy and his choice of wardrobe, between an individual and his/her known quantity, between thought and action, process and result — the exception is to make it appear seamless."[102] Given that he seemingly strives to eliminate the distance between a dandy and his "choice of wardrobe," this statement might seem contradictory, yet it animates the space Fanon identifies between a black man and his representational uniform. Udé is a seamless investigator of and reveler in all the elements that compose his identity as an Afro-cosmopolitan, "post-colonial flaneur."[103] He is, as his "Cover Girl" parody of *Time* magazine declares, "Man of the Year: Prince I.K.," a royal restored to the throne because, as a banner across the masthead indicates, "Male Subjectivity [is] at the Margins."[104]

More than any other artist of New Dandyism, Udé playfully and ironically deliberates on dandyism's ability to self-fashion identity in a world in which fashion and media have so much sway over identity and its representation. At every turn, he styles disjunction by means of ironic displacement. For example, his cover images, film advertisements, and texts are almost completely at odds with expectation. Udé appears on the cover of *Town & Country* in a suit and cravat, made up in the modified guise of a Wodaabe Geerewol ritual celebrant, a member of a northern Nigerian/Southern Niger group obsessed with male beauty.[105] The headline states "The Noble Savage is Dead: L. A. Harris Reports from Lagos," suggesting an interesting, provocative but uncertain relationship between supposed savagery, civilization, and native and nonnative dandyism. In an article about the rise of contemporary African artists in Western artistic circles in the mid-1990s, when Udé and Shonibare were getting their first press, the art historians and critics Okwui Enwezor and Octavio Zaya speculated that with this new group of artists, "we are jarringly confronted with questions around the possibility of an autonomous postcolonial enunciation."[106] As I read the dandyism displayed by Udé (and all of these artists), this possibility seems both emancipatory and potentially deferred in their work. It is liberating because, according to Enwezor and Zaya, these artists flirt with imaging contemporary African identities outside of the old paradigms, even those generated in opposition to racist images. It is potentially deferred because this statement also calls into question whether this possibility really exists at all. It is this kind of disjunctive frisson that electrifies Udé's dandyism. Udé continually uses and displays a dandyism that seriously, but playfully, questions the line between the savage and civilized, the traditional and cosmopolitan, consumption practices and the concept of a free market. He does so even as he either symbolically or actually capitulates to or profits from that same market.

Considering another Udé piece, an image similar to "The Regarded Self" poster, the *Glamour* cover from the magazine parody "Cover Girl" series, Lauri Firstenberg notes that "Udé is confronted by his own gaze as his image is duplicated in the magazine cover, literalizing the mirror stage as self-staged, as a means of visualizing identification via self-determination."[107] This cover is, then, a glimpse of what a dandy-generated "autonomous postcolonial enunciation" could look like. As *Glamour* cover girl, Udé looks at his reflection in a mirror as the story headlines arranged around his dual image announce, "Genesis of Obsession," "MY GOD: Who's that Girl?," "Variations on Loneliness and Aloneness," "Plus: Bill T. Jones, Isaac Julien, Quentin Crisp, Nina Simone and Others." The art and the text signal what to expect inside the "cover" and indicate what this man sees when he looks in the mirror. As his own supermodel, Udé does not see an other, a racist depiction of the self that would be alienating (he experiences *variations* on loneliness and aloneness). Instead, he sees a self that calls into question gender identity (who's that girl?), sexual preference, and national belonging, through references to the black Brit Julien, the gay icons Jones and Crisp, and the exile in France Simone. In fact, as a revision of cross-dressing and imposture, the "Cover Girl" series manipulates both African practices (the adanma masquerade and Wodaabe Geerewol) and the world of Western high fashion, taking the portraits well beyond their apparent signification as either ethnically or culturally traditional or as drag.[108] Instead, they are the efforts of a diasporic dandy to claim his "entitles," to name his own favorite "designers," to practice the possibility of a self-enunciation.

A similar effort is visible in "The Rebel Genius" movie poster. Here, Udé, in his signature makeup and suit, presents an image of his head neatly divided into quadrants labeled with their putative contents, indicating the "price of the ticket" for entry into this dandy's mind. Udé grants complementary entrance, labeled "COMP" on his head, to the likes of Aimé Césaire, Fanon, [Wole] Soyinka, [Chinua] Achebe, Fela Kuti, [Toni] Morrison,

33. Iké Udé, "The Rebel Genius" from *Celluloid Frames* (1995). Courtesy of the artist.

[bell] hooks, [Cheikh Anta] Diop, and [Michel] Foucault. Jacques Derrida enters "at a discount," Friedrich Nietzsche is given a "cover charge." Only "The Bell Curve" is given "no admission." Again, the credits of this film are illustrative. The film's executive producer is the diasporic slave narrative author "Olaudah Equiano"; the music is by an interesting triumvirate of black male icons, "Fela Kuti, Miles Davis, Michael Jackson"; coexecutive producers include "L.A. Harris and [Anthony] Appiah."[109] The genius of this effort is that it imagines a black cosmopolitan dandy's cultural perspective, names the origins of his rebelliousness, and "cause[s] the viewer to construct his/her own narrative of what such a movie should or would be like."[110] This rebellion and Udé's rebellion in general will not be that of an angry revolutionary, but that of a sophisticated, theoretically elegant exercise in media masquerade.

Udé sees the "regarded self" and its imbrication in image and fashion as the mechanism for both the erasure and instantiation of his self-identity and that of the many groups with which he affiliates. In his haute couture and media parodies he signals an awareness of the dandy's origin in a world of material and symbolic exploitation. Like Harris, he uses masquerade to look backward and forward at the ways in which blackness, masculinity, and sexuality have been imaged; as he lives the life of an aesthete, he signifies in and on the world of mass consumption and media. On the cover of *Rolling Stone*, this time in an extreme close-up of his face that is captivatingly blurred, one reads that dandy "dj IK gets trickier without apologies." In Udé's oeuvre, his trick is not just to use his dandy masquerade to ironize and thus wittily repair images of Africans and African Americans through media appropriations, but, in other pieces, like his magazine *aRude*, his "Beyond Decorum" clothing series, and his planned film "The Exquisites," to take his dandyism into a much more conceptual realm that both deepens and frustrates the critique.

In 1995 Udé began publishing Iké Udé's *aRude*, a "New York international magazine [of] style, art, fashion, culture, scenes and beyond," a "public extension of the 'Cover Girl'" project from the previous year.[111] The magazine has since been fine-tuned as ARUDE: *the index of elegance.* Udé's editorship of *aRude* takes his self-stylization to the masses under the ideology, stated in the magazine's "Elements of Style" section, that a dandy's "style is not just about form and substance. It is also about the luxurious deliberation of intelligence in the face of boundaries."[112] There could not be a better definition of dandyism as practiced by blacks historically, especially by these artists. Refigured by them as "intelligence," style becomes the process and fact of self-knowledge, part of the process of accessing the past as a means of reaching the "future perfect." In *aRude*, Udé's dandyism is not itself on display, as his own fashioned body is not seen (except in the "society page" section of the magazine, which sometimes shows Udé at parties, openings, etc.). Instead, *aRude* operates as a purchasable artifact that is a total product of Udé's dandyish lifestyle and world vision—what the reader sees inside is equal parts haute couture and downtown chic, Lagos, New York, Tokyo, multicultural, multiracial, international, high- and lowbrow. In *aRude*, Afro-cosmopolitan dandyism is reified and made available for purchase.[113]

How this foray into the commercial affects Udé's dandyish practice is difficult to read. On the one hand, it does seem a natural representation of his aesthetic, while, on the other hand, it commercializes that representation. That Udé knows his dandy and black dandy history, a history that is also a negotiation between exploitation and subversion, inevitably helps here. For example, on his cover of GQ, in which the headlines read "Hot New Designers," "Real Men Wear Makeup: How-To Tips Inside," "Conservative Skirts for the Working Man," and, oddly, "What is the Average Man's Penis Size? Find Out," one learns, more importantly, of "The Importance of Chevalier de St. Georges before Beau Brummell."

A mixed-race man who was the son of a slave woman from Guadeloupe and a prominent Frenchman, Joseph Boulogne, the Chevalier de Saint-Georges, was a well-known composer, fencer, and darling of eighteenth-century Europe (he was known as the black Mozart). Mentioned in the same breath as Julius Soubise, the subject with which this book begins, the Chevalier was one of the first black men to use his own "preciousness" to his advantage.[114] That Udé invokes as originary to his project this strikingly beautiful, stylish man, himself a product of imperialism and his own talent, is not an accident. That Udé bases his artistic practice in a historical sense of the nexus that produced his own black style—which includes African, European, and American strains of dandyism—hints that he knows that being a dandy always means being simultaneously a slave to fashion and fashion's slave. As was said in reference to his planned film "The Exquisites," a dandy "revenge fantasy"—"dandy is as dandy does."[115]

"Beyond Decorum," the exhibition in 2001 that lent its name to his first solo show plus retrospective, takes this reification or dandy conceptualization even further. Not an installation, mock magazine cover, faux film poster, or even a magazine, "Beyond Decorum" goes straight to the dandy's true foundation, clothing, consisting of a series of shirts, jackets, and shoes redesigned to reveal the true emotion behind how and why we dress—desire. Characteristically, Udé goes well "beyond decorum" here—the labels and linings of each designer piece, whether clothing or shoe, have been replaced by textual and visually pornographic personal ads. The piece thus literalizes and exaggerates desire even while secreting it in the lining of a coat, on the label of a crisp white shirt, or in the lining of a gloriously sequined shoe. The label of a starched white shirt has an advertisement from "Robert," who is "25 years old, blond, brown eyes, 5'9", 150 lbs, 9' cock," who "would love to bend you over and do it doggie style." The lining of a well-tailored plaid double-breasted coat shows men and women in poses far removed from respectability. "Beyond Decorum" irreverently presents the equal parts grotesque and titillating obsession every fashionista has with appearance. Displayed like clothing in a high-end department store or designer boutique (some pieces are under glass) and materializing the idea of clothing as fetish, these jackets, shirts, and shoes "appeal to our consumer mentality to construct identity through outward experience," even as their labels turn that "consumer mentality" away from the clothing and back to the body.[116] This turn is interesting and a little bit dangerous, as it highlights the risks one takes in fulfilling any desire, but especially those desires that are filled by actual, rather than symbolic consumption. For a black dandy in particular, what is at risk in a performance of or life as a dandy is, in fact, ownership of the body and its representation. Udé punctuates this particular point by displaying clothes and shoes that have been previously worn. "Beyond Decorum" shows how joyous and truly costly fashion can be, how fantastic and fragile is the concept of redemptive narcissism.

Belle of the Ball

Describing how he is perceived in the art world, the artist Yinka Shonibare, who was born in London and raised in Lagos, Nigeria, says he understands that "when people see an artist of African origin, they think: oh, he's here to protest." Shonibare admits, "Yes, okay, I'm here to protest" but adds, provocatively, "but I am going to do it like a gentleman. It is going to look very nice."[117] A self-confessed "beauty hugger" who has "found beauty one of the most radically subversive strategies to counter Eurocentric hegemony on the use of beauty," Shonibare has used the beautiful, especially his meticulously tailored fabric sculptures and gorgeously styled photographic narratives, to remind people, continually, of the importance of appearance and the tendency of appearance to deceive.[118] For him, an art practice that is gentlemanly and prizes beauty is not at all antithetical to a radical critique of all expectations. Shonibare's protest is against rhetorical simplicity and essentialist thinking about identity and

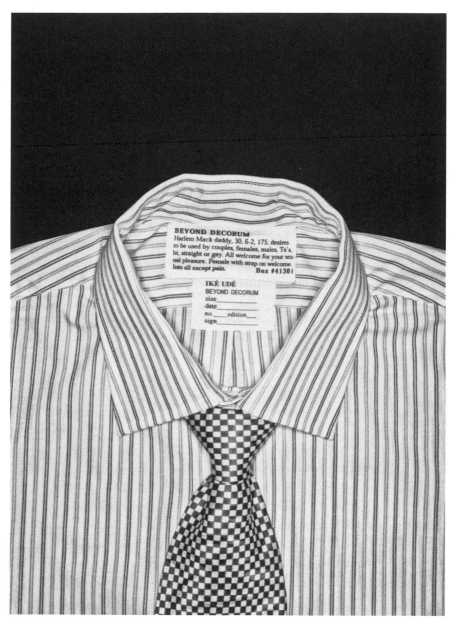

34. The label inside the shirt reads, "BEYOND DECORUM. Harlem Mack Daddy, 30, 6-2, 175, desires to be used by couples, females, males, Ts's, bi, straight or gay. All welcome for your sexual pleasure. Female with strap on welcome. Into all except pain. Box #41301." Iké Udé, "Harlem Mack Daddy" from *Beyond Decorum* (1999). Courtesy of the artist.

aesthetics and for a complexity that makes an "easy read" of him and his work as a dandy impossible.

Although Shonibare, like Udé, would disdain many of the labels that could be used to describe him (postcolonial hybrid, Afro-British, black, Nigerian, or African), the one marker he has taken on is that of poet, in an effort to reclaim beauty and the aesthetic for himself (see the epigraph above).[119] Despite the fact or maybe even because Thomas Carlyle once pejoratively described the dandy as "inspired with Cloth, a Poet of Cloth" and dandies as merely "Clothes-wearing men" who "dress to live and live to dress," Shonibare dares to appropriate such a designation and make it true, on his own terms.[120] As a "poet of cloth" who is also a self-described trickster, Shonibare uses fabric, clothing, and dandyism as a language to express, as poets do, the ineffable, the transcendent, the shockingly ordinary, and the achingly complex with precision, elegance, and irony. He explains his hermeneutic in literary terms: "I want to look at my practice in the area of the poetic. Speech—direct speech, or journalism—is sure to declare itself and its intentions clearly; that is the nature of straight speech or journalism. The poet finds another thing, which is the use of words to become another order of signification. Then that becomes an integral part of speech. One has expression, but the artist can never be as sure as the critic, because the artist is skeptical by nature, so that what is expressed is always contradicting itself. In other words, my work occupies the space of contradiction."[121] As a poet, Shonibare metaphorizes this space of contradiction as the black dandy and dandyism; in so doing, he fashions costumes and whole mise-en-scènes that narrate tales of beautifully coy confusion, tales that seduce and surprise.

Self-described also as a rascal, Shonibare defines the artist's task as "to entertain, to seduce, to provoke, to challenge and be historically relevant."[122] No phrase could better describe his sculptures, tailored from African Dutch wax fabric, which he affectionately calls his dresses. Walking into a Shonibare exhibit is like entering a black hole, a space of temporal and geographic travel, a place that connects the past, present, and future representations of blackness and its intersections with gender, sexuality, class, colonialism and imperialism, consumption, and globalization. Of course, in true trickster form, Shonibare's black hole is not at all a dark aporia, but a riot of color, a confusion of cultures. As the designer of the sculpture "Affectionate Men" (1999), he positions two male mannequins standing as if in intimate conversation. The man on the left wears a three-piece suit and bow tie, all in "African fabric," an outfit that uses the disparately colored (orange, black, yellow, blue) and patterned fabric to both blend and contrast the Western style of the suit with the ethnic cloth out of which it is fashioned. One cannot help noticing, for example, that the man's vest features a yellow design dominated by a large blue eye printed on it, suggesting a watchfulness or surreality.[123] His friend wears a similar outfit, a jacket styled in colors of orange and pink, pants in yellow and black, although this chap is less formal, wearing a more standard shirt and tie, in contrast to the high-collared shirt of his friend. A work of the same year, "Gay Victorians," seems a companion piece to this one, as it features two exquisitely tailored female figures, styled in a more recognizably Victorian-era costume, standing abreast of each other in a half-embrace. In these female pieces, the African fabric cascades down the back of the figures as it forms a bustle, revealing a differently patterned and contrastingly colored petticoat underneath. These dresses beg for narrative, given that they are figured as if in secret communication. Yet, what story do they tell each other with all of this color and pattern? What narrative can or should one attach to these figures? Are they African, European, Victorian, or contemporary? Are their closeness and quiescence, their affection and gayness coded? What to make of their headlessness and their lack of hands? The only definitive thing about them is that their clothing is beautifully crafted, finely tailored—clearly the handiwork of a "poet of cloth" extremely invested in making beauty from chaos and contradiction.

In Shonibare's oeuvre, looking nice and playing fair are not the same thing. He has faced the problem of finding an appropriate aesthetic throughout his career, and it has driven him from fashioning dresses to exploring dandyism less abstractly in photography and film. Predictably, in the late 1980s, when he was in art school in London working on conceptual painting on the theme of perestroika, he was asked by a professor why he was not working on Africa, producing "authentic traditional African art, like any good colonial, indeed postcolonial should."[124] After getting over what he describes as the trauma of this Fanonian "Look, a Negro!" moment that he says "negated his experience with modernism and modernization," he decided to respond by "creat[ing] a confusion." Shonibare's fabric sculptures were initially a gentlemanly response to the

35. Yinka Shonibare, MBE, "Affectionate Men" (1999). © Yinka Shonibare, MBE. Courtesy of the artist and Stephen Friedman Gallery, London.

aesthetic demands of his tutor and the seeming demands of history. Yet, even as he critiques the history of imperialism, African independence, and migration, Shonibare does so in a way that does not put any of this contestation to rest, saying instead, "I will locate myself in the area of confusion because confusion is more honest on my part, it is a closer expression of where I am. I don't mean confusion negatively."[125] As a result of this conversation with his tutor, Shonibare went out into London in search of what Africa meant to him (to paraphrase Countee Cullen's famous words) and came back with this fabric from the Brixton market out of which he shapes images of his own self-regard.

Eager to "tailor" a conversation about African identity and aesthetics, he began to use African fabric literally as a canvas in the early 1990s, first painting on it abstractly and arranging discrete squares and circles of it on blue and pink walls, and eventually sewing it into pieces like "Affectionate Men" and "Gay Victorians."[126] In these displays of African and European hybridity, one experiences a fantastically simple, witty critique of the demands of cultural and artistic authenticity. Nineteenth-century dress in African fabric spectacularly reveals the exploitation of Africans that fueled the imperialist project and resulted in the enormous wealth that was most lavishly displayed in Victorian dress, salons, estates—the trappings of the leisured lifestyle during the heyday of the empire's ruling classes (all on display now in London's Victoria and Albert Museum). Given that the fabric is also indelibly associated with African pride, independence, and nationalism, these sculptures must be read also as manifestations of the empire striking back, fashioning a new view of what it means to be African, British, and of the African diaspora then and now. Marking Shonibare's deep, ironic understanding of history and his return to the modern, these sculptures gloriously display the wit that characterizes European modernism's most famous fashioned creature, the dandy. "Affectionate Men" and "Gay Victorians" seemingly embody the black or African dandy's revenge, literally and figuratively materialized.

But do they? Since Shonibare always insists on the humor and jouissance of his work, saying "pleasure's central to my practice," one should never forget that the trickster usually does not reveal his disguise so easily and that great poems, of words or cloth, stand up to multiple interpretations.[127] Looking at these sculptures carefully, one sees that the hem of the fabric, where one might expect to find some indication of the fabric's Africanness such as "Made in Nigeria" or "Fabrique à Senegal," says, "Dutch wax." A little investigation reveals that this fabric is not African at all or even, really, Dutch. Originally from Indonesia, where it was hand-made by laborious, expensive batik methods, the cloth was brought to Europe by nineteenth-century Dutch and British colonials involved in the East India trade. The colonials, in turn, manufactured it in Holland and Manchester, England, for export back to Indonesia. The Indonesians rejected this industrially made cloth as a bad imitation of their own arti-sanal fabric. Therefore, it was reexported to Europe and then to the West African colonies, where it became valued by Africans, initially for being not African at all but foreign. In Africa, the fabric became especially popular after the independence movements of the 1950s and 1960s, when its designs were altered to reflect specifically African concerns. For example, Diawara recalls that during his childhood in Guinea in the late 1950s the market women were fond of a print that featured a portrait of the revolutionary Sekou Touré.[128] Later, supposedly African fabric enjoyed a vogue in post–civil rights America in the 1970s as a result of the growing popularity of black nationalism and its subsequent consumerist manifestation in the dashiki, head wrap, and mu-mu. Cheaper cotton versions of this fabric are now produced in Africa (and, until recently, Japan); but the most fancy version of the fabric, the Dutch or Super Wax, is still manufactured only in Holland and Manchester, England, for export to the African diaspora.

Therefore, this material sign of putatively authentic Africanness is both a lie and the truth of an African identity. Contra the hopes of Shonibare's tutor, the African who fashioned these dresses does not passively receive and then outrightly reject colonial influence for a return to the so-called native or expression of the postcolonial. Rather, his sculptures done in the fabric, such as "Affectionate Men," "Gay Victorians," and "Big Boy" (2002) embody and wear a hybridity that travels an unsuspected route, bringing a beautiful perplexity with them. Just as the Africanness of these figures is destabilized by the origins and contemporary uses of the fabric, the supposed course of their desires is similarly undone by the way in which the fabric is worn on same-sex bodies experiencing a spatial, stylish intimacy. That one destabilization leads to many others is also seen in other signature pieces like "Big Boy," in which a Victorian man's suit is topped with a feminized flamboyant coat of ruffles, and "Boy/Girl" and "Girl/Boy"

36. Yinka Shonibare, MBE, "Big Boy" (2002). © Yinka Shonibare, MBE. Courtesy of the artist and Stephen Friedman Gallery, London.

(1998), which features Victorian women's high-bustle dresses topped by waistcoats, tailcoats, and bow ties. A "full-throttle griffin—a fashion plate gender blend, a colonial couturier's nightmare that is simultaneously ameliorated and exaggerated by the skirmish between fabric and costume, surface and shape," a piece like "Boy / Girl" requires the viewer to "look both [or all] ways" at gender, sexuality, race, and power.[129]

Indeed, in "Big Boy" and the other pieces, Shonibare enunciates many other cross-cultural and transtemporal debates that include inquiries into his own sense of blackness, Africanness, diaspora, and cosmopolitanism. For example, when his sculptures were exhibited in Dakar, Senegal, he faced an unexpected local inquiry and complaint about the perceived waste of the cloth, which was so valuable to the local residents.[130] When the work appeared at The Studio Museum in Harlem, on 125th Street, it occupied a space that is also home to an increasing number of African immigrants who very visibly mark their origins through a mix of Dutch wax dress and Western styles as they sell their wares in the African market down the street. The sculptures also meditate on more specifically British concerns that extend beyond a simple postcolonial critique and take on the more contemporary politics of globalization; for example, those who labor to produce this fabric in Manchester are predominantly South East Asian, once the subjects of the same empire on which the sun never set. When these dresses are displayed in places like Dakar, New York, and London, they are always headless, implying an exercise of power that also can be seen both ways: either the heads of Europeans have been removed, as in the French Revolution, or, if one reads the figures as African, then perhaps their headlessness indicates an irrationality or lack of vitality. Indeed, these figures might be so stylized as to be impotent. Shonibare also deliberately frustrates the viewer's need to discern them racially— his dresses nearly always adorn handless mannequins with limbs whose skin color does not indicate race—some are pink, others tawny, making it impossible to know if they are Victorians in Africa or African Victorians. With so much unknown, what comes to matter is not only what a figure like "Big Boy" is wearing, but also how he wears it, how he works the costume. Standing tall in bold confusion, a figure in the midst of an unspoken, but extremely provocative Afro-cosmopolitan narrative, he performs a gesture of announcement and demands appreciation.

One wonders if, with these signifying sculptures, Shonibare is indicating that "he wants us to get over colonial (and post-colonial) ideology and rhetoric" and is using the dandy and dandyism and play with clothing, gesture, and wit as a fabulous illustration of this new sentiment.[131] As Evence Verdier suggests in trying to situate Shonibare's dandyism, "The dandy, like the libertine, or the rake defined [defied?] conventional values and social norms to experiment with a new unique individuality. Shonibare wields that power of disquiet, the force of nonconformity and the resources of pleasure against the unshakable optimism that was modernism's signature and that now characterizes the advocates of globalization."[132] This tendency of Shonibare originates in his sense of himself as a cosmopolitan, a new kind of African artist imaging a host of "post-'s," including, perhaps, post-blackness. As noted, Shonibare was born in London, in 1962, and raised in Lagos, Nigeria, a city then "pulsating" with a heady mix of postindependence pride (Nigeria became independent in 1960), British colonial influence, Islamic, Catholic, and native religious culture, Bollywood cinema, and American kung-fu films.[133] According to his own report, "The Australian program *Scoopy* [sic; actually *Skippy*] *the Kangaroo*, the American [television shows] Batman and Robin, and Soul Train" were the cultural markers he discussed at home in Yoruba, even while learning "perfect" English at a "very strict private school."[134] Born into an aristocratic family and the son of a successful lawyer, Shonibare traveled in style—he was chauffeured to that strict private school and he summered in London until he was sixteen, when he was sent to England permanently to an "upper-class boarding school."[135] Against his parent's wishes, he earned a bachelor of arts degree in art and then took his masters from the prestigious Goldsmith's College of Art. A perhaps perfect example of the postcolonial cosmopolitan when he debuted on the art scene in 1994, he was well positioned to blend his multicultural, international, high-low cultural upbringing with the materials to which he was exposed at art school: what he identifies as feminist theory, especially as exemplified by the work of Cindy Sherman and Barbara Kruger, and the "conceptual work and theory [of] . . . Foucault and Derrida."[136] Through Sherman's work in particular he found a mode of inquiry that led him into the dandy's masquerade. For Shonibare, Sherman "did not apologize for the beauty of what she did," and he admired her performativity, saying, "I guess some of my own photographic work was influenced by her approach. Except, I wanted to expand the performance beyond the single person and sought ways to relate my own identity to a broader context."[137]

As his medium has moved from painting to sculpture to photography and, most recently, to film, Shonibare's practice of dandyism and exploration of black cosmopolitan possibilities has expanded across media and well beyond his personal concerns. As he takes on the black dandy figure as the vehicle of his productive confusion, he continues to intrigue and to warn of the potential dangers of the dandy's redemptive narcissism, of the possible missteps attendant to his masquerade. As an artist who works on dandyism, he is aware of the politics of the trend within the art world (for example, who or what will be the next big thing). In fact, he is not only aware of trends, but also knows that he must profit from them when he can. In the late 1990s and early 2000s, his fabric sculptures became extremely popular—there was a time when a Shonibare piece could be included in nearly any group exhibition on contemporary African art, postmodernism, costume, gender masquerade, to name but a few. When asked in 2004 during a residence in Stockholm why he made a model of Sweden's national treasure, the famous ship *Vasa*, in African fabric, he responded that he did so not to reveal an uncovered story of a Swedish colonial past in Africa, but simply because the fabric has become his signature.[138] "Yinka Shonibare" has become a brand, a kind of collection of which everyone would like to have a piece. The fabric which was once used primarily to signal a profound ambiguity and ambivalence is now, at times, a definitive mark of Shonibare's design. Taking advantage of the market, Shonibare reveals here, if anything, that "dandy" does not mean fool, that black dandyism has always operated in relationship to the market. Even the profit from Shonibare's work will not be one-dimensional; just as he gains from the marketing of his work he provides a lesson from which dandy-watchers will profit also. While displayed in no uncertain terms in his work in Sweden, such an awareness seemingly permeates his work in other media, including his most explicitly dandy pieces, his large-format photograph series titled "Diary of a Victorian Dandy" (1998) and "Dorian Gray" (2001).

Shonibare playing the dandy himself was perhaps inevitable—as one critic says, "If the public wants to pin a given identity on a complex and hence ambiguous experience like his, he, an aristocrat by birth and unconventional by upbringing, is bound to wear the mask of the most sophisticated epicene and cosmopolitan dandy."[139] While he has not yet worn any of his dresses, Shonibare nevertheless identifies as a black dandy and with the figure's history since, despite his protests to the contrary, he does occasionally take on at least the trappings of the subversive stylist: once, Shonibare went to an exhibit of his work "accompanied by two formally dressed attendants."[140] While a sculpture like "Big Boy" challenges the viewer to fill in a context around the dandified figure (as most of the sculptures are displayed without a background, as "naked" tableaux), Shonibare's photographic work presents the dandy's context in the same kind of meticulous, wry detail that characterizes the fabric folds in his sculpture. Here, the dandy as Shonibare plays him is definitively African; his setting is at once the Enlightenment, Victorian England, and altogether contemporary. Like the works of the other dandy artists under discussion here, "Diary of a Victorian Dandy" and "Dorian Gray" are simultaneously self-portraits and histories of black representation. But Shonibare's work looks at the history of black representation explicitly through the dandy's history — the mirror he holds up to himself is one that reflects the history recounted in this book. The narcissism in Shonibare's photography is redemptive, like that of Julien, Harris, and Udé, and simultaneously comments on and critiques the possibility of redemption in the black dandy's narcissism specifically. Whereas critics, myself included, have read skepticism into the power of black dandyism as it meets the market in work like that of Udé, Shonibare, as the dandy and artist himself, performs this same critical function in his work. His skepticism about the ability of the dandy's subversive style to image or imagine "one startling step beyond" or a post-blackness infects his photographic work even as it presents a black dandy in all of his velvet-clad glory.

"Diary of a Victorian Dandy" startles. Shot like film stills — a decision exploited much further in "Dorian Gray" and culminating later in the film "Un Ballo in Maschera" (2004) — "Diary of a Victorian Dandy" consists of five large-format photographs (seventy-two by ninety inches) chronicling the day of a black dandy from his morning toilet through his late night / early morning revels. Shonibare brings to this series all the tricks associated with his dresses — in each image "masquerade, fantasy, and camouflage" that confuse race and power, gender and sexuality, intersect with history as he uses the series to experiment not only with "a whole series of historical questions," but also with a set of aesthetic questions.[141] While some have questioned whether "Diary of a Victorian Dandy" is a "biopic on some recently discovered historical figure, or a fictional fantasy," others have attempted to name that figure, saying that it "alludes to the likes of Ignatius Sancho, an African man of letters . . . who also enjoyed life in the upper echelons of 18th-century English society."[142] Of course, both interpretations are almost right as "Diary of a Victorian

Dandy" signifies transhistorically as it reimagines the black dandy's origins and classic European dandy locations (Victorian England), while
also bringing the figure to the threshold of the twentieth century. In this
piece, Shonibare calls on William Hogarth, Wilde, Julien, Harris, and Udé
to narrate the black dandy's more recent exploits.

Though Shonibare said of his paintings, "I'm not just making pretty,
pretty objects. I try to locate them in the history of art," the same sentiment applies to "Diary of a Victorian Dandy."[143] In this series, Shonibare
references Hogarth's rendition of the dandy's history and his engagement
with representations of blacks caught up in elite milieu. As the first chapter of this book shows, black dandyism had its origins in Enlightenment
England, when young black boys from Africa and the Caribbean were
forced into foppery as examples of the fabulous wealth of their masters.
Some of these boys, like Ignatius Sancho (who, before his life as a diarist
and merchant, was also a prestige servant), took advantage of their spectacularity and exploited, to the degree they could, the social world that
confused their status as subjects and objects. As an artist, Hogarth played
a fascinating role in recording this phenomenon. Early in his career, he
painted portraits of aristocratic families in which the presence of ostentatiously dressed black servants emphasizes the wealth and whiteness of
their masters and mistresses. These blacks might be positioned in the
background of a scene, as decoration, or in the foreground, actively
serving their masters and mistresses. Later in his career, just as some
of these servants were making real and symbolic bids for their freedom,
Hogarth also devoted himself to paintings and prints that, in their satiri-
zation of the upper classes, recorded the life and viewpoints of the lower
orders, black and white.

According to David Dabydeen, some of Hogarth's satiric paintings
and prints effectively reread his earlier aristocratic portraits by granting the black figures within them a critical perspective that does not fail
to "acknowledg[e] the wealth and colonial connections of [their] masters."[144] For example, Dabydeen reads the ostentatiously dressed black
servants in some of Hogarth's best-known work, for example, plate 4 of
Marriage à la Mode (1743), as the only "natural" and "civilized" people
depicted in the painting, "us[ed] . . . positively as the norm against which
the inadequacies of [the] masters are measured."[145] An elaborate scene
that takes place in a mistress's bedroom, where she is being entertained

37. William Hogarth, *Marriage à la Mode, IV* (The Countess's Morning Levee) (1743).
© National Gallery, London.

by an Italian opera singer and attended by her lover, friends, and servants, this plate elaborately comments on the dissipation of the wealthy. In the painting, Hogarth exposes their leisure as that which emanates from or participates in a deviance and barbarity that are enabled by the labor of prestige blacks. Presiding over the scene is a black man serving chocolate with a sly smile on his face; he seems to know that his mistress will have no success with the opera singer, who is more interested in the castrato sitting next to him. Objects in the room, among them an empire-derived American and African *objet* on the floor in front of the singer, reinforce the artist's point that elite spaces are often characterized by loose morals and economic exploitation. In depicting the black perspective, Hogarth leads the viewer to the inevitable conclusion that white elites have been corrupted by their ultrafashionable, wholly self-gratifying way of life. This

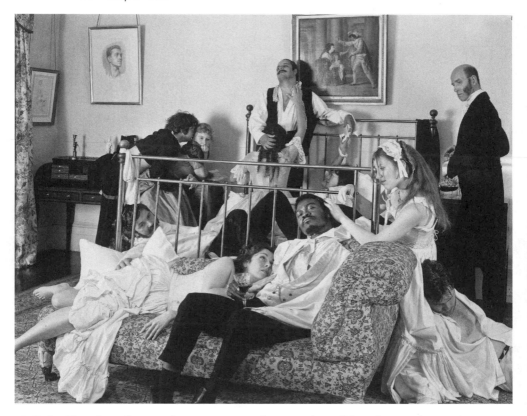

38. Yinka Shonibare, "Diary of a Victorian Dandy: 03:00 hours" (1998). © Yinka Shonibare, MBE. Courtesy of the artist and Stephen Friedman Gallery, London.

perspective shift revises and re-presents the place of the ostentatiously dressed black by styling him as a visible and visual critique within this elite narrative.

In "Diary of a Victorian Dandy," Shonibare implicitly references the black boys of *Marriage à la Mode* while explicitly inserting them into another Hogarthian cautionary tale, "The Rake's Progress" (1735; engraved 1822). In the original sequence of "The Rake's Progress," a dandy is made and unmade. The first scenes introduce young Tom Rakewell, recently graduated from Oxford; he has just inherited his father's wealth and, in celebration, is being outfitted in a costume and environment appropriate for his new aristocratic station. Tom's costume seems to fit him well, as he is soon gambling and whoring with the best of them. Quickly becoming

39. Yinka Shonibare, "Diary of a Victorian Dandy: 19:00 hours" (1998). © Yinka Shonibare, MBE. Courtesy of the artist and Stephen Friedman Gallery, London.

insolvent, Tom is arrested and forced to marry a wealthy widow to pay his debts and restore his fortune. Predictably, he continues his rakish ways and, too late, pledges reform. Reform does not last, and Tom soon finds himself in jail and, later, in the madhouse. A comment on the excesses of luxury and their culmination in the degeneracy of the individual, the class, the nation, "The Rake's Progress" both delights in and censures the young man in question, drawing with equal relish his rise and fall.

Hogarth's rake is Shonibare's dandy, transported to Victorian England and present-day London. His dandy makes progress as well, but he progresses through the stages of his own pleasure, not toward any punishment. One does not see this dandy made, but meets him in medias res, suggesting his haunting omnipresence (who or what he haunts is the question). Given that this is the dandy's diary, rather than a rake's progress, what one looks at in Shonibare's sequence is what this black dandy wants one to see. Here, instead of being relegated to the margins of a print, this dandy is central to each image. Instead of wearing a livery and being at someone else's service, this dandy is served, again and again. There is no scene here in which the dandy does not appear totally in control: indeed, "3 hours" shows the dandy being not only served, but also serviced, as he lounges in a pink waistcoat on the bed, surrounded by servants in various stages of sexual exploration of him and each other. His presence animates this orgiastic setting—throughout the sequence, all eyes devour him when he is either in the bedroom or the boardroom. The black dandy alone is desired. Fawned over, attended to, obeyed, and finally applauded, this Victorian dandy demands notice. In all of these images, his clothing is the richest and most colorful, as all the other figures are positioned, it seems, to get a good view. Finally, at "19 hours," he is being toasted for his accomplishment—for privileging the subjectivity, rather than the objectivity of Hogarth's black boys, for inserting his interrogative body within this frame, practicing a redemptive narcissism. Whether he exposes Enlightenment and Victorian society as dependent on his heretofore invisible or marginal presence or gives one a glimpse of a colonial Lagos inhabited by his own aristocratic family, in the "Diary of a Victorian Dandy," as in his entire oeuvre, Shonibare "would proffer a fiction of difference, like the devil's hand in a card game."[146]

The staged quality of these images and the settings in which they appear do impact how one reads the narcissism within them; when exhibited in a gallery, the images are shown in elaborate, heavy, gilt frames. Though seemingly triumphant, Shonibare as Victorian dandy within these scenes seems both in command and awkwardly positioned, alienated within them. The dandy's body is stiff and still, his face blank, in marked contrast to the eager-to-please faces and much more expressive bodies of his servants, attendants, and audience. Though the figure's disposition in these photos is partly due to Shonibare's physical limitations (he was nearly crippled by a viral infection while in his first year of art school), his dis-ease within the frame is both actual and symbolic. This dandy might be, like his Hogarthian predecessors, imprisoned within this image, all grown up (a "Big Boy") but with no discernible way out of the frame that raised him. Additionally, when reproduced in exhibition catalogs, the scene most raw in its desire, the orgy scene "3 hours," is positioned sometimes as the first photograph in the series, sometimes as the last. Thus, "Diary of a Victorian Dandy" has a distinctive circularity about it. The dandy's narcissism in these elaborate self-portraits both redeems and traps.

The dandy here may not only invade the eighteenth-century scene and revise its Victorian legacy, but also offer a comment on the cosmopolitan nature of twentieth- or twenty-first century blackness in doing so. As important as the staged quality of the work is the venue in which it first appeared in 1998, the London Underground, or subway, and also its potential relationship to the other dandy work with which this chapter is concerned. Commissioned by the International Institute for Visual Arts and first seen by Londoners in transit, "Diary of a Victorian Dandy" has a strange but intriguing association with travel, movement, and the mobility of the multicultural laboring masses, an association that asks one to see its black dandy differently still. Even if the dandy is arrested within the frame of the photographs, he would have been seen in fleeting glances and also in more contemplative moments in Underground stations, from an endless number of perspectives. The dandy here could be triumphant and defeated, invader and occupant, confrontational and melancholy, dead and alive, depending on who is looking and from what perspective. Audience matters here, and when looking at this work one might also consider that some of the Underground riders and certainly those who encountered this work in galleries all over the world perhaps discerned its relationship to the dandyism in the work of Harris and Udé. Thus, at the same time that Shonibare builds a stage on which to play out the dandy's beautiful wink and snarl at history, he also inhabits that set, creating with "Diary of a Victorian Dandy" a mirror that does not lie.

In "Dorian Gray," Shonibare asks a related but slightly different set of questions about the politics of the look and "appropriate aesthetics" through the dandy figure. As in the "Diary of a Victorian Dandy" series, Shonibare is once again rewriting a classic, taking on Wilde's famous tale of decadence. This time, however, Shonibare works not to expose its suppressed African connections, but to more explicitly explore both the danger and pleasure of the narcissism that fuels these images and dandy art in general. Again, there is a doubling in this piece, as Shonibare's "Dorian Gray" references two versions of "The Picture of Dorian Gray" and the time periods from which they emanate. Obviously, Wilde's story of 1890 set in London is the main referent, but, unexpectedly, the series also references an American film of the story from 1945, directed by Albert Lewin. As a twenty-first-century "copy" of two earlier originals, Shonibare's "Dorian Gray," like "Diary of a Victorian Dandy," disturbs stories of origin as it initiates, once again, a contest between the real and the representation, the original and the copy. Deliberately shot in the form of twelve film stills that correspond in mood, but not always in content, to the Lewin film, "Dorian Gray" follows the Wildean story, which, like "Diary of a Victorian Dandy," celebrates and reviles the dandy figure. Perhaps because it is rendered in black and white, like the film, and strives to take advantage of the medium's light and shadow as psychological effects, "Dorian Gray" seems less triumphant and even more cautionary about the subversiveness and liberatory quality of Shonibare's — or any artist's — dandy masquerade.

Just as "Diary of a Victorian Dandy" follows a black rake through his day, "Dorian" follows a black dandy through his encounter with Wilde's "New Hedonism." Initiated into the dandy's life by Lord Henry, Shonibare's Dorian presides over a gloomy Gothic narrative that because of its black protagonist and fateful entanglement both with Lord Henry and Sybil Vane could read as much like *Othello* as like Wilde's novel. The moments of Dorian's tale that Shonibare chooses to represent and the way in which he represents them are curious, leading one to surmise that, as interpreted by Shonibare's camera, what is at stake in this "Dorian Gray" are not only the Wildean themes concerning the moral compass of aestheticism or the ethical problem of psychological influence, but the power of self-regard. The sequence opens with Lord Henry admiring Basil's picture of Dorian; this is followed not by the moment in which Lord Henry meets Dorian and brings him under his influence, but by Dorian gazing laconically at himself in a mirror. Next is a shot of Sibyl Vane singing (she is a chanteuse, rather than an actress, in the film), and then Dorian's introduction to Sibyl, the only image in the Shonibare oeuvre in which the black dandy smiles. Next, Lord Henry and Dorian meet in the park, seemingly solidifying Henry's influence over him; then Basil confronts Dorian about his reputation (in two shots), which results in the scene of Dorian's murder of Basil after revealing to him the secret of the aging, putrefying, somaticizing picture. Missing here is a shot of the dis-

40. Yinka Shonibare, "Dorian Gray" (detail) (2001). © Yinka Shonibare, MBE. Courtesy of the artist and Stephen Friedman Gallery, London.

solution of his relationship with Sibyl, his initial realization that the portrait reveals his decadence and cruelty, the effort he makes to drown his guilty dissipation in drink, drugs, the collection of exotic *objets*, and the sexual exploitation of both the high- and lowborn—all potentially interesting dandy moments worth imaging. In the next-to-last still, Shonibare presents a shot of Dorian alone in a park. At last, the viewer sees him finally gazing upon his degradation in the one shot that Shonibare renders in color, followed by a final image of his subsequent death. Tellingly in Shonibare's "Dorian Gray" it is not the destruction of the painting that leads to Dorian's death, but the destruction of Basil, the painter, that kills the dandy.

Since major moments in the plot of both the novel and the film are missing in this series, the drama of this particular narrative is not what

41. Yinka Shonibare, "Dorian Gray" (detail) (2001). © Yinka Shonibare, MBE.
Courtesy of the artist and Stephen Friedman Gallery, London.

Shonibare is after. What he privileges in these scenes seems to be a dandy's
contemplation, rather than his status as a provocateur or pleasure-seeker.
In shot after shot Dorian is either contemplating his own image or involved in what looks like guarded conversation with others; the image
of Dorian in the park is particularly telling, as its presence illustrates his
physical isolation from others and perhaps even from himself (his back is
to the camera, as in the murder scene). Nowhere is the sexuality depicted
in "Diary of a Victorian Dandy," in Wilde's story, and in Lewin's film in
evidence in this series; it is empty of any scenes of charged assignations
between Dorian and Sybil or of homoerotic banter between Lord Henry,
Basil, or Dorian. Shonibare empties out the queer content of one of the

English language's most prototypically queer texts.[147] Therefore, "Dorian Gray" must function as something other than an eccentric retelling of Wilde's masterpiece. I read it as a metatext about race and regard. Black and dandy, the outsider status of this figure rather than his sartorial fabulousness or seductive power is on display. If anything is emphasized in this series, it is the melancholy of this lonely position.

In full color and lavish style, the earlier "Diary of a Victorian Dandy" announces the black dandy's presence partially by means of color. The black-and-white "Dorian Gray" flashes into color only when the dandy faces himself in the mirror, when, in the story, he would have looked at his painting for confirmation of his depravity (the flash into color is consistent with the film). The 1945 film version of "The Picture of Dorian Gray" was one of the first Hollywood films to use color. In the film, the Technicolor shots of Dorian's picture are literally and figuratively brilliant, absolutely captivating—beautiful and deadly. In choosing to render the Wildean story through this film, Shonibare uses the contrast between black and white and color and changes the picture to a mirror to teach his own lesson about the consequences of aestheticism. What the young, white Dorian gets away with in the novel and the film, the black dandy of this photographic series does not. In Shonibare's series there is no displacement of this dandy's narcissistic depravity onto a separate object, the picture of the title, for the picture of Dorian that appears in the first frame never reappears. Instead, a mirror replaces it and reveals his degradation, suggesting that Dorian's evil has been internalized. In these moments of introspection, his ruin is revealed in his own reflection, in its color, its blackness. The space between skin and costume is here completely dissolved. I read this series not as a specific comment on Wilde's story or Lewin's film, but as a comment on the black dandy's heretofore colorful postcolonial re-dressing, his bold attempt at redemptive narcissism. Prostrate on the floor, his face destroyed and looking diseased, this dandy dies a victim of his hubris. He is, perhaps, provocatively, hopelessly, and fatally fascinated with his own beauty and self-fashioning. With "Dorian Gray," Shonibare seemingly critiques his own project (and that of others) of re-visioning colonial objectification and postcolonial narcissism through the dandy figure.

In an interview, Shonibare said, "My work is read in contradictory ways, sometimes by the same critics, and I enjoy that. I think the value of resolving something is overstated. I don't necessarily think that resolution is what a poet should be seeking."[148] With this in mind, I turn to one of Shonibare's latest efforts, the film "Un Ballo in Maschera (A Masked Ball)" (2004). Taking its title and putative subject from Giuseppe Verdi's opera of 1859 about the assassination in 1792 of King Gustav III of Sweden at a masked ball, "Un Ballo in Maschera" is a fascinating turn in Shonibare's practice in terms of both form and content. "Un Ballo in Maschera" animates the fabric sculptures within the lavish, aristocratic settings featured in his photographs, intersecting the tricksterism and masquerade that is constitutive of each piece. The film is set in what appears to be an eighteenth-century period room and features a stylized dance performed by figures clad in versions of his African costumes. Characteristically gender bending and playful with sexuality, Shonibare casts the king and his assassin as women, heightening the sexual tension between them. While the Swedish nature of the subject may not matter—as Shonibare says that with the setting he was primarily searching for a metaphor—some of the local circumstances are, nevertheless, intriguing. Gustav III (1746–92) was Sweden's Enlightenment king, a patron of the arts and a lover of theater. He lived and died by masquerade, as he was reportedly a slovenly person who "liked to be surrounded by splendour and elegance" and who modeled his court on that of Louis XIV even while he placed many new restrictions on noble power. He even engineered a war with Russia by having Swedes dressed as Russians fire on Swedish troops. As a result of that war and of the cultural fallout from the French Revolution, he was assassinated at a masquerade ball at the opera in 1792.[149] Of uncertain sexuality and a bon vivant who loved to act and appear on stage himself, Gustav III, metaphor or not, is a fascinating character given his propensity for theatricality and dissembling.

Shonibare indicates that when he decided to do a film about power during his time in Sweden, "Un Ballo in Maschera" emerged as a way to speak indirectly about current political events in a world increasingly defined by the phrase "You are either with us or against us."[150] Wanting to once again "challenge opposites," he decided to use the dance and death of an overly confident, foreign king to image the beautiful ambivalence of revenge. But just as every Shonibare work can be read in multiple, even contradictory, ways, "Un Ballo in Maschera" is as much about Shonibare's current practice as it is about current events. In the film, the king

42. Yinka Shonibare, "Un Ballo in Maschera (A Masked Ball)."
Film still. (2004). © Yinka Shonibare, MBE. Courtesy of the artist and
Stephen Friedman Gallery, London.

(as noted, a woman in man's clothing), accompanied by two courtiers,
dances his way into a room, glides purposefully about the floor, displaying his command of the space and everyone in it with a coy smile. During
the dance, he is lifted high above everyone else and with his gracious
and commanding steps clears a path through the crowd with his kinetic
power. When he finishes his last move, throwing his arms up in the air as
if to say, "Aha!" the courtiers erupt in applause. As the king basks in his
accomplishment, a group of male courtiers attending a lavishly dressed
woman answers his challenge. In an ever-changing formation which both
reveals and envelops the woman at their center, the courtiers dance in
deference to and in defiance of the king, displaying an uncertain obedi-
ence to his powerful presence. Eventually, the woman stops directly in
front of the king, and he acknowledges her presence by kissing his lips
with his fingers and moving his hand slowly toward her face. As the dance

ends, the king looks away, and the woman points a revolver at him and shoots him dead. Courtiers rush to his side and pick him up — revived and smiling, the king begins the dance again.

In "Un Ballo in Maschera," the king and his assassin enter the room, the king dances and dies three times, simulating a loop effect characteristic of film in gallery settings. Each time, the dance is slightly, almost imperceptibly different. At the end of the third iteration, there is a change — the film is rolled backward, the king steps out of the room and the assassin steps down the stair she uses to enter the building. At once an illustration of "history repeating" and the inevitability of repetition with a difference, "Un Ballo in Maschera" demonstrates the possibility of resuscitation and renewal — as Shonibare says, "The impossible happens within the film." If one sees the king here alternatively as the black dandy and Shonibare as dandy artist, then this dance is as much about the power of an aesthetic that turns on masquerade, subversive style, and redemptive narcissism as it is about political power. As such, "Un Ballo in Maschera" is a manifestation of the repeated and even impossible success and failure of the dance of dandyism as an aesthetic tool to define and redefine blackness and cosmopolitanism. Though threatened by his own overweening power, the narcissist lives for Shonibare, forewarned oxymoronically by the past and the future.

Notes

Introduction

1. The servant boy is pictured with his owner, James Drummond of Scotland, the Second Titular Duke of Perth. The phrase "African American Gentlemen's Movement" was first coined by the valet/rapper/entrepreneur Fonzworth Bentley. For more on Andre 3000 as a style icon, leading a change in hip-hop dress from sportswear to Savile Row, see Richard L. Eldredge, "Andre 3000 Togs a '10' with Esquire," *Atlanta Journal-Constitution*, August 12, 2004; "Andre 3000 Gets Style from Prince Charles," *UPI*, September 9, 2004; Lynn Hirschberg, "The Originals," *New York Times*, September 19, 2004.

2. "Virginia in 1732, The Travel Journal of William Hugh Grove," ed. Gregory A. Stiverson and Patrick H. Butler III, quoted in Baumgarten, "'Clothes for the People': Slave Clothing in Early Virginia," 28.

3. *Runaway Slave Advertisements*, compiled by Windley, 78.

4. Ibid., 167.

5. When I use "performance" and "performativity," I follow other literary scholars and scholars of performance studies who, in trying to account for what E. Patrick Johnson calls the "aesthetic, cultural and social communicative events, interpretive practices and critical methodologies" of people of color, refer to a critical methodology that is an intersection between the high theory of deconstructive social semioticians such as Judith Butler and the critical interventions seen or experienced in interrogative, culturally and historically specific behaviors of people of color. See Johnson, *Appropriating Blackness*, 6.

6. Elam, "The Device of Race," *African American Performance and Theater History*, ed. Elam and Krasner, 4.

7. For more on the emergence of "black" and "African" as self-description for the enslaved, see Michael A. Gomez, *Exchanging Our Country Marks*. The black dandy's sartorial performativity thus makes manifest this sense of identity and tailors it to more specific black needs or ends.

8. I borrow this phrase from E. Patrick Johnson and Mae G. Henderson,

"Introduction: Queering Black Studies / Quaring Queer Studies," *Black Queer Studies*, ed. E. Patrick Johnson and Mae G. Henderson, 1.

9. Elam, "The Black Performer and the Performance of Blackness," *African American Performance and Theater History*, ed. Elam and Krasner, 290.

10. Beerbohm, "Dandies and Dandies," *The Bodley Head Max Beerbohm*, ed. David Cecil, 190.

11. The classic texts of European dandyism include Beerbohm; Charles Baudelaire, *Selected Writings on Art and Literature*, trans. P. E. Charvet; George Gordon Byron, *Byron: A Self-Portrait, Letters and Diaries, 1798 to 1824*, ed. Peter Quennell; Albert Camus, *The Rebel: An Essay on Man in Revolt* (*L'Homme Revolte*); Thomas Carlyle, *Sartor Resartus*; Jules Barbey D'Aurevilly, *Dandyism* (*du dandysme et Georges Brummell*), trans. Douglas Ainslie; Jean Paul Sartre, *Baudelaire*, trans. Martin Turnell; Oscar Wilde, *The Complete Works of Oscar Wilde*.

12. "Fop," *Oxford English Dictionary*, 2d edn.

13. "Dandy," *Oxford English Dictionary*, 2d edn.

14. The etymology of "dandy" in the *Oxford English Dictionary* indicates that the word's origin is unknown, although it is perhaps a form of "jack-a-dandy," related to the French words *dandiprat*, a small coin, or, *dandin / dandiner*, to waddle; in addition, "dandy" is a form of Andrew in Scotland. In chapter 4 of this book, I speculate about the association between "dandy" and "dandiprat" in a discussion of father-son inheritance in James Weldon Johnson's *The Autobiography of an Ex-Coloured Man*.

15. Laver, *Dandies*, 10.

16. Moers, *The Dandy*, 13.

17. For more on dandyism's semiotics, see Domna Stanton, *The Aristocrat as Art*, in which she avers that a dandy's resignification of flamboyant dress and attitude, along with a characteristic exhibition of "innovation and eccentricity, paradox and hyperbole," "transform[s] every pertinent element of [the dandy's] body, dress or ornamentation, manners, speech into a system of poetic signs laden with secret, nondiscursive meanings," 173. For the most recent book-length interventions in fashion theory generally, see Berg Publisher's excellent series *Dress, Body, Culture*; Berg also publishes the journal *Fashion Theory* and in 2009 will release *The Men's Fashion Reader*, ed. Peter McNeil and Vicki Karaminas, the most comprehensive, historically informed collection of articles on the semiotics and politics of men's dress currently available.

18. E. Patrick Johnson, "'Quare Studies,'" *Black Queer Studies*, ed. E. Patrick Johnson and Mae G. Henderson, 125.

19. Ferguson, *Aberrations in Black*, 5. Like Ferguson, I would like to ac-

knowledge that the first group of theorists to oppose and challenge "ideologies of discreteness" were women of color feminists; queer theorists of color or quare theorists owe a great intellectual and spiritual debt to these pioneering women, who refused to theorize their identities in ways different from how they experienced them — as intersections of race, gender, sexuality, class, and nation.

20. Muñoz, *Disidentifications*, 28.

21. See Feldman, *Gender on the Divide*, and Garelick, *Rising Star*. The Prince reference is to Garelick.

22. Unfortunately, only *Black British Style* produced a catalog of essays along with it, *Black Style*, ed. Carol Tulloch. The cocurators of *Black Style Now* in New York, Michael Henry Adams and Michael McCollom, have both published books on black style in architecture, home decoration, and fashion. See especially Adams, *Style and Grace*, and McCollom, *The Way We Wore*.

23. Fillin-Yeh, "Preface," *Dandies*, ed. Susan Fillin-Yeh, ix.

24. Powell, "Sartor Africanus," in *Dandies*, ed. Susan Fillin-Yeh, 224.

25. Ibid., 225.

26. Roach, *Cities of the Dead*, xi.

27. Signifying was first famously theorized by Henry Louis Gates Jr. as a vernacular oral tradition that encompasses "marking, loud-talking, testifying, calling out (of one's name), sounding, rapping, playing the dozens," in *The Signifying Monkey*, 52. Caponi, "Introduction: The Case for an African American Aesthetic," *Signifyin(g), Sanctifyin,' and Slam-dunking*, 22.

28. Elam on Homi Bhabha, in "The Black Performer," in *African American Performance and Theater History*, ed. Elam and Krasner, 289.

29. Diamond, "Introduction," *Performance and Cultural Politics*, quoted in Diana J. Paulin, "Acting Out Miscegenation," *African American Performance and Theater History*, ed. Elam and Krasner, 266, note 5.

30. Diamond, "Introduction," *Performance and Cultural Politics*, quoted in Elam, "The Device of Race," 9.

31. Elam, "The Device of Race," *African American Performance and Theater History*, ed. Elam and Krasner, 5.

32. Scott, "From Weapons of the Weak," *The Cultural Resistance Reader*, ed. Stephen Duncombe, 90.

33. Ibid., 93, 90.

34. Ibid., 93.

35. Kelley, "Introduction: Writing Black Working Class History from Way, Way Below," *Race Rebels*, 4. For more on the zoot suit, see Cosgrove, "The Zoot Suit and Style Warfare," *History Workshop Journal*. For more on subcultural style in general, see Hebdige, *Subculture*.

36. White and White, *Stylin'*, 2, 4.

37. Kelley, "'We Are Not What We Seem,'" *Journal of American History*, 86.

38. For more on these ironies, see Greenberg, *'Or Does it Explode?,'* and Weems, *Desegregating the Dollar*.

39. Weems quotes an article from an African American marketing researcher, David Sullivan, who states in 1943 that, "the U.S. Chamber of Commerce says, and facts prove, that Negroes spend more money for clothes per capita than do white people in New York City and other large cities," *Desegregating the Dollar*, 32.

40. Feldman, *Gender on the Divide*, 9.

41. According to Colin Campbell, "Those who dedicate themselves to keeping up with fashion—even more interestingly, to 'taking the lead' in fashion—can be said, quite justifiably, to be striving to bring their lives in line with the ideal of beauty . . . [a] high-minded pursuit of a serious ideal"; see "Consuming Goods and the Good of Consuming," *Consumer Society in American History*, ed. Glickman, 29.

42. Phelan, *Unmarked*, 97.

43. Ibid., 180.

44. Udé echoes José Muñoz, whose work posits the performativity of minoritarian subjects as a "utopian blueprint for a possible future, while at the same time, staging a new political formation in the present," Muñoz, *Disidentifications*, 200.

45. Udé, "Elements of Style," *aRude*.

46. I borrow this phrase from the recent book *Black Cultural Traffic*, ed. Elam and Jackson.

47. Carby, *Race Men*, 12.

48. Certainly, during the intervening fifty years, black people were still stylin' out, yet in a different spirit or way. Even though the glamorous dress of Little Richard (and many of his Motown colleagues), the uniform-like disciplined clothing of the Black Panthers, funky and flashy polyester jumpsuits, and over-the-top boas of Blaxploitation-era heroes and pimps share some of the traits and functions of black dandyism, they are nevertheless separate from the phenomena I explore in this book. With a few exceptions, these clothing practices lack a certain combination of irony and seriousness, a sartorial and attitudinal wink and nod ventured for survival when in dire straits. Because these efforts are, perhaps, more choices of wardrobe than gestures fundamentally constitutive of self-fashioning, I choose to conclude this book with the dandyism that emerges in the 1990s, after another signal moment of transition for black people. It is not until then, after the multiple libera-

tion movements in the mid- to late twentieth century (postcolonial, civil rights, gay and lesbian rights) that the dandy reappears in a truly sassy, avant-garde form, ready, once again, with a critique and idealization of a "freedom dream."

49. Hall, "What Is This 'Black' in Black Popular Culture?," *Black Popular Culture*, ed. Gina Dent, 27.

CHAPTER ONE Mungo Macaroni

1. Fahrner, "David Garrick Presents *The Padlock*," 58.

2. Cooley, "An Early Representation of African-American English," 51–52, and Fahrner, "David Garrick Presents *The Padlock*," 57.

3. See Pentzell, "Garrick's Costuming," 18–42, and the section titled "Black Looks Onstage and Off," below.

4. Other performances in which blackface would have been used included *Othello* and *Oroonoko*, two plays very popular during the eighteenth century.

5. De Bolla, "The Visibility of Visuality," 65.

6. Fahrner, "David Garrick Presents *The Padlock*," 52.

7. Ibid., 63.

8. "Mungo," *Oxford English Dictionary*, 2d ed.

9. Cervantes, "The Jealous Extremaduran," 15. The stories were first translated into English in 1640 by James Mabbe, who was also known as Don Diego Puede Ser.

10. Bickerstaffe, *The Padlock* (1768), n. pag. or i.

11. Cervantes, "The Jealous Extremaduran," 180.

12. Cooley, "An Early Representation of African-American English," 55. A survey of eighteenth-century drama yields very few plays with any substantial parts for black characters in the Restoration and eighteenth century. Well-known plays like Southerne's *Oroonoko* (1695), *Paul and Virginia* (1799), *Laugh When You Can* (1799), and *The Africans* (1808 / 1843) do not include black characters that resemble Mungo; instead the plays as a group are much more in the noble savage school. In one of the earliest surveys of literary attitudes concerning blacks in English literature, the historian Carter G. Woodson places *The Padlock* in the post-*Oroonoko*, post–noble savage school of depictions of blacks "who deeply moved the English public" during the period of the British slave trade. He claims that between *The Padlock* in 1768 and a play called *The West Indian* (1771), "with the exception of the usual presentation of *Othello* with varying interpretations as to the parts the Blackamoor played no other dramatization based upon the life of the Negro deeply moved the

English public until we come to *Uncle Tom's Cabin* [1852]." Woodson is in error about *The West Indian*, a play by Richard Cumberland. He may have been misled by the title—while "West Indian" in the twentieth century almost always connotes black residents of Jamaica and other former British colonies in the Caribbean, earlier it almost always referred to white, British planters resident (at least for a time) in those colonies. The play itself is about a planter returning to London. Though the West Indian in question is an illegitimate son of a white Englishman, the first scene of the play goes out of its way to establish his mother as being white also. While my research has found other plays produced between 1768 and 1852, Woodson's chronology is correct if one looks at truly popular and well-known depictions of blacks on the English stage. To his credit, Woodson is one of the few historians or literary critics to note the importance of *The Padlock* to literary representations of blacks. See Woodson, "Some Attitudes in English Literature," 27–85.

13. "Bastinado," *Oxford English Dictionary*, 2d ed.

14. Fahrner, "David Garrick Presents *The Padlock*," note 11. In the poem, the lines are slightly different: "Be to her Virtues very kind: / Be to her Faults a little blind: / Let all her Ways be unconfin'd: And clap your PADLOCK—on her mind." In later nineteenth-century adaptations of *The Padlock*'s finale, these last lines are eliminated and the character of the wife gets the last word.

15. Mungo may not be a threat to the young wife as a suitor in Don Diego's eyes, but he appears to be a potential general threat to the safety of others. When Diego returns from the country late at night to find his house seemingly open to the public and guarded by a drunken slave, his immediate reaction is to incriminate Mungo:

> *Dieg.* Wretch do you know me?
> *Mung.* Know you—damn you.
> *Dieg.* Horrid creature! what makes you here at / this time of night; is it with a design to surprise the / innocents in their beds, and murder them sleeping?
> *Mung.* Hush, hush—make no noise—hic—hic (II, vi).

Such a reaction might be taken as a general sign of the dis-ease that accompanies enslavement in general and especially, as seen here, the employment of house slaves with whom masters live closely.

16. Bickerstaff, *The Padlock* (1823), ii–iii.

17. Ibid.

18. "Stereotype," *Oxford English Dictionary*, 2d ed.

19. Freeman, *Character's Theater*, 1.

20. Ibid., 16.

21. Ibid., 27.

22. In "An Early Representation of African-American English," Cooley notes of the Cervantes pre-text that "the story is narrated with little dialogue and no dialect representation of Luis's speech either in the original Spanish or in Mabbe's 1640 English translation," 53.

23. Among many examples, see *Birth of a Consumer Society*, ed. Neil Mc-Kendrick, John Brewer, and J. H. Plumb; *Consumption and the World of Goods*, ed. John Brewer and Roy Porter; *Consumption and Culture, 1600–1800*; Blackburn, *The Making of New World Slavery*; Smith, *Consumption and the Making of Respectability*; Breen, *The Marketplace of Revolution*.

24. Brewer, *The Pleasures of the Imagination*, xxv.

25. Orr, *Empire on the English Stage*, 274.

26. In "Visuality and Visibility," Peter de Bolla uses Adam Smith's development of the theory of the "impartial spectator" in *The Theory of Moral Sentiments* (1759) to elaborate on the connection between the visual and identity. For de Bolla, "vision figures Enlightenment thought" (65). Subjectivity and the visual were so implicated in each other that their interaction matters not just for preeminently visual social forms like the theater or the art world (painters and their portraits), but for Enlightenment culture at large.

27. Orr, *Empire on the English Stage*, 19.

28. Ibid., 135.

29. This engraving also appeared in *Dramatic Characters, or, Different Portraits of the English Stage* (London, 1770), Fahrner, "David Garrick Presents *The Padlock*," 60. The same illustration appears in Dr. Doran, *Annals of the English Stage from Thomas Betterton to Edmund Keane*, ed. and rev. Robert W. Lowe, 272. These portraits also appear as figures in Fahrner's article. The illustration of Dibdin with the hat, dating from 1769, can be seen in White, *The Rise of English Opera*.

30. Pentzell, "Garrick's Costuming," 21. Garrick was responsible for many other reforms as well, most notably the removal of spectator seats on the stage itself and also the dimming of the lights in the audience; all of these reforms were designed to change theatrical performance into an event to be watched, rather than one in which to participate. It is tempting to read Mungo's costume as a part of this increased emphasis on spectatorship.

31. Fahrner, "David Garrick Presents *The Padlock*," 59, and Doran, *Annals of the English Stage from Thomas Betterton to Edmund Keane*, 249.

32. Doran, *Annals of the English Stage from Thomas Betterton to Edmund Keane*, 249–53.

33. Pentzell, "Garrick's Costuming," 19.

34. Ibid., 19.

35. The suit is called the "Iachimo suit" by the theater historian Muriel St. Clare Byrne. Byrne chronicles the way in which the suit was used in *Macbeth* as a supposed version of ancient Scots dress. Like Pentzell, she debunks the mythology surrounding the efforts of Garrick and others to present historically accurate costumes on stage, noting the limitations with which he worked and imposed upon himself in terms of his own preferences as an actor on stage. See Byrne, "The Stage Costuming of *Macbeth* in the Eighteenth Century," and Pentzell, "Garrick's Costuming," 32.

36. Pentzell, "Garrick's Costuming," 33.

37. Ibid., 32.

38. In *Staying Power*, Peter Fryer notes that in the seventeenth century, "rich people would often display their wealth and good taste by dressing their black slaves in special costume: either obviously expensive garments or some kind of showy livery," 25. This practice took a particularly ostentatious form in the eighteenth century, when, as a result of the British slave trade and attendant trading enterprises, a greater portion of the population became wealthy enough to own other human beings and use them as part of a growing ethos of conspicuous consumption. See also Shyllon, "Black Body Servants," *Black Slaves in Britain*, and Gerzina, "Princes and Paupers," *Black London: Life Before Emancipation*.

39. Fryer, *Staying Power*, 22, and Shyllon, *Black Slaves in Britain*, 9. The padlocked collar suggests an economic and sexual bondage, a limitation of Mungo as a laborer and a lover. I thank Maurice Wallace for this insight. In his film *The Attendant* (1992), the filmmaker Isaac Julien might be seen to have subversively signified on this phenomenon when he depicts a black man's encounter with the tools of domination and submission. The film animates the s&m fantasies of a black museum guard who gazes on a painting of a slave in bondage, proposing the presence of a complicated pleasure in the reuse of collars, whips, and chains. For more on Julien, see chapter 5.

40. See editions printed in Boston (1795), New York (1805), and London (1823). Actors at the time were well known for taking liberties with the text, adding signature ad-libs to what the playwright furnished. I am indebted to Marianne Cooley's "An Early Representation of African-American English" for her analysis of Mungo's dialect and her focus on Mungo's speech as being African American, or, in the case of the first production of *The Padlock*, in 1768, spoken by an African seemingly once resident in the West Indies or the Americas. In addition, the dialect's combination of real and imagined aspects of black speech had a locatable origin in the writing of the play. The part of Mungo was originally written for John Moody, who had been to the West Indies and founded a theater company in Jamaica, where he gained an

apparent familiarity with West Indian speech. See Fahrner, "David Garrick Presents *The Padlock*," 57.

41. Cooley, "An Early Representation of African-American English," 53.

42. Cooley writes, "In fact, too consistent a representation [of dialect] may be distracting or stereotypical while too accurate a representation may be unintelligible. Perhaps the more important principle is that, given audience reaction to the play, Mungo's speech did not contrast with what the audience accepted or expected an African-American to sound like," ibid., 55.

43. Freeman, *Character's Theater*, 12.

44. De Bolla, "The Visibility of Visuality," 70.

45. Freeman, *Character's Theater*, 27.

46. Barthelemey, *Black Face, Maligned Race*, x.

47. Hall, *Things of Darkness*, 59.

48. Hall asserts that these reports "have the secondary purpose of developing a sense of English identity; allowing English readers to know themselves by seeing others," *Things of Darkness*, 59.

49. The term "Moor" was used in the period to define a range of people who hailed from Africa, the Middle East, and the Far East. As is the case with the most famous Moor, Othello, much critical ink has been spilled trying to determine if Shakespeare and other playwrights really meant for their Moors to be black Africans or North African white Moors. In general, regardless of how dark the Moor's hue, he or she was undeniably other in religion, culture, temperament, and ethnicity. Aaron's costume of villainy is noted in Eldred Jones, *Othello's Countrymen*, 53. Jones does not connect this rhetorical costume with other actual costumes of blackness, as I do later in this chapter.

50. For more on early methods of "blackening up," see Tokson, *The Popular Image of the Black Man in English Drama*; Jones, *Othello's Countrymen*; and Hall, *Things of Darkness*.

51. Tokson, *The Popular Image of the Black Man in English Drama*, 104–05.

52. Orr, *Empire on the English Stage*, 27.

53. Nussbaum, *Limits of the Human*, 136.

54. Orr says, "It is their [the plays of the Restoration and earlier] exploitation of the particular affective and spectacular possibilities offered by theatricality which enabled them [playwrights] to provide peculiarly pleasurable and apparently successful ways of processing aspirations to empire and curiosity about exotic societies," *Empire on the English Stage*, 27.

55. *Gentlemen's and London's Magazine*, 687–90.

56. Cowhig, "The Black in English Renaissance Drama and the Role of Shakespeare's *Othello*," 7. The schizophrenic response to blacks resident in Britain before the abolition of slavery resulted in a remarkably diverse black

community in eighteenth-century England. That community and some of its "darlings" are discussed below.

57. The first Africans came to England in 1555 as a result of John Lok's journey to West Africa. Natives of Guinea, the five black men came as emissaries from their government. In 1563, Africans became private property in England in the first recorded sale of slaves. For a more complete history of blacks in Britain, see Fryer, *Staying Power*; Shyllon, *Black People in Britain*; Walvin, *Black and White*; Edward Scobie, *Black Brittania*; and Gerzina, *Black London* and *Black Victorians / Black Victoriana*.

58. Linda Colley, *Britons*, 8, 17; quoted in Cynthia Lowenthal, *Performing Identities on the Restoration Stage*, 79.

59. Many of the literary histories of blacks on the English stage exclude works by Shakespeare, especially *Othello* and *The Tempest*, in their discussions. Authors like Tokson and Jones distinguish these plays by virtue of the unusual psychological complexity given to the characters which separate a Moor like Othello from his black countrymen. Even Aaron in *Titus Andronicus* is said to have a certain amount of self-consciousness as a black character, in that he communicates an understanding of his position when talking to his young son. Given Caliban's uneasy designation as an African, Afro-Caribbean, Native American, human, or "animal," these authors choose to leave him out of the history entirely. For more on this, see the introductions to Tokson and Jones.

60. Cowhig, "The Black in English Renaissance Drama and the Role of Shakespeare's *Othello*," 4.

61. Hall, *Things of Darkness*, 128.

62. Ibid.

63. For more on *The Masque of Blackness*, see Hall, *Things of Darkness*, 136.

64. Also relevant here is Queen Elizabeth's edicts of 1596 and 1601 expelling blacks from England in order to preserve British resources for "true Englishmen." These events take place in Scotland and England as the two countries come to form Great Britain in 1605, which, under the moniker of empire, will eventually also encompass the African and American territories then being explored. See File and Power, *Black Settlers in Britain 1555–1958*, 6. For more on Elizabeth and her personal use of blackness as a tool of power, see *Staying Power*, 8, and Gerzina, *Black London*, 4–5.

65. The text for these pageants is extant from 1585 onward. See Barthelemy, *Black Face, Maligned Race*, 44.

66. The scripts for the pageants make a distinction between black characters: "Negroes" are black people and "blacks" are whites in black costume.

For more on the difficulty of distinguishing Africans from Indians and whites in black costume, see ibid., 47.

67. Ibid., 47–48.

68. Ibid., 48 n. 10.

69. Nussbaum, *Limits of the Human*, 157, 195.

70. Illustrations from Behn's novel in 1722 and 1769 can be found in *Oroonoko*, Norton Critical Edition, ed. Joanna Lipking.

71. Nussbaum, *Limits of the Human*, 179.

72. Ibid.

73. Oroonoko as a savage Highlander has other imperial overtones, reminding one that just as England was trading Africans abroad, it had other perceived barbarians at the gate closer to home.

74. Ibid., 237.

75. Ibid., 195.

76. Fryer, *Staying Power*, 31.

77. Shyllon, *Black People in Britain*, 10, and "The Black Man," 490.

78. Walvin, *Black and White*, 10.

79. Fryer, *Staying Power*, 8.

80. Walvin claims that slavery recruiting patterns in Africa caused more of these luxury slaves to be boys. Recently, Jennifer Morgan has disputed this for later time periods, particularly in the Americas. See Walvin, *Black and White*, 48; Morgan, *Laboring Women*; David Eltis, David Richardson, Stephen D. Behrendt, and Herbert S. Klein, *The Trans-Atlantic Slave Trade: A Database on CD-ROM*. While I will concentrate on the stylization of black men and boys, Nussbaum explores how the relative dearth of black women and girls affected depictions of women in the eighteenth century. See *Limits of the Human*, 151–88.

81. "The Black Man," 490. See also *Black Africans in Renaissance Europe*, ed. T. F. Earle and K. J. P. Lowe.

82. Walvin, *Black and White*, 48.

83. Fryer, *Staying Power*, 25. Fryer culls his descriptions from Hue and Cry ads placed in the *London Gazette* for runaway slaves in January 1685 (no. 1996) and July 1715 (no. 5343). The genealogy of black dandies in America from overdressed black slaves in England is given credence in the costume, especially the blue coats. Blue coats were seemingly so popular for European servants in the eighteenth century that the nobility carefully avoided them; the tradition of dressing servants in blue apparently crossed the ocean with the English. A century later in America, the black dandy, a figure popular in blackface minstrel shows as an uppity slave or servant or a northern free Negro with pretension to airs, was known as Long-Tail Blue, which was a

reference to the tails of his blue overcoat. See Maza, *Servants and Masters in Eighteenth-Century France*, and Cunnington, *Costume of Household Servants*.

84. Hall, *Things of Darkness*, 212.

85. Noting that jewels adorned with portraits of Africans were circulated in the same way that sonnets were among the upper class in the early modern period, and that when the vogue in jewels passed it was replaced by portrait painting which included black slaves, Hall argues that these phenomena were two of the important ways in which aristocratic identity was formed and marked in the early days of exploration and trade. See Hall, *Things of Darkness*, 214.

86. In fact, the servant's evanescence is born out in that a version of the painting in the collection at Colonial Williamsburg shows Lady Mary Churchill in the exact same pose but without the black servant. This painting came into the collection through William Byrd III, a Virginia colonist, who was a friend of the duchess and her father, the Duke of Marlborough. Boughton House, the Montagu/Buccleuch family seat, who owns the painting with the page, attributes it to Enoch Seeman, while the Colonial Williamsburg version is attributed to the Kneller Studio, for which Seaman (their spelling) may have worked. It is impossible to know why the page is omitted from the Colonial Williamsburg painting, but Barbara R. Luck, the curator of paintings, drawings, and sculpture at Colonial Williamsburg, guesses that the reason could be as simple as cost — eliminating the page would have made the copy of the painting much cheaper (email correspondence, May 31, 2007). In addition, luxury slavery like that depicted in the painting did not occur in the North American colonies because given the large number of slaves there and the kind of labor they performed black ostentation was more of a threat in America than in Britain. For more on the distinction between slaves as luxury and labor in England and America, see chapter 2 of this book. For more on the provenance of the paintings, see Thorne, "The Duchess and William Byrd." I thank Barbara Luck for this reference.

87. Shyllon, *Black People in Britain*, 9.

88. "The Black Man," 491, from Hue and Cry Advertisements of 1688 and 1694. The question of racial designation in these ads appears in the "The Black Man."

89. *Tatler* 245, November 2, 1710, in Fryer, *Staying Power*, 473.

90. I am grateful to Jim Basker for his assistance in reading this painting. Although I read the stylization here as a comment on different modes of slaveholding, Basker cautions me that the stylization might also be a result of an exaggerated nineteenth-century depiction of this eighteenth-century incident.

91. Cunnington, *Costume of Household Servants*, notes that servants' dress continually flouted sumptuary laws; for example, in 1597 laws "forbade the use of silk to working men," with the exception of royal servants (23); Queen Elizabeth also reserved velvet for certain degrees of nobility (63); James I dictated kinds and lengths of fabric appropriate for servants and others (64). Maza, *Servants and Masters*, records that "from the seventeenth century on, royal legislation [in France] attempted to contain the elaborateness of servants' attire by prohibiting the wearing of gold or silk, or by prosecuting masters who dressed their servants up in the royal colors of scarlet, white and blue. But the authorities never really succeeded in putting a check on the expensive habits of status-hungry employers" (121).

92. Fryer, *Staying Power*, 73. Kim Hall notes that in portraits the androgyny of these boys is emphasized, allowing white masters the power of constructing their own gendered identities. Perhaps such androgyny is also a bid to delay their impending maturation into men. See Hall, *Things of Darkness*, 241.

93. Hecht, "Continental and Colonial Servants in Eighteenth-Century England," 43, 44.

94. Scobie optimistically notes that "in 18th-century England many masters showed great consideration, giving their slaves wages, arranging for them to be educated, to be taught crafts and trades and even bequeathing them freedom and money," *Black Brittania*, 37.

95. Gerzina, *Black London*, 29. There is considerable evidence for black social life in eighteenth-century London. See especially chapters 1 and 2 of *Black London*.

96. Nussbaum, *Limits of the Human*, 197.

97. This list of occupations is derived from those described in Fryer, *Staying Power*, Scobie, *Black Britannia*, Walvin, *Black and White*, and Shyllon, *Black People in Britain*. In the late eighteenth century and early nineteenth black musicians became increasingly popular in military bands. Dressed in oriental costumes that approximated the livery look, blacks were originally employed as drummers, but their popularity soon dictated that they comprise the whole band. There may be a link between these regiments, known as the Coldstream Guards and Connaught Rangers, and later blackface minstrel groups in England (where they were known in the nineteenth century as Ethiopian Serenaders) and America. In the American case, a brass band typically announced the performance of a blackface minstrel group by parading around the town in which the group was engaged. See chapter 2 for more on this possible connection.

98. Biddulph, *Kitty, Duchess of Queensberry*, 1.

99. Scobie, *Black Brittania*, 89. For more on Kitty's eccentricities, see Nussbaum, *Limits of the Human*, 6–9.

100. Scobie, *Black Brittania*, 89.

101. Fryer, *Staying Power*, 73.

102. In *Black Brittania*, Scobie identifies the "Mungo Macaroni" print by Matthew and Mary Darly (1772) as a caricature of Julius Soubise (3). This print is also mentioned by Ogborn, who places this print as one of "an extensive series of engravings—including The Clerical Macaroni, The Macaroni Haberdasher, and A Mungo Macaroni, which satirized both social types and individuals" (447–48). Gerzina, along with the British Museum's *Catalogue of Prints*, identifies the image as possibly both Soubise and Jeremy Dyson, a member of Parliament known for the fickleness of his politics (like Mungo, he is "here, dere, and everywhere"). See the *Catalogue of Political and Personal Satires Preserved in the Department of Prints and Drawings in the British Museum, 1771–1783*, ed. Mary Dorothy George, vol. 5, 82. As we've seen, Soubise is both a type and an individual, making him an ideal subject for the satiric portrait.

103. Said of Sir Novelty Fashion in Colley Cibber's, *Love's Last Shift, or The Fool in Fashion* (1695–6) in *Colley Cibber*, III.1.

104. Robbins, *The Servant's Hand*, 19.

105. See Yi-Fu Tuan, *Dominance and Affection*, for more on the inevitability of "animate luxury items" growing beyond their borders.

106. None of Soubise's letters are extant; the only piece that may be his writing is a love letter reprinted in *Black Writers in Britain, 1760–1890*, ed. Edwards and Dabydeen, 82. The letter originally appeared in the anonymously written *Nocturnal Revels, or the History of King's Place*, London 1779, a satirical piece which included mockeries of contemporary personalities, among them the Mungo Macaroni. Characterized by what could be a cheeky riff on the master-slave convention in love letters, the letter's centerpiece is Soubise's declaration that he is not merely a slave to his beloved, but his beloved's "*Negro Slave*."

107. Scobie, *Black Brittania*, 49.

108. The following paragraphs on Soubise's life are culled from four major sources (Scobie, *Black Brittania*; Biddulph, *Kitty, Duchess of Queensberry*; Henry Angelo, *The Reminiscences of Henry Angelo*, vol. 1; and J. D. Aylward, *The House of Angelo*) that offer basically the same information, in varying degrees of exegesis. The most complete rendition of his life is told by Scobie, which is based in large part on Angelo's *Reminiscences*; almost all of Angelo is reproduced in Scobie. In addition, Scobie omits an important incident concerning the alleged cause of Soubise's expulsion from England, which is

noted tacitly in Biddulph and explicitly in Fryer and Shyllon. This incident will be discussed in the body of the chapter. Rather than footnote excessively, I will note references to direct quotations only. Recently Vincent Carretta updated Soubise's biography in the *Oxford Dictionary of National Biography*, culling from these major sources. See Carretta, "Soubise."

109. Angelo, *The Reminiscences of Henry Angelo*, 447.

110. Biddulph, *Kitty, Duchess of Queensberry*, 215.

111. Angelo, *The Reminiscences of Henry Angelo*, 448.

112. Scobie, *Black Brittania*, 89, 90.

113. Angelo, *The Reminiscences of Henry Angelo*, 448.

114. Scobie, *Black Brittania*, 90.

115. Angelo, *The Reminiscences of Henry Angelo*, 450–51.

116. Ibid., 453, and Scobie, *Black Brittania*, 90, 91. During this time, it was important for servants, especially footmen, to have well-formed legs, especially calves. Since many servants' legs fell short of the ideal, they were required to pad them under their tights in the calf area. The costume collection of the Metropolitan Museum of Art has contemporary examples of these calf pads.

117. Angelo, *The Reminiscences of Henry Angelo*, 449.

118. Scobie, *Black Brittania*, 91.

119. Ibid., 92.

120. Scobie, *Black Brittania*, 92; Biddulph, *Kitty, Duchess of Queensberry*, 217.

121. Angelo, *The Reminiscences of Henry Angelo*, 451. Soubise and Ignatius Sancho were also correspondents; for more on this, see chapter 2 of this book.

122. Biddulph, *Kitty, Duchess of Queensberry*, 217; Scobie, *Black Brittania*, 92–93.

123. Scobie, *Black Brittania*, 92.

124. Ibid., 94.

125. Fryer, *Staying Power*, 73.

126. Nussbaum reads the print of them fencing with each other as a parody of their intimacy and as a sign of how each (an older, eccentric woman and a young, attractive foppish African) compromised the other's integrity or even dignity. *Limits of the Human*, 6–9.

127. Carretta, "Soubise."

128. In *Dominance and Affection* Yi-Fu Tuan argues, "Blacks were openly offered for sale in shops, warehouses, and coffeehouses. Metropolitan and provincial newspapers regularly announced their availability," 141. This observation is corroborated by many historians; see also the runaway slave ads

below. Most of those ads direct inquiries to coffeehouses and other gentlemen's clubs.

129. According to the Restoration scholar Robert Heilman, the fop's "hyperbolic stylishness" originated in the circumstances surrounding the return of King Charles from the Continent in 1660, resulting in a time of "reactions against the [Puritan] Commonwealth, its secular sense of the elect, the nonelect, and the too-elect, and its awareness of a French style that could be both compelling and overbearing and hence conducive to both xenophobia and xenophilia." Heilman, "Some Fops and Versions of Foppery," 366. Once used to describe a fool, the word "fop" did not identify swells until the late seventeenth-century. The *Oxford English Dictionary* defines the word by 1672 as "one foolishly attentive to and vain of his appearance, dress or manners; a dandy, an exquisite." For more on King Charles II's influence on fashion and masculine style, see Edward Kutcha, *The Three Piece Suit and Modern Masculinity.*

130. Williams, *The Restoration Fop,* 14.

131. See Kimmell, "From Lord and Master to Cuckhold and Fop," 93–109, and Carter, "An 'Effeminate' or 'Efficient' Nation?," 429–43.

132. For more on elite dress in the eighteenth century, see Ribeiro, *Dress in Eighteenth-Century Europe* and *The Art of Dress.*

133. Ogborn, "Locating the Macaroni," 447, 448.

134. Steele, "The Social and Political Significance of Macaroni Fashion," 101–02.

135. Ibid., 102.

136. Ibid.

137. See McNeil, "'That Doubtful Gender,'" 411–47. A contemporary pamphlet published after a group of Macaronies got into an infamous scrape in Vauxhall Gardens included the following ditty: "But *Macaronies* are a sex / Which do philosophers perplex; / Tho' all the priests of Venus's rites / Agree they are *Hermaphrodites.*" Quoted in Shearer West, "The Darly Macaroni Prints and the Politics of 'Private Man,'" 170.

138. Ogborn, "Locating the Macaroni," 450, 453.

139. Ibid., 453.

140. Ibid., 455, 456–57.

141. Ibid., 448–49.

142. Lynch, *The Economy of Character,* 24.

143. See Lynch, *The Economy of Character,* and Freeman, *Character's Theater.*

144. West, "The Darly Macaroni Prints and the Politics of 'Private Man,'" 174–75.

145. Rauser, "Hair, Authenticity and the Self-Made Macaroni," 114, and

West, "The Darly Macaroni Prints and the Politics of 'Private Man,'" 176. Nussbaum reads anomaly in the period differently—as segregating the raced, gendered, and differently abled from the emerging "normalized modern subject"—but even she would agree that there was a negotiated space between the anomalous and the distinctive in the period.

146. I will use the term "stylist of subjectivity," coined by Lauri Firstenburg, again in chapter 5 of this book, in reference to what I call artists of New Dandyism, such as Iké Udé.

147. Rauser, "Hair, Authenticity and the Self-Made Macaroni," 102.

148. Nussbaum notes that the word "mungo" is also perhaps of Scots origin; thus, as Mungo Macaroni, Soubise was also perhaps being imputed as Scots and made doubly foreign and uncivilized by the association. Nussbaum, *Limits of the Human*, 8.

149. In "The Social and Political Significance of Macaroni Fashion," Steele notes that despite all of its extravagance macaroni dress was considered too democratic because of its distinctive style (it could easily be imitated). She quotes a contemporary pundit who fears the macaroni ethos because "'all ranks of people' might fall into absurdity of dress; and a 'butcher's son' might be able 'to afford to appear in lace and embroidery,' but his 'false pretensions to gentility' were attacked as ridiculous and his dress inappropriate, as well as intrinsically foppish." Steele, 101, quoting from the *Macaroni and Theatrical Magazine* (October 1772) as it appears in M. Dorothy George, *Hogarth to Cruikshank: Social Change in Graphic Satire*, 368.

150. Castle, *Masquerade and Civilization*, 24 and Rauser, "Hair, Authenticity and the Self-Made Macaroni," 105.

151. The Sierra Leone scheme of 1786 to remove Britain's entire black population to West Africa, is, of course, the starkest example of British confusion and anxiety over the influx of black residents. For a time, Olaudah Equiano participated in the scheme, hoping to manage it in the interests of his fellow blacks. Eventually he realized the malice behind the motives and execution of the plan and became a vociferous critic of the project. Though he goes about self-fashioning differently from Soubise, Equiano seems to understand the legitimacy a good suit can give to a tale of slavery and imperialism, as seen in the frontispiece to his *Narrative* and also in the epigraph to my next chapter. The recent controversy over the veracity of Equiano's history (that he was born in South Carolina instead of West Africa) also suggests that he knew a great deal about literary self-fashioning and could tailor his literary and actual look as needed. For more on Equiano's origins, see Vincent Carretta, "Olaudah Equiano or Gustavus Vassa?" See also Carretta's book-length study, *Equiano the African*.

152. Walvin, *Black and White*, 61.

153. *Public Advertiser*, June 27, 1772, File and Power, *Black Settlers in Britain*, 20.

154. Oldfield, "The 'Ties of Soft Humanity,'" 9 notes 22, 23.

155. Mungo, *The Padlock Open'd or Mungo's Medley*, 226.

156. Fahrner, "David Garrick Presents *The Padlock*," 66. The joke was in reference to Jeremy Dyson.

157. Ibid., note 40.

158. Lindfors, "The Signifying Flunkey," 1–11.

159. For more on this alleged disappearance from a nineteenth-century perspective, see "Black Man," *All the Year Round*, 489.

160. See Gerzina, ed., *Black Victorians / Black Victoriana*.

161. Ibid., 51.

162. Ibid.

163. Ibid., 52.

164. Ibid.

165. Fahrner, "David Garrick Presents *The Padlock*," 66. This statement is not exactly true, as many histories of blackface do not mention Mungo at all. However, the connection between Mungo, the blackface minstrel show's black dandy character, and indigenous African American race and class cross-dressing traditions (such as Pinkster, Negro Election Day, John Canoe festivals) is not to be denied. During the two-hundredth anniversary of David Garrick's death in 1979, the Old Vic Theatre in London revived two of his most famous plays as a producer, including *The Padlock*. The performance was controversial and was "rejected by the Arts Council as unsuitable for touring." See George Rowell, *The Old Vic Theatre*, 160, and clipping files, "The Padlock," Theatre Museum of London.

166. Bickerstaffe, "The Padlock" (1823).

CHAPTER TWO   Crimes of Fashion

Concerning the chapter's third epigraph, White and White quote a variation of the statement that appeared originally in *Mary Chesnut's Civil War*, ed. C. Vann Woodward: "One of our sins as a nation, the way we indulged them [blacks] in sinful finery. We let them dress too much. It led them astray. We will be punished for it." See *Stylin',* 30.

1. Mowatt, *Fashion*, in *Staging the Nation*, ed. Wilmeth, 127.

2. Ibid., 127.

3. Ibid., 151.

4. Ibid., 137.

5. Ibid., 152, 164.

6. "Fashion (1845)," *Early American Drama*, ed. Richards, 305. *Fashion* had a record-breaking run in 1845 (45 performances in New York and Philadelphia) and since its initial success, it has enjoyed numerous revivals, especially in the early twentieth century, when it was in production nearly continuously from 1923 to 1946 (232 performances alone in the 1923–24 season). It was also transformed into a musical in the 1970s. For more on the production history, see clipping files in the Billy Rose Theater Collection, New York Public Library for the Performing Arts.

7. For more on Mowatt's career and iconoclasm as a writer and actress, see Alison Piepmeier, *Out in Public: Configurations of Women's Bodies in Nineteenth-Century America*.

8. For a dissenting view about the play's originality, see Poe, "The Theatre: The New Comedy by Mrs. Mowatt," *Broadway Journal*, March 29, 1845. Royall Tyler's *The Contrast* (1787), which features a culture war between decadent values and manners and good old Yankee sincerity, is actually the first comedy produced professionally in the United States, beginning the long tradition of American social satire. In *The Contrast*, Tyler questions how much of Europe to retain in a postcolonial United States, while Mowatt wonders if the only way to communicate sophistication and cultural arrival is through recourse to the affectations of foreign high culture. If Tyler's comedy embodies late eighteenth-century sentiment about fashion and foreignness and Mowatt's *Fashion* does the same for mid-nineteenth-century America, then, one notices a significant difference between the two. There is no Zeke or mention of African American dandies in *The Contrast*. Tyler does not rely on African American characters and the contrast of their disposition and behavior with other characters' to make its point about Americanness. Once perhaps not numerous or threatening enough to warrant theatrical ridicule, blacks increasingly became subjects of mainstream cultural concern as the nineteenth century dawned. Part of American cultural maturity, at least as traced in the history of social comedy (from *Contrasts* to *Fashions*), requires the inclusion of African Americans — but only in a way that communicates and facilitates their exclusion from the larger American project. Over time, the black, especially as a figure serving to boost white status by virtue of his position as an excessively fashionable house servant, joins the European as a troubling influence on American sensibilities.

9. The review in *The Express* thought *Fashion* truly extraordinary: "The production of a new play, written in our own city, by one of our own citizens, with our own society, hotels, houses, customs, virtues, vices, foibles and fol-

lies as the subject matter, is an event looked forward to as a thing resting somewhere on the outer verge of possibility, but far beyond the known limits of the probable," Barnes, *The Lady of Fashion*, 142.

10. Ibid., 142.

11. Prior to Mowatt's time, the theater was a dangerous place for a woman, literally and by association. Women on stage—actresses, dancers, "ballerina girls"—were, in the public imagination, hard to separate from women "watching" the stage, the prostitutes working the third tier. See Pipemeier's *Out in Public*.

12. Barnes, *The Lady of Fashion*, 136–37.

13. Ibid., 139.

14. Ibid., 140.

15. Ibid., 144. The assessment of Poe's reaction is Barnes's. Poe wrote two reviews of the play, both mixed, and was, despite his reservations, apparently fascinated, as he saw it eight times in a row.

16. The many revivals of *Fashion* since its debut similarly make little of him except, in the twentieth century, to decry his characterization as evidence of the racist discourse operating at the time. Notices of the play in its revival in New York in 1959 mention that Zeke is played in blackface, saying, for example, in the *Herald Tribune* for January 21, 1958, that "you will also find . . . Stephen Daley, in blackface that does not quite meet his powdered wig and various other suitably stylized mementos of an earlier, more innocent time." A review of the musical on February 22, 1973, in the *Village Voice* makes no mention of the blackface but does declare that the play's "unconscious racism" "really make[s] you wince." The production is praised for its historical honesty and accuracy. *Fashion* clipping files, Billy Rose Theater Collection, New York Public Library for the Performing Arts.

17. "Fashion (1845)," *Early American Drama*, ed. Richards, 307. This anonymous author goes on to say, "While [Zeke] may remind us uncomfortably of the 'race' humor of the later *Amos 'n' Andy* radio and television series, Zeke can also be seen in the context of the 1840s as an advancement in the portrayal of African-American characters by white playwrights," 307. Given that he seems entirely derived from blackface tradition, but without the minstrel show's challenging carnivalesque treatment of race and gender, this analysis seems naïve. For more on black dandies and minstrel tradition, see below in this chapter.

18. While America lacked a professional or national theater for over a hundred years after the first Europeans landed, festivals and holidays of Native American, European, African, and African American design were an important part of the establishment and communication of group identity and soli-

darity. For both free and slave, these festivals fostered a sense of local and national belonging. They highlighted visually the presence and performance traditions of these other, emergent American cultures.

19. "It is commonly suggested that early modern Europe privileged observation, and 18th-century British North America certainly shared this bias," Prude, "'To Look Upon the Lower Sort,'" 127.

20. See Piersen, *Black Yankees*, Platt, "Negro Governors," and Fabre, "Pinkster Festival," for more on European precedents and other similar celebrations in the Caribbean.

21. The frequently cited sources for these festivals are Fenn, "'A Perfect Equality Seemed to Reign'"; Baldwin, "The Cakewalk"; Bettelheim and Ortiz, eds., *Cuban Festivals*; and Kiddy, "Who Is the King of Kongo?" For more on the cakewalk, see below.

22. Turner, *The Ritual Process*, 167.

23. Ibid., 168–69.

24. Douglass quotation from the *Narrative of Frederick Douglass, An American Slave, Written by Himself*, in Verter, "Interracial Festivity," 423 note 5, and Bakhtin, *Rabelais*, 10. For more on the carnivalesque and its potential for subverting societal structures, see Bakhtin, *Rabelais*, and Davis, *Society and Culture in Early Modern France*. In *The Ritual Process*, Turner argues that for the "structural superiors" involved, the ritual is one of "penance" undergone in the hope of "achieving a symbolic communitas" (203). In my reading, Turner's analysis of the ultimate effect of "rituals of reversal" seems too optimistic, not wholly applicable to festivals between masters and slaves. The communitas of which Turner speaks is one that includes social hierarchies, but not legal ownership of some of that community's constituents. The symbolic nature of African American festivals deepens and becomes even more ironic in the case of slaveholding America.

25. See Verter, "Interracial Festivity," 423 note 5.

26. The best sources for more details on Election Day in New England are Piersen, *Black Yankees*; Platt, "Negro Governors"; White, *Somewhat More Independent*; and White and White, *Stylin.'* For Pinkster, see Fabre, "Pinkster Festival, 1776–1811"; Wade, "'Shining in Borrowed Plumage'"; Williams-Meyers, "Pinkster Carnival: Africanisms in the Hudson Valley"; and Verter, "Interracial Festivity." While I rely on these historians for excellent archival research and cogent arguments concerning the cultural context in which these festivals took place (especially White and White and Verter), none of these historians has yet understood how this process of play with clothing, in the days before blackface minstrelsy, might have influenced the representation of dandies and the black middle class in later nineteenth-century literature. I explore this theme in later sections of this chapter.

27. Shelton, "The New England Negro," 535. The 1750 date is from Platt, "Negro Governors." In *Black Yankees*, William Piersen lists Newport, 1756, as one of the first festivals.

28. Williams-Meyers, "Pinkster Carnival," 8.

29. Fabre, "Pinkster Festival," 14.

30. Ibid., 15.

31. Shelton, "The New England Negro," 537; Piersen, *Black Yankees*, 120–21.

32. Turner, *The Ritual Process*, 185.

33. Piersen, "Puttin' On Ole Massa," 20–21. As a result of the completion of the Trans-Atlantic Slave Trade database, it is now known that most slaves in the United States came from West and Central West Africa, two regions which shared some broad cultural traditions concerning government and ritual life. While most research into the African origins of Negro Election Day and Pinkster references West Africa as the source of its dances and parodic structure (see especially Sterling Stuckey), much of this research was done before West Central Africa assumed such a prominent place in studies of U.S. slavery. See *The Trans-Atlantic Slave Trade Database*, ed. Eltis, Richardson, Behrendt, and Klein. My use of "African" here is admittedly general, pertaining to West Africa primarily, and is perhaps inadequate for a more detailed discussion of the "Africanness" of the festivals. Debate continues as to how varied particular communities of African population were in colonial America; some, like Thornton, in *Africa and Africans in the Making of the Atlantic World, 1400–1800*, acknowledge that although the slave population often constituted multiple (as many as two dozen) ethnic and language groups, nevertheless, the groups can be aggregated into three larger cultural entities from which generalities can be made. Gomez's *Exchanging Our Country Marks*, a study of the ethnicity of slave populations and their acculturation in the South, identifies which ethnic groups were in contact with one another in various regions of the South and what cultural traditions they might have retained and negotiated with each other and the majority population. As of yet, no such detailed study exists for the North.

34. Williams-Meyer, "Pinkster Carnival," 10; Piersen, *Black Yankees*, 129; Verter, "Interracial Festivity," 419–20.

35. Piersen, *Black Yankees*, 134.

36. Ibid., 130. For more on the Samuel Huntingtons, see Frances M. Caulkins, *History of Norwich, Connecticut* (1866).

37. Eights, "Pinkster Festivities in Albany," 45.

38. White, *Somewhat*, 199. For more on the dancing, see Stuckey, "The Skies of Consciousness," *Going Through the Storm*.

39. In the introduction to *Feasts and Celebrations*, Fabre claims that festivals in general "offer a way of performing experience and of identifying 'sites of memory'" for the communities that perform them (6).

40. Verter, "Interracial Festivity," 411.

41. Cooper, *Satanstoe*, 61.

42. Ibid., 65.

43. Gomez, *Exchanging Our Country Marks*, 5.

44. Ibid., 10.

45. Ibid.

46. Ibid., 3, 11.

47. Ibid., 13.

48. Piersen, *Black Legacy*, 38. See Foster, 'New Raiments of Self,' 21–43, for a discussion of the relationship between African nakedness and Islamic and European clothing traditions concerning modesty and the achievement of "civilization."

49. As early evidence of this, Thornton records the remarks of a German traveler to the Gold Coast in 1688 who "chided the people for their vanity in hoarding and displaying cloth and for the great public show that wealthier members (and even commoners) of society made when going out." Willem Johan Muller in Thornton, *Africa and Africans*, 51.

50. Piersen, *Legacy*, 38. Thorton argues that the Africans were certainly self-sufficient before the arrival of Europeans, so the European trade was, for a long time, a luxury market, not one for essential goods; "purchasers were responding far more to the changing fashions of nonessential commodities than [to] a real need to trade to satisfy essential wants" (52). According to Foster, trade networks predating even those of the Europeans would have brought variety in the form of the foreign, the stuff of fashion, to West Africa—for example, Indian cottons and Muslim cuts and styles of dress. Foster provides an amazing list of cloth types available in Benin from the early 1500s to the early 1770s, noting that over time "Indian cloth in the early years [Cambay and silk, 1505] gives way to luxury European cloths [Breton linen, Rouen cotton, Nîmes silk, early 1770s] by the early eighteenth century" (61). That these goods were all traded by Europeans suggests that Europeans entered the market in the 1500s by trading what was already available (cloth from India) and quickly began to offer fabric of European manufacture, such as Bruges green satin, available by 1535; see 'New Raiments of Self,' 61–62, 64. In *What Clothes Reveal*, Baumgarten notes that Native Americans also wore combinations of Western and native clothing from the point of contact, 70–71.

51. Foster, 'New Raiments of Self,' 29.

52. Ibid., 34–35. Foster also notes that there was an indigenous West Afri-

can precedent for the practice of presenting cloth and other luxury items to African kings; thus, Europeans found a custom already congenial to their needs.

53. An interesting exception is an account recorded by Captain John Adams, ca. 1800: "The king whose name is Otoo appeared about sixty years of age. . . . He had on a white satin waistcoat trimmed with silver lace, a silk purple coat much embroidered, black satin small-clothes, with knee buckles, coarse thread stockings, shoes and buckles, and a large black hat trimmed round the edge with red feathers; all of which appeared to us of Portuguese fabric, except the coat and waistcoat, which, there is little doubt, had, at a former period, been worn by some noble peer or knight at the court of St. James," Foster, 'New Raiments of Self,' 32.

54. Ibid., 34.

55. Ibid., 40. Foster notes that "Africans sometimes unraveled European trade cloth and rewove the threads in patterns which more conformed to African aesthetics," 57.

56. Ibid., 69. "Cultural exchange" when one speaks of slavery has an undeniable relationship to the slave trade's commodification of African bodies, whether or not they were dressed in fancy clothes. Africans perpetrated crimes of fashion even as they were victimized by them — Gomez records a series of stories in which African Americans lament the way in which "commodity attraction" tricked their ancestors into captivity with the promise of red flannel cloth, "party gew-gaws — red handerchiefs, dress goods, beads, bells, and trinkets in bright colors," from Europeans. *Exchanging Our Country Marks*, 201, esp. 200–206.

57. Genovese, *Roll, Jordan, Roll*, 555. Baumgartner records that slave men were issued a waistcoat with sleeves, breeches or trousers, and two shirts, a pair of summer breeches and trousers. Women were given a jacket, petticoat and two shifts, and linen petticoats for summer. *What Clothes Reveal*, 135. Gomez notes that after slaves came on board the ships naked, "some order and sense had to be fashioned out of the New World disorder." For Gomez, this "new life in death" was symbolized by the issuance of Western dress and the adjustment to it. See *Exchanging Our Country Marks*, 167–72.

58. Foster, 'New Raiments of Self,' 139.

59. Ibid., 144–45. Ex-slave testimony records that even though house slaves were the best-dressed laborers on the plantation, they understood that their appearance was a direct result of their master's pride and bid for social regard.

60. White and White, *Stylin'*, 12, 19–22; see also Baumgarten, *What Clothes Reveal*.

61. Foster, *'New Raiments of Self,'* 77.

62. *Pretends to be Free*, ed. Hodges and Brown, 91.

63. *Runaway Slave Advertisements*, compiled by Windley, 366.

64. Ibid., 318–19, 167, 356, 361, 408–09.

65. According to White and White, "slaves bought, sold, bartered, and traded garments in an underground economy that easily and quietly absorbed items of questionable origin." *Stylin',* 15. See also White, *Somewhat More Independent*, for more on underground clothing markets in eighteenth-century New York City.

66. See Foster, *'New Raiments of Self,'* 134; White and White, *Stylin',* 9; and Genovese, *Roll, Jordan, Roll*, 559. For sumptuary laws for whites in the North, see Earle, *Customs and Fashions in Old New England*, which argues that despite having a reputation for restraint in all things, Puritans, especially the men, were very vain and concerned about who was allowed to "wear the garb of a gentleman" (317). *Customs and Fashions* also includes a section on Negro Election Day, but Earle does not connect the clothing excesses of the black holiday to concerns about the fashions of white colonists and early Americans.

67. Foster includes a short section on the relationship between gender identities and clothing in which she cites some literary and real-life examples of black women escaping or subverting slavery by assuming male dress (for example, Harriet Jacobs, Harriet Tubman, Ellen Craft), *'New Raiments of Self,'* 160, 171. I will discuss the black dandy's engagement with gender identities in depth in the next section (on blackface minstrelsy) and in the final sections of this chapter concerning "crimes of fashion" in Stowe, Melville, Twain, and Chesnutt.

68. See Piersen, *Black Yankees*, 159, for more on lower-class white resentment; Reidy, "'Negro Election Day,'" and Williams-Meyers, "Pinkster Carnival," for more on the festivals' later perceived threat to law and order.

69. Southern, *The Music of Black Americans*, 54 note 28. Events similar to Pinkster and Negro Election Day did occur in the South, the Caribbean, and Brazil, and they were plagued by whites' fears that blacks, who outnumbered them, would use the occasions as opportunities to plan or carry out an insurrection.

70. For the increasing number of black slaves recently freed, the raucousness of Pinkster in particular came to be seen as increasingly outré and in need of being stopped in order to present new potential black citizens in their best light. White and Verter disagree somewhat about the true nature of the festival's cessation, Verter arguing that White puts too much emphasis on black elite censure and not enough on the political situation in Albany at

the time, which would have seen an elite Dutch culture being superseded by a more multicultural one, symbolized by Pinkster festivities. See White, *Somewhat*, and Verter, "Interraciality."

71. "De Genteel Fine Ole Nigga" of this section's title was a variant title for the minstrel song, "The Fine Old Colored Gentleman," which, despite its title, was not a song about a black dandy, but actually about a "happy slave" content with life on the plantation. See Dennison, *Scandalize My Name*, 98.

72. Stowe, *Uncle Tom's Cabin*, ed. Ammons, 1.

73. Ibid., 1.

74. Ibid., 141.

75. Ibid., 289.

76. Ibid., 142.

77. Ibid., 142, 143.

78. Foreman, "'This Promiscuous Housekeeping," 59. Foreman's article and Borgstrom's "Passing Over" are the only articles I have found that focus on Adolph's dandyism and its potential disturbance of how one reads the master–slave relationship in *Uncle Tom's Cabin*. Foreman's work emphasizes the homosocial and potential homosexual triangle between Tom, St. Clare, and Adolph in order to acknowledge the vulnerability or penetrability of black men under slavery; Borgstrom argues that Adolph serves as a sign of the way in which Stowe, in spite of herself, perhaps, reads race, class, and gender in an intersectional way, arguing for the construction of identity despite the stereotypes of blackness she puts forth in depicting other characters. My reading of Adolph largely squares with Borgstrom's; see the next section of this chapter for more.

79. Moody, *America Takes the Stage*, 33.

80. Ibid., 38–39.

81. See Lott, *Love and Theft*. Lott argues for the origin of the show in an incident that occurred between T. D. Rice and a black man named Cuff on the docks in Pittsburgh. Apparently, Rice had observed Cuff and friends earning money by presenting their open mouths as targets or receptacles for tossed coins. After blacking up, Rice persuades Cuff to lend him his outfit and goes on stage as a Negro, dancing and singing, or "jumping Jim Crow." For a different origin for blackface performance, see the introduction to Lhamon's *Jump Jim Crow*. As in his earlier book, *Raising Cain*, Lhamon argues that more attention should be paid to minstrelsy's "mulatto character" and miscegenistic origin and tendencies, in order to acknowledge it as a "symbol of demotic brotherhood in black" (*Jump Jim Crow*, 8) in the earliest example of cross-racial working-class culture and an important predecessor for current white and black performance practices. Although I generally agree with the

spirit of Lhamon's analysis of blackface performance and the potential of its "mulatto-ness" or what *Jump Jim Crow* calls its "Ethiopian mobility," for re-thinking relationships between black and white peoples and cultures, I find that his insistence on how early minstrelsy "provides an earlier—even en-thusiastic—version of the American obsession with blackness" does not fully account for the forceful legacy of the stereotypes it generated. Even if racial play produces stereotypes that are not fixed, such play does not erase the felt presence of those stereotypes and the need for blacks to continually address their often negative power. Lhamon's perspective also causes him to not fully acknowledge the multipronged class critique present in blackface perfor-mance that mocks the elite. In his analysis, Rice's black dandy characters (in-cluding Mungo in *The Padlock*) only mock white elite pretension; black elites are not mentioned as a potential target of satire. See *Jump Jim Crow*, 31–36.

82. That blackface minstrelsy originated in the North is now a common-place fact; before more contemporary histories of minstrelsy, like Toll's *Black-ing Up* (1974), there was still some debate surrounding whether or not the show had its origins in the South and the degree to which its performers faithfully represented (rather than imitated or manipulated) the folklife of southern blacks.

83. Mahar, *Behind the Burnt Cork Mask*, 90.

84. See Lott, *Love and Theft*: "At the very least, these events [Negro Elec-tion Day and Pinkster] set off a train of racial burlesque and counterburlesque that surely helped inspire blackface miming, a less efficient control of inde-pendent black practices than proscription, perhaps, but more lucrative and engaging" (46). Lott's description of the festivals, blackface, and its legacy as "burlesque and counterburlesque" will become important in my analysis of literature's grappling with this cyclical process. W. T. Lhamon Jr. also identi-fies a link between blackface performance and the festivals Pinkster and John Canoe when he calls the festivals "little-known local secrets until blackface performers started trucking abstracted combinations of them to the Atlantic populace. Blackface not only stepped in, it primarily brought in and broad-casted blackness" (*Raising Cain*, 149). See also Mahar, *Behind the Burnt Cork Mask*, 90; Shane White, "'It Was a Proud Day,'" 25–27.

85. Moody, *America Takes the Stage*, 44.

86. Lott, *Love and Theft*, 46.

87. Foster's research reminds one that some ex-slaves found themselves in a situation markedly different from Equiano's: some were fortunate enough to celebrate their freedom with a new suit, while others were without suffi-cient clothing at all. See '*New Raiments of Self*,' 208–13.

88. Toll characterizes the War of 1812 as a second declaration of indepen-

dence from Europe: "After the War of 1812, many Americans expressed the need for native forms, symbols, and institutions that would assert the nation's cultural distinctiveness as clearly and as emphatically as the war had reaffirmed its political independence." *Blacking Up*, 3. The blackface minstrel show became one of these new forms, and the show's dandy a figure that satisfied a particularly American need to critique a lingering reverence for the European as well as the visibility of American blacks' upward mobility.

89. White and White identify the sliding significance of the dandy figure during the time of minstrelsy's development when they write that "for many whites, a well-dressed black was an at least slightly comic figure, but there was also often, in whites' observations, an underlying sense of disquiet, a fretful complaint at the blurring of what had seemed relatively clear-cut racial boundaries." *Stylin,'* 91. In *Stylin,'* they include a chapter, "Dandies and Dandizettes," on free black expression and white responses in the nineteenth century that while thoroughly documenting the public debate around black visibility and mobility does not meditate on the consequences of the events and situations they describe for black representation and self-stylization then and now.

90. White and White, *Stylin,'* 133 and note 35.

91. When recounting the minstrel show's intersection with blackface acts in the circus, especially a P. T. Barnum sketch that featured the potential effects of a weed that turned Negroes white, Lott argues that these "instances of imaginary racial transmutation literalize one train of thought responsible for the minstrel show. They are less articulations of difference than speculations about it." *Love and Theft*, 77. As a figure that in black and blackface has a close relationship to whiteness (through the play with elite clothing, rather than the ingestion of a race-transforming weed), the dandy figure particularly embodies this speculatory impulse.

92. Toll, *Blacking Up*, 34. Toll includes an illustration of sheet music of "Ethiopian Melodies" that juxtaposes caricatures of "refined" dandies and more grotesque "Ethiopians of the Southern States," 34. In *Behind the Burnt Cork Mask*, Mahar claims that even though minstrel show playbills frequently list "dandyisms" of the North as the first part of the show, followed by the "Peculiarities of the Southern Plantation Negroes," "most ensembles mixed-up their offerings so much that the songs and instrumental numbers could hardly be characteristic of [geographical] distinctions in African American behaviors," 23. It is possible that the dandyism in these playbills and sheet music may refer to certain parts of the performance, say, the clothing, rather than to the conjunction of men dressed as dandies singing the songs that came to define the figure; in any case, the minstrels' point would be made, as

seeing "Negroes" dressed in elite clothing burlesquing opera is just as funny as seeing those same dandy Negroes singing plantation songs.

93. Nathan, *Dan Emmett and the Rise of Early Negro Minstrelsy*, 57.

94. Dennison, *Scandalize My Name*, 76. *Scandalize My Name* and Mahar's *Behind the Burnt Cork Mask* provide the best collections of song lyrics outside of contemporary songsters. For minstrel sketches, see Engle's *This Grotesque Essence*; *Inside the Minstrel Mask*, ed. Bean, Hatch, and McNamara; and Lhamon, *Jump Jim Crow*.

95. Lewis, "Daddy Blue," *Inside the Minstrel Mask*, ed. Bean, Hatch, and McNamara, 258. Lewis and Mahar provide the most thorough discussion of dandy minstrel types. Lewis focuses on the transformation of the figure from Long-Tail Blue to Zip Coon, while Mahar uses the figure to exemplify a group of songs he identifies as concerned with "male display." Because he does not acknowledge the longer history of dandyism, Mahar labels the dandy "a pretender, a charlatan, a confidence man who is insincere and ignorant of the values associated with social station or power" (209), rather than a trickster who imitates class, race, and gender roles, all with an edge. Lewis's work is much more attentive to the dandy's multiply oppositional power.

96. Lewis, "Daddy Blue," *Inside the Minstrel Mask*, ed. Bean, Hatch, and McNamara, 269. Lewis compares illustrations of Long-Tail Blue and Zip Coon accompanying the sheet music and notes that "with Coon, the image of the stately and affluent black male is deformed or 'crowed,' signaling that whatever 'good' qualities Blue might have had, they would be diminished in his coon-ish brother," 268.

97. Dennison, *Scandalize My Name*, 138, 140.

98. Ibid., 140.

99. Lott, "Blackface and Blackness," *Inside the Minstrel Mask*, ed. Bean, Hatch, and McNamara, 13. Mahar seemingly writes *Behind the Burnt Cork Mask* specifically against this kind of psychoanalytic reading of the minstrel show. In so doing, he takes pains to argue that minstrelsy was much more about class (white middle-class pretensions) than about race, as it started not in burlesques of black folk, but in adaptations and mockeries of white European musical forms, especially Italian opera. While he is willing to admit that blackface performers, "whether rudely stereotyped or ethnographically scrupulous, had consciously or unconsciously entered into a multilayered satire of Anglo-American life" (41), he will not allow for the possibility that blackface was as much about cultural forms as it was about both black and white image making. His close analysis of the music excludes attention to the larger cultural causes and effects of the performances.

100. Lott, *Love and Theft*, 119.

101. For more on urban blacks in the North, see especially White, *Somewhat*, and Nash, *Forging Freedom*.

102. White and White, *Stylin',* 128.

103. Fabre argues that at Pinkster, King Charley (even in his fantastical dress) was seen as a preeminent embodiment of black dignity: "The king could also facilitate the acculturation of his fellow slaves and free blacks: this 'civilized' Negro could bring composure and refinement. One witnesses here the unusual reversal of stereotypes — the official recognition of African royalty and gentility, instead of the more common association of Africanness with savagery or lack of culture." Fabre, "Pinkster," 18. In addition, Reidy argues that the festivals were important for building black middle-class consciousness through the organizational effort they required, as well as the way in which they "internally adjudicated standards of acceptable behavior for the black community"; see "'Negro Election Day,'" 111.

104. White, "It Was a Proud Day," 43. For more on the problematics of attempts by black elites in the nineteenth century to "uplift the race," see the early chapters of Gaines's *Uplifting the Race*.

105. Nash, *Forging Freedom*, 5, 7.

106. Ibid., 217–18. For an excellent literary example of the relationship of sober dress and fine fabrics to respectability, see *The Garies and Their Friends* (1857) by Frank Webb.

107. Lorini, "Public Rituals and the Cultural Making of the New York African American Community," 35. Lorini's work charts the popularity and later disappearance of the nineteenth-century African American parade, focusing on it as a mechanism for the display of African American presence and respectability after abolition in the North. See also Lorini's *Rituals of Race*. In "'It Was a Proud Day,'" White similarly argues that when African Americans gave up or were forced to abandon the Negro festivals, they turned to the parade as an outlet for announcing their presence and expressing their unique culture. Blacks paraded to mark funerals, celebrate the anniversary of abolition, on the Fourth of July, or as part of publicizing their new social organizations, such as the Masons and other benefit societies. Dressing up and looking good while in the public eye, en masse, obviously played a part in this display, and thus a public event drew commentary from black and white alike.

108. Nash, *Forging Freedom*, 219.

109. Ibid., 222.

110. For more on caricatured images of blacks, see Nash, *Forging Freedom*, and White and White, *Stylin'.* In reading an illustration from 1863 of black dandies on Broadway in New York City, Domosh makes the point that even blacks trying to be extremely assimilative, outfitting themselves in exactly

the right white elite clothing and accessories, were still a major affront; see "'Those Gorgeous Incongruities.'"

111. Toll, *Blacking Up*, 97. Dandies did not disappear from the minstrel stage entirely. Toll's history of later minstrelsy in its sentimental and most spectacular forms in the 1880s finds dandies in the following guises: as part of military burlesques ridiculing black participation in the Civil War; in white-face, beau-ish and foppish in a bid for prestige in the "Mastodon period," when minstrel troupes employed hundreds of performers in an effort to reap large profits; in skits depicting black prosperity in heaven (after the spirituals were further incorporated into the show in the 1870s and 1880s); and finally, most poignantly, in late nineteenth-century performances by blacks in blackface like Bob Mack, George Walker, and Bert Williams. See *Blacking Up*, 120, 154, 187, 249–51; Webb, "The Black Dandyism of George Walker"; for a recent fictional treatment of Bert Williams, see Phillips, *Dancing in the Dark*; for more recent critical studies, see Louis Chude-Sokel, *Bert Williams*, and Forbes, *Bert Williams*.

112. Stowe, *Uncle Tom's Cabin*, ed. Ammons, 143–44.

113. Ibid., 187.

114. Ibid., 177.

115. Ibid., 143.

116. Ibid., 132.

117. Ibid., 141.

118. See Foreman, "This Promiscuous Housekeeping."

119. In "Passing Over," Borgstrom makes a very similar argument about Adolph's dandyism and effect in the text. For him, Adolph "cannot be recuperated in the text because his dandified behavior fuses spheres that should remain separate and thereby violates the discrete gender classifications on which abolitionism relies" (1298), and "Adolph's dandyism acts as a refusal of slavery's obliteration of gender through race and class" (1299).

120. Adolph's "refusing to act like an authentic black male slave . . . implies that it is possible to reject such taxonomic classifications." Borgstrom, "Passing Over," 1294.

121. Stowe, *Uncle Tom's Cabin*, ed. Ammons, 288.

122. Borgstrom, "Passing Over," 1294.

123. Stowe, *Uncle Tom's Cabin*, ed. Ammons, 288, 289.

124. In "Fathering and Blackface in *Uncle Tom's Cabin*," Zwarg argues that Stowe's placement of blackface elements in the text shows the author actively disrupting the stereotypes that seem to bind her characterization of the blacks in the novel. Concentrating on Uncle Tom and Sam, Zwarg does not examine all the characters whose actions and appearance exhibit black-

face elements; however, these other characters, Adolph and George, do, in fact, expose the full force of her argument. According to Zwarg, Stowe links George Harris to a blackface portrait of Founding Father George Washington that hangs in Uncle Tom's cabin through their shared name; she reads the portrait's presence as a kind of wink indicating that Tom and others know and signify on the color of patriarchy and patriotism under which they toil. Even so, Stowe does not allow George Harris to capitalize on the deconstructive power the portrait potentially "unleashes" in the text. Stern does mention Christina Zwarg's argument and also finds it limited in scope: "Zwarg's reading of Samboism is convincing, her analysis of the blackface George Washington is less so, precisely because it is not attuned to the disturbing implications of Stowe's 'raucous' minstrel-show comedy. The Founding Father in blackface constitutes another tableau that, like Spanish masquerade, bears multiple and contradictory valences." Stern, "Spanish Masquerade," 103.

125. Stern, "Spanish Masquerade," 109.

126. Ibid., 107, 110, 111–12.

127. Ibid., 103, and passim.

128. For more, see Zwarg, "Fathering and Blackface in *Uncle Tom's Cabin*."

129. The relationship between masculinity and freedom is a tricky one in Stowe's text—the fact that George's wife, Eliza, must cross-dress as a man to escape slavery both validates and troubles George's own reliance on manhood as a marker of liberty. For more on Eliza's transvestism, see Garber's chapter "Black and White TV" in *Vested Interests*.

130. Stern, "Spanish Masquerade," 121, 100. When choosing an independent black republic to live in, George selects Liberia over Haiti because on the island the men are "worn out [and] effeminate." Stowe, *Uncle Tom's Cabin*, ed. Ammons, 374. George will take his manhood very seriously, at home and abroad. See chapter 3 below for W. E. B. Du Bois's use of the dandy figure to negotiate the relationship between political and cultural freedom and masculinist potency.

131. Melville, *Benito Cereno, Billy Budd and Other Stories*, 176–77. Other discussions of *Benito Cereno* that were useful to me in their consideration of stereotype, the text's relationship to minstrelsy, and the performative and sartorial aspects of Babo's mutiny include Sundquist's chapter on *Benito Cereno* in *To Wake the Nations*; Hilfer, "The Philosophy of Clothes in Melville's 'Benito Cereno'"; Fagan Yellin, "Black Masks"; and Dooley, "Fixing Meaning."

132. Melville, *Benito Cereno*, 184.

133. Ibid., 258.

134. Sundquist, *Nations*, 139.

135. Melville, *Benito Cereno*, 187, 217.

136. Sundquist, *Nations*, 159. Sundquist says this specifically in relation to the shaving scene.

137. Melville, *Benito Cereno*, 258.

138. As Morris suggests, the text is "rich with masquerading, with layering of clothing, with cross-dressing and misleading gender markers, with foppery, veiling and unveiling, and with clothing as cues (and mis-cues) to sexual and racial identity." "Beneath the Veil," 37.

139. Twain, *Pudd'nhead Wilson and Those Extraordinary Twins*, ed. Berger, 14.

140. Jehlen makes this point in her article "The Ties that Bind," 45.

141. Twain, *Pudd'nhead Wilson*, ed. Berger, 23–24.

142. Jehlen's reading of *Pudd'nhead Wilson* emphasizes the way in which Tom's assumption of women's clothing, added to the Negro bellringer's dandified mockery of him, feminizes him and, by implication, black men. See "The Ties that Bind."

143. Morris, "Beneath the Veil," 50; Jehlen, "The Ties that Bind," 45.

144. Twain, *Pudd'nhead Wilson*, ed. Berger, 114.

145. For Jehlen, Twain is "caught between radical criticism and an implicit conservatism expressed in the refusal, or the inability, to imagine significant change." "The Ties that Bind," 54.

146. Chesnutt, *The Journals of Charles Chesnutt*, 125–26.

147. Ibid., 126.

148. Sundquist, *Nations*, 47.

149. Ibid., 433.

150. Chesnutt, *The Marrow of Tradition*, 283.

151. Sundquist, *Nations*, 273, 279. In his discussion of Chesnutt, Eric Sundquist identifies the cakewalk as the governing metaphor of the author's life and work.

152. Ibid., 308.

153. For a good history of the cakewalk, see Baldwin's "The Cakewalk."

154. Sundquist suggests that, as Chesnutt's narrative strategy, the cakewalk made it possible to dance one's status from slave to New Negro by "subvert[ing racial, cultural, and social norms] not by parodic attack alone but by replacement, by recalling in performative expression a cultural meaning separate from and prior to enslavement." The African "roots" that Sundquist calls on as support for this statement are primarily dance and music; he does not emphasize that the black encounter with "big house fashion" had occurred with clothing itself, and even earlier than he may have imagined. Sundquist, *Nations*, 280.

155. Chesnutt, *The Marrow of Tradition*, 119.

156. Ibid.

157. Ibid.

158. Ibid., 23.

159. Ibid., 26.

160. Ibid., 204.

161. Ibid., 23, 25.

162. Ibid., 225.

163. Ibid., 36.

164. Ibid., 87.

165. Ibid., 238.

166. Ibid., 50, 251. The *Oxford English Dictionary* defines "fallal" as "a piece of finery or frippery, a showy adornment in dress; affectation in manner, fussy show of politeness," *Oxford English Dictionary*, 2d edn.

167. Ibid., 250–51.

168. Ibid., 252.

169. Ibid., 75.

170. Ibid., 48.

171. Ibid., 49.

172. Ibid., 61.

173. Ibid., 65.

174. Ibid., 277.

175. Ibid., 285.

176. Ibid., 280.

177. Ibid., 282.

178. Ibid., 288.

179. Ibid., 289–90, and 291.

180. Ibid., 294.

181. Ibid., 282.

182. Du Bois, "Chesnutt," in *Writings*, 1234.

CHAPTER THREE Du Bois's Diasporic Race Man

1. W. E. B. Du Bois, *Dark Princess*, 7.

2. Ibid.

3. Ibid., 104.

4. Ibid., 200, 201.

5. Tate, "Introduction," *Dark Princess*, ix. Claudia Tate indicates that Du Bois says this on page 270 of *Dusk of Dawn* but does not indicate the edition of *Dusk* to which she refers.

6. Though Matthew Towns's story is very different from that of Du Bois, the two share a certain kind of sensibility. One could say that Matthew's narrative exposes some of the contentious parts of Du Bois's own life in terms of his relationship to black folk, political and social justice activism, and the relationship of activism to the aesthetic. See Levering Lewis, *W. E. B. Du Bois*.

7. Rampersad, *The Art and Imagination of W. E. B. Du Bois*, 265. In recent years, the novel *Dark Princess* has emerged as a signal text for the investigation of Du Bois's gender and sexual politics, especially as they relate to his internationalism. Important articles on Du Bois's masculinism and "erotics" by Tate, Carby, and James established this new inquiry into Du Bois studies. This chapter and its pre-text, my article "W. E. B. Du Bois and the Dandy as Diasporic Race Man" (2003) participates in this field and thus has much in common with a new collection on Dubois, *Next to the Color Line*, ed. Gillman and Weinbaum. Focusing on "the simultaneous juxtaposition of issues of race, gender and sexuality and the submerging of their express connection," the essays in the collection aim to illuminate the ways in which Du Bois's work both does and does not "give expression to sexual and gendered logics and their relation to the logics of race" (7, 18). Articles in that volume that are in particular conversation with my work here include the introduction by Weinbaum and Gillman and articles by Weinbaum, Edwards, Elam, and Taylor. My reading of *Dark Princess* as a "dandified text" brings together some of the arguments in this volume, even as they disagree with each other on the issue of Du Bois's (emergent?) feminism. For me, reading Du Bois's protagonist as a dandy and, as such, part of a long line of black and European queer revolutionaries, allows for an understanding of how *Dark Princess* can be a text that imagines men differently, sometimes within a logic of feminism and sometimes without. As this book hopes to make clear, this is the essential position of the dandy, queer or "quare" because of his complicated position on the spectrum of masculinities, sexualities, and races.

8. Carby, *Race Men*, 25.

9. Du Bois, *Souls*, 365.

10. West, *Race Matters*, quoted in Carby, *Race Men*, 21.

11. Carby, *Race Men*, 21.

12. Ibid., 12, 14, 16.

13. Gates in Gooding-Williams, "Du Bois, Aesthetics, Politics," *Public Culture*, 205.

14. Carby, *Race Men*, 16, 12.

15. Coopan, "The Double Politics of Double Consciousness," *Public Culture*, 301.

16. Du Bois, *Dark Princess*, 272.

17. Townsend, *Manhood at Harvard*, 11.

18. Du Bois, *The Autobiography of W. E. B. Du Bois*, 137.

19. Townsend writes "by the end of the century, 'masculine'—once used simply to differentiate traits distinguishing men from women ('masculine clothing' or 'masculine occupations,' for example)—had become useful to men looking for ways to describe and explain the authority they sought to establish. By 1890, the noun 'masculinity' was in the *Century Dictionary*." *Manhood at Harvard*, 17. *The Oxford English Dictionary* records the word "masculinity" extant as early as 1748. Townsend cites the *Century Dictionary* in order to emphasize the American usage of the word.

20. Here and throughout this chapter, I use "queer" to describe Du Bois's "anxious masculinism," primarily in the sense that E. Patrick Johnson does in defining a black version of queer or "quare" as "odd and slightly off kilter." For more on how queer is deployed in this book, see the introduction. In my readings of Du Bois's explorations of masculinity, the queerness of his differently masculine men is sometimes sexual, sometimes not. In all cases, the Du Boisian dandy is a figure whose "sexual and gender identities always already intersect with racial subjectivity." Johnson, "Quare Studies," *Black Queer Studies*, 125. In *Dark Princess* and other texts in which Du Bois attempts to define or promote different masculinities, he is especially concerned with the political potential of those raced, gendered, sexualized figures.

21. Du Bois, "Jefferson Davis as a Representative of Civilization," in *Writings*, 811.

22. Ibid.

23. Ibid., 813–14.

24. Ibid., 813.

25. Ibid.

26. In his critique of Booker T. Washington in *Souls*, Du Bois also calls upon the feminine or effeminate and sexualizes black–white cultural and political relations, this time to shame Washington for prostituting black America to the interests of the white majority. The "Jefferson Davis" speech helpfully contextualizes this rhetoric—Washington does not express his "Submission" like a man, it seems; therefore, he does not escape imputations of "cowardice, laziness or stupidity, such as the world never saw before." Du Bois, "Jefferson Davis," 813.

27. Nero, "Queering *The Souls of Black Folk*," *Public Culture* 259, 255. Nero's reading of gender and sexuality in *Souls* inspired me to rethink this entire chapter with an eye to Du Bois's unwitting foray into queerness in *Souls* and *Dark Princess*.

28. See especially Wehilye, "The Grooves of Temporality," *Public Culture*, for a meta-reading of the way in which *Souls* sounds.

29. Carby does say in *Race Men* that what *Souls* as a whole dramatizes is that "integral to the 'problem' of simultaneously being black and being American is coming into manhood." The failed resolution of this problem "results in their [black men] being denied a full role in the patriarchal and political order," 32–33. In this last statement she echoes Nero but does not then attribute the status of queer to this denial of masculine privilege.

30. Nero cites, among other moments, black John's longing gaze at the dead body of white John, "Queering *The Souls of Black Folk*," 271.

31. Although Carby does not pay a great deal of attention to "Of the Coming of John" in *Race Men*, her analysis of the story also points out that the killing of white John shores up black John's masculinity. Her reasons differ from Nero's: for her, black John's violent assault on his white double is an effort to deny the passivity of black men in the face of white racial violence. See *Race Men*, 25.

32. For more on "gender inversion" and "homosexual panic" in *Souls*, see Nero, "Queering *The Souls of Black Folk*."

33. Nero, "Queering *The Souls of Black Folk*," 276.

34. Townsend also cites the essay "The Conservation of Races" (1897) and *Souls* as places in which Du Bois considers the "Submissive Man's role in the formation of American Culture." Townsend indicates that in "The Conservation of Races," Du Bois creates a figure "destined to soften the whiteness of the Teutonic"; and in *Souls* the "[seemingly feminine man] is made integral to the fulfillment of the 'greater ideals of the American Republic.'" *Manhood at Harvard*, 253, Du Bois, *Souls*, 370. Townsend is obviously on the same track as Nero but does not push his inquiry into *Souls* toward an exploration of the intersection of gender and sexuality in that text.

35. Townsend, *Manhood at Harvard*, 253.

36. Du Bois, "The Negro in Literature and Art," 862.

37. Ibid., 866.

38. Du Bois, "The Criteria of Negro Art," 993.

39. Ibid., 1000.

40. Ibid., 1001.

41. My reading of "The Criteria of Negro Art" owes a debt to Keith Byerman's *Seizing the Word*. Byerman provides an extended reading of the essay that emphasizes the way in which Du Bois sought to redefine (or seize) certain concepts like propaganda and beauty for his own use. Despite paying attention to Du Bois's use of femininity as a positive value and beauty as a goal in a progressive political project, Byerman does not apply his idea of the femininity of beauty to gender politics in *Dark Princess*.

42. Du Bois, *Dark Princess*, 12. Du Bois's language indicates that he was, at the time, thinking of African America's predicament partially within a Hegelian system.

43. Ibid., 48, 101.

44. Ibid., 3, 6.

45. Du Bois's review of *The New Negro* in *Crisis* (January 1926), quoted in Rampersad, *The Art and Imagination of W. E. B. Du Bois*, 194. According to Herbert Aptheker, white and black reviewers alike were challenged by the flamboyance and melodrama of Du Bois's text, which he himself called, modestly, a "romance with a message." White reviewers took the genre mix—a combination of sociology, didacticism, love story, and adventure—as evidence that the "Negro problem" had grown so dire that it needed such multifarious coverage or, more typically, as a failure of Du Bois's art. See Aptheker, "Introduction to *Dark Princess*," in *Dark Princess*, 5–29. In her introduction to the novel, Tate records an anecdote found in a letter from Alain Locke to Langston Hughes in which Locke lamented his fate as a reviewer of the novel. He writes, "Tonight I have to do *Dark Princess* for [*New York Herald Tribune*] Books. God help me." Tate, "Introduction," *Dark Princess*, xxiv.

46. Du Bois, *Dark Princess*, 114, 119.

47. Ibid., 143, 152.

48. Ibid.,132, 137.

49. Ibid., 153.

50. Du Bois, "The Talented Tenth," in *Writings*, 861, 847.

51. Du Bois, *Dark Princess*, 200.

52. Ibid., 159.

53. Ibid., 16, 17.

54. Ibid., 18.

55. Ibid., 20.

56. Ibid., 24.

57. Ibid., 25.

58. Ibid., 26.

59. Sima Godfey, "The Dandy as Ironic Figure," *Sub-stance*, 27.

60. In fact, when Oscar Wilde traveled to America, he was often caricatured as a black dandy in the press. See Posnock, *Color and Culture*, and Marez, "The Other Addict."

61. Du Bois, *Dark Princess*, 27.

62. Du Bois, *The Souls of Black Folk*, 537, 536.

63. Advocacy of the Sorrow Songs contrasts with a silence surrounding another folk-derived, uniquely African American art form, jazz. With roots in juke joints and the like, jazz was viewed with trepidation by those like Du

Bois who adhered to "the politics of respectability." Though jazz was young in 1903 when *Souls* was published, it was all the rage when *Dark Princess* came out in 1928. One wonders about the implications for *Dark Princess* if Matthew had played a charleston rather than sung a Sorrow Song. Later in the novel, Matthew has a drunken night of debauchery with a dancer in a speakeasy. Jazz and its culture function as a release and a distraction in the novel, since Matthew "falls" only because he has not heard from the princess concerning the status of the revolution. Such distinctions reveal a hierarchy among aesthetic experiences for Du Bois; this certainly complicates his appeal to the aesthetic as a category that reveals and enables black equality.

64. Herring, "Du Bois and the Minstrels," 4.

65. For more on minstrel show dandyism as a critique of attempted class mobility on the part of blacks in the nineteenth century, see chapter 2 above.

66. Du Bois, *Dark Princess*, 42.

67. Ibid., 125.

68. Ibid., 128.

69. Ibid.

70. Ibid., 193.

71. Ibid., 147–48.

72. Ibid., 207.

73. Ibid., 63.

74. Ibid., 210, 213.

75. Ibid., 286.

76. See Lewis's biography of Du Bois and Tate's introduction to the novel, in which she notes that many of Du Bois's Harlem Renaissance colleagues may have regarded the novel's eroticism and exoticism as part of "a dirty old man's fantasy that should never have been published." Tate, "Introduction," *Dark Princess*, xxiv.

77. Ross Posnock designates this place above or beyond the color line as one in which the souls of black folk would be "uncolored," "How It Feels to Be a Problem," 325. Additionally, he coins the phrase "aesthetic politics" to describe Du Bois's ideology in *Dark Princess* and names the figure practicing such politics a "political aesthete," as a descriptive of Du Bois's early-century work, in "The Distinction of Du Bois." Posnock's work focuses on Du Bois as an elitist or intellectual who used the pragmatic philosophy of William James as a methodology to think "in and through paradox," in an effort to turn the "aesthetic into a form of praxis," 509, 505. Posnock's thesis in this article and in "How It Feels to Be a Problem" that Du Bois's conception of the aesthetic is "beyond race" and that aesthetic contemplation plays a role in reaching

this liberating place figures prominently in my argument about the dangers and rewards of Du Bois's attempted rehabilitation of the dandy figure. Certainly Posnock's description of Du Bois as a political aesthete who insists on the political potential of aesthetics expands one's understanding not only of Du Bois's own aesthetic inclinations but also of the interrelatedness of art and politics in African American struggles for equality. However, Posnock's designation of the ultimate goal of Du Bois and the other African American authors—a place in which souls are uncolored—does not do justice to their lifelong efforts to eradicate racism and prejudice. Though Du Bois and others, like James Weldon Johnson, worked to bring about a world in which dark skin color did not automatically erase people from consideration in terms of social and political justice and recognition as cultural producers, I believe that they wanted to defuse, rather than eliminate, the difference that race or culture makes. Above the veil, souls would only be uncolored as long as color mattered below. Posnock's articles from 1995 and 1997 appeared before the book-length study I cite later in this chapter, *Color and Culture*. In this chapter, I cite from both articles and the book, as the longer study recontextualizes the earlier articles. My argument with Posnock's reading of Du Bois relies, in part, on the rhetoric in all three sources.

78. Posnock, "Distinction," 504.

79. Du Bois, *Dark Princess*, 279–80.

80. Ibid., 280.

81. Posnock, "Distinction," 515, 502.

82. In "The Criteria of Negro Art," Du Bois references as examples four beautiful things that take different forms: a European cathedral, an African landscape, an Italian sculpture, and the spirituals. While this is just an example in a single essay in his copious oeuvre, the exclusion of anything American simultaneously makes a bid for African American culture as American culture as well as denies worth to those things American that, in Du Bois's opinion, do not engage African America. Though hardly a full or adequate explanation of why Du Bois reveres the icons of modern European visual art, that he sees Africa in them (the "Congo flooding the Acropolis") helps one understand his predilection for them. One must note that although he wants to add ideology to art in service of the African American cause, he fails to acknowledge the ideological conditions that produce and inform the European art he admires. However, as we have seen in his discussions of blackface minstrelsy, Du Bois has a definite sense of the potency of art forms that deprecate (black) humanity. From the 1920s on, as his pan-African concerns and socialism deepen in response to American racism, xenophobia, and militarism, Du Bois sees less and less beauty in the United States.

83. Posnock, "Distinction," 506.

84. Du Bois, *Dark Princess*, 272.

85. Ibid., 273, 261.

86. Ibid., 271.

87. Ibid., 272.

88. Du Bois, "The Criteria of Negro Art," 1001.

89. Du Bois, *Dark Princess*, 310–11. *Dark Princess* and this scene specifically have become the subject of much new scholarship on the relationship between Du Bois's internationalism in the 1920s and his sexual, racial, and nationalist politics. For a reading of the "sexual logic" of *Dark Princess* that focuses on the problematics of "black maternity," rather than on those of black paternity (my focus here), see Weinbaum, "Reproducing Racial Globality," *Social Text*.

90. Du Bois, *Dark Princess*, 308.

91. Posnock, "How It Feels to Be a Problem" 344, 326.

92. Ibid., 346.

93. Ibid., 349.

94. Posnock, *Color and Culture*, 5.

95. Ibid., 46.

96. In fact, the oxymoronic quality of the lexicon of *Color and Culture* does not stem from an appreciation of an intellectual's "double aims" against racialism through a sometimes strategic essentialism; rather, the true object of Posnock's critique is revealed as what he calls our present essentialism-harboring "epoch of postmodern tribalism," otherwise known as the phenomenon of "multiculturalism," 47.

97. Gilroy, *The Black Atlantic*, 144.

98. Edwards, *The Practice of Diaspora*, 1.

99. Ibid., 1.

100. Lewis, *W. E. B. Du Bois*, 129.

101. Du Bois, *Autobiography*, 153.

102. Ibid., 156–57.

103. Du Bois, *Dusk of Dawn*, 45, 47.

104. Gilroy, *Black Atlantic*, 17.

105. For example, he describes Matthew and Kautilya's idyllic retreat from the revolution as, "He goes to work. She cooks curry." *The Black Atlantic*, 143.

106. Ibid., 44.

107. Ibid., 144.

108. This seems especially true, as Asian men are often stereotyped as effeminate, not normatively masculine. In fact, one might see the marriage and

its progeny as doubly emasculated, given the English attitude toward Kautilya in the novel; though royal, she is still considered a "nigger" by her former British fiancee. *Dark Princess*, 239. See Said's *Orientalism* or Suleri's *The Rhetoric of English India* for more on the feminized "oriental man" and culture.

109. Gilroy, *Black Atlantic*, 136.

110. Posnock, *Color and Culture*, 183.

111. Ibid., 183.

CHAPTER FOUR Dandyism and the Politics of Visuality

1. Baker, *Modernism and the Harlem Renaissance*, xvi, xiii. For details on the ways in which critics have judged the success and failure of the Harlem Renaissance, see especially chapter 2 of *Modernism and the Harlem Renaissance* and David Levering Lewis's preface to the 1997 edition of *When Harlem Was in Vogue*.

2. Baker, *Modernism*, 8, 7, 4.

3. Ibid., 7.

4. Ibid., 9, xiv.

5. Ibid., 106; Baker, *Turning South Again*, 33.

6. Baker, *Turning South Again*, 70.

7. Ibid., 75.

8. Ibid., 33.

9. Levy uses the term in his biography of Johnson, *James Weldon Johnson*, 20; Baker, *Modernism*, 3.

10. I borrow this phrase from Robin Kelley's *Freedom Dreams*.

11. In *Turning South Again*, Baker also mentions the way in which Booker T.'s dandyism feminizes him; for Baker this feminization is, like the dandyism, dangerous rather than a potential experiment with masculine styles. In *Turning South Again*, both "mulatto" and "feminization" are "bad" words. For more on how the dandy's play with gender might be liberating, see especially chapter 3 above.

12. Huyssen, "Mass Culture as Woman," 44–62.

13. Feldman, *Gender on the Divide*, 4.

14. Ibid., 9.

15. Huyssen, "Mass Culture as Woman," 52.

16. Baudelaire, "The Painter of Modern Life," 402.

17. Both Baker's rethinking in *Modernism and the Harlem Renaissance* and my own bring us to the black dandy, but our very different conclusions on how to read the figure reveal the different purposes of our projects. For Baker, as

for Washington in *Up from Slavery*, dandyism is frivolous; see *Up from Slavery*, chapter 8, in which Washington rails against the "educated Negro, with high hat, imitation gold eye-glasses, a showy walking stick, kid gloves, fancy boots and what not," a distraction from what Baker calls the "achievement of a black citizenship that entails documented mobility (driver's license, passport, green card, social security card) and access to a decent job at a decent rate of pay." *Turning South Again*, 33. For me, black dandyism is a practice that reveals the black imaginary, is a location of one kind of expressive or creative response to oppression in the field of representation.

18. Gates, "The Trope of the New Negro and the Reconstruction of the Image of the Black," 132.

19. Ibid.

20. James Weldon Johnson, *Black Manhattan*, 4.

21. Ibid., 144.

22. Ibid., 147.

23. Ibid., 281.

24. Douglas, *Terrible Honesty*, 326.

25. Ibid., 326.

26. Ibid., 328.

27. Ibid., 323, 324.

28. Lewis, *When Harlem Was in Vogue*, 3–5.

29. "On Seventh Avenue," *Baltimore Afro-American*, December 27, 1930, 9, quoted in George Chauncey, *Gay New York*, 249.

30. The white female impersonator Robert Brennan quoted in George Chauncey, *Gay New York*, 244.

31. "Gracious Me! Dear, 'Twas To-oo Divine," *New York Amsterdam News*, March 7, 1936, 8.

32. Ibid.

33. "Men Step Out in Gorgeous Finery of Other Sex to Vie for Beauty Prizes," *New York Amsterdam News*, March 2, 1932, 2.

34. Chauncey, *Gay New York*, 261.

35. Johnson died in 1938, eight years after *Black Manhattan* was published; after 1930, he was increasingly interested in self- and cultural history as he wrote his autobiography, *Along This Way*, in 1933 and revised *The Book of American Negro Poetry*, originally published in 1922, in 1931.

36. Johnson, *Along This Way*, 47.

37. Ibid., 47–48.

38. Ibid.

39. Levy, *James Weldon Johnson*, 17.

40. Ibid., 20.

41. Ibid., 50, 47, 52.

42. Ibid., 52.

43. Ibid., 59.

44. Ibid.

45. Ibid., 65. Later in life, this language ability landed him an appointment in the United States Consular service, an unusual opportunity for an African American in the early twentieth century.

46. Ibid., 171–72.

47. Ibid., 88.

48. Ibid., 80.

49. Johnson, "Double Audience Makes Hard Road for Negro Authors," *The Selected Writings of James Weldon Johnson*, ed. Wilson, vol. 2, 410.

50. Johnson, *Black Manhattan*, 3.

51. Ibid., 161.

52. Ibid.

53. Ibid.

54. Ibid., 171.

55. Ibid., 283. This phrase first appears in an essay, "Harlem: The Culture Capital," that Johnson published in the *Survey Graphic* number that later became the *New Negro* volume.

56. Douglas, *Terrible Honesty*, 324.

57. Johnson, *Black Manhattan*, 231.

58. Ibid., 164.

59. Ibid., 162–63.

60. See White and White, "Strolling, Jooking, and Fixy Clothes," *Stylin.'*

61. Ibid., 97.

62. Ibid., 228.

63. Johnson, *Black Manhattan*, 260.

64. Ibid., 281.

65. Douglas, *Terrible Honesty*, 323, 213.

66. Johnson, "A Poetry Corner," *New York Age*, January 7, 1915, *The Selected Writings of James Weldon Johnson*, vol. 1, 252.

67. Johnson, "Some New Books of Poetry and Their Makers," *New York Age*, September 7, 1918, *Selected Writings*, vol. 1, 273.

68. Johnson, *The Autobiography of an Ex-Coloured Man*, 5.

69. Ibid., 6.

70. "Dandy," *Oxford English Dictionary*, 2d ed.

71. Johnson, *The Autobiography of an Ex-Coloured Man*, 6.

72. Kawash, "*The Autobiography of an Ex-Coloured Man*," 62.

73. Johnson, *The Autobiography of an Ex-Coloured Man*, 7.

74. Ibid., 16.

75. Kawash quotes an unpublished paper by Barbara Johnson, "Fanon and Lacan," delivered at the University of North Carolina, Chapel Hill, March 28, 1991. See Kawash, *"The Autobiography of an Ex-Coloured Man,"* 67.

76. Johnson, *The Autobiography of an Ex-Coloured Man,* 17.

77. See chapter 5 below for more on the relationship of black dandyism to narcissism, including its potential to be redemptive rather than hopelessly solipsistic, for black subjects. In *Queering the Color Line,* Somerville also argues that the Ex-Coloured Man's gaze here is erotic and narcissistic as well as "distinctly feminized, recalling descriptions of the highly eroticized mulatta of nineteenth-century fiction," 113. I am indebted to Somerville's reading of *The Autobiography of an Ex-Coloured Man*'s queerness, as it is essential to my argument about his dandyism and the way in which Johnson wants to figure a "cosmopolite self-concept" very differently in his nonfiction and fiction.

78. Johnson, *The Autobiography of an Ex-Coloured Man,* 18.

79. Ibid., 46.

80. Ibid.

81. Kawash, *"The Autobiography of an Ex-Coloured Man,"* 63.

82. Somerville, *Queering,* 114.

83. Johnson, *The Autobiography of an Ex-Coloured Man,* 121.

84. Ibid., 129, 130.

85. Somerville, *Queering,* 121.

86. Johnson, *The Autobiography of an Ex-Coloured Man,* 148.

87. Ibid., 157.

88. Ibid., 173, 182.

89. Kawash makes this same point: "Race is not a physical or psychological fact but a legal fiction. The basis of distinction is completely arbitrary. Nevertheless, once the law has defined 'a few drops of Negro blood,' as the line separating black from white, the cultural definition of blackness becomes a naturalized fact." *"The Autobiography of an Ex-Coloured Man,"* 71.

90. Johnson, *The Autobiography of an Ex-Coloured Man,* 190.

91. Ibid., 204, 210.

92. Ibid., 200. Somerville points out the importance of this line as well, *Queering,* 125.

93. Bontemps, "Introduction," *Autobiography of an Ex-Coloured Man,* vii. Somerville makes a similar argument—by the late 1920s, Harlem was seemingly sufficiently queer to handle this destabilizing text. See *Queering,* 127.

94. Huggins, *Harlem Renaissance,* 95.

95. Thurman, *Infants of the Spring,* 267.

96. Ibid., 280–81.

97. Ibid., 24, 56.

98. Ibid., 280.

99. Ibid., 24, 21.

100. Ibid., 235.

101. Ibid., 236, 237.

102. Ibid., 280–81.

103. Ibid., 241.

104. Ibid., 59.

105. Cobb, "Insolent Racing, Rough Narrative," 341.

106. Ibid., 337.

107. Ibid., 338 (quoting Thurman, 197).

108. Thurman, *Infants of the Spring*, 44.

109. Ibid., 223, 224.

110. Feldman, *Gender on the Divide*, 9.

111. Thurman, *Infants of the Spring*, 282–83.

112. Ibid., 284.

113. Paul's subversive exuberance also contrasts with that of another dandy figure in the book, the washed-up "gentleman" singer Eustace Savoy. Preoccupied with classical music and unwilling to sing the spirituals, costumed in a cloak and surrounded by "cloisonné bric-a-brac, misty etchings, antique silver pieces, caviar and rococo jewelry," Eustace's dandyism is read by Elisa Glick as "a preoccupation with dress and exterior elegance, stripped of the social rebellion that is the badge of the bohemian dandy." "Harlem's Queer Dandy," 432. When Eustace does wander out of his carefully contrived element and, desperate for a job, performs the spirituals at an audition, he fails miserably and becomes a "shell," "a mere shadow of his former self." Just as his earlier reverence for Western classics prevented him from joining either the New Negro or avant-garde artistic projects in Niggerati Manor, his failure to perform the spirituals well similarly isolates him and, in effect, destroys any path available for his art. He becomes, as Glick argues, reified, as his dandyism functions as mere self-commodification in contrast to that of Paul, which productively challenges conformist attitudes.

114. Thurman, *Infants of the Spring*, 144–45.

115. Cobb, "Insolent Racing, Rough Narrative," 340.

116. Ibid., 347.

117. Ibid., 337.

118. Glick, "Harlem's Queer Dandy," 437; Thurman, *Infants of the Spring*, 284.

119. Ibid., 437.

120. James Weldon Johnson says of Hughes in *Black Manhattan*, "Langs-

ton Hughes is a cosmopolite. Young as he is, he has been all over the world, making his way. Consciously he snaps his fingers at the race, as he does a great many other things. He belongs to the line of rebel poets," 207.

CHAPTER FIVE Visual Histories of Black Cosmopolitanism

1. Golden, "Introduction: Post . . . ," *Freestyle*, 14.

2. Ibid.

3. Ibid., 15.

4. Ibid.

5. Kim Hall borrows this phrase from Frantz Fanon's *Black Skin, White Masks* in her *Things of Darkness*.

6. I borrow this phrase from Robin Kelley, *Freedom Dreams*.

7. Gates, "The Black Man's Burden," 233.

8. Diawara, "The Absent Ones," 209; Hemphill, "*Looking for Langston*," 177.

9. Gates, "Looking for Modernism," 203.

10. Diawara, "The Absent Ones," 206.

11. Muñoz, "Photographies of Mourning," 340.

12. Hughes, "The Negro Artist and the Racial Mountain," *The Nation*, June 23, 1926.

13. Grundmann, "Black Nationhood and the Rest in the West," 28.

14. Ibid., 28.

15. Arroyo, "Look Back and Talk Back," 331.

16. When asked by *Cineaste* in 1995, "Why is everyone so beautiful in *Looking for Langston*?" Julien replied, "The film is about fantasy, about reinscribing an idealized gay iconography, it never set out to represent everybody. It deliberately appropriates a certain genre of gay and black photography of Robert Mapplethorpe and George Platt Lynes." Grundmann, "Black Nationhood and the Rest in the West," 28. My goal here is to link this "idealized gay iconography" to dandyism and its new New Negro, potentially post-black aesthetics.

17. Julien and Mercer, "True Confessions," 171.

18. Mercer, "Avid Iconographies," 81.

19. Deitcher, "A Lovesome Thing," 232.

20. hooks, "Seductive Sexualities," 200.

21. *Looking for Langston* was also presented as a performance piece in 1991, titled "Undressing Icons." In an unrelated interview with Julien that same year, Essex Hemphill describes the film's impact when he says, "For many,

Hughes is a 'sacred icon,' an icon saddled with what Julien astutely refers to as 'the burden of representation,' a burden that effectively obscured questions of Hughes' sexual identity until Julien chose to gently undress him, or, more appropriately, ease him out of the closet." "*Looking for Langston*," 174. For me, what is important about the film is not the "disrobing" or exposure of Hughes, but how and to what effect Julien uses dress to represent Hughes's social and cultural circle and its aesthetic goals.

22. The sartorial style might also be a function of what Julien and Mercer describe in "True Confessions" in 1991 as "recent trends in [white or mainstream] gay style." In this article, they indicate that "after the clone imagery in which gays adopted very straight signifiers of masculinity—moustaches, short hair, workclothes—in order to challenge stereotypes of limp-wristed 'poofs,' there developed stylistic flirtations with s&m, leather, quasi-military uniforms and skinhead styles. The racist and fascist connotations of these new styles escaped gay consciousness," 167. In *Looking for Langston*, Julien may be offering the tuxedo as an alternative to that of the offensive mainstream look and the "poof."

23. Locke, *The New Negro*, 50; quoted in Diawara, "The Absent Ones," 217.

24. Chauncey, *Gay New York*, 248.

25. Ibid., 266; hooks, "Seductive Sexualities," 195. Julien did not know of Chauncey's excellent work when the film was made, although he does mention reading Eric Garber's work. In fact, in 1991 Julien stated, "If one wanted to look in an archive to find specific images of black gay dance halls one would be undertaking a journey that would have no beginning because such places did not exist then. Sensuality and desire were issues that really weren't at stake. But there were issues that were at stake: it was very important to construct images of dreams. One can only view that world from an imaginary position." Hemphill, "*Looking for Langston*," 178. He is wrong about the existence of dance halls, but after Chauncey's work, his "dream" seems prescient.

26. For more on the introduction of the short black dinner jacket, see Laver, *Costume and Fashion*.

27. Diawara, "The Absent Ones," 206.

28. Deitcher, "A Lovesome Thing," 16.

29. For fancy clothes citations, see Diawara, "The Absent Ones"; hooks, "Seductive Sexualities"; and B. Ruby Rich, "Interview with Isaac Julien," 50; for remarks on the nakedness, see hooks and Gates, "Looking for Modernism."

30. Hollander, *Sex and Suits*, 113.

31. Ibid.

32. The black men and the nudes in this film are many-hued; Julian does not reproduce color politics as he works against gender and sex politics.

33. hooks, "Seductive Sexualities," 196.

34. Gates, "Looking for Modernism," 203, 204, and Mercer, "Busy in the Ruins of a Wretched Phantasia," 35.

35. hooks, "Seductive Sexualities," 199.

36. Ibid., 195.

37. Deitcher, "A Lovesome Thing," 16. He is responding to bell hooks's reading of the film explicitly.

38. "There was a lot of work done around picture and visual research," Julien says, explaining that while he was in the United States conducting research he visited the Schomburg Center, Roy DeCarava, Donna Mussenden Van Der Zee (James's widow), and Robert Mapplethorpe's agent. Hemphill, "*Looking for Langston*," 176. With this in mind, it seems fitting that the film's overall "faggy sense of style" derives from that which Julien absorbed from Van Der Zee and Robert Mapplethorpe.

39. Kelley, "Foreword," *Reflections in Black*, ix.

40. Barry Gaither, quoted in the "Introduction" to Willis, *Reflections in Black*, xv; and bell hooks, "In Our Glory," 48.

41. hooks, "In Our Glory," 53.

42. Willis-Braithwaite, "Introduction," *Van Der Zee*, 11.

43. Ibid., 16.

44. Hemphill, "If His Name Were Mandingo," and Muñoz, "Photographies of Mourning." For more on this, see Kobena Mercer's "Reading Racial Fetishism: The Photographs of Robert Mapplethorpe."

45. That the photographer and many of the subjects of these images have since died adds to the urgency of seeing these photographs as celebratory rather than funerary. See Muñoz, "Photographies of Mourning."

46. Ibid., 349, 354.

47. Ibid., 356.

48. "Interview with Isaac Julien," *Struggles for Representation*, 364.

49. For more on the affirmative capacity of mourning, see Muñoz, "Photographies of Mourning." I take the term "redemptive narcissism" from Lyle Ashton Harris in Cohen, "Lyle Ashton Harris," 107.

50. Sarkar, "Tangled Legacies," 228.

51. Hemphill, "*Looking for Langston*," 180.

52. Yinka Shonibare was awarded the title MBE (Member of the Order of the British Empire) in 2005 and now uses it as a part of his artistic name.

53. Shonibare in Griffin, "Global Tendencies."

54. Sarkar, "Tangled Legacies," 221.

55. Hall, "New Ethnicities," 443.

56. There was a Fanon vogue in black (British) cultural studies from about 1985 to 1996, from the publication of Homi Bhabha's foreword to the Pluto Press edition of *Black Skin, White Masks* in 1985 through the Mirage exhibit and *Fact of Blackness* volume in 1996. Since then, the Bhabha school of reading Fanon has been attacked by many cultural critics for analyzing Fanon ahistorically, psychoanalytically, and without sufficient attention to the cultural milieu about which the book was written (1950s Martinique). In any event, the dandy artists I study here were an initial part of that vogue, and their work reflects an engagement with this reading of Fanon, for better or worse.

57. Hall, "The After-Life of Frantz Fanon," 34. Here Hall cites Benita Parry's "Signs of the Times," *Third Text*.

58. Fanon, *Black Skin, White Masks*, 34.

59. Ibid., 114.

60. Ibid., 110–12.

61. Ibid., 194.

62. Ibid., 10.

63. Ibid., 23; James Smalls uses the same quotation to make a similar point in his "African-American Self-Portraiture," 54, 58.

64. Bhabha, "Foreword," *Black Skin, White Masks*, xxiv.

65. For Bhabha, *Black Skin, White Masks* presents and then shies away from its own liberatory moments, as if Fanon were "fearful of his most radical insights." "Foreword," xx.

66. Fanon, *Black Skin, White Masks*, 232.

67. Ibid., 229.

68. Ibid.

69. Hall, "Afterlife," 20. In the full quotation, Hall indicates that he coined the phrase "new black narcissus" elsewhere; the note to this indicates that this source is in the forthcoming *Race, Ethnicity, and Diaspora* from Harvard University Press. I have been unable to locate this book.

70. Robbins, "Introduction," *Cosmopolitics*, 3.

71. Cohen, "Lyle Ashton Harris," *Flash Art*, 107.

72. Ibid.

73. For more on this, see especially the essays by Mercer and Young in *The Fact of Blackness*.

74. Harris and Harris, "Black Widow," *The Passionate Camera*, ed. Bright, 249.

75. Ibid.

76. Carter, "Artists After Stonewall," 63.

77. Smalls, "African-American Self-Portraiture," *Third Text*, 47.

78. Ibid., 49, 50.

79. Ibid., 58.

80. Carter, "Artists After Stonewall," 63.

81. Ibid.

82. Udé was born in 1962 in Makurdi, Nigeria, and grew up in Lagos. He came to New York in the 1980s and attended Hunter College.

83. Harris and Harris, "Black Widow," *The Passionate Camera*, ed. Bright, 252.

84. Ibid., 248.

85. Smalls mentions Harris's "rhetoric of the pose to perform a subversive act of narcissism," and the fact that he "challenges codes of masculinity and femininity through a focus on artificiality, performative gestures and props," on 57 and 59, respectively, in "African-American Self-Portraiture."

86. Harris and Harris, "Black Widow," *The Passionate Camera*, ed. Bright, 255–56.

87. Other portraits that use the "nationalist" background include "For Cleopatra," "Venus Hottentot," "Alex and Lyle," and "The Child."

88. Harris and Harris, "Black Widow," 255.

89. Seward, "Lyle Ashton Harris at Jack Tilton Gallery," 83.

90. Firstenberg, "A Stylist of Subjectivities."

91. In reading a similar image in Udé's "Cover Girl" series, the *Glamour* cover, Firstenberg notes that "Udé is confronted by his own gaze as his image is duplicated in the magazine cover, literalizing the mirror stage as self-staged, as a means of visualizing identification via self-determination." "A Stylist of Subjectivities," 172. While I am not going to follow through on the Lacanian reading of Udé that this quote suggests, I do believe, along with Firstenberg, that Udé's work offers a very different model of "othering."

92. Udé, "The Regarded Self," 16.

93. Ibid.

94. Firstenberg, "A Stylist of Subjectivities," 171.

95. Patrick McDonald, "The High Brow."

96. Shirin Neshat says to Udé in an interview in 2001, "You, more than any artist I know, live your art. One can't look at your work without being drawn into the world you exist in. You have surrounded yourself with multiple groups of talents in fashion, art, film, popular culture, and intellectuals. Your mere physical presence and style are a work of art." "Iké Udé," 92. In 2002, Udé said a similar thing to his friend and fellow dandy Patrick McDonald: "Simply put, I'm invariably inspired by beautiful things, be it a gesture

of one's hand, a silhouette, a certain fabric or cut of a garment, a smile, a redeemable shyness, a touch of perversity, style, intelligence or that indeterminate something that few possess. Ultimately, my work and life are nearly indistinguishable." McDonald, "The High Brow."

97. Udé, "Magnificent Futility," 125.

98. Firstenberg, "A Stylist of Subjectivities," 170. Udé voices his disapproval of all labels, especially "queer of color," in "Magnificent Futility." His objection to the label seems to reveal that he considers queer to be a description of gay or same-sex sexuality, not of an oppositional identity that can incorporate, but is not limited to, same-sex sexual practices. See Udé, "Magnificent Futility," 124–25. In correspondence with me, he clarifies: "I've always deemed myself as an exceptional individual with the entitlement and liberty to do as I please with due respect to law but not stigma or uninformed stereotype that make people — men and women — afraid to realize and live a fully realized individualistic life." Email, June 2008.

99. Udé and Enwezor, "Between Mask and Fantasy," 71.

100. Ibid.

101. Mercer, "Iké Udé," 32; Mercer borrows the term from James Clifford's *Routes*.

102. Neshat, "Iké Udé," 92.

103. This is the title of Kobena Mercer's article on Udé in *Camera Austria*.

104. This is an homage to Kaja Silverman's groundbreaking book of 1992 of the same name. This particular piece was included in the Second Johannesburg Biennale and was "mass-produced and posted on lampposts in downtown Johannesburg and its suburbs." Firstenberg, "A Stylist of Subjectivities," 173.

105. The Wodaabe or Bororo celebrate the annual festival with weeklong male beauty contests in which elaborate dress, makeup, and dancing skill are judged. For more on the Geerewol festival and the Wodaabe, see Werner Herzog's film *Wodaabe: Herdsmen of the Sun* (2001), and Mette Bovin, *Nomads Who Cultivate Beauty*.

106. Enwezor and Zaya, "Moving In," 84.

107. Firstenberg, "A Stylist of Subjectivities," 172.

108. Ibid., 171.

109. Iké Udé did not know at the time how appropriate his reference to Equiano would become — recently, Equiano's narrative, at least the part that recalls his capture in Africa and his middle passage, has been revealed as the product of his imagination. In my opinion, rather than rendering his narrative inauthentic this revelation recalls once again the inventiveness of people of African descent and their sometime ability to self-fashion in order to take advantage of the market. See recent work by Carretta.

110. Mercer, "Post-colonial Flaneur," 34.

111. Patrick McDonald, "The High Brow."

112. Udé repeats this phrase when he talks about style in general or about a dandy's style. I first read it in the "Elements of Style" section in *aRude*. He repeats it in the "Post-colonial Flaneur" interview with Mercer in *Camera Austria*.

113. Udé's latest venture is *Style File: The World's Most Elegantly Dressed* (HarperCollins, 2008), which profiles contemporary and historical style icons and explains in words and illustrations the importance of a number of the twentieth-century's most influential looks. As advertised, *Style File* is a "comprehensive, gorgeous book" that is "a rich exploration of personal style that belongs in every well-dressed library." Udé, *Style File*, front flap.

114. See the recent biography of the Chevalier by Guede, *Monsieur de Saint-Georges*.

115. MacDonald, "The High Brow."

116. Bessire, "Iké Udé's 'Beyond Decorum,'" 8.

117. Guldemond and Mackert, "To Entertain and Provoke," 41.

118. Griffin, "Global Tendencies," 152.

119. "Post-colonial hybrid" is the term the Tate Britain used in promoting Shonibare's work for the Turner Prize in 2004; it also appears in the most comprehensive volume of his work, *Double Dutch*. Even though Shonibare himself seems to assent to this label, my reading of his work reveals its limitations. I believe the term questions the preeminence of the postcolonial as the only hermeneutic for analyzing his work.

120. Thomas Carlyle, *Sartor Resartus*, part 3.

121. Enwezor, "Of Hedonism, Masquerade, Carnivalesque and Power," 166.

122. Turner Prize lecture, November 2004, on Tate Britain Web site. Second quotation from Guldemonde and Mackert, "To Entertain and Provoke," 35.

123. See especially John Picton's work on the history and meaning of the fabric for more on how Shonibare might be using the pattern for a further double entendre—for example, some of his women's dresses use fabric with the Chanel "double C" sign printed on them, while other pieces, such as "19th-Century Kid (Queen Victoria)," feature a child's dress in a pattern found on soccer balls. Additionally, Shonibare plays with the way in which certain patterns have come to signify in West African societies; for example, patterns known as "money has wings" and "the mat," a euphemism for female genitalia, are used to dress women and girls in his oeuvre.

124. Enwezor, "Of Hedonism, Masquerade, Carnivalesque and Power," 166.

125. Ibid., 167.

126. These abstract pieces are read in art history terms as Shonibare's experiments with the modernist grid. See Oguibe on Shonibare's first piece in this vein, "Double-Dutch and the Culture Game," catalogue essay for "Yinka Shonibare: Be-Muse," Rome, 2001: www.camwood.org.

127. Enwezor, "Of Hedonism, Masquerade, Carnivalesque and Power," 173.

128. Diawara, "The Independence Cha-Cha," 17–18.

129. Weinstein, "Yinka Shonibare," 175.

130. Picton, "Undressing Ethnicity," 66.

131. Verdier and Torgoff, trans., "YS: Eloge de Decoratif Veneneux / Re-Stitching the Social Fabric," 32.

132. Ibid.

133. Oguibe, "Double-Dutch and the Culture Game."

134. Holmes, "The Empire's New Clothes," 120.

135. Ibid.

136. Griffin, "Global Tendencies," 152ff. Hynes, "Re-Dressing History," 60–65. In this article Hynes says that Shonibare found Foucault and Derrida "very important for his work. Their approach to the deconstruction of categories, the structural problem of the signifier and signified, and the idea of power structure created through various systems of signification gave Shonibare a powerful interpretive framework for his personal experiences as an artist from the African continent living and working in London."

137. Guldemond and Mackert, "To Entertain and Provoke," 36.

138. Turner Prize lecture, November 2004.

139. Corbetta, "Dietro la maschera dell'arte / Behind the Mask of Art," 16.

140. Fisher, "Yinka Shonibare," 186.

141. Enwezor, "Of Hedonism, Masquerade, Carnivalesque and Power," 176, and McRobbie, "The African Dandy," 64.

142. Hynes, "Re-Dressing History," and Hylton, "Yinka Shonibare," 101.

143. Turner Prize lecture, November 2004.

144. Dabydeen, *Hogarth's Blacks*, 85. See also Bindman, "'A Voluptuous Alliance between Africa and Europe.'"

145. Dabydeen, *Hogarth's Blacks*, 74.

146. Oguibe, "Double-Dutch and the Culture Game."

147. I thank Caroline Levin for this insight.

148. Enwezor, "Of Hedonism, Masquerade, Carnivalesque and Power," 177.

149. Swedish history and biography of Gustav III from Lagerqvist, *History of Sweden*. Although Sweden does not have a colonial history in Africa, it did

have a Caribbean colony, St. Barthélemy, acquired from the French in 1784. Additionally, Sweden has a history of black luxury slavery. For more on this, see the story of Badin, a slave from St. Croix, who was at the Swedish court during Gustav II's and Gustav III's reign in Pred, *The Past Is Not Dead*.

150. This and the following remarks on "Un Ballo" are from Shonibare's Turner Prize lecture.

Bibliography

Adams, Michael Henry. *Style and Grace: African Americans at Home.* New York: Bulfinch Press, 2006.

"Andre 3000 Gets Style from Prince Charles." *UPI*, September 9, 2004.

Angelo, Henry. *The Reminiscences of Henry Angelo.* Vol. 1. London: Colburn and Bentley, 1834.

Appiah, Anthony. "The Uncompleted Argument: Du Bois and the Illusion of Race." *Race, Writing, and Difference.* Chicago: University of Chicago Press, 1985.

Aptheker, Herbert. "Introduction." *Dark Princess: A Romance.* Millwood, N.Y.: Kraus-Thomason Organization Limited, 1976.

Arroyo, José. "The Films of Isaac Julien: Look Back and Talk Back." *Cinemas of the Black Diaspora.* Detroit: Wayne State University, 1995.

Aylward, J. D. *The House of Angelo.* London: Batchworth Press, 1953.

Bailey, David A. "Mirage: Enigmas of Race, Difference and Desire." *Mirage: Enigmas of Race, Difference and Desire*, ed. by Ragnar Farr, 56–80. London: Institute of Contemporary Art and Institute of International Visual Arts, 1995.

Baker, Houston. *Modernism and the Harlem Renaissance.* Chicago: University of Chicago Press, 1989.

———. *Turning South Again: Re-Thinking Modernism / Re-Reading Booker T.* Durham: Duke University Press, 2001.

Bakhtin, Mikhail. *Rabelais and His World.* Translated by Helen Iswolsky. Cambridge, Mass.: MIT Press, 1968.

Baldwin, Brooke. "The Cakewalk: A Study in Stereotype and Reality." *Journal of Social History* 15 (Winter 1981), 205–18.

Barnes, Eric Wollencott. *The Lady of Fashion: The Life and Theatre of Anna Cora Mowatt.* New York: Scribner, 1954.

Barthelemy, Anthony Gerard. *Black Face, Maligned Race: The Representation of Blacks in English Drama from Shakespeare to Southerne.* Baton Rouge: Louisiana State University Press, 1987.

Barthes, Roland. *The Fashion System.* Translated by Matthew Ward and Richard Howard. Berkeley: University of California Press, 1990.

Baudelaire, Charles. "The Painter of Modern Life." *Selected Writings on Art and Literature*. Translated and edited by P. E. Charvet. New York: Penguin, 1992.

Baumgarten, Linda. "'Clothes for the People': Slave Clothing in Early Virginia." *Journal of Early Southern Decorative Arts* 14 (November 1988), 26–70.

———. *What Clothes Reveal: The Language of Clothing in Colonial and Federal America*. Williamsburg, Va., and New Haven: Colonial Williamsburg Foundation and Yale University Press, 2002.

Bean, Annemarie, James V. Hatch, and Brooks McNamara, eds. *Inside the Minstrel Mask: Readings in Nineteenth-Century Blackface Minstrelsy*. Hanover, N.H.: University Press of New England, 1996.

Beerbohm, Max. "Dandies and Dandies." *The Bodley Head Max Beerbohm*. Edited by David Cecil. London: Bodley Head, 1970.

Behn, Aphra. *Oroonoko*. Edited by Joanna Lipking. New York: W. W. Norton, 1997.

Belton, Don, ed. *Speak My Name: Black Men on Masculinity and the American Dream*. Boston: Beacon Press, 1995.

Bermingham, Ann, and John Brewer, eds. *Consumption and Culture, 1600–1800: Image, Object, Text*. New York: Routledge, 1995.

Bernard, Emily. *Remember Me to Harlem: The Letters of Langston Hughes and Carl Van Vechten*. New York: Vintage, 2001.

———. "What He Did for the Race: Carl Van Vechten and the Harlem Renaissance." *Soundings* 80.4 (Winter 1997), 531–42.

Bessire, Aimée. "Iké Udé's *Beyond Decorum*: The Poetics and Politics of Fashionable Selves." *Beyond Decorum: The Photography of Iké Udé*, ed. by Mark H. C. Bessire and Lauri Firstenberg, 8–9. Cambridge, Mass.: MIT Press, 2000.

Bessire, Mark H. C., and Lauri Firstenberg, eds. *Beyond Decorum: The Photography of Iké Udé*. Cambridge, Mass.: MIT Press, 2000.

Bettelheim, Judith, and Fernando Ortiz, eds. *Cuban Festivals: A Century of Afro-Cuban Culture*. Princeton: Marcus Weiner, 2001.

Bhabha, Homi K. "Are You a Man or a Mouse?" *Constructing Masculinity*, ed. by Maurice Berger, Brian Wallis, and Simon Watson, 57–68. New York: Routledge, 1995.

———. "Foreword: Remembering Fanon." *Black Skin, White Masks*. London: Pluto Press, 1986.

———. "Interrogating Identity: Frantz Fanon and the Postcolonial Prerogative." *The Location of Culture*. New York: Routledge, 1994.

———. "Of Mimicry and Man: The Ambivalence of Colonial Discourse." *The Location of Culture*. New York: Routledge, 1994.

———. "The Other Question: Stereotype, Discrimination and the Discourse of Colonialism." *The Location of Culture*. New York: Routledge, 1994.

———. "Signs Taken for Wonders: Questions of Ambivalence and Authority under a Tree Outside Delhi, May 1817." *The Location of Culture*. New York: Routledge, 1994.

Bickerstaff[e], Isaac. *The Padlock: A Comic Opera in Two Acts. Dolby's British Theatre*. London: T. Dolby, Brittania Press, 1823.

———. *The Padlock: A Comic Opera*. London: W. Griffin, 1768. *Literature Online (LION) English Prose Drama Full-Text Database*. Cambridge: Chadwyck-Healey, 1996.

———. *The Padlock: A Comic Opera*. Boston: William Spotswood, 1795. *Early American Imprints* I, no. 28296. New York: Readex Microprint, 1985.

———. *The Padlock: A Comic Opera in Two Acts*. New York: D. Longworth, 1805. *Early American Imprints*, 2d ser., no. 8016. New Canaan, Conn.: Readex Microform, 1990.

Biddulph, Violet. *Kitty, Duchess of Queensberry*. London: Ivor Nicholson and Watson, 1935.

Bindman, David. "A Voluptuous Alliance Between Africa and Europe: Hogarth's Africans." *The Other Hogarth: Aesthetics of Difference*, ed. by Bernadette Fort and Angela Rosenthal, 260–69. Princeton: Princeton University Press, 2001.

Blackburn, Robin. *The Making of New World Slavery: From the Baroque to the Modern, 1492–1800*. London: Verso, 1997.

"The Black Man." *All the Year Round: A Weekly Journal*, n.s. 13. 327 (March 6, 1875), 89–493.

Bogle, Donald. *Toms, Coons, Mulattoes, Mammies, and Bucks*. New York: Continuum, 1994.

Bontemps, Arna. "Introduction." *The Autobiography of an Ex-Coloured Man*. New York: Hill and Wang, 1995.

Borgstrom, Michael. "Passing Over: Setting the Record Straight in *Uncle Tom's Cabin*." PMLA 118.5 (2003), 1290–1304.

Boskin, Joseph. *Sambo: The Rise and Demise of an American Jester*. New York: Oxford University Press, 1986.

Bovin, Mette. *Nomads Who Cultivate Beauty: Wodaabe Dances and the Visual Arts in Niger*. Uppsala: Nordiska Africaninstitutet, 2001.

Breen, T. H. *The Marketplace of Revolution: How Consumer Politics Shaped American Independence*. New York: Oxford University Press, 2004.

Brewer, John. *The Pleasures of the Imagination: English Culture in the Eighteenth Century*. Chicago: University of Chicago Press, 1997.

Brewer, John, and Roy Porter, eds. *Consumption and the World of Goods*. New York: Routledge, 1994.

Brody, Jennifer DeVere. *Impossible Purities: Blackness, Femininity, and Victorian Culture*. Durham: Duke University Press, 1998.

Brown, Richard E. "The Fops in Cibber's Comedies." *Essays in Literature* 9.1 (Spring 1982), 31–41.

Bruzzi, Stella. *Undressing Cinema: Clothing and Identity in the Movies*. New York: Routledge, 1997.

Byerman, Keith. *Seizing the Word: History, Art and the Self in the Work of W. E. B. Du Bois*. Atlanta: University of Georgia Press, 1994.

Byron, Gordon George. *Byron: A Self-Portrait, Letters and Diaries, 1798 to 1824*. Edited by Peter Quennell. Oxford: Oxford University Press, 1990.

Byrne, Muriel St. Clare. "The Stage Costuming of *Macbeth* in the Eighteenth Century." *Studies in English Theatre History*. London: Society for Theatre Research, 1952.

Campbell, Colin. "Consuming Goods and the Good of Consuming." *Consumer Society in American History: A Reader*, ed. by Lawrence B. Glickman, 19–32. Ithaca: Cornell University Press, 1999.

Canfield, J. D. *Tricksters and Estates: On the Ideology of Restoration Comedy*. Lexington: University Press of Kentucky, 1997.

Caponi, Gina Dagel. "Introduction: The Case for an African American Aesthetic." *Signifyin(g), Sanctifyin,' & Slam-dunking: A Reader in African American Expressive Culture*, ed. by Gina Dagel Caponi. Amherst: University of Massachusetts Press, 1998.

Carby, Hazel. *Race Men*. Cambridge, Mass.: Harvard University Press, 1998.

Carlyle, Thomas. *Sartor Resartus: The Life and Opinions of Herr Teufelsdrockh*. New York: AMS Press, 1974.

Carretta, Vincent. *Equiano the African: Biography of a Self-Made Man*. Athens: University of Georgia Press, 2005.

———. "Olaudah Equiano or Gustavus Vassa? New Light on an Eighteenth-Century Question of Identity." *Slavery and Abolition* 20.3 (December 1999), 96–105.

———. "Soubise." *Oxford Dictionary of National Biography*. Oxford: Oxford University Press, 2004.

Carter, Holland. "Art after Stonewall: 12 Artists Interviewed." *Art in America* 82 (June 1994), 56–65.

Carter, Philip. "An 'Effeminate' or 'Efficient' Nation? Masculinity and Eighteenth-Century Social Documentary." *Textual Practice* 11.3 (1997), 429–43.

Casey, Moira E. "The Fop: 'Apes and Echoes of Men': Gentlemanly Ideals and the Restoration." *Fools and Jesters in Literature, Art, and History*, ed. by Vicki K. Janik, 207–14. Westport, Conn.: Greenwood Press, 1998.

Castle, Terry. *Masquerade and Civilization*. Stanford, Calif.: Stanford University Press, 1986.

Catalogue of Political and Personal Satires Preserved in the Department of Prints and Drawings in the British Museum, 1771–1783. Vol. 5. Edited by Mary Dorothy George. London: British Museum Publications, 1978.

Caulkins, Frances M. *History of Norwich, Connecticut (1866)*. Norwich, Conn.: John Trumbull Press, 1989.

Cervantes, Miguel de. "The Jealous Extremaduran." *Exemplary Stories*. Translated by C. A. Jones. Middlesex: Penguin Books, 1972.

Chauncey, George. *Gay New York*. New York: Basic Books, 1994.

Chesnut, Mary Boykin. *A Diary from Dixie*. Edited by Ben Ames Williams. Cambridge, Mass.: Harvard University Press, 1980.

Chesnutt, Charles W. *The Journals of Charles Chesnutt*. Edited by Richard H. Brodhead. Durham: Duke University Press, 1993.

———. *The Marrow of Tradition*. New York: Penguin, 1993.

Chude-Sokel, Louis. *Bert Williams: Black-on-Black Minstrelsy and the African Diaspora*. Durham: Duke University Press, 2005.

Cibber, Colley. *The Careless Husband. Colley Cibber: Three Sentimental Comedies*. Edited by Maureen Sullivan. New Haven: Yale University Press, 1973.

———. *Love's Last Shift, or The Fool in Fashion. Colley Cibber: Three Sentimental Comedies*. Edited by Maureen Sullivan. New Haven: Yale University Press, 1973.

Clemens, Samuel Langhorne (Mark Twain). *Pudd'nhead Wilson and Those Extraordinary Twins*. Edited by Sidney E. Berger. New York: W. W. Norton, 1980.

Cobb, Michael L. "Insolent Racing, Rough Narrative: The Harlem Renaissance's Impolite Queers." *Callaloo* 23.1 (2000 Winter), 328–51.

Cohen, Michael. "Lyle Ashton Harris." *Flash Art* 188.29 (May–June 1996), 107.

Colley, Linda. *Britons: Forging the Nation*. New Haven: Yale University Press, 1993.

Cooley, Marianne. "An Early Representation of African-American English." *Language Variety in the South Revisited*, ed. by Bernstein, Nunnally, and Sabino, 51–58. Tuscaloosa: University of Alabama Press, 1997.

Coopan, Vilashini. "The Double Politics of Double Consciousness: Nationalism and Globalism in *The Souls of Black Folk*." *Public Culture* 17(2), 299–318.

Cooper, James Fenimore. *Satanstoe: or, the Littlepage Manuscripts, A Tale of a Colony*. Albany: State University of New York Press, 1990.

Corbetta, Caroline. "Dietro la maschera dell'arte / Behind the Mask of Art." *Domus* 845 (February 2002), 14–16.

Cosgrove, Stuart. "The Zoot Suit and Style Warfare." *History Workshop Journal* 18 (Autumn 1984), 77–91.

Cowhig, Ruth. "The Black in English Renaissance Drama and the Role of Shakespeare's *Othello*." *The Black Presence in English Literature*, ed. by David Dabydeen, 1–23. Manchester: Manchester University Press, 1985.

Crowne, John. *Sir Courtly Nice, or It Cannot Be*. Edited by Charlotte Bradford Hughes. The Hague: Mouton, 1966.

Cunnington, Phillis. *Costume of Household Servants: From the Middle Ages to 1900*. London: Adam and Charles Black, 1974.

Dabydeen, David. *Hogarth's Blacks: Images of Blacks in Eighteenth-Century English Art*. Athens: University of Georgia Press, 1987.

Dabydeen, David, and Paul Edwards. *Black Writers in Britain, 1760–1890*. Edinburgh: University of Edinburgh Press, 1991.

D'Aurevilly, Jules Barbey. *Dandyism (du dandysme et Georges Brummell)*. Translated by Douglas Ainslie. New York: PAJ Publications, 1988.

Davis, Natalie Zemon. *Society and Culture in Early Modern France: Eight Essays*. Stanford, Calif.: Stanford University Press, 1975.

de Bolla, Peter. "The Visibility of Visuality." *Vision in Context: Historical and Contemporary Perspectives on Sight*, ed. by Teresa Brennan and Martin Jay, 63–81. New York: Routledge, 1996.

Deitcher, David. "A Lovesome Thing: The Film Art of Isaac Julien." *The Film Art of Isaac Julien*. Annandale-on-Hudson, N.Y.: Bard College Center for Curatorial Studies, 2000.

Dennison, Sam. *Scandalize My Name: Black Imagery in American Popular Music*. New York: Garland, 1982.

Diawara, Manthia. "The Absent One: The Avant-Garde and the Black Imaginary." *Representing Black Men*, ed. by Marcellus Blount and George P. Cunningham, 205–24. New York: Routledge, 1996.

———. "The Independence Cha-Cha: The Art of Yinka Shonibare." *Yinka Shonibare: Double Dutch*. Rotterdam: Museum Boijmans Van Beuningen Rotterdam / Nai Publishers, 2004.

Domosh, Mona. "Those 'Gorgeous Incongruities': Polite Politics and Public Space on the Streets of Nineteenth-Century New York." *Annals of the Association of American Geographers* 88.2 (1998), 209–26.

Dooley, Reinhold J. "Fixing Meaning: Babo as Sign in 'Benito Cereno.'" *American Transcendental Quarterly* 9.1 (March 1995), 41–50.

Doran, John. *Annals of the English Stage from Thomas Betterton to Edmund Keane*. Vol. 3. Edited by Robert W. Lowe. London: John C. Nimmo, 1888.

Douglas, Ann. *Terrible Honesty: Mongrel Manhattan in the 1920s.* New York: Farrar, Straus and Giroux, 1994.

Du Bois, W. E. B. "The American Girl." *Against Racism: Unpublished Essays, Papers, Addresses, 1887–1961.* Amherst: University of Massachusetts Press, 1985.

———. *The Autobiography of W. E. B. Du Bois: A Soliloquy on Viewing My Life from the Last Decade of Its First Century.* New York: International Publishers, 1968.

———. "Chesnutt." *Writings.* New York: Literary Classics of the United States (Library of America), 1986.

———. "Criteria of Negro Art." *Writings.* New York: Literary Classics of the United States (Library of America), 1986.

———. *Dark Princess: A Romance.* Jackson: University Press of Mississippi, 1995.

———. *Darkwater: Voices from Within the Veil.* Millwood, N.Y.: Kraus-Thomson Organization, 1975.

———. "Does Education Pay?" *Writings by Du Bois in Periodicals Edited by Others.* Vol. 1, *1891–1909.* Millwood, N.Y.: Kraus-Thomson Organization, 1982.

———. *Dusk of Dawn.* New Brunswick: Transaction Publishers, 1995.

———. "Jefferson Davis as a Representative of Civilization." *Writings.* New York: Literary Classics of the United States (Library of America), 1986.

———. "The Negro in Literature and Art." *Writings.* New York: Literary Classics of the United States (Library of America), 1986.

———. *The Souls of Black Folk. Writings.* New York: Literary Classics of the United States (Library of America), 1986.

———. "The Talented Tenth." *Writings.* New York: Literary Classics of the United States (Library of America), 1986.

———. "Tom Brown at Fisk in Three Chapters." *Creative Writings by W. E. B. Du Bois: A Pageant, Poems, Short Stories, and Playlets.* White Plains, N.Y.: Kraus-Thomson Organization, 1985.

Earle, Alice Morse. *Customs and Fashions in Old New England.* Detroit: Singing Trees Press, 1968.

Earle, T. F., and K. J. P. Lowe, eds. *Black Africans in Renaissance Europe.* Cambridge: Cambridge University Press, 2005.

Edwards, Brent Hayes. "Late Romance." *Next to the Color Line: Gender, Sexuality, and W. E. B. Du Bois,* ed. by Susan Gillman and Alys Eve Weinbaum, 124–49. Minneapolis: University of Minnesota Press, 2007.

———. *The Practice of Diaspora: Literature, Translation, and the Rise of Black Internationalism.* Cambridge, Mass.: Harvard University Press, 2003.

Edwards, Paul, and David Dabydeen, eds. *Black Writers in Britain*. Edinburgh: Edinburgh University Press, 1991.

Edwards, Paul, and Polly Rewt. "Introduction." *The Letters of Ignatius Sancho*. Edinburgh: Edinburgh University Press, 1994.

Eights, James. "Pinkster Festivities in Albany." *Readings in Black American Music*, ed. by Eileen Southern, 41–47. New York: W. W. Norton, 1983.

Elam, Harry J., Jr. "The Black Performer and the Performance of Blackness." *African American Performance and Theater History: A Critical Reader*, ed. by Harry J. Elam Jr. and David Krasner. Oxford: Oxford University Press, 2001.

Elam, Harry J., Jr., and Kennell Jackson, eds. *Black Cultural Traffic: Crossroads in Global Performance and Popular Culture*. Ann Arbor: University of Michigan Press, 2005.

Elam, Harry J., Jr., and David Krasner, eds. *African American Performance and Theater History*. Oxford: Oxford University Press, 2001.

———. "The Device of Race: An Introduction." *African American Performance and Theater History*, ed. by Harry J. Elam Jr., and David Krasner. Oxford: Oxford University Press, 2001.

Elam, Michelle, and Paul C. Taylor. "Du Bois' Erotics." *Next to the Color Line: Gender, Sexuality, and W. E. B. Du Bois*, ed. by Susan Gillman and Alys Eve Weinbaum, 209–33. Minneapolis: University of Minnesota Press, 2007.

Eldredge, Richard L. "Andre 3000 Togs a '10' with Esquire," *Atlanta Journal-Constitution* (August 12, 2004).

Eltis, David, David Richardson, Stephen D. Behrendt, and Herbert S. Klein, eds. *The Trans-Atlantic Slave Trade: A Database on CD-ROM*. Cambridge: Cambridge University Press, 1999.

Engle, Gary. *This Grotesque Essence: Plays from the American Minstrel Stage*. Baton Rouge: Louisiana State University Press, 1978.

Enwezor, Okwui. "Of Hedonism, Masquerade, Carnivalesque and Power: The Art of Yinka Shonibare." *Looking Both Ways: Art of the Contemporary African Diaspora*, ed. by Laurie Ann Farrell, 163–67. New York: Museum for African Art, 2003.

Enwezor, Okwui, and Octavia Zaya. "Moving In: Eight Contemporary African Artists." *Flash Art* 186 (January–February 1996), 84–89.

Equiano, Olaudah. *The Interesting Narrative of the Life of Olaudah Equiano, or Gustavus Vassa, the African*. *The Classic Slave Narratives*, ed. by Henry Louis Gates Jr., 3–182. New York: Mentor / Penguin, 1987.

Etherege, George. *The Man of Mode*. *Restoration and Eighteenth-Century Comedy*, ed. by Scott McMillin, 8–168. New York: W. W. Norton, 1997.

Fabre, Geneviève. "Introduction." *Feasts and Celebrations in Northern American*

Ethnic Communities, ed. by Ramón Gutiérrez and Geneviève Fabre, 1–12. Albuquerque: University of New Mexico Press, 1995.

———. "Pinkster Festival, 1776–1811: An African-American Celebration." *Feasts and Celebrations in Northern American Ethnic Communities*, ed. by Ramón Gutiérrez and Geneviève Fabre, 13–29. Albuquerque: University of New Mexico Press, 1995.

Fahrner, Robert. "David Garrick Presents *The Padlock*: An 18th-Century Hit." *Theatre Survey: The American Journal of Theatre History* 13.1 (1972), 52–70.

Fanon, Frantz. *Black Skin, White Masks*. New York: Grove Press, 1982.

Fashion by Anna Cora Mowatt clipping files, Billy Rose Theater Collection, New York Public Library for the Performing Arts.

Feldman, Jessica. *Gender on the Divide: The Dandy in Modernist Literature*. Ithaca: Cornell University Press, 1993.

Fenn, Elizabeth. "'A Perfect Equality Seemed to Reign': Slave Society and Jonkonnu." *North Carolina Historical Review* 65 (April 1988), 127–53.

Ferguson, Roderick. *Aberrations in Black: Toward a Queer of Color Critique*. Minncapolis: University of Minnesota Press, 2004.

File, Nigel, and Chris Power. *Black Settlers in Britain 1555–1958*. London: Heinemann Educational Books, 1981.

Fillin-Yeh, Susan. Preface. *Dandies: Fashion and Finesse in Art and Culture*, ed. by Susan Fillin-Yeh, xi–xii. New York: New York University Press, 2001.

Firstenberg, Lauri. "Stylist of Subjectivities: Interface in the Photography of Iké Udé." *Beyond Decorum: The Photography Iké Udé*, ed. by Mark H. C. Bessire and Lauri Firstenberg, 166–73. Cambridge, Mass.: MIT Press, 2000.

Fisher, Jean. "Yinka Shonibare: Camden Arts Centre." *Artforum International* 39.1 (September 2000), 86.

Flugel, J. C. *Psychology of Clothes*. London: Hogarth Press, 1930.

Forbes, Camille. *Introducing Bert Williams: Burnt Cork, Broadway, and the Story of America's First Black Star*. New York: Basic Civitas, 2008.

Foreman, P. Gabrielle. "'This Promiscuous Housekeeping': Death, Transgression, and Homoeroticism in *Uncle Tom's Cabin*." *Representations* 43 (summer 1993), 51–72.

Foster, Helen Bradley. *"New Raiments of Self": African American Clothing in the Antebellum South*. New York: Berg, 1997.

Fowler, William C. *The Historical Status of the Negro in Connecticut*. Charleston: Walker, Evans, and Cogswell, 1901.

Francklyn, Thomas. *The Earl of Warwick*. London: T. Davies, R. Baldwin and W. Griffin, 1766. *Literature Online (LION) English Verse Drama Full-Text Database*. Cambridge: Chadwyck-Healey, 1994.

Frederickson, George M. *The Black Image in the White Mind: The Debate on*

Afro-American Character and Destiny, 1817–1914. New York: Harper and Row, 1971.

Freeman, Lisa. *Character's Theater: Genre and Identity on the Eighteenth-Century Stage*. Philadelphia: University of Pennsylvania Press, 2001.

Fryer, Peter. *Staying Power: The History of Black People in Britain*. London: Pluto Press, 1984.

Gaines, Kevin K. *Uplifting the Race: Black Leadership, Politics, and Culture in the Twentieth Century*. Chapel Hill: University of North Carolina Press, 1996.

Garber, Marjorie. *Vested Interests: Cross-Dressing and Cultural Anxiety*. New York: HarperPerennial: 1992.

Garelick, Rhonda. *Rising Star: Dandyism, Gender, and Performance in the Fin de Siècle*. Princeton: Princeton University Press, 1988.

Gates, Henry Louis, Jr. "The Black Man's Burden." *Fear of a Queer Planet*, ed. by Michael Warner, 230–38. Minneapolis: University of Minnesota Press, 1993.

————. "Looking for Modernism." *Black American Cinema*, ed. by Manthia Diawara, 200–207. New York: Routledge, 1993.

————. *The Signifying Monkey: A Theory of African American Literary Criticism*. New York: Oxford University Press, 1988.

————. "The Trope of the New Negro and the Reconstruction of the Black Image." *Representations* 24.4 (fall 1988), 129–55.

Gebhard, Caroline. "Reconstructing Southern Manhood: Race, Sentimentality, and Camp in the Plantation Myth." *Haunted Bodies: Gender and Southern Texts*, ed. by Anne Goodwyn Jones and Susan V. Donaldson, 132–55. Charlottesville: University of Virginia Press, 1997.

Genovese, Eugene D. *Roll, Jordan, Roll: The World the Slaves Made*. New York: Vintage Books, 1976.

Gentleman and London's Magazine (November 1768), 687–90.

George, M. Dorothy. *Hogarth to Cruikshank: Social Change in Graphic Satire*. London: Penguin Press, 1967.

————. *London Life in the Eighteenth Century*. New York: Capricorn Books, 1965.

Gerzina, Gretchen. *Black London: Life Before Emancipation*. New Brunswick, N.J.: Rutgers University Press, 1995.

Gerzina, Gretchen, ed. *Black Victorians / Black Victoriana*. New Brunswick, N.J.: Rutgers University Press, 2003.

Gillman, Susan, and Alys Eve Weinbaum. "Introduction: W. E. B. Du Bois and the Politics of Juxtaposition." *Next to the Color Line: Gender, Sexuality, and W. E. B. Du Bois*, ed. Susan Gillman and Alys Eve Weinbaum, 1–34. Minneapolis: University of Minnesota Press, 2007.

Gillman, Susan, and Alys Eve Weinbaum, eds. *Next to the Color Line: Gender, Sexuality, and W. E. B. Du Bois.* Minneapolis: University of Minnesota Press, 2007.

Gilroy, Paul. *The Black Atlantic: Modernity and Double-Consciousness.* Cambridge, Mass.: Harvard University Press, 1993.

Glick, Elisa. "Harlem's Queer Dandy: African-American Modernism and the Artifice of Blackness," *MFS: Modern Fiction Studies* 49, no. 3 (fall 2003), 414–42.

Godfrey, Sima. "The Dandy as Ironic Figure." *Sub-stance* 36.11.3 (1982), 21–33.

Golden, Thelma. "Introduction: Post . . ." *Freestyle.* New York: Studio Museum in Harlem.

Gomez, Michael. *Exchanging Our Country Marks.* Chapel Hill: University of North Carolina Press, 1998.

Gooding-Williams, Robert. "Du Bois, Aesthetics, Politics: An Introduction." *Public Culture* 17.2, 203–15.

"Gracious Me! Dear, 'Twas To-oo Divine." *New York Amsterdam News*, March 7, 1936, 8.

Green, Alan W. C. "'Jim Crow,' 'Zip Coon': The Northern Origins of Negro Minstrelsy." *Massachusetts Review* 11.2 (1970), 385–97.

Greenberg, Cheryl Lynn. *"Or Does It Explode?": Black Harlem in the Great Depression.* New York: Oxford University Press, 1997.

Greene, Lorenzo J. *The Negro in Colonial New England.* New York: Atheneum, 1969.

———. "The New England Negro as Seen in Advertisements for Runaway Slaves." *Journal of Negro History* 29.2 (1944), 125–46.

Griffin, Tim. "Global Tendencies: Globalism and the Large-Scale Exhibition (A Roundtable)." *Artforum* 42.3 (2003), 152–63.

Grundmann, Roy. "Black Nationhood and the Rest in the West: An Interview with Isaac Julien." *Cineaste* 21.1–2, 28–31.

Guede, Alain. *Monsieur de Saint-Georges: The American.* New York: Picador, 2004.

Guldemond, Jaap, and Gabrielle Mackert. "To Entertain and Provoke: Western Influences in the Work of Yinka Shonibare." *Yinka Shonibare: Double Dutch.* Rotterdam: Museum Boijmans Van Beuningen Rotterdam / Nai Publishers, 2004.

Hall, Kim F. *Things of Darkness: Economies of Race and Gender in Early Modern England.* Ithaca: Cornell University Press, 1995.

Hall, Stuart. "The After-Life of Fanon: Why Fanon? Why Now?" *The Fact of Blackness: Frantz Fanon and Visual Representation*, ed. by Alan Read, 12–37. Seattle: Institute of Contemporary Art and Bay Press, 1996.

————. "New Ethnicities." *Stuart Hall: Critical Dialogues in Cultural Studies*, ed. by David Morley and Kuan-Hsing Chen, 441–49. New York: Routledge, 1996.

————. "Subjects in History: Making Diasporic Identities." *The House that Race Built*, ed. by Wahneema Lubiano, 289–99. New York: Pantheon Books, 1997.

————. "What Is This 'Black' in Black Popular Culture?" *Black Popular Culture*, ed. by Gina Dent. Seattle: Bay Press, 1992.

Harper, Phillip Brian. *Are We Not Men?: Masculinity, Anxiety, and the Problem of African-American Identity*. New York: Oxford University Press, 1996.

Harris, Lyle Ashton, and Thomas Allen Harris. "Black Widow: A Conversation." *The Passionate Camera: Photography and Bodies of Desire*, ed. by Deborah Bright, 248–62. New York: Routledge, 1998.

Hebdige, Dick. *Subculture: The Meaning of Style*. London: Routledge, 1979.

Hecht, J. Jean. "Continental and Colonial Servants in Eighteenth-Century England." *Smith College Studies in History* 40 (1954), 1–61.

Heilman, Robert B. "Some Fops and Versions of Foppery." *ELH* 49.2 (Summer 1982), 363–95.

Hemphill, Essex. "If His Name Were Mandingo." *Ceremonies: Prose and Poetry*. San Francisco: Cleis Press, 2000.

————. "*Looking for Langston*: An Interview with Isaac Julien." *Brother to Brother: New Writings by Black Gay Men*, ed. by Essex Hemphill, 174–80. New York: Alyson Books, 1991.

Herring, Scott. "Du Bois and the Minstrels." *MELUS* 22.3 (1997), 3–17.

Herzog, Werner, director. *Wodaabe: Herdsmen of the Sun*. Interama Video, 1989.

Hilfer, Anthony Channell. "The Philosophy of Clothes in Melville's 'Benito Cereno.'" *Philological Quarterly* 61.2 (spring 1982), 220–25.

Hill, Bridget. *Servants: English Domestics in the Eighteenth Century*. Oxford: Clarendon Press, 1996.

Hirschberg, Lynn. "The Originals." *New York Times*, September 19, 2004.

Hodges, Graham Russell, and Alan Edward Brown, eds. *Pretends to be Free: Runaway Slave Advertisements from Colonial and Revolutionary New York and New Jersey*. New York: Garland, 1994.

Hollander, Anne. *Sex and Suits*. New York: Kodansha International, 1994.

Holmes, Pernilla. "The Empire's New Clothes." *Artnews* (October 2002), 119–20.

hooks, bell. "In Our Glory." *Picturing Us: African American Identity in Photography*, ed. by Deborah Willis, 42–53. New York: New Press, 1994.

————. "Seductive Sexualities." *Yearning: Race, Gender, Cultural Politics*. Boston: South End Press, 1990.

Huggins, Nathan Irvin. *Harlem Renaissance*. New York: Oxford University Press, 1971.

Hughes, Langston. "The Negro Artist and the Racial Mountain." *The Nation* (June 23, 1926), 692–94.

Hutton, Laurence. *Curiosities of the American Stage*. New York: Harper and Brothers, 1891.

Huxley, Elspeth. "Blacks Next Door." *Punch* (January 29, 1964), 154–57.

Huyssen, Andreas. "Mass Culture as Woman: Modernism's Other." *After the Great Divide: Modernism, Mass Culture, Postmodernism*. Bloomington: Indiana University Press, 1986.

Hylton, Richard. "Yinka Shonibare: Dressing Down." *Third Text* 46 (Spring 1999), 101–03.

Hynes, Nancy. "Re-Dressing History." *African Arts* 34.3 (Autumn 2001), 60–65.

"Interview with Isaac Julien." *Struggles for Representation: African American Documentary Film and Video*, ed. by Phyllis Klotman and Janet K. Cutler, 364–71. Bloomington: Indiana University Press, 1999.

James, Joy. *Transcending the Talented Tenth: Black Leaders and American Intellectuals*. New York: Routledge, 1997.

Jehlen, Myra. "The Ties that Bind: Race and Sex in *Pudd'nhead Wilson*." *American Literary History* 2 (1990), 39–55.

Johnson, Charles S. "The New Frontage on American Life." *The New Negro*, ed. by Alain Locke, 278–98. New York: Atheneum, 1992.

Johnson, E. Patrick. *Appropriating Blackness: Performance and the Politics of Authenticity*. Durham: Duke University Press, 2003.

———. "'Quare Studies': or (Almost) Everything I Know About Queer Studies I Learned from My Grandmother." *Black Queer Studies: A Critical Anthology*, ed. by E. Patrick Johnson and Mae G. Henderson, 124–57. Durham: Duke University Press, 2006.

Johnson, E. Patrick, and Mae G. Henderson. "Introduction: Queering Black Studies / Quaring Queer Studies." *Black Queer Studies: A Critical Anthology*, ed. by E. Patrick Johnson and Mae G. Henderson, 1–17. Durham: Duke University Press, 2006.

Johnson, James Weldon. "A Poetry Corner." *New York Age*, January 7, 1915. *The Selected Writings of James Weldon Johnson*. Vol. 1. Edited by Sondra Kathryn Wilson. New York: Oxford University Press, 1995.

———. *Along This Way*. New York: Viking Press, 1968.

———. *The Autobiography of an Ex-Coloured Man*. New York: Hill and Wang, 1995.

———. *Black Manhattan*. New York: Da Capo Press, 1991.

———. "Double Audience Makes Hard Road for Negro Authors." *The*

Selected Writings of James Weldon Johnson. Vol. 2. Edited by Sondra Kathryn Wilson. New York: Oxford University Press, 1995.

———. "Some New Books of Poetry and Their Makers." *The Selected Writings of James Weldon Johnson*. Vol. 1. Edited by Sondra Kathryn Wilson. New York: Oxford University Press, 1995.

Jones, C. A. "Introduction." *Exemplary Stories*, by Miguel Cervantes. Translated by C. A. Jones. Middlesex: Penguin Books, 1972.

Jones, Eldred. *Othello's Countrymen: The African in English Renaissance Drama*. London: Oxford University Press, 1965.

Jordan, Winthrop. *White Over Black: American Attitudes toward the Negro, 1550–1812*. Chapel Hill: University of North Carolina Press, 1968.

Julien, Isaac, director. *Frantz Fanon: Black Skin, White Masks*. Produced by Mark Nash. California Newsreel, 1996.

———. *Looking for Langston*. Produced by Nadine Marsh-Edwards. Water Bearer Films, 1989.

Julien, Isaac, and Kobena Mercer. "True Confessions: A Discourse on Images of Black Male Sexuality." *Brother to Brother: New Writings by Black Gay Men*, ed. by Essex Hemphill, 167–73. New York: Alyson Books, 1991.

Kawash, Samira. "The Autobiography of an Ex-Coloured Man: (Passing for) Black, Passing for White." *Passing and the Fictions of Identity*, ed. by Ellen K. Ginsberg, 59–74. Durham: Duke University Press, 1996.

Kelley, Robin D. G. Foreword. *Reflections in Black: A History of Black Photography, 1840 to Present*, by Deborah Willis. New York: W. W. Norton, 2000.

———. *Freedom Dreams: The Black Radical Imagination*. Boston: Beacon Press, 2000.

———. "Introduction: Writing Black Working-Class History from Way, Way Below." *Race Rebels: Culture, Politics, and the Black Working Class*. New York: Free Press, 1994.

———. "'We Are Not What We Seem': Rethinking Black Working-Class Opposition in the Jim Crow South." *Journal of American History* 80.1 (June 1993), 75–112.

Kiddy, Elizabeth. "Who is the King of Kongo? A New Look at African and Afro-Brazilian Kings in Brazil." *Central Africans and Cultural Transformations in the American Diaspora*, ed. by Linda M. Heywood, 153–82. New York: Cambridge University Press, 2002.

Kimmel, Michael S. "From Lord and Master to Cuckhold and Fop: Masculinity in Seventeenth-Century England." *University of Dayton Review* 18.2 (Winter–Spring 1986–87), 93–109.

Kutcha, Edward. *The Three Piece Suit and Modern Masculinity, England 1550–1850*. Los Angeles: University of California Press, 2002.

Lagerqvist, Lars O. *A History of Sweden*. Stockholm: Swedish Institute, 2002.

Lapsansky, Emma Jones. "'Since They Got Those Separate Churches': Afro-Americans and Racism in Jacksonian Philadelphia." *American Quarterly* 32.1 (1980), 54–78.

Laver, James. *Costume and Fashion: A Concise History*. London: Thames and Hudson, 1995.

————. *Dandies*. London: Weidenfeld and Nicolson, 1968.

Levine, Lawrence. *Black Culture and Black Consciousness*. New York: Oxford University Press, 1977.

Levy, James. *James Weldon Johnson: Black Leader, Black Voice*. Chicago: University of Chicago Press, 1973.

Lewis, Barbara. "Daddy Blue: The Evolution of the Dark Dandy." *Inside the Minstrel Mask: Readings in Nineteenth-Century Blackface Minstrelsy*, ed. by Annemarie Bean, James V. Hatch, and Brooks McNamara, 257–74. Hanover, N.H.: University Press of New England, 1996.

Lewis, David Levering. *W. E. B. Du Bois: Biography of a Race, 1868–1919*. New York: Henry Holt, 1993.

————. *When Harlem Was in Vogue*. New York: Penguin, 1997.

Lhamon, W. T., Jr. *Jump Jim Crow: Lost Plays, Lyrics, and Street Prose of the First Atlantic Popular Culture*. Cambridge, Mass.: Harvard University Press, 2003.

————. *Raising Cain: Blackface Performance from Jim Crow to Hip Hop*. Cambridge, Mass.: Harvard University Press, 1998.

Lindfors, Bernth. "The Signifying Flunkey: Ira Aldridge as Mungo." *Literary Griot* 5.2 (Fall 1993), 1–11.

Little, Kenneth. *Negroes in Britain: A Study of Race Relations in English Society*. London: Kegan Paul, Trench, Trubner, 1948.

Locke, Alain. "The New Negro." *The New Negro*, ed. by Alain Locke. New York: Atheneum, 1992.

Lorini, Alessandra. "Public Rituals and the Cultural Making of the New York African-American Community." *Feasts and Celebrations in Northern American Ethnic Communities*, ed. by Ramón Gutiérrez and Geneviève Fabre, 29–46. Albuquerque: University of New Mexico Press, 1995.

————. *Rituals of Race: American Public Culture and the Search for Racial Democracy*. Charlottesville: University of Virginia Press, 1999.

Lott, Eric. "Blackface and Blackness: The Minstrel Show in American Culture." *Inside the Minstrel Mask: Readings in Nineteenth-Century Blackface Minstrelsy*, ed. by Annemarie Bean, James V. Hatch, and Brooks McNamara, 3–33. Hanover: University Press of New England, 1996.

————. *Love and Theft: Blackface Minstrelsy and the American Working Class*. New York: Oxford University Press, 1995.

Lowenthal, Cynthia. *Performing Identities on the Restoration Stage*. Carbondale: Southern Illinois University Press, 2003.

Lurie, Alison. *The Language of Clothes*. New York: Henry Holt, 2000.

Lynch, Deidre. *The Economy of Character: Novels, Market Culture, and the Business of Inner Meaning*. Chicago: University of Chicago Press, 1998.

Mahar, William J. *Behind the Burnt Cork Mask: Early Blackface Minstrelsy and Antebellum Popular Culture*. Urbana: University of Illinois Press, 1999.

Marez, Curtis. "The Other Addict: Reflections on Colonialism and Oscar Wilde's Opium Smoke Screen." *English Literary History* 64 (1997), 257–87.

Maza, Sarah C. *Servants and Masters in Eighteenth-Century France: The Uses of Loyalty*. Princeton: Princeton University Press, 1983.

McCollum, Michael. *The Way We Wore: Black Style Then*. New York: Glitterati Press, 2006.

McDonald, Patrick. "The High Brow: Interview with Iké Udé." *Papermag*, October 10, 2002. www.papermag.com.

McKay, Nellie Y. "W. E. B. Du Bois: The Black Women in His Writings, Selected Fictional and Autobiographical Portraits." *Critical Essays on W. E. B. Du Bois*, ed. by William Andrews, 230–52. Boston: G. K. Hall, 1985.

McKenrick, Neil, John Brewer, and J. H. Plumb, eds. *Birth of a Consumer Society: The Commercialization of Eighteenth-Century England*. Bloomington: Indiana University Press, 1982.

McNeil, Peter. "'That Doubtful Gender': Macaroni Dress and Male Sexualities." *Fashion Theory* 3.4 (December 1999), 411–48.

McRobbie, Angela. "The African Dandy." *Yinka Shonibare: Double Dutch*. Rotterdam: Museum Boijmans Van Beuningen Rotterdam / Nai Publishers, 2004.

Melville, Herman. *Benito Cereno, Billy Budd, and Other Stories*. New York: Penguin, 1986.

"Men Step Out in Gorgeous Finery of Other Sex to Vie for Beauty Prizes." *New York Amsterdam News*, March 2, 1932, 2.

Mercer, Kobena. "Avid Iconographies." *Isaac Julien*. London: Ellipsis, 2001.

———. "Busy in the Ruins of a Wretched Phantasia." *Mirage: Enigmas of Race, Difference and Desire*, ed. by Ragnar Farr, 15–55. London: Institute of Contemporary Art and Institute of International Visual Arts, 1995.

———. "Decolonization and Disappointment: Reading Fanon's Sexual Politics." *The Fact of Blackness: Frantz Fanon and Visual Representation*, ed. by Alan Read, 115–31. Seattle: Institute of Contemporary Art and Bay Press, 1996.

———. "Iké Udé: A Dandy in the Naked City." *Beyond Decorum: The Photography of Iké Udé*, ed. by Mark H. C. Bessire and Lauri Firstenberg, 30–35. Cambridge, Mass.: MIT Press, 2000.

————. "Post-colonial Flaneur." *Camera Austria* 73 (February 2001), 33–44.

————. "Reading Racial Fetishism: The Photographs of Robert Mapplethorpe." *Welcome to the Jungle*. New York: Routledge, 1994.

Merish, Lori. "Sentimental Consumption: Harriet Beecher Stowe and the Aesthetics of Middle-Class Ownership." *American Literary History* 8.1 (Spring 1996), 1–33.

Meserve, William J. *An Outline History of American Drama*. Totowa, N.J.: Littlefield, Adam, 1965.

Miller, Monica L. "W. E. B. Du Bois and the Dandy as Diasporic Race Man." *Callaloo* 26.3 (2003), 738–65.

Moers, Ellen. *The Dandy: Brummell to Beerbohm*. New York: Viking Press, 1960.

Moody, Richard. *America Takes the Stage: Romanticism in American Drama and Theatre, 1750–1900*. Bloomington: Indiana University Press, 1955.

Morgan, Jennifer. *Laboring Women: Reproduction and Gender in New World Slavery*. Philadelphia: University of Pennsylvania Press, 2004.

Morison, Samuel E. "A Poem on Election Day in Massachusetts about 1760." *Transactions 1915–1916, Publications of the Colonial Society of Massachusetts*, February 18, 1915 (reprint. 1992): 54–62.

Morris, Linda A. "Beneath the Veil: Clothing, Race, and Gender in Mark Twain's *Pudd'nhead Wilson*." *Studies in American Fiction* 27.1 (Spring 1999), 37–52.

Morrison, Toni. "Home." *The House that Race Built*, ed. by Wahneema Lubiano, 3–12. New York: Pantheon Books, 1997.

Mowatt, Anna Cora. *Fashion* (1845). *Early American Drama*, ed. by Jeffrey H. Richards, 304–67. New York: Penguin Books, 1997.

————. *Fashion; or Life in New York*. *Staging the Nation: Plays from the American Theater, 1781–1909*, ed. by Don B. Wilmeth, 125–80. Boston: Bedford Books, 1997.

Mungo. *The Padlock Open'd: or, Mungo's Medley*. London: C. Corbett, 1771.

Muñoz, José Esteban. *Disidentifications: Queers of Color and the Politics of Performance*. New York: Routledge, 1999.

————. "Photographies of Mourning: Melancholia and Ambivalence in Van Der Zee, Mapplethorpe, and *Looking for Langston*." *Race and the Subject of Masculinities*, ed. by Harry Stepcopoulos and Michael Uebel, 337–60. Durham: Duke University Press, 1997.

Nash, Gary B. *Forging Freedom: The Formation of Philadelphia's Black Community, 1740–1840*. Cambridge, Mass.: Harvard University Press, 1988.

Nash, Mark, Isaac Julien, Martina Attile, Raoul Peck, and Homi K. Bhabha. "Filmmaker's Dialogue." *The Fact of Blackness: Frantz Fanon and Visual Rep-*

resentation, ed. by Alan Read, 167–177. Seattle: Institute of Contemporary Art and Bay Press, 1996.

Nathan, Hans. *Dan Emmett and the Rise of Early Negro Minstrelsy*. Norman: University of Oklahoma Press, 1962.

Nero, Charles I. "Queering the Souls of Black Folk." *Public Culture* 17(2), 255–76.

Neshat, Shirin. "Iké Udé: Between a Dandy and His Choice of Clothes." *Flash Art* 34.217 (March–April 2001), 92–93.

Nussbaum, Felicity. *Limits of the Human: Fictions of Anomaly, Race, and Gender in the Long Eighteenth Century*. Cambridge: Cambridge University Press, 2003.

Ogborn, Miles. "Locating the Macaroni: Luxury, Sexuality, and Vision in Vauxhall Gardens." *Textual Practice* 11.3 (1997), 445–61.

Oguibe, Olu. "Finding a Place: Nigerian Artists in the Contemporary Art World." *Art Journal* 58.2 (Summer 1999), 30–41.

———. "Double-Dutch and the Culture Game." Yinka Shonibare: Be-Muse Rome, 2001. www.camwood.org.

Oldfield, J. R. "The 'Ties of Soft Humanity': Slavery and Race in British Drama, 1760–1800." *Huntington Library Quarterly* 56.1 (Winter 1993), 1–14.

Orr, Bridget. *Empire on the English Stage, 1660–1714*. Cambridge: Cambridge University Press, 2001.

The Padlock by Isaac Bickerstaffe clipping files, Theatre Museum of London.

Park, Robert E. *Race and Culture: Essays in the Sociology of Contemporary Man*. Glencoe, Ill.: Free Press, 1950.

Parry, Benita. "Signs of Our Times: A Discussion of Homi Bhabha's *The Location of Culture*." *Third Text* 28–29 (Autumn / Winter 1994), 5–24.

Paulin, Diana J. "Acting Out Miscegenation." *African American Performance and Theater History*, ed. by Harry J. Elam Jr. and David Krasner, 251–70. Oxford: Oxford University Press, 2001.

Pentzell, Raymond J. "Garrick's Costuming." *Theatre Survey* 10 (May 1969), 18–42.

Pfeiffer, Kathleen. "Introduction." *Nigger Heaven*, by Carl Van Vechten. Urbana: University of Illinois Press, 2000.

Phelan, Peggy. *Unmarked: The Politics of Performance*. New York: Routledge, 1993.

Phillips, Caryl. *Dancing in the Dark*. New York: Knopf, 2005.

Picton, John. "Undressing Ethnicity." *African Arts* 34.3 (Autumn 2001), 66–73.

Piepmeier, Alison. *Out in Public: Configurations of Women's Bodies in Nineteenth-Century America*. Chapel Hill: University of North Carolina Press, 2004.

Piersen, William D. *Black Legacy: America's Hidden Heritage.* Amherst: University of Massachusetts Press, 1993.

———. *Black Yankees: The Development of an Afro-American Subculture in Eighteenth-Century New England.* Amherst: University of Massachusetts Press, 1988.

———. "Puttin' Down Ole Massa: African Satire in the New World." *African Folklore in the New World*, ed. by Daniel J. Crowley, 20–34. Austin: University of Texas Press, 1977.

Platt, Oliver H. "Negro Governors." *Papers of the New England Historical Society* 6 (1900), 315–35.

Poe, Edgar Allan. "The Theatre: The New Comedy by Mrs. Mowatt." *Broadway Journal*, March 29, 1845.

Posnock, Ross. *Color and Culture: Black Writers and the Making of the Modern Intellectual.* Cambridge, Mass.: Harvard University Press, 1998.

———. "The Distinction of Du Bois: Aesthetics, Pragmatism, Politics." *American Literary History* 3.3 (1995), 500–24.

———. "How It Feels to Be a Problem: Du Bois, Fanon, and the 'Impossible Life' of the Black Intellectual." *Critical Inquiry* 23.2 (1997), 323–49.

Powell, Richard. "Sartor Africanus." *Dandies: Fashion and Finesse in Art and Culture*, ed. by Susan Fillin-Yeh, 217–42. New York: New York University Press, 2001.

Pred, Allan. *The Past Is Not Dead: Facts, Fictions, and Enduring Racial Stereotypes.* Minneapolis: University of Minnesota Press, 2004.

Prude, Jonathan. "To Look Upon the 'Lower Sort': Runaway Ads and the Appearance of Unfree Laborers in America, 1750–1800." *Journal of American History* 78 (June 1991), 124–59.

Rampersad, Arnold. *The Art and Imagination of W. E. B. Du Bois.* New York: Schocken Books, 1990.

Rauser, Amelia. "Hair, Authenticity and the Self-Made Macaroni." *Eighteenth-Century Studies* 38.1 (Fall 2004), 101–17.

Reidy, Joseph P. "'Negro Election Day' and Black Community Life in New England, 1750–1860." *Marxist Perspectives* 1.3 (1978), 102–17.

Ribeiro, Aileen. *The Art of Dress: Fashion in England and France, 1750–1820.* New Haven: Yale University Press, 1995.

———. *Dress in Eighteenth-Century Europe, 1715–1985.* New Haven: Yale University Press, 2002.

Rich, B. Ruby. "Interview with Isaac Julien." *Art Journal* 61.2 (Summer 2002), 50–67.

Richardson, Gary A. *American Drama from the Colonial Period through World War I: A Critical History.* New York: Twayne Publishers, 1993.

Roach, Joseph. *Cities of the Dead: Circum-Atlantic Performance*. New York: Columbia University Press, 1996.

Robbins, Bruce. "Introduction: Part I: Actually Existing Cosmopolitanism." *Cosmopolitics*, ed. by Pheng Cheah and Bruce Robbins, 1–19. Minneapolis: University of Minnesota Press, 1998.

———. *The Servant's Hand: English Fiction from Below*. Durham: Duke University Press, 1986.

Robbins, Sarah. "Gendering the History of the Antislavery Narrative: Juxtaposing *Uncle Tom's Cabin* and *Benito Cereno*, *Beloved* and *Middle Passage*." *American Literary History* 9.3 (1997), 531–73.

Rowell, George. *The Old Vic Theatre: A History*. Cambridge: Cambridge University Press, 1993.

Said, Edward. *Orientalism*. New York: Vintage, 1994.

Samuels, Shirley. "Miscegenated America: The Civil War." *American Literary History* 9.3 (Fall 1997): 482–501.

Sancho, Ignatius. *The Letters of Ignatius Sancho*. Edited by Paul Edwards and Polly Rewt. Edinburgh: Edinburgh University Press, 1994.

Sarkar, Bhaskar. "Tangled Legacies: The Autos of Biography." *Rethinking History* 7.2 (2003), 215–34.

Sartre, Jean-Paul. *Baudelaire*. Translated by Martin Turnell. Norfolk, Conn.: James Laughlin, 1950.

Saxton, Alexander. *The Rise and Fall of the White Republic: Class Politics and Mass Culture in Nineteenth-Century America*. New York: Verso, 1990.

Scobie, Edward. *Black Brittania: A History of Blacks in Britain*. Chicago: Johnson, 1972.

Scott, James C. "From Weapons of the Weak." *The Cultural Resistance Reader*, ed. by Stephen Duncombe, 89–93. London: Verso, 2002.

Seward, Keith. "Lyle Ashton Harris at Jack Tilton Gallery." *Artforum International* 33 (December 1994), 83.

Shelton, Jane DeForest. "The New England Negro: A Remnant." *Harper's Magazine* 88.526 (1894), 533–38.

Shonibare, Yinka. Turner Prize Lecture. www.tate.org.uk.

Shyllon, Folarin. *Black People in Britain 1555–1833*. London: Oxford University Press, 1977.

———. *Black Slaves in Britain*. London: Oxford University Press, 1974.

Smalls, James. "African-American Self-Portraiture: Repair, Reclamation, Redemption." *Third Text* 54 (Spring 2001), 47–62.

Smith, Woodruff D. *Consumption and the Making of Respectability: 1600–1800*. New York: Routledge, 2002.

Sollors, Werner, Caldwell Titcomb, and Thomas A. Underwood, eds. *Blacks at*

Harvard: A Documentary History of the African-American Experience at Harvard and Radcliffe. New York: New York University Press, 1993.

Somerville, Siobhan B. *Queering the Color Line: Race and the Invention of Homosexuality in American Culture*. Durham: Duke University Press, 2000.

Southern, Eileen. *The Music of Black Americans: A History*. New York: W. W. Norton, 1971.

Stafford, Barbara Maria. *Body Criticism: Imaging the Unseen in Enlightenment Art and Medicine*. Cambridge, Mass.: MIT Press, 1992.

Stanton, Domna. *The Aristocrat as Art: A Study of the Honnête Homme and the Dandy in Seventeenth and Nineteenth Century France*. New York: Columbia University Press, 1980.

Starke, Barbara M. "Nineteenth-Century African-American Dress." *Dress in American Culture*, ed. by Patricia A. Cunningham and Susan Voso Lab, 66–79. Bowling Green: Bowling Green State University Press, 1993.

Staves, Susan. "A Few Kind Words for the Fop." *Studies in English Literature, 1500–1900* 22.3 (Summer 1982), 413–28.

Steele, Valerie. "The Social and Political Significance of Macaroni Fashion." *Costume* 19 (1985), 101–02.

Stern, Julia. "Spanish Masquerade and the Drama of Racial Identity in *Uncle Tom's Cabin*." *Passing and the Fictions of Identity*, ed. by Ellen K. Ginsberg, 103–30. Durham: Duke University Press, 1996.

Stowe, Harriet Beecher. *Uncle Tom's Cabin*. Edited by Elizabeth Ammons. New York: W. W. Norton, 1994.

Stuckey, Sterling. "The Skies of Consciousness: African Dance at Pinkster in New York, 1750–1840." *Going Through the Storm: The Influence of African American Art in History*. New York: Oxford University Press, 1994.

Suleri, Sara. *The Rhetoric of English India*. Chicago: Chicago University Press, 1992.

Sundquist, Eric J. "Introduction." *New Essays on Uncle Tom's Cabin*, ed. by Eric J. Sundquist, 1–44. Cambridge: Cambridge University Press, 1986.

———. *To Wake the Nations: Race in the Making of American Literature*. Cambridge, Mass.: Harvard University Press, 1993.

Tate, Claudia. "Introduction." *Dark Princess: A Romance*, by W. E. B. Du Bois. Jackson: University of Mississippi Press, 1995.

Thorne, Thomas. "The Duchess and William Byrd." *Antiques* (November 1963), 562–65.

Thornton, John. *Africa and Africans in the Making of the Atlantic World, 1400–1800*. 2d ed. New York: Cambridge University Press, 1998.

Thurman, Wallace. *Infants of the Spring*. Boston: Northeastern University Press, 1992.

Tokson, Elliot. *The Popular Image of the Black Man in English Drama, 1550–1688*. Boston: G. K. Hall, 1982.

Toll, Robert C. *Blacking Up: The Minstrel Show in Nineteenth-Century America*. New York: Oxford University Press, 1974.

Townsend, Kim. *Manhood at Harvard: William James and Others*. Cambridge, Mass.: Harvard University Press, 1996.

Tuan, Yi-Fu. *Dominance and Affection: The Making of Pets*. New Haven: Yale University Press, 1984.

Tulloch, Carol, ed. *Black Style*. London: Victoria and Albert Museum Publications, 2004.

Turner, Grady. "Lyle Ashton Harris at Jack Tilton." *Art in America* 85 (March 1997), 99–100.

Turner, Victor. *The Ritual Process: Structure and Anti-Structure*. New York: Aldine, 1969.

Twain, Mark [Samuel Clemens]. *Pudd'nhead Wilson and Those Extraordinary Twins*. Edited by Sidney E. Berger. New York: W. W. Norton, 1980.

Tyler, Royall. *The Contrast. Staging the Nation: Plays from the American Theater, 1781–1909*, ed. by Don B. Wilmeth, 11–59. Boston: Bedford Books, 1997.

Udé, Iké. "Elements of Style." *aRUDE* 12 (1999), 9–10.

———. "Magnificent Futility." *Beyond Decorum: The Photography of Iké Udé*, ed. by Mark H. C. Bessire and Lauri Firstenberg, 124–25. Cambridge, Mass.: MIT Press, 2000.

———. "The Regarded Self." *NKA* 3 (Fall/Winter 1995), 16.

———. *Style File: The World's Most Elegantly Dressed*. New York: Harper Collins, 2008.

Udé, Iké, and Okwui Enwezor. "Between Mask and Fantasy: A Conversation Between Iké Udé and Okwui Enwezor." *Beyond Decorum: The Photography of Iké Udé*, ed. by Mark H. C. Bessire and Lauri Firstenberg, 70–73. Cambridge, Mass.: MIT Press, 2000.

Ugwu, Catherine. "Live Art." *Mirage: Enigmas of Race, Difference, and Desire*, ed. by Ragnar Farr, 82–96. London: Institute of Contemporary Art and Institute of International Visual Arts, 1995.

Van Vechten, Carl. *Nigger Heaven*. Urbana: University of Illinois Press, 2000.

Verdier, Evence. "Yinka Shonibare: Eloge de Decoratif Veneneux/Re-Stitching the Social Fabric." Translated by L. A. Torgoff. *Art Press* 288 (March 2003), 29–32.

Verter, Bradford. "Interracial Festivity and Power in Antebellum New York: The Case of Pinkster." *Journal of Urban History* 28.4 (May 2002), 398–428.

Wade, Melvin. "'Shining in Borrowed Plumage': Affirmation of Community in the Black Coronation Festivals of New England, (c.1750–c.1850)." *Western Folklore* 40.3 (1981), 211–31.

Walvin, James. *Black and White: The Negro in English Society, 1555–1945.* London: Allen Lane, Penguin Press, 1973.

Washington, Booker T. *Up from Slavery.* New York: Dover Publications, 1995.

Webb, Barbara. "The Black Dandyism of George Walker: A Case Study in Genealogical Method." *Drama Review* 45.4 (Winter 2001), 7–24.

Webb, Frank. *The Garies and Their Friends* (1857). Baltimore: Johns Hopkins University Press, 1997.

Weems, Robert E., Jr., *Desegregating the Dollar: African American Consumerism in the Twentieth Century.* New York: New York University Press, 1998.

Weheliye, Alexander G. "The Grooves of Temporality." *Public Culture* 17.2 (Spring 2005), 319–38.

Weinbaum, Alys Eve. "Interracial Romance and Black Internationalism." *Next to the Color Line: Gender, Sexuality, and W. E. B. Du Bois,* ed. by Susan Gillman and Alys Eve Weinbaum, 96–123. Minneapolis: University of Minnesota Press, 2007.

——. "Reproducing Racial Globality: W. E. B. Du Bois and the Sexual Politics of Black Internationalism." *Social Text* 67.19 (Summer 2001), 15–39.

Weinstein, Jeff. "Yinka Shonibare: Studio Museum in Harlem, NY." *Artforum International* 40.9 (May 2002), 175.

West, Shearer. "The Darly Macaroni Prints and the Politics of 'Private Man.'" *Eighteenth-Century Life* 25 (spring 2001), 170–82.

White, Eric. *The Rise of English Opera.* New York: Da Capo Press, 1972.

White, Shane. "'It Was a Proud Day': African Americans, Festivals, and Parades in the North, 1741–1834." *Journal of American History* (June 1994), 13–50.

——. *"Somewhat More Independent": The End of Slavery in New York City, 1770–1810.* Athens: University of Georgia Press, 1991.

White, Shane, and Graham White. *Stylin': African American Expressive Culture from its Beginnings to the Zoot Suit.* Ithaca: Cornell University Press, 1998.

Wilde, Oscar. *The Complete Works of Oscar Wilde.* New York: Harper and Row, 1989.

Williams, Andrew P. "The Centre of Attention: Theatricality and the Restoration Fop." *Early Modern Literary Studies* 4.3 (January 1999).

——. *The Restoration Fop: Gender Boundaries and Comic Characterization in Later Seventeenth-Century Drama.* Lewiston, N.Y.: Edwin Mellen Press, 1995.

Williams-Meyers, A. J. "Pinkster Carnival: Africanisms in the Hudson Valley." *Afro-Americans in New York Life and History* 9.1 (1985), 7–18.

Willis, Deborah. *Reflections in Black: A History of Black Photographers from 1840 to the Present*. New York: W. W. Norton, 2002.

Willis-Braithwaite, Deborah. "Introduction: They Knew Their Names." *Van Der Zee: Photographer, 1886–1983*. New York: H. N. Abrams, 1993.

Windley, Nathan A., comp. *Runaway Slave Advertisements: A Documentary History from the 1730s to 1790*. Vol. 2. *Maryland*. Westport, Conn.: Greenwood Press, 1983.

Woodson, Carter G. "Some Attitudes in English Literature." *Journal of Negro History* 22.1 (January 1935), 27–85.

Woolf, Cynthia Griffin. "'Masculinity' in *Uncle Tom's Cabin*." *Speaking the Other: American Women Writers*, ed. by Jeanne C. Ressman, 3–26. Athens: University of Georgia Press, 1997.

Wycherly, William. *The Gentleman-Dancing-Master. The Complete Plays of William Wycherly*, ed. by Gerald Weales, 125–250. New York: New York University Press, 1967.

Yarborough, Richard. "Strategies of Black Characterization in *Uncle Tom's Cabin* and the Early Afro-American Novel." *New Essays on Uncle Tom's Cabin*, ed. by Eric J. Sundquist, 45–84. Cambridge: Cambridge University Press, 1986.

Yellin, Jean Fagan. "Black Masks: Melville's *Benito Cereno*." *American Quarterly* 22 (1970), 678–89.

Young, Lola. "Missing Persons: Fantasizing Black Women in *Black Skin, White Masks*." *The Fact of Blackness: Frantz Fanon and Visual Representation*, ed. by Alan Read, 86–101. Seattle: Institute of Contemporary Art and Bay Press, 1996.

Zamir, Shamoon. *Dark Voices: W. E. B. Du Bois and American Thought, 1888–1903*. Chicago: University of Chicago Press, 1995.

Zwarg, Christina. "Fathering and Blackface in *Uncle Tom's Cabin*." *Novel* 22.3 (Spring 1989), 274–87.

Index

MONICA L. MILLER IS AN ASSISTANT PROFESSOR

OF ENGLISH AT BARNARD COLLEGE.

Library of Congress Cataloging-in-Publication Data
Miller, Monica L.
Slaves to fashion : black dandyism and
the styling of black diasporic identity / Monica L. Miller.
p. cm.
Includes bibliographical references and index.
ISBN 978-0-8223-4585-5 (cloth : alk. paper)
ISBN 978-0-8223-4603-6 (pbk. : alk. paper)
1. African American men — Clothing — History.
2. African American men — Race identity.
3. Fashion — United States.
4. Dandyism — United States.
5. Clothing and dress — United States.
I. Title.
E185.89.F37M55 2009
305.38'896073 — dc22 2009013116